C0-ATA-955

INDIA AND BRITAIN : 1947-68

INDIA AND BRITAIN

1947-68

The Evolution of Post-Colonial Relations

ARUN KUMAR BANERJI

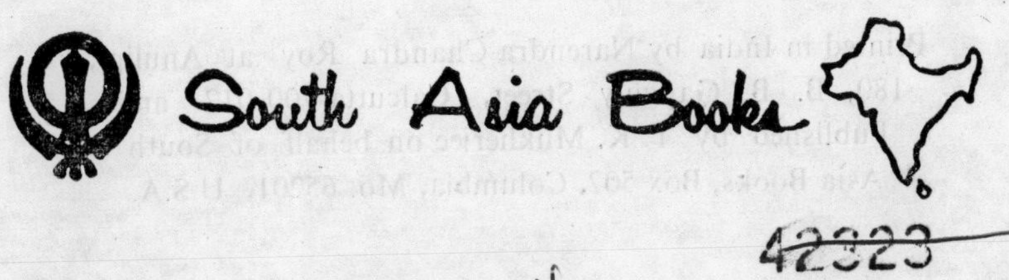

SOUTH ASIA BOOKS
Box—502 : Columbia, Mo. 65201. U.S.A.
By arrangement with
Minerva Associates (Publications) Pvt. Ltd.
7B, Lake Place : Calcutta-700 029
INDIA

First Published : 1978
ISBN : 0-88386-903-9

Printed in India by Narendra Chandra Roy at Anulipi, 180, B. B. Ganguly Street, Calcutta-700 012 and Published by T. K. Mukherjee on behalf of South Asia Books, Box 502, Columbia, Mo. 65201, U.S.A.

To

D.N.B.

who initiated me to the process of learning

To:

D.N.B.

who initiated me to the process of learning

PREFACE

INDIA WAS the first colony to become independent, after the Second World War. The evolution of India's relationship with Britain in the post-colonial years as revealed through inter-governmental exchanges, and through the attitudes of the ruling political elites in the two states, is the subject of this study. A number of factors contributed to the shaping of Indo-British relations : the memories of a shared history, similarities in legal and political institutions, and their mutually advantageous links in the political, economic and military spheres. The history of their relations, though free from major upheavals, had some important turning points. There were also some recurrent causes of disagreements between the two governments leading to much misunderstanding and tensions in their diplomatic relations. Nevertheless the underlying theme of the evolution of Indo-British relations during the first two decades since India's independence, is one of gradual decline in Britain's importance to India. This cannot be explained solely, or even primarily, by reference to their political differences. Rather this is the consequence of a number of developments : (a) emergence of a new generation of social and political elites in Britain and India, (b) changes in their concepts of national interests leading to corresponding changes in their political and economic links, and (c) relative decline in Britain's international standing in a world dominated by the two super Powers.

The present work is a modified version of my thesis presented to the University of London in early 1972 for the Ph.D. degree. For a work of this nature there is no natural *terminus ad quem*. But the year 1968 was, nonetheless, significant as it seemed to mark the beginning of a quest for a new order in Indo-British relations based on the concept of maturity. The principal focus of attention has been on the evolution of Indo-British relations between the years 1947-68 ; references to events beyond this date have, however, been made whenever these were found necessary.

A number of individuals and institutions helped me in various ways. I am particularly indebted to my supervisors, Dr Peter Lyon of the Institute of Commonwealth Studies, London, and Mr James Mayall of the London School of Economics and Political Science, for their encouragement, advice and ungrudging help.

I take this opportunity to thank all those who kindly agreed to talk to me on various issues affecting Indo-British relations. Mr A. Madhavan, formerly of the Indian High Commission, London, helped me in obtaining some valuable information about the organisation of the Indian High Commission. Mr S. S. Khera read and commented on an earlier draft of Chapters I and III. I would also like to thank the staff of the various libraries I have used in London and Oxford ; and later, in New Delhi and Calcutta.

My grateful thanks are also due to the Government of West Bengal for awarding me a State Scholarship which made this study possible, to Mr Sushil Mukherjea of the Minerva Associates, and to my wife Soumitri but for whose constant prodding the work would have never been published.

The Indian Council of Social Science Research deserves grateful thanks for partly subsidizing the publication of this study. The responsibility for the facts stated, opinion expressed or conclusions reached in this book is entirely that of the author and the ICSSR has no responsibility for them.

Presidency College,
Calcutta, Nov. 1977

Arun Kumar Banerji

CONTENTS

ABBREVIATIONS

C.R.O.	Commonwealth Relations Office
G.O.I.	Government of India
I.C.W.A.	Indian Council of World Affairs
M.E.A.	Ministry of External Affairs
M.I.T.	Massachusetts Institute of Technology
O.U.P.	Oxford University Press
R.B.I.	Reserve Bank of India
R.I.I.A.	Royal Institute of International Affairs
S.C.O.R.	Security Council Official Records
G.A.O.R.	General Assembly Official Records

INTRODUCTION

THE BRITISH *withdrawal* from India, unlike the French *retreat* from Indo-China or Algeria, was a comparatively smooth process, and brought to an end an era of frustration, hatred and misunderstanding that had undermined Indo-British relations for the preceding half-century. No special privileges were asked for the protection of British interest, nor was any alliance suggested. Nevertheless, the dissolution of the British empire in India did not mean a complete break with the past. The decision of the Indian leaders to invite the last Viceroy to become the first Governor-General of independent India was as much symbolic of the sense of continuity as it was politically significant.

Indeed, the ties between the two states were too numerous to be severed by a single Act of Parliament. This was recognised by informed observers in both Britain and India. K.M. Panikkar and Guy Wint, in two separate studies, emphasised the need for close cooperation between Britain and India not only for their own mutual advantages but also for the general good of post-war Asia[1]. India's decision to continue her membership of the Commonwealth strengthened many of the existing links between the two states, and widened the area of co-operation between them.

The changing nature of India's relationship with Britain since 1947, the main causes of tension in their relations, and the factors which contributed to the decline of Britain's importance to India are the subject of this study.

With the transfer of power in August 1947, the British Government was faced with the problem of an immediate change in its attitudes and policies towards the sub-continent. The problem had really two aspects. First, the liquidation of the British empire in India called for a new relationship between London and New Delhi ; the administrative and political norms of the pre-independence days were no longer applicable to this changed context. Secondly, the transfer of power in India also involved the partition of the former Raj, and this meant that the British Government now had to deal with two main centres of power in the sub-continent—one in New Delhi and the other in Karachi (later Rawalpindi and then Islamabad). If relations between India and Pakistan had been amicable, the division of the sub-continent, by itself, would not have created many problems for Britain. But the very fact that partition had to take place made it unlikely that India and Pakistan would beable to establish amicable relations easily. In fact, the two neighbours were at odds with each other from the beginning of their emergence as independent states, and British attitudes and policies towards these two states, therefore, became an important factor in the development of Indo-British relations. Throughout the period under study, the twists and turns in Indo-Pakistani relations posed acute problems for Britain.

In addition to Indo-Pakistani disputes, there were a number of issues in the international sphere such as military alliances, colonialism, and the attitude towards racial discrimination, especially the attitude towards the racialist regime in South Africa, which were recurrent causes of disagreement between the two Governments. Partly this was the result of differences in the historical experience of the two states ; but in many cases disagreements also reflected differences in their interests, as perceived by the foreign policy-making elites in Britain and India. The decision of the British Government to join SEATO in 1954 and to form the Baghdad Pact in 1955, the Anglo-French invasion of Suez and the Russian military intervention in Hungary both in 1956, India's annexation of Goa in 1961, the war between India and China in 1962 (and the subsequent attempts by the British and American Governments to link up military aid to India with a satisfactory settlement of the Kashmir dispute), the Indo-Pakistani war of 1965, and the British Government's attitude to it—all these had important consequences for Indo-British relations.

The almost total liquidation of the British empire by the end of the period under study, the burden of Britain's overseas commitments—especially because of the role of Sterling as an international currency, and the maintenance of military bases east of Suez—led to the devaluation of the Pound sterling in 1967, and forced the British Government (much more decisively than had its earlier devaluation in 1949) to think in terms of readjusting Britain's national and international priorities in a European context. During the latter half of the 1960s, on the other hand, India became more pre-occupied with internal problems. In external relations, hostilities with two of her neighbours—China and Pakistan—and the growing collusion between them ; and the re-alignment of powers in the international scene as a result of the development of the Sino-Soviet conflict, and the emergence of China as a new centre of power in Asia, impelled India closer to the Soviet Union.

There were also a number of significant developments affecting economic relations between Britain and India. Their patterns of trade changed in direction as well as in composition. Commonwealth preferences, so important during the 1950s, became less important during the 1960s ; and the importance of sterling as a link diminshed too. Secondly, India's need for development capital, especially in the sphere of official economic aid, far exceeded what Britain alone could contribute, thus increasing India's reliance on other states, although foreign aid became an important ingredient of Indo-British relations. There was also a decline in the rate of flow of private capital from Britain to India. In the sphere of defence, similarly, India's reliance on Britain declined, particularly after the Sino-Indian conflict of 1962. With the retirement of the 'Sandhurst' men from the Indian Army, the link between the 'elite' cadres of the defence forces of the two states was further weakened.

Demographic movements—not so important in the 1950s—added a new dimension to Britain's relations with the former colonial territories. The movement of people from countries in Africa, Asia and the West Indies to UK, and the British Government's attempt to stem the flow of immigration by enacting laws, introduced a source of tension in Indo-British relation. In terms of social costs, the migration of skilled personnel from India to Britain, no doubt, involved a loss of trained manpower for the country of origin ; this was partly offset by the financial remittances of Indians overseas. What was, however, more important in the context of Indo-British relations, was the emergence of racial tensions in UK, particularly in the late 1960s and 1970s.

The dominant attitudes of the political elites of the two states also underwent important changes. No less significant were the changes in the nature and composition of the bureaucratic elites in India resulting from an erosion of British influence on the higher civil service[2]—for the Indian Civil Service was an ascriptive body with a pronounced 'ethos' of its own, an ethos which in the past was very much a legacy of the British.

Literature on Indo-British relations is voluminous and growing, and very variable in character and quality. It takes many forms : published documents, state papers, parliamentary debates, memoirs, biographies and accounts by participant observers, histories as well as imaginative fiction and even poetry. Each of these throws some valuable light on different aspects of Indo-British relations. But most of the published accounts of Indo-British relations still relate to the pre-independence period and especially to the tortuous course of events leading to partition and transfer of power in 1947. Few serious attempts have been made to focus attention centrally, on the evolution of relations between the two states during the post-colonial years[3]. In India, relations with Britain have been viewed more often through the lens of India's relations with the Commonwealth, which represents not so much the neglect of interest in Britain as the tendency to equate the United Kingdom with the Commonwealth. And in most cases, serious analysis of Indo-British relations hitherto has been confined to the study of British attitudes and policies towards such general themes as non-alignment[4], or to such particular issues as Kashmir and Goa.

In Britain, interest in India has been shown by those who were personally connected with the Raj in some way—as civil servants, academics, ex-servicemen, journalists, or as businessmen. After independence, they constituted what may be called a group of 'India-experts' in Britain. Much has been written already by participant observers as well as by historians to throw light on the attitudes and assumptions of those who governed India[5]. But not enough has been said to explain the attitudes of those who were to deal with an independent India on the basis of equality. Maurice and Taya Zinkin are still almost alone with their important contribution to the understanding of the subject[6].

The Zinkins, however, did not attempt to analyse, systematically, the evolution of post-imperial relations between Britain and India. The present study seeks to provide a general context for the analysis of Indo-British relations, particularly between the transfer of power in 1947, and Mr Michael Stewart's visit to India in 1968. That visit was quite significant as the main purpose of Mr Stewart was to explain the changes in British attitudes and policies towards India (as well as to the commonwealth in general) in the context of Britain's new non-imperial role. Some mention of events before 1947, or after 1968, has at times been necessary to maintain thematic unity. It has, of course, been necessary to be selective in deciding what are the central issues and then to treat them in some depth, while leaving aside many other matters which are interesting, but are of peripheral importance to the understanding of Indo-British relations.

Some questions are particularly significant but not self-evidently simple to answer. To what extent, for example, were the attitudes and assumptions of the political and administrative elites prevailing in the colonial days carried over to the post-independence years ? And how did they affect Indo-British relations ? What were the principal causes of disagreement between the British and the Indian Governments during the period under study ? Has the shift of emphasis in India's foreign policy away from Britain been deliberate, or is it a natural result of the evolution of post-colonial relationship ?

The emphasis here is on the study of *India's* relations with Britain—how British policies and attitudes affected India, how important Britain was in India's foreign policy perspectives, and what are the reasons that account for the changes in Indian attitudes towards Britain ? This does not mean that India did not have any influence on British policies. The fact that the

British Government were willing and eager to keep India within the Commonwealth, even after the latter decided to adopt a Republican constitution, in itself shows the importance attached by Britain to India. During the late 1940s and early 1950s the British Government's policies in Asia, especially policy towards China, were considerably influenced by Indian views. This was particularly evident in 1950 when the British Government granted recognition to the Government of the People's Republic of China[7]. This official British-Indian identity of approach towards some of the major problems of Asia was also evident during the early stages of the Korean war. The two Governments co-operated in bringing to an end the Korean war, especially, during the Prisoners-of-war negotiations in 1953 ; and in 1954, for bringing an end to the war in Indo-China.

One sphere where India has exercised some influence on British policy, though perhaps in a less obvious way, is in the evolution of the Commonwealth, and more particularly, in helping to shape British attitude towards colonialism.

This study has been divided into theree distinct but closely related parts. The first part deals with the nature and composition of the foreign policy elites in the two states, their attitudes towards each other, and the formal structure of their relationship, as without this background it is difficult to appreciate the richness and variety in Indo-British relations. The issues which have been recurrent causes of disagreement between the two Governments will be discussed in the second part. Part three deals with those areas of interaction between them—trade, aid, investment and military link – where the interests of the two states are mutually complementary. But different aspects of relations between states cannot be separated completely, even for analytical purposes ; the treatment of certain issues is, therefore, bound to overlap. The method of approach in this study is thematic, though an attempt has been made to maintain the historical chronology of events in dealing with particular themes.

During his visit to India, the then Foreign and Commonwealth Secretary Mr Michael Stewart said at a press conference in New Delhi, on 2 December, 1968 :

"We must neither of us see the relationship between our two countries as solely a heritage from the past... the previous relationship between Britain and India has now receded into history, and although I hope the fact that we were so closely in touch for centuries is something that can help in our mutual understanding, we must look to our relationship to day in the light of the facts of the present time and on the proper recognition of each other's interests."[8]

This statement breathes pragmatism, a readiness to accept change, which is so important in the conduct of relations between states. Have Indo-British relations really been based on and characterised by pragmatism ? The rest of the study is broadly an attempt to answer this question.

NOTES AND REFERENCES

1. See K.M. Panikkar : *The Basis of an Indo-British Treaty* (O·U.P. for I.C.W.A., New Delhi, 1946), and Guy Wint : *The British in Asia* (Faber, London, 1947).

2. For a discussion on this, see R. Braibanti : 'Elite Cadres in the Bureaucracies of India, Pakistan, Ceylon and Malaya since Independence' in W.B. Hamilton et. al. (eds) ; *A Decade of the Commonwealth 1955-64,* (Duke University Press, Durham, N.C., 1966).

3. Michael Lipton and John Firn ; *The Erosion of a Relationship* : *India and Britain Since 1960* (OUP for RIIA, 1975), is an exception.

4. See for example, S.R. Sharma ; *India's Foreign Policy* : *The British interpretations* (Gyan Mandir, Gwalior, 1961).

5. To take one example, P. Woodruff (pseud,) ; *The Men who Ruled India* ; vol. I, *The Founders*, and Vol. II, *The Guardians* (Cape, London, 1953 and 1954).

6. Maurice and Taya Zinkin ; *Britain and India* : *Requiem for Empire* (Chatto and Windus, London, 1964).

7. For recollections of Mr Krishna Menon of this phase of Indo-British relations see, M. Brecher ; *India and World Politics* : *Krishna Menon's View of the World* (O.U.P., London, 1968) pp. 137-38.

Also see, P. Gordon Walker ; *The Commonwealth* (Mercury Books, London, 1965), p. 315.

8. British Information Service ; *Survey of British Commonwealth Affairs* (London). vol. 3, No. 1, 3 January 1969, p. 19.

CHAPTER I

ELITE ATTITUDES AND FOREIGN POLICY : THE ROLE OF THE FOREIGN POLICY ELITES IN SHAPING INDO-BRITISH RELATIONS

RELATIONS BETWEEN any two states are influenced and determined, to a very large extent, by the 'image' of each state as perceived by the foreign policy making elite in the other.[1] But this image is not formed in a vacuum. There are always a number of factors which contribute to its formulation, such as the psychological disposition of the foreign policy elites arising out of their memories of past associations and of future expectations. These may create a friendly, a hostile or neutral attitude, towards another state.

The elite groups in Britain and India which participate in the process of foreign policy initiation and formulation may broadly be divided, in terms of different levels of communication and interaction, into two categories : (a) official and (b) non-official. The former may be further subdivided into (1) political elites which include the elected political leaders of the Government (Ministers), who participate in the decision-making process, as well as the Members of Parliament having particular interest in foreign affairs ; and (2) bureaucratic or administrative elites, which include not only the diplomats but also the bureaucrats in the foreign office and in other departments of government whose policies affect the state's external relations. The non-official elites include the leader-writers and diplomatic correspondents of the 'quality press', intellectual discussion groups[2] and the business communities. Membership of these groups is by no means exclusive. These various elites exercise different types of influence over the policy-making process, and have different types of relationship with their 'constituents'.[3]

Within the foreign policy elite, there are bound to be different groups with different 'images' which advocate different, and even, conflicting policies. Nevertheless, it is possible to talk of dominant images meaning thereby those identical views held by the majority of members within the foreign policy elite.

I

Factors Influencing Elite Attitudes in Britain And India

In India the immediate effect of the transfer of power was the creation of a favourable image of the British. The British Raj left a number of legacies which made cooperation between the two states possible and even desirable. India inherited from the Raj an efficient and highly anglicised bureaucracy, an army organised on the British pattern, equipped with British weapons, and with a good number of Sandhurst men among its senior officers; and a legal system based on the English conception of rule of law. The two countries had also developed close economic links over the years, and any sudden rupture in that relationship would have had adverse effects on both sides. The United Kingdom was not only India's most important trading partner,[4] but also her biggest source of foreign capital[5] and India had large sterling balances in London, greatly swollen as a result of the credits accumulated during the Second World War.[6]

In the sphere of ideas, British influence acted as the chief foreign source. English education inevitably introduced in India the British concept of polity, and a generation of Indian leaders had grown up with these ideas which gradually became a part of the national tradition.

Thus at the time of independence there were many forces naturally impelling India towards Britain, and facilitating co-operation between the two states. But there were certain countervailing forces as well. There were, for example, the unpleasant memories of colonial rule, with all the concomitant feelings of political and economic exploitation. During the days of British rule in India the middle-class mentality of many British officials and businessmen, who preserved an insular and somewhat narrow outlook, had tended to alienate many educated Indians, and created an image of the British which surely did not represent Britain at her best.[7] Indeed, in the world of India's caste system the Europeans constituted a separate caste, "the 'white Brahmins', with the usual features of the caste system—endogamy, commensality and mutual control by members."[8]

There was also the widely-held belief among Indians that in the ultimate analysis the partition of the former Raj was the result of a deliberately planned act by the departing British Government. Born out of this belief was a suspicion of the motives of the British Government's policy towards the newly independent states in the sub-continent, a suspicion which increased over the year because of Britain's alleged Pro-Pakistan bias in the Indo-Pakistani dispute over Kashmir. In the immediate aftermath of independence, the presence of these feelings in India militated against the possibility of close formalised co-operation with Britain. Finally, so far as relations with Britain were concerned, it seemed on occasions that many Indians failed to shake-off their inhibitions of the colonial days and tended to voice even their positive claims in the language of grievence.[9] Because of the simultaneous operation of the forces of antipathy and friendliness, Indians' attitudes towards Britain have remained ambivalent, variable and diffuse.

On the British side, the transformation of a former colony into an independent and equal partner in the Commonwealth called for considerable readjustment of thought and action in many fields. This was not always easy to achieve. There were a number of factors which concealed the fact that Indo-British relations had undergone a fundamental change, once the decision was taken to dismantle the empire. The British withdrawal from India was effected without any traumatic experience on either side, and the apparent ease with which the old empire was transformed into the new Commonwealth in the years 1947-49 obscured the fact that Britain could no longer have the same influence in the world as she had in the heyday of the empire. To many people in Britain, not least to the official classes, the Commonwealth appeared to be a substitute for the old imperial relationship, and this had important consequences for British policy. Expressions such as 'our Commonwealth' reflected what Professor Mansergh has well called 'the possessive imperial attitude';[10] and this attitude of mind stood in the way of the development of relationships on the basis of equality. This was particularly true in the context of Indo-British relations, as many Indians felt that even after the liquidation of the empire the British behaved in a way as if they were still the rulers.[11] There was a tendency to regard Indians as honorary Englishmen, and to assume that with the end of the struggle for independence, Britons and Indians could settle down to a relationship of mutual friendship based on an identity of views on major issues.[12] Such innocent but false assumptions caused a great deal of harm to Indo-British relations, as they showed a lack of appreciation of Indian views and sentiments.

British attitudes towards India were also influenced by a sense of guilt which some Britons felt about the effects of British rule in India, especially about the policies that ultimately led to the partition. A friend of Gaddhi wrote to him about this on 6 July, 1947 in the following words : 'I feel terribly ashamed, sad and distressed...I cannot escape the condemnation of my own conscience. We the British have done so much to bring India to this spiritual tragedy."[13] This feeling of guilt, in later years, led British Indophiles to view with sympathy many of the problems which India faced in her attempts to establish a secular democratic system. The fact that India had chosen the democratic way was a matter of considerable satisfaction for many Britons who had spent the best part of their life in India working for that development.

Membership of the Commonwealth

India's decision to remain in the Commonwealth, even after the adoption of a republican constitution, was of considerable importance both for the subsequent development of the organization, and in establishing a framework for the subsequent development of Indo-British relations. Some analysis of the political background to this decision is, therefore, necessary as it will shed some light on the factors that influenced the attitudes of the foreign policy elites in Britain and India, during 1947-49.

Power was transferred to India on the basis of dominion status. This was done partly as a matter of convenience ; it would be easier for the British Parliament to pass a law making India a dominion under the Statute of Westminster than to pass a law making India a republic, which would call for new type of legislation. It was with this end in view that the Indian leaders, despite their earlier opposition, agreed to the transfer of power on the basis of dominion status. It was fully recognised in India, as indeed it was recognised by the Statute of Westminster, that a dominion could withdraw from the Commonwealth at any time. Dominion status, therefore, did not mean a limitation on India's sovereignty.

Nevertheless, on attaining independence, India's Constituent Assembly continued to work on the declared objective of making India a republic. This posed new problems for her membership of the Commonwealth. Could a 'Republic' continue to be a member of the Commonwealth with the crown as its head ? The problem was as much political as legal, and its solution demanded political skill and a willingness for accommodation on both sides. As the negotiations later revealed, this willingness was present in both Britain and India.

The earlier opposition of Indian leaders to any form of association with Britain gradually gave way to pragmatism, as the prospect for independence draw nearer. On 22 January, 1947, Nehru told the Constituent Assembly,

> "At no time have we ever thought in terms of isolating ourselves in this part of the world from other countries or of being hostile to countries which have dominated over us...We want to be friendly to all. We want to be friendly with the British people, and the British Commonwealth of Nations."[14]

Once independence was achieved, the need for maintaining close relations with UK became even more apparent. India had close economic and military links with UK which could be fostered and promoted by her membership of the Commonwealth. There was also the realisation that if India withdrew from the Commonwealth while Pakistan remained, the latter could be in an advantageous position vis-a-vis India to influence British policy towards Indo-Pakistani disputes. It was, moreover, recognised that membership of the Commonwealth would enable India to look after the interests of the overseas Indians living in British colonies, and dependencies.[14a]

There were some difficulties as well, especially because of South Africa's membership of the association. Membership of the Commonwealth might be interpreted by the critics, in India, as condoning South Africa's policy of racial discrimination. The Communists were opposed to it ; even the non-Communist left-wing opposition parties criticised the Government for their decision to keep India within the Commonwealth.

The rank and file within the Congress Party did not have any definite idea on the issue, although Nehru and some of his senior colleagues in the party were quite keen on continuing India's membership of the association because of the advantages that would follow from this link. But even Nehru was not prepared to "break his neck over it",[15] as he had also to think of other problems. At one time it seemed that Krishna Menon was "the one single person who wanted to keep membership of the Commonwealth", and in this matter, he claimed later, he was given a virtual *carte blanche* by the Prime Minister, to negotiate with the British Government.[16] Krishna Menon was exaggerating. No doubt, as India's High Commissioner in London he had played a vital role in the process of negotiations. The fact that he enjoyed Nehru's confidence and had contacts with many influential members of the Labour Party, lent more weight to his negotiations. But Krishna Menon had also his critics both in Britain and in India ; Nehru was aware of this, and sought to strengthen his position by winning the party's support for his policy. He succeeded in this. At the Jaipur session of the Congress in 1948, a resolution was passed in favour of India's continued association with the Commonwealth. It is quite evident now that although Prime Minister Nehru himself was responsible for India's external relations, on the issue of India's membership of the Commonwealth he was in continuous communication with Sardar Patel during the crucial months preceding the commonwealth Prime Ministers' conference in April, 1949, and also during the conference ; and Patel supported his policy.[16a]

The British Government were also willing to keep India within the Commonwealth. Speaking to the House of Commons on 15 March, 1946, Attlee said ; "I hope that the Indian people may elect to remain within the British Commonwealth. I am certain that she (India) will find great advantages in doing so."[17] Again, on 10 July 1947, while speaking on the Indian Independence Bill he expressed the desire that India and Pakistan would continue their association with the Commonwealth, giving and receiving benefits.[18]

Even the Conservatives were willing to keep India within the Commonwealth. After India's independence, Leopold Amery, a former Secretary of State for India, took a personal interest in the matter, and in a series of letters to Prime Minister Attlee suggested a 'formula' by which India's Republican status could be reconciled with her membership of the Commonwealth.[19] While recognising the difficulties in finding a formula that would be acceptable to all, he wrote to the Prime Minister of the disastrous consequences that might follow from a complete severance of India's links with the Commonwealth. "It would be difficult to sustain Pakistan as a member, or even an associate, if India broke away completely", he wrote. Moreover, the Commonwealth would lose one of its strongest justifications as "the great world nation group which transcends the boundaries of race and colour."[20] The British Government were aware of these, and were, therefore, willing to keep India within the Commonwealth. But they showed no signs of bending over backwards, as this might be misinterpreted as an attempt to re-impose some sort of British supremacy over India. Probably Krishna Menon was nearest to the truth when he said, later : "They (the British) were quite willing to have us if we wanted to come."[21]

The lynch-pin of the Commonwealth was the allegiance to the crown, and it was the status of the crown that proved to be the most difficult problem to solve. The Foreign Office lawyers said that there could not be a Republic within the Commonwealth, nor could there be anything such as Commonwealth citizenship. This was a strictly legalistic definition of the Commonwealth which, if pursued to its logical extreme, could have wrecked the association. The political leaders recognised this danger. Leo Amery suggested, in his letters to Attlee, that the Indians should be persuaded to include in their constitution a "declaration of free association with the Commonwealth and with the crown as the historic symbol of that association and, if possible, a further declaration that the crown is represented or personified by the Head of the Indian State."[22] Failing that, he suggested, India should be offered the status of an Associate member[23]—a suggestion that received some attention both in London and New Delhi where some Indian officials were thinking along the same line. Lord Mountbatten suggested that the legal problem raised by India's republican status could be solved by putting the Union Jack in the middle of the Indian flag.[24] As the King, rather than the crown, constituted the real link in the Commonwealth—suggested Attlee—it would be advantageous to retain the King in the Indian constitution by having, for example, a King's representative in India to be appointed by him on the recommendation of the Prime Minister.[24a]

A solution to the vexed problem could ultimately be found by defining the King as the Head of the Commonwealth. As the Final Communique of the Commonwealth Prime Ministers' Conference (1949) recorded it :

> "...The Government of India have informed the other Governments of the Commonwealth of the intention of the Indian people that under the new constitution... India shall become a sovereign independent republic. The Government of India have however declared and affirmed India's desire to continue her full membership of the Commonwealth of Nations and her acceptance of the King as the symbol of the free association of its independent member nations and *as such the Head of the Commonwealth.*
>
> The Governments of the other countries of the Commonwealth, the basis of whose membership is not hereby changed, accept and recognizc India's continuing membership in accordance with the terms of the declaration."[25]

Krishna Menon, as mentioned earlier, played an important role in the long-drawn negotiations with the British Government, preceeding the Commonwealth Prime Ministers' Conference of 1949. The actual drafting of the final declaration was made by him and Norman Brook (later Lord Normanbrook) who was the Secretary to the British Cabinet at the time, though a number of other persons contributed to the idea behind it.[26] By defining the King as 'the symbol' of the free association of the Commonwealth's independent nations, and 'as such' the Head of the Commonwealth, this declaration made it possible for India to remain within the Commonwealth, and thus laid the foundation for the future development of Indo-British relations on a firm footing. So far as Krishna Menon was concerned, perhaps this was his most important achievement during his tenure of office as the Indian High Commissioner.

The decision of the Commonwealth Prime Ministers was of historic significance. It involved a notable departure from the doctrine embodied in the Preamble to the Statute of Westminister in which the members of the Commonwealth were said to be 'united by a common allegiance to the crown.'[27] Explaining the significance of the 1949 declaration, Nehru said in the Indian Constitutent Assembly on 16 May, 1949 :

> "This declaration, therefore, states that this new Republic of India, completely sovereign and owing no allegiance to the King, as the other Commonwealth countries owe, will, nevertheless, be a full member of this Commonwealth and it agrees that the King will be recognized as a symbol of this free partnership or association."[28]

Republicanism, which in the past was regarded as equivalent to seccession, was now accepted as compatible with full membership. It was maintained at the time that this compatibility extended only to the case of India ; but later on when other members of the Commonwealth become Republican, notably Pakistan and Ghana, but not South Africa, they were allowed to continue their membership on the same basis.

This declaration of 1949, went a long way towards reconciling 'constitutional forms with political realities'.[29] The 1948 conference of Commonwealth Prime Ministers had already extended the full membership of the Commonwealth beyond the circle of the self-governing European peoples. The 1949 declaration had strengthened its base. India had made a valuable contribution towards this development. If she decided to withdraw from Commonwealth, with Burma and Ireland already out by 1948, it is doubtful whether the Commonwealth would ever have become a multi-racial, multi-cultural association of independent states. The use of the term 'Commonwealth of Nations' in later paragraphs of the Prime Ministers' declaration (1949), as distinguished from the 'British Commonwealth of Nations' in the first, reflected a significant change in the composition and outlook of the Commonwealth as an association.[30]

Britain had every reason to welcome the Indian decision, and the new Commonwealth born out of the deliberations of 1949. As the leader of a multi-racial community of independent states, her voice carried greater weight in world affairs, particularly in Washington, than was warranted by her military strength. She could claim to speak not only for herself, but also with the knowledge of the aspirations of the emergent nations in Asia,[31] and her role in the Commonwealth provided a counter-weight to her growing dependence on the United States.[32]

Defending the Government's decision to continue India's membership of the Commonwealth, Nehru said in the Constituent Assembly that "it was an agreement by free will to be terminated by free will."[33] Other members of the Commonwealth, while regretting India's decision to become a republic, welcomed the new type of association as an evidence of its flexibility. (During the conference, only Pakistan was a little uncoperative). Even Winston Churchill, a long opponent of India's demand for independence, welcomed this new settlement. Speaking in the House of Commons on 28 April, 1949, he said :

> "I am unfeignedly glad that an impassable gulf has not opened between the new India and the British Empire and Commonwealth of Nations or between our famous past in India and our anxious present all over the world ...It seems to me that the personal dignity of the King is not impaired by the conditions under which India remains in the Commonwealth. The final significance

> and value of the Monarchy seems to be enhanced by the way in which the King is acknowledged by the Republic of India and by the Commonwealth monarchies alike."[34]

But the advantages were by no means one-sided. As Nehru told the Constituent Assembly on 16 May, 1949 :

> "We join the Commonwealth, obviously because we think it is beneficial to us and to certain causes in the world that we wish to advance. The other countries in the Commonwealth want us to remain, because they think it is beneficial to them."[35]

During the late 1940s and early 1950s, the British Government's policy in Asia, especially policy towards the Peoples' Republic of China, was considerably influenced by the views of the Indian Government ; as India was then in a unique position because of her friendly relationship with Peking, to communicate with the Government of the People's Republic. This influence was particularly evident in 1950, when the British Government granted recognition to the People's Republic of China.[36] Through her membership of the Commonwealth, Indian diplomacy also became more effective in influencing the policies of the Great Powers. As Nehru himself said in the Indian Parliament on 17 March 1954 :

> "I think we have gained positively by being in the Commonwealth...During the past five years specially, many avenues have opened out to us which may not have been open if we had not been there...Secondly, I think we have somewhat affected world politics, not directly in so far as we can, but to some extent indirectly also, through the Commonwealth, and I think that it is to our and the world's advantage."[37]

It was the consideration of these advantages, and the economic benefits which India derived from the Commonwealth link that influenced the decision of the Indian leaders to keep India within the Commonwealth, despite the frequent demands for the termination of the link voiced by different sections of political opinion in India.

II

Nature and Composition of the Foreign Policy Elites

(a) The Political Elites : (i) Ministerial

In Britain, relations with India, prior to the transfer of power, were primarily the responsibility of the India Office. After the transfer of power, the Commonwealth Relations Office (CRO) —itself created by the merger of the Dominion Office and the India Office in 1947—became responsible for the conduct of relations with India, until it was merged with the Foreign Office in 1968.[38]

According to the Memorandum[39] submitted by CRO to the Sub-Committee (K) of the Select Committee of Estimates, of the 1958-59 Parliamentary session, the Commonwealth Secretary, and under his instructions the Office, were responsible, for :

(a) advising the Ministers on every aspect of policy affecting the other members of the Commonwealth ;

(b) co-ordinating the work of the various UK departments in so far as the Commonwealth countries were concerned ;

(c) arranging consultations, as necessary, with other members of the Commonwealth ; and

(d) acting as the channel of communication between London and other Commonwealth capitals on matters of mutual interest such as foreign policy.

The over-riding responsibility of the Commonwealth Secretary, according to a former Minister, "was to maintain the distinction of Commonwealth Relations".[40] Relations with India, as a member of the Commonwealth, were based on a doctrine mainly propounded by Britain, which asserted that Commonwealth relations were neither international relations, nor governed by international law. This '*inter se* doctrine', as Professor Robinson [41] has called it, was not accepted with equal enthusiasm in India. At least this was not reflected in the organisation of the governmental machinery ; because, at the level of policy formulation, no distinction was made between a Commonwealth country and a foreign country.[42]

Though the Commonwealth Secretary, as the head of CRO, was primarily responsible for the formulation of policy towards India, other Ministers and Ministries had also influenced the Government's policy. The Labour Government's policy towards India during 1945-51 was almost certainly influenced by the views of Prime Minister Attlee and of Cripps, who had long experience of Indian affairs. Apart from the CRO, the Foreign Office, the Board of Trade, the Treasury and the Ministry of Overseas Development—all had interests in India, and at different times influenced the British Government's policy. Even the activities of some of the home departments, apart from the Treasury, had at times considerable impact on relations between Britain and India—the Commonwealth Immigrants Acts are examples. Within British bureaucracy, the immigration policy of the British Government is primarily the responsibility of the Home Office ; but when the British High Commission Offices in India issue work permits to prospective immigrants, they in fact act for the Home Office and the Department of Employment.

India is an important power in South Asia and, therefore, the Foreign Office attached some importance to the views of the Indian Government, especially in matters affecting the security of Asia. This was particularly evident in 1954, from the differences between Foreign Secretary Sir Anthony Eden (later Lord Avon), and the then US Secretary of State John Foster Dulles. Both Dulles and Eden agreed on the need for a regional security organisation for South East Asia, but they could not agree on its form and membership.[43] The British Foreign Secretary wanted to have a 'Locarno Type' arrangement for the security of South East Asia, and would have liked to include India in it ; whereas Dulles was against the inclusion of India. Significantly, initiatives for consulting the Government of India's opinion on the proposed security system for South East Asia were taken by the Foreign Secretary and not by CRO.[44]

By the end of the 1960s economic aid had established itself as one of the instruments of British foreign policy. The Government's policy towards India was, therefore, likely to be affected by the views of the Ministry formulating and administering aid programmes. Until 1961 economic and technical aid to the developing countries was distributed through the Colonial Office, the Commonwealth Relations Office, or the Foreign Office (FO), depending on the relationship of the state concerned, with the UK Government. In 1961, management of the aid scheme was concentrated in the Department of Technical Co-operation under a Minister of State. But the Commonwealth, Foreign and Colonial Secretaries continued to be responsible for matters of general policy. In 1964, a new Ministry of Overseas Development (MOD) was established by the Labour Government with a Cabinet Minister as its head.[45] To what extent MOD could influence the policy of CRO, or later, of the Foreign and Commonwealth Office, towards India is, however, difficult to determine.

All modern governments face the problem of co-ordinating the work of different ministries whose operations necessarily overlap, and who are thereby likely to produce distinct and sometimes even conflicting plans. This was particularly true of the British Government's external policies before 1968. There were at least two different ministries—the Commonwealth Relations Office and the Foreign Office—concerned with Britain's external relations, manned by officers with different departmental loyalties, career structures and with different ministers each having his own ideas, interests and aspirations. The Foreign Office often argued, and rightly perhaps, that it had a comprehensive experience and expertise in dealing with Britain's external relations which CRO lacked. After all, CRO was manned by a much smaller staff,[46] had to depend on the Foreign Office and its Ambassadors as the source for the "vast amount of diplomatic and international information sent to the rest of the Commonwealth."[47] Moreover, the very existence of CRO was justified on the basis of a distinction between Commonwealth relations and foreign affairs, which the Foreign Office refused to recognise. "It was on this question that I had my only serious disagreement with Ernest Bevin," Mr Gordon Walker wrote later.[48] Much would, however, depend on the personality of the Commonwealth Secretary, and his influence and political standing in the Cabinet.

When matters affecting Britain's external relations came up for discussion in the Cabinet, the line taken by CRO could be

quite different from that of the Foreign Office. On several occasions, these two ministries were advocating different, and even conflicting policies on issues affecting Indo-British relations. Take, for example, their attitudes towards the question of India's membership of the Commonwealth. During early 1949, this issue was discussed in a number of meetings of the Commonwealth Affairs Committee of the Cabinet. In these discussions, CRO strongly advocated the policy of retaining India within the Commonwealth, even after the adoption of the republican constitution, while Foreign Secretary Bevin, backed by the Foreign Office lawyers, took a legalistic view according to which republicanism was incompatible with membership of the Commonwealth.[49] Mr Gordon Walker wrote later,

> "Bevin argued the Foreign Office line...that it was not worth keeping India within the Commonwealth ; it was not going to be morally committed to us, but we to it. To keep India in would lead to the breakdown of the old Commonwealth. In course of the discussion, Bevin warmed up and made some positive suggestions."[50]

Such differences between FO and CRO arose over other issues as well. For example if FO took the Portuguese line on Goa, CRO would point out its implications for Indo-British relations. In 1954, during a period of tension in Indo-Portuguese relations over the Goa issue, the Foreign Office issued a statement which was considered in New Delhi to be unfavourable to India and gave rise to indignation.[51] Later, the Under-Secretary of State for Commonwealth Relations made a statement in Parliament, stressing the British Government's neutrality in the Indo-Portuguese dispute.[52] Apparently this neutral attitude of CRO seemed to be different from that of the Foreign Office. Whether this was the result of a lack of co-ordination between the two ministries, or of differences of policies and attitudes between them is, however, difficult to determine.

It was recognised quite early, that the division of responsibility between FO and CRO would pose problems of co-ordination. Attempts were, therefore, made to maintain continuous liaison between the two which ensured that out of the mass of material coming to FO, all was passed on to other Commonwealth Governments that was necessary to keep them informed of all aspects of foreign affairs. There was also some exchange of staff between the two Offices, so that each could learn the ways of the other. It was a regular practice to appoint either the High Commissioner or his Deputy in New Delhi from the Foreign Office ; and during his term of office, he would be responsible to the Commonwealth Secretary.[53]

But the dual machinery for the conduct of Britain's external relations was far from satisfactory, and in 1964 it was criticised by the Plowden Committee that was set up to study the working of Britain's representational services overseas. The report of the Committee pointed out that the division of responsibility between CRO and FO impeded the development and execution of a coherent policy.[54] While the merger of the two offices was to be the ultimate aim, the Committee recommended as "an intermediate and urgently needed reform, the creation of a unified Service which will take in the duties, personnel and posts of the Foreign Service."[55] The unified service, known as Her Majesty's Diplomatic Service, was set up on 1 January 1965.[56] The two Offices were finally merged in October, 1968.

The Indian Government did not have a separate Ministry to deal with Commonwealth countries.[57] Relations with all foreign countries are dealt with by the Ministry of External Affairs (MEA), which was set up in 1947 with the title of 'Ministry of External Affairs and Commonwealth Relations', by amalgamating the two Departments of 'External Affairs' and 'Commonwealth Relations' of the pre-independence Indian Government.[58] Two years after independence, the appendage Commonwealth Relations was dropped ; and the Indian foreign office came to be known as the Ministry of External Affairs.

The foreign policy elite in India consisted of a very small group ; and during Nehru's premiership, especially till the end of the 1950s, the making of foreign policy was virtually his personal monopoly. He was not only the Prime Minister, but also the Foreign Minister of India. Because of his long experience as the acknowledged spokesman of the Congress

Party in international affairs since the middle of the 1930s, and also because of the absence of a body of men trained in the art of diplomacy, Nehru became 'the philosopher, the architect', and 'the engineer' of independent India's foreign policy.[59] He completely dominated not only MEA, but also the Cabinet, in matters affecting India's foreign relations.

Apart from MEA, the working of the defence, trade and, economic ministries also influenced India's foreign relations and, to that extent, India's relations with Britain. There were two Standing Committees of the Cabinet—the Committee on Foreign Affairs, and the Committee on Defence—directly concerned with India's foreign affairs. Their membership was almost identical. Besides the Prime Minister, they included the Home Minister, the Finance Minister and the Defence Minister.

Even before Mr Krishna Menon became the Defence Minister in 1957, he used to sit on the Foreign Affairs Committee, during his tenure of office as the Minister without Portfolio (1956) ; another member of the Cabinet, Maulana A.K. Azad, became a member of the Committee, not in his capacity as the Minister for Education, but by virtue of his status as a national leader. These two Committees included most of the senior members of the Cabinet ; but in practice, they exercised very little influence on the formulation of foreign policy.[60] Nehru was too dominating a man to allow criticisms to emanate from his Cabinet colleagues, and apart from Krishna Menon, few of his senior ministerial colleagues had much interest in foreign affairs.

This did not mean that he had an absolute freedom in the conduct of foreign affairs. He had to face criticisms in the Parliament, from the Opposition parties, and at times, even from the members of his own party. In terms of policy formulation, however, his private discussions with his advisers in MEA, or outside it, were likely to be more influential and effective than criticisms in the Parliament where, because of the overwhelming majority of the Congress Party, the Government could expect to secure the necessary votes.

In shaping India's relations with UK, Krishna Menon was one of Nehru's closest confidants and advisers, first during his tenure of office as the Indian High Commissioner in London (1947-52), and later as a Minister in Nehru's Cabinet (1956-62). Both of them were highly anglicised, both were educated in England, and had personal friends amongst men who were Britain's leaders during the early phase of Britain's withdrawal from empire. Both were committed to Parliamentary and social democracy, in much the same general terms as the political leaders of post-War Britain. Such intellectual affinities produced among them a sentimental attachment towards Britain, notwithstanding their dislike for British colonialism, and successive British Governments' policy towards the Kashmir dispute. There were also others, both in the Government and outside, who had influenced Nehru's policy towards Britain, at various times, and on various issues.[61] Principal among them were the Mountbattens, whose main role was to strengthen India's links with the Commonwealth, Mrs V.L. Pandit, and Dr S. Radhakrishnan who was a Professor of Philosophy at Oxford, and later became the President of India. Nehru always acted as a moderating influence to tone down anti-British feelings in India, whenever demands for India's withdrawal from the Commonwealth were made in the Parliament. Even Krishna Menon was pro-British in his own idiosyncratic way. Nothing illustrates it better than his conversations with Michael Brecher.[62] During his years of power, despite his frequent criticism of British policy on Kashmir, and his sharp reaction to the Anglo-French invasion of Suez in 1956, he never advocated a policy of withdrawal from the Commonwealth. In later years, explaining the causes for the recurrence of anti-British outbursts in India he said : "The British lend themselves to it, because, quite unnecessarily, they hang on to the Americans and identify themselves with U.S. reaction."[63] This is, perhaps, a mirror-image of Krishna Menon's view of the world. Much of his polemics against the West were directed against USA ; and UK was blamed for hanging on to 'U.S. reaction'. Even on colonial issues, in many debates before the Trusteeship Council, he paid handsome tribute to the British Government for the way they had carried on the process of decolonisation. As an acute English diplomat once said to one of his Australian colleagues,

Krishna Menon "has been at once the worst enemy and the best friend of Britain in India."[64] With the emergence of a new generation of political leaders in the two states, these important personal links have inevitably weakened.

India had, from the very beginning, one single ministry to deal with foreign (political) policy,[65] and thus could avoid many of the shortcomings experienced in UK because of the division of responsibility between CRO and FO. Even then, lack of coordination between the different ministries, at times, led to the pursuit of conflicting goals by them. On many occasions, this became quite evident in the context of Indo-British relations.

The Ministry of External Affairs was bound by the Rules of Business of the Government which assigned foreign affairs to MEA, but placed commerce exclusively under the jurisdiction of the Ministry of Trade and Industry, and the Ministry of Finance.[66] Within MEA, an economic division was set up in 1949 which was abolished in 1951 for want of financial resources ; it was re-established with a smaller staff in 1961.[67] The Ministry of External Affairs could not always keep in touch with the vastly expanded foreign *economic* policy of the Government of India except inefficiently and begrudgingly in the field of commerce. The Economic Committee of the Cabinet was expected to act as the coordinator between political and economic aspects of the Government's foreign policy. But as an Indian writer observed, "there is no evidence to suggest that this Committee ever concerned itself, during Nehru's time, with the economic, military or other related aspects of foreign policy."[68] As a result, on several occasions the objectives of India's foreign economic policy were at variance with those of foreign political policy. In 1957, for example, the spokesmen for India's foreign political policy were critical of the British Government's role in the Security Council debates on Kashmir, and even hinted at the possibility of withdrawal from the Commonwealth. On the other hand, the spokesmen for India's foreign *economic* policy, faced with a severe foreign exchange crisis, were seeking British help and cooperation in the field of foreign aid and investment, which was the purpose of the then Finance Minister Mr

Morarji Desai's visit to London and to other western capitals in September 1957. Again, Indo-British-disagreements over the cotton textiles issue came to a head in the summer of 1971.[69] The handling of the issue by the then Minister for Foreign Trade in India revealed the differences between the actions and policies of MEA (the principal spokesman for the country's foreign political policy), and those of the Ministry of Trade. The Minister for Trade, the late Mr L.N. Mishra, criticised the British Government's decision to impose, unilaterally, a 15 per cent tariff on all cotton textiles imported from India, and threatened to take retaliatory measures against British interests in India which would have included the nationalisation of British investments and a ban on the repatriation of profits.[70] This threat came at a time when India needed Britain's support over the Bangladesh crisis. The Indian Foreign Minister visited London in June, 1971, with this end in view, and "expressed appreciation of the sympathy and support for the refugees from East Pakistan given by the people and Government of Britain."[71]

During the 1960s, because of Britain's considerable, though declining involvement in India's economic sector—by way of trade, aid and investment—the economic ministries of the Government of India attached more importance to UK than that by MEA. Perhaps, it is not without significance that while the annual Report of MEA has, in successive years, devoted only a few paragraphs to Indo-British relations,[72] the annual *External Assistance* of the Ministry of Finance, has devoted a separate chapter in dealing with Indo-British economic relations.

(ii) *Parliamentary Groups*

The political elites include, besides the Ministers, members of Parliament with special interest in foreign affairs. An analysis of the attitudes and policies of the different groups within the Labour and the Conservative parties, towards certain issues affecting Indo-British relations—as reflected, chiefly, through their actions in the Parliament—reveals a wide spectrum of views about India, from a feeling of antipathy and even hostility to one of friendliness and even camaraderie.

During 1948-49, as we have seen, both the Labour and the Conservative parties were willing and anxious to keep India within the Commonwealth. But this 'bi-partisanship' broke down on many other issues affecting Indo-British relations. It is surprising to see the depth of hostility which a section of the Conservative party, led by Winston Churchill, felt towards Nehru and his policies, during the early years of independence. Take, for example, the attitude of the Conservative party, especially of Churchill, to the Hyderabad issue.[73] On several occasions the Prime Minister and his colleagues had to point out that this attitude of the Leader of the Opposition was biased against Nehru and the Hindus, and that this was causing more harm than good to Indo-British relations.[74]

For a number of reasons, Indians came to look upon the Labour party as being more favourable to India than the Conservative party. It was the Labour party which had long campaigned for Indian independence ; and many of its members were actively associated with the India League. After 1945, the Labour government reopened negotiations with Indian leaders which ultimately led to the transfer of power. Ideologically Nehru and many of his colleagues within the Congress party were closer to the Fabian socialists in Britain, and radicalism in Indian political thinking during the fifties was the radicalism of Laski and of the *New Statesman* rather than that of the Marxists. In Britain, the left-wing of the Labour party had long adulated Nehru, and on many issues took their cue from the policies and actions of Nehru. On the occasion of Nehru's visit to London to attend the Commonwealth Prime Ministers' Conference, in June 1956, Jennie Lee wrote an article in the *Tribune* paying handsome tribute to Nehru and his Government's socialist policies. "British socialists should at least feel proud that India chooses the democratic way forward..."[75] she commented. Referring to the preamble to India's *Second Five-Year Plan*, which declared that the achievement of a socialist pattern of society was the objective of the Government's economic policy, she wrote :

> "I would give three cheers if I could be sure that an official publication from a British Labour Government,

while it is in power, would be equally clear in its avowals."[76]

But it was not only Nehru's commitment to socialism that won the applause of the left-wing of the Labour party. As Professor Finer has pointed out, "In adulating India, pacifism, socialism, democracy and anti-colonialism find common ground ; and these form the syndrome of the 'Left'."[77] Within the Parliamentary Labour Party, there were many backbenchers who supported Nehru's policy of opposition to colonialism, his emphasis on the peaceful settlement of international disputes, and his plea for the non-proliferation of nuclear weapons, and disarmament. In 1955 when the British government were equivocating in their attitude towards the Indo-Portuguese dispute over Goa, a group of Labour MPs formed a Goa Committee in association with the Movement for Colonial Freedom, to support the demand of the Goans for self-determination.[78] They sponsored a motion in the Parliament asking the British government to mediate in the Indo-Portuguese dispute over Goa so as to create conditions under which the Goans could "decide their own future."[79] Three Labour MPs also wrote a letter to *The Times* urging the British government to try to bring about a settlement of the dispute between Portugal and India.[80]

Some of the anti-colonialists within the Labour Party, especially those belonging to the political Left, shared Nehru's ambivalent attitude towards the Soviet Union. This was clearly demonstrated by one incident during the Hungarian crisis in 1956. On 12 December, 1956, a motion was tabled in the House of Commons which, while welcoming the decision of the British government to withdraw their forces from Egypt, and deploring the continued use of violence in Hungary, ended with the suggestion that the Government should invite Nehru

> "to use his good offices to secure withdrawal of Russian military forces from Hungary, and to use his influence to effect a reconciliation between Russia and the Western Powers, which would make possible a new approach to a peaceful solution of world problems."[81]

Such a move was surprising in view of Nehru's strong criticism of British action in Suez, and his initial equivocation over

Hungary. Unlike their Conservative colleagues, the sponsors of the motion, while shocked at the suppression of the people of Hungary, were not quite willing to come out with an outright condemnation of the Soviet Union. This motion, signed by more than 100 members, was in fact intended to be an indirect appeal to Nehru, through his sister Mrs Pandit who was then the Indian High Commissioner in London. A deputation of MPs presented a copy of the motion to Mrs Pandit who accepted it with great warmth ;[82] but nothing ultimately came out of it.

But it was on the Anglo-French invasion of Suez that Nehru's criticism of the British Government's action was matched by equally vigorous criticism of the Labour Party. In October 1956, when the Conservatives, especially the 'Suez die-hards'[83] were criticising Nehru for his double standards over Suez and Hungary, a Labour commentator warned the Government not to forget India. "Whereas under the Labour Government India's views had high priority," he wrote, "now it seemed that Delhi ranked alongside, for Conservative Cabinet purposes, Baghdad, Saigon and Taipei."[84] Perhaps an exaggeration ; but from a casual reading of the editorial comments on India in *The Daily Express*, *The Daily Telegraph* and even in *The Times*, during the Suez crisis of 1956, and from the speeches of the various Conservative MPs in the House of Commons, it becomes quite evident that Nehru and Krishna Menon were the principal targets for criticism, alongside President Nasser, and for different reasons, Dulles.

On occasions, when the policy of the Labour left was in conflict with that of the official policy of the Labour party, the former often tried to justify its position with reference to Nehru's policy. In 1957, for example, during the Labour Party's annual conference in Brighton, when Aneurin Bevan spoke against committing the Party to a policy of unilateral renunciation of nuclear weapons, shouts of 'Nehru has no bomb' were raised by the unilateralists.[85]

Because of Nehru's popularity with the 'Labour left', he and his policies were disliked by a section of the Conservatives. The Conservative party, at least its Parliamentary wing, being much more homogeneous in social composition, and educational and occupational backgrounds, the distinction between the 'Right' and the 'Left' is slightly misleading in the case of the Tories.[86] Nevertheless, it may be said that so far as Nehru and his policies were concerned, the severest critics were the empire loyalists, and those who constituted what has been described as the 'Foreign Policy Right.'[87] Even after Indian independence some Conservatives, led by Winston Churchill, could not forget that it was the Congress party which led the agitation against the British, ultimately leading to the liquidation of the British empire in India. There was also a tendency in a section of the British press, particularly in the group of newspapers controlled by Lord Beaverbrook to take an overtly anti-Indian attitude on any issue in which India was involved in a dispute with another state.[88] This is partly because Nehru stood for so much in English radical tradition which the Conservatives did not like. They also disliked his pontifical utterances on issues such as colonialism, and his constant reminders that the days of European dominance over Asia were at an end.

This point, however, should not be stretched too far. For one thing, during the 1950s both the Labour and the Conservative parties attached considerable importance to India's continued membership of the Commonwealth. Within the conservative party, even the 'empire stalwarts' were generally 'Commonwealth loyalists', and were aware of the value of India's membership of the Commonwealth. Above all, given the social composition of the Conservative party, even the Tories could count Nehru as a member of their class ; for he was an aristocrat by birth, had a public school education in England, followed by education at Cambridge and a few years at one of the Inns of Court. Though he was the hero of the Left, his words had a wider audience because he spoke their language in a way which was understood by the British public. Finally, within the Parliament there are all-party organisations such as the Indo-British Parliamentary Group which work for the promotion of Indo-British co-operation and understanding.

In the 1960s, both the Labour and the Conservative parties lost much of their earlier enthusiasm for the Commonwealth.

With the Labour party, the first cause for disillusionment with Nehru and his policies, was his decision to send troops to Goa in December, 1961. It was the friends and not the enemies of India who felt the greatest shock, wrote a commentator in the *New Statesman.*[89] Later events, especially the Sino-Indian conflict of 1962, the political turmoil in India in the post-Nehru era, and the Indo-Pakistani war of 1965, contributed to the decline in India's prestige among both the political parties in Britain.

In India the government's policy towards Britain has been formulated mainly by the Congress party.[90] For all practical purposes, the closeness of relationship with UK has been equated in India, with the membership of the Commonwealth, as Britain was not only the dominant partner, but also the centre of that association. The attitudes of the different political parties towards the Commonwealth may, therefore, be taken as an indicator of their attitudes towards Britain. Outside official circles, there has been very little appreciation of the value of India's membership of the Commonwealth, and opposition to the link has been voiced from time to time. Almost every single Opposition party (with the exception of the Swatantra party) demanded the termination of the Commonwealth link at one time or another.[91] It is indeed a matter of conjecture whether any non-Congress Government in Delhi at any time between the years 1947-68 would have led India out of the Commonwealth.

The Communist Party of India[92] was opposed to India's membership of the Commonwealth, from the time of independence. In 1949, the CPI bitterly criticised the decision of the Indian government to continue India's membership of the Commonwealth on the ground that this would compromise India's stand on such issues as colonialism and racialism, and would lead to increasing dependence on UK. In 1953, during the debate on the appropriations Bill in the Lok Sabha, Mr Hiren Mukherjee, a leading member of the Communist Party of India, launched a scathing attack on Britain and on India's membership of the Commonwealth for what he called "the domination of British imperialism" over Indian economy.

> "We know", he said, "that British capital controls some of our major industries. It makes enormous profits and exports them out of the country. These, together with the profits which are earned by the British banks, insurance companies and shipping companies enable Britain to exercise over our economy a sort of dominating influence. Britain has a sort of lien over our foreign trade. Britain has deciding voice ; with whom and how much we shall trade. There are powerful foreign exchange banks, for example, who rule the roost, who make us depend upon not only the British Commonwealth, but the United States of America for the disposal of our produce."[93]

In foreign affairs, he complained, membership of the Commonwealth limited India's freedom of action.[94] The opposition of CPI to close relations with Britain was based, therefore, mainly on ideological grounds, though Britain's policy on such issues as the Indo-Pakistani dispute over Kashmir or the Indo-Portuguese dispute over Goa also came in for criticism. During the Suez crisis, Mr A.K. Gopalan, speaking for the party, asked the Government to quit the Commonwealth not because it posed a threat to India, but because it gave Britain the prestige which enables it to deceive the world public opinion.[95] In later years, even after the division within the Communist party, the opposition of the various factions to the Commonwealth link remained unabated.

Apart from the Communists, the Socialists were also opposed to India's membership of the Commonwealth. In December 1948, the National Executive of the Socialist Party declared that it could not be a party to India remaining within the British Commonwealth.[96] After its merger with the Kishan Majdoor party (in 1952), the Socialist Party (now renamed the Praja Socialist Party), maintained its opposition to India's continued membership of the Commonwealth, mainly on the ground that this would tie India to the 'apron strings' of the British Government, in foreign affairs. This opposition intensified over the years because of what the PSP thought to be the anti-Indian stance of the British Government on the Kashmir and Goa issues, and because of their attitude to the racialist regime in South Arica.

Even the Hindu nationalist party, the Jan Sangh, was opposed to India's membership of the Commonwealth, mainly because of the British Government's attitude towards the Kashmir dispute. The Anglo-French invasion of Suez (1956) led to a chorus of demand from all sections of Indian Parliament, with the exception of the Jan Sangh, for the termination of India's Commonwealth membership.

Of all the major opposition parties in India only the Swatantra was in favour of India's continued association with the Commonwealth. As one of its chief spokesmen said in a debate in the Rajya Sabha on 19 February 1964 :

> "...We are not in the Commonwealth for the blue eyes of British statesmen, nor even for the blue eyes of the present aristocratic Prime Minister of England. We are in the Commonwealth because it serves our interests to be in the Commonwealth, because it helps our national and international position. We are there because it is useful to us, not because of any ideal or theory, international or national."[97]

This stand of the party was consistent with its economic policy of free enterprise, and with the political policy of closer association with the West.

During the sixties, the image of Britain declined among almost all the major political parties in India, for a number of reasons. The most important of them were : (1) the British Government's criticism of Indian military occupation of Goa in 1961 ; (2) their role during the Indo-Pakistani war of 1965 ; (3) the Government's handling of the Rhodesian problem, and last, but not the least, (5) the immigration laws introduced by the British Government to control the influx of coloured population from the Commonwealth countries in Asia, Africa and the West Indies. The Commonwealth Immigrants Act of 1968, in particular, was interpreted by most Indians as Britain's overzealousness to withdraw from her post-imperial responsibilities.

By the time of the fourth general elections in India in 1967, both the relationship with Britain and the question of India's continued membership of the Commonwealth had become non-contentious issues in Indian politics. Only the Swatantra Party stressed the value of India's Commonwealth link, whereas the Communist Party (Marxist) demanded that India should quit the Commonwealth.[98] In foreign policy, relations with China and Pakistan were the major preoccupation of all the political parties. While this was not unnatural given the hostile posture of these two neighbours, it also revealed the extent to which Indo-British relations had ceased to dominate India's foreign policy perspectives.

(*iii*) *The Administrative Elites*

Apart from the political executives (the Ministers), the other group with most influence on the foreign-policy making process is the elite cadre in the bureaucracy, especially, the senior officials in the foreign office,[99] and in other departments of government whose policies affect the external relations of the state. Their outlook, attitudes and preferences are, therefore, likely to have some influence on the government's foreign policy.

In India, during the first two decades after independence, the majority of senior officials in MEA, as well as in other departments of government belonged to the Indian Civil Service (ICS).[100] This was a legacy of the Raj. Indian ICS officers had a spell of training in UK, and the experience of working with British officers in India. They believed in many British ideas and practices about government and bureaucracy. This does not mean that all of them were consciously pro-British ; but by virtue of their education, up-bringing and training they were likely to have pro-West, if not always pro-British, inclinations. As a former Secretary-General of MEA, a member of the Indian Civil Service, once remarked to Professor Brecher, "after all, senior officials in the Ministry were very Pro-British."*

Similarly, at the time of independence, all the senior officers of the Indian Army were Sandhurst men,[101] trained in the British army's tradition. It is difficult to say to what extent these men influenced India's policy towards Britain ; but in the matter of purchase of arms and equipment for the defence forces, they generally preferred to buy from Britain, if for no other reason than that they were better acquainted with the British weapons system. Both in the army and in the civil service the men at the top have generally been replaced by members of a generation who do not have such sentimental links with Britain.

In UK, many of the senior officials in CRO had long acquaintance with affairs in the Indian sub-continent. They worked either in the India Office, or in the Dominion Office before joining CRO ; and some of them held important diplomatic assignments in the sub-continent[102]. Even for those who did not work in India, an intimate knowledge of Indian affairs was possible because of the small size of CRO[103], and also because of the small number of states with which it had to deal[104]. Some of these officials, perhaps because of their past experience, came to develop partisan attitudes in India-Pakistan conflicts. This had important implications for British policy towards India and Pakistan. For example, during the Indo-Pakistani war of 1965, the then British Prime Minister Mr Harold (now Sir Harold) Wilson issued a statement accusing India of aggression. This created great anger and resentment in India, and rapidly induced a deterioration in Indo-British relations. Mr Wilson wrote later that the statement was too influeneed by the advice of a pro-Pakistani faction in CRO.[105]

With the gradual retirement of the generation of officials who were inducted to CRO from the India Office or from the Dominion Office, and with the creation of a single diplomatic service in 1965, followed by the merger of the Commonwealth Relations Office and the Foreign Office in 1968, the sense of a personal and, at times even emotional, involvement which some British officials felt in Indo-Pakistani affairs, is likely to decline. One may also expect a qualitative change in the style of diplomacy—from "the practice of a maternal relationship, the proud and tolerant kindness of the mother country towards her adolescent brood",[106] which was so characteristic of CRO, to the thorough professionalism of the diplomats in the Foreign Office.

III

Non-official Elites

The General nature of British foreign policy, or for that matter, British policy towards India cannot be fully comprehended merely by studying the composition and function of the governmental machinery for the formulation and implementation of foreign policy. To understand the working of the British political process, one has to look to the special relationships of those who take part in it. In the first place, among many of the principal participants, there is a "*continuing mutual but loose acquaintanceship*" as a result of initial contacts at school, university, at the Services during the Wars, or in the initial stages of their careers ; and secondly, "the degree of respect for ability and personality rather than status which such a system of social relationship is likely to bring with it."[107] This generates a dialogue between the *policy-makers* of the Government, and those who *influence* the policy-making process in various ways—Members of Parliament having special interest in foreign affairs, members of the 'quality press', and the intellectual discussion groups ; and this has its political implications.

It is important to recognise this relationship in order to be able to explain the role of the foreign policy elites in Britain. In shaping relations with colonies and ex-colonies, the elites included not only those identified by D.C. Watt, [108] but also the members of what J.M. Lee calls the 'official class'.[109] In shaping Britain's relations with India, the influence of the old 'India hands'—those who had worked in India either in the Civil Service or in the Army, or as journalists or educationists —was probably of some importance ; but this subject has not yet been explored in depth. Many of these ex-'India hands', after their return to Britain, continued to take interest in the affairs of the sub-continent, and constituted a group of 'experts' on South Asia. They did not necessarily constitute a closely-knit cohesive group with identity of views on all issues ; in fact, often there were sub-groups advocating different and even conflicting policies. Most of them, because of their past experience in India, tended to think of Indo-Pakistani differences in terms of Hindu-Muslim conflict. Their stand on the issues in dispute between India and Pakistan was bound to be influenced by this attitude of mind, as well as by their personal acquaintance with those members of the administrative and political elites in undivided India, who, in later years, became leaders in either India or Pakistan. As one member of this broadly identifiable, but by no means formal, group once told me, it was difficult for men of his generation and background not to be partisan in Indo-Pakistani conflicts despite their protestation of neutrality. To what extent the British Government's policy towards India has been influenced by such extra-Parliamentary groups is extremely difficult to determine. It is difficult, if not impossible, to demonstrate that in the early 1950s, British policy towards the Indo-Pakistani conflict over Kashmir was to some extent influenced by the views of men such as Sir Olaf Caroe, Lord Birdwood or Sir William Barton[110]. But it would be implausible, in the context of the social relationships mentioned above, to deny them any impact at all given their undoubted energy, experience and knowledge.

In the developed countries of the West, like UK and USA, organised pressure groups, especially the business community and other interest groups, do influence the shaping of foreign policy. During the 1960s, for example, the British Government's economic policy towards India has been influenced by the views of the business community,[111] and by the 'Aid Lobby'.[112]

The role of the non-official elites has been relatively insignificant in India, in influencing the government's foreign policy. In Britain, as mentioned earlier, there is a continuous 'dialogue' between the *makers* of foreign policy and those who *influence* it; but this was not the situation in India, at least during the 1950s. The social relationships and the intellectual climate which make such 'dialogues' possible in London, were absent in New Delhi. There were not many people in India who had knowledge of international affairs ; and between 1947-68, there were very few academic institutions[113] for a systematic analysis of the country's defence and foreign policies.

Secondly, unlike the situation in the industrially developed states of Western Europe and North America, business communities in India have not played any important role in influencing foreign policy.[114] However, they have tried to influence the government's domestic economic policy which, incidentally, affected British economic interests in India. The ambivalent attitudes of Indian business to foreign capital—which swung from outright hostility to one of cautious welcome —is an example.[115] Nevertheless, the influence of the Indian business community on the government's policy towards Britain has been relatively insignificant.

IV

The attitudes of the political and administrative elites in Britain and India towards each other, as discussed above, have changed over time. In India, the elite cadres in the bureaucracy as well as in the defence forces, who had part of their training in UK, have generally been replaced by younger men who do not have such links with Britain. After India's independence, it was decided not to send the IAS (the successor to the ICS) officers to England for training. By 1963, only 10 per cent of the total cadre of IAS officials had received their training in UK,[116] and by 1968, there were only 117 ICS officers in the Indian Administrative Service out of a total cadre of 2459.[117] Similar trends were seen also in the Army.[118]

By itself, this break in traditional training pattern may not have changed the attitudes of the bureaucratic elites in India. As an Indian writer, a former member of the Indian Civil Service commented later, when the British left India, "their administrative traditions, indeed the whole corpus of their administrative precept left with them."[119] This was because, he thought, British administrative ethos was accepted by the Indian members of ICS "merely as an expedient, to be cast aside as soon as independence and the resurgence of Indian way of life made it possible."[120] Perhaps an exaggeration. But when one considers the change in the composition of the elite cadres of the civil service along with the sharp diminution of direct British participation immediately after independence, the relative decline in the importance of the cadre as an institutional matrix for the diffusion of British norms became quite significant.[121]

Along with the changes in the composition of the elite structure in the bureaucracy, the composition of the political elites has also changed in the two states. Men of the generation of Churchill and Attlee in Britain, and of Gandhi and Nehru in India, have passed from the political scene, and the effective leadership of the political parties has passed on to those who no longer have the same sentimental involvement in Indo-British affairs as that of their predecessors. While this may lead to the establishment of Indo-British relations on a more realistic appraisal of each other's interests, this may also lead to an attitude of indifference and apathy towards each other's problems and difficulties.

NOTES AND REFERENCES

1. See, K.E. Boulding : 'National Images and International Systems' in James N. Rosenau (ed.) ; *International Politics & Foreign Policy* (Free Press of Glencoe, 1961).

2. In the context of Indo-British relations this would include, for example, the 'India Study Group' of the Royal Institute of International Affairs at the Chatham House (London), the Institute for Strategic Studies (London), the Royal United Services Institution (London), the Institute of Commonwealth Studies (at the Universities of London and Oxford), the Centre for South Asian Studies at the University of Sussex, in Britain ; and the Indian Council of World Affairs (New Delhi), and the Indo-British Historical Association (Madras), in India. This list is not exhaustive. A list of such groups is given in Appendix VI.

3. See, G.A. Almond : *The American People and Foreign Policy* (Praeger, N. York, rev. edition, 1960), p. 139.

4. In 1948-49, for example, imports from UK constituted 28.6% of total imports into India, and exports to that country constituted 23.2% of total exports. See, Appendix-II, Table-I.

5. In mid-1948, British investments in India amounted to Rs. 206.0 crores, out of a total foreign investment of Rs. 255.8 crores. See Appendix-II, Table-III.

6. On 14 August, 1947, the Government of India had £ 1160m in London as sterling balances. See *Cmd.* 7195.

7. See G. Schuster and G. Wint : *India and Democracy* (Macmillan, London 1941. pp. 417-18). For a characteristic example of the disdainful attitude of the British officials towards Indians, especially educated Indians, see F.W. Tuker ; *While Memory Serves* (Cassell, London, 1950). But the best description of this attitude is in E.M. Forster : *Passage to India*, first published in 1924.

8. E. Thompson and G.T. Garratt ; *The Rise and Fulfilment of British Rule in India* (Macmillan, London, 1934), p. 533.

9. This point has been developed in Nirad C. Chaudhuri : 'Blaming India's British Friends' in *The Times* (London), 21 September, 1971.

10. N. Mansergh : *The Commonwealth Experience*, (Weidenfeld & Nicolson, London, 1969), p. 403.

11. Mrs V.L. Pandit said in the Lok Sabha on 24 September 1965 that the British often forgot that they could not run the Commonwealth in the same way as they ran the empire. See, *Parliamentary Debates* (Lok Sabha) 3rd series, Vol. XLVI, No. 29, cols. 7528-29. Mrs Pandit. Nehru's sister, was Indian High Commissioner to the United Kingdom (1952-61). For further information see Chap. 2, p. 60 below.

12. John Freeman : *Pattern of Independence* (Tagore Memorial Lecture, London, 1968) mimeo. Mr Freeman was British High Commissioner to India (1965-68).

13. Cited in Pyarelal : *Mahatma Gandhi* : *The Last Phase* (Navajivan Publishing House, Ahmedabad, 1958), vol. II, p. 302.

14. *Jawaharlal Nehru's Speeches*, vol. I, September 1946-May 1949. (Publications Division, Ministry of Information and Broadcasting, Government of India, New Delhi, 2nd edition, 1958), p. 21.

14a. On 3 February, 1950, Nehru informed the Lok Sabha that one important reason for India remaining in the Commonwealth was the large number of Indians living abroad in the British colonies. "By our remaining in the Commonwealth, these Indians are in a better position than they would be otherwise.... Had we left the Commonwealth, it would have put millions of our people in a difficult position...", said Mr Nehru, see, *Jawaharlal Nehru's Speeches*, vol. II, p. 273.

15. See Krishna Menon's interview with Prof. Brecher in M. Brecher : *India and World Politics* : *Krishna Menon's View of the World*, p. 20.

16. Ibid.

16a. See Durga Das (ed.) ; *Sardar Patel's Correspondence 1945-50*, Vol. 8 (Navajivan Publishing, Ahmedabad, 1973), Ch. 1. See, particularly, Nehru's letters to Patel dated 12.1.49, 14.3.49, 26.3.49, 14.4.49 ; and telegrams Nos. 6-8, 10 & 11 (dated 23.4.49) ; Nos. 13-18 (dated 26.4.49), and telegram No. 20 (dated 23.4.49), No. 19 (dated 27.4.49).

17. *Hansard* (Commons), 5 series, vol, 420, col. 1421.

18. *Ibid*, vol. 439, col. 2446.

19. See Leo Amery's letters to Attlee, written on 30 November, 1948, 14 April 1949, and 19th April 1949, in *Private Papers of Attlee*, University College Library, Oxford, file no. 4.

20. *Ibid.* See letter of 14.4.49, p. 1. There were others, such as Lord Wavell who thought that it would be highly dangerous to have Pakistan in the Commonwealth and India out of it. See, Penderel Moon (ed.) ; *Wavell : The Viceroy's Journal* (O.U.P., London, Karachi, New Delhi, 1973) p. 437.

21. See M. Brecher ; *op, cit.*, p. 21. The Service chiefs in Britian, however, were toying with the idea of establishing a base in Pakistan and letting India go, if she wished. See P. Moon (ed) ; *op. cit.* p. 437.

22, See his letter to Attlee on 30th November 1948, p.l., *Private Papers of Attlee.*

23. *Ibid.*, See his letter of 14th April, 1949, p. 2.

24. See Krishna Menon's interview with M. Brecher in M. Brecher *op. cit.*, p. 21.

24a. See Durga Das (ed.) : *op. cit.* p. 8. Attlee's suggestion was made in his letter to Nehru dated 20 March, 1949. In forwarding the same to Patel, Nehru dismissed it as 'a naive document.'

25. See, *Hansard* (Commons), 5 series, vol. 464, col. 370, 28 April, 1949. Italics added.

26. See, M. Brecher ; *op. cit.*, p. 24. Also, see T.J.S. George ; *Krishna Menon : A Biography* (Cape, London, 1964), pp. 161-62.

27. For the text, see N. Mansergh ; *Documents and Speeches on British Commonwealth Affairs 1931-52*, vol. I (O.U.P. for R.I.I.A., London, 1953), p.1.

28. *Ibid.*, vol. 11, p. 848.

29. See, M. Mansergh ; *Survey of British Commonwealth Affairs : Problems of War-time Co-operation and Post-war Change 1939-52* (O.U.P. for R.I.I.A., London, 1958), p. 252.

30. *Ibid.*, p. 253.

31. For further discussion on this, see J.D.B. Miller ; *The Commonwealth in the World* (G. Duckworth, London, 3rd edn., 1965), pp. 111-12.

32. See Oliver S. Franks : *Britain and the Tide of World Affairs* (B.B.C. Reith Lectures, 1954. O.U.P., London, 1955), p. 15.

33. See his speech on 16 May, 1949, in N. Mansergh ; *Documents 1931-52*, vol II, p. 848.

34. *Hansard* (Commons), 5 series, vol. 464, cols. 372-73.

35. N. Mansergh ; *Documents* 1931-52, vol. II, p. 853.

36. See, Patrick Gordon Walker : *The Commonwealth* (Mercury Books, London, 1965), p. 351. Mr Gordon Walker was Under-Secretary of State for Commonwealth Relations (1947-50), and the Secretary of State for Commonwealth Relations (1950-51) ; Secretary of State for Foreign Affairs (Oct. 1964-Jan. 1965) ; Minister without Portfolio (1967) and Secretary of State for Education (1967-68).

Also see M. Brecher : *India and World Politics : Krishna Menon's View of the World*, pp. 137-138.

37. See, N. Mansergh ; *Documents and Speeches on Commonwealth Affairs 1952-62* (O.U.P. for R.I.I.A. London, 1963), p. 754, Also see. Nehru's speech to the Lok Sabha on 8 April, 1953. He said, inter alia, "I think that our being in the Commonwealth...in a sense gives us larger freedom in international activity than otherwise, to a certain extent. And we have utilised that freedom and we propose to utilise it." See *Parliamentary Debates* (Lok Sabha), 3 series, vol. III No. 8, pt. II, col. 3961. Krishna Menon, also, said later ; "...I have said many times that by being an equal member of this society (i.e. the Commonwealth) we have influence in the Commonwealth,...that is quite true. When I was High Commissioner they (the British) did practically what I asked them." See M. Brecher ; *op. cit.*, p. 26.

38. See Foreign & Commonwealth Office : *A Year Book of the Commonwealth 1971* (H.M.S.O., London, 1971), p. 4.

39. *The Third Report from the Select Committee on Estimates*, 1958-59 session, see The Memorandum submitted by CRO on 29 Jan. 1959 (H.M.S.O. London 1959).

40. Patrick Gordon Walker : "Commonwealth Secretary" in the *Journal of Commonwealth Political Studies*, vol. 1, No.1, p. 25.

41. K. Robinson : 'The Intergovernmental Machinery of Consultation and Co-operation' in W. B. Hamilton et al, (eds) ; *A Decade of the Commonwealth 1955-64* (Duke University Press, Durham, N.C., 1966), p.89.

42. Though there was no separate minister for the conduct of India's relations with the Commonwealth countries, there was a division of responsibility within MEA between a foreign Secretary dealing with India's external relations in general and an Addl. Secretary looking after relations with the Commonwealth.

43. See, Anthony Eden : *Full Circle : Memoirs of Sir Anthony Eden* (Cassell, London, 1960), pp. 94-99.

44. Ibid.

45. Later on, the Minister ceased to be a member of the Cabinet. When the Conservatives came to power in 1970, MOD was merged with the Foreign and Commonwealth Office, to be separated again in 1974.

46. In 1949-50, the home establishment of CRO consisted of 972 men ; the figures for 1956-57, 1957-58 and 1958-59 were 957, 726 and 737 respectively. See *Third Report from the Select Committee on Estimates*, CRO Memorandum of 29 January, 1959, pp. 6-7. In 1956, the Administrative Staff of CRO totalled only 135 ; 70 of them working in London and the rest in the various UK posts in the Commonwealth. See, W.J.M. Mackenzie and J.W. Grove : *Central Administration in Britain* (Longmans, London, 1957) p. 225. After 1959, with the rapid increase in the number of Commonwealth members CRO also expanded.

47. Patrick Gordon Walker : 'The Commonwealth Secretary', p. 25.

48. *Ibid.*

49. See Patrick Gordon Walker : *The Cabinet* (Cape, London, 1970), pp, 135-37,

50. *Ibid.*, p. 137.

51. For the text of the statement, see *The Times*, 7 August, 1954. For a brief discussion on this, see Chap. 4.

52. For the statement by Mr Dodds-Parker, the then Under-Secretary of State in CRO, see *Hansard* (Commons), 5 series, vol. 531, col. 242, 25 October, 1954. The statement has been quoted in Chap. 4.

53. Patrick Gordon Walker : 'The Commonwealth Secretary', p. 25.

54. *Report of the Committee on Representational Services Overseas* (Plowden Report), *Cmnd*, 2276 (H.M.S.O., London, 1964), p. 12.

55. *Ibid.*, p. 13.

56. *The Diplomatic List 1970* (H.M.S.O., London, 1970), p. iii.

57. Though there was no separate ministry to deal with India's relations with the Commonwealth countries, within the Ministry of External Affairs, there was a division of responsibility between a 'Foreign Secretary' dealing with India's external affairs in general, and an 'Additional Secretary', in charge of India's relations with the Commonwealth countries. In course of time, the latter come to be known as the 'Commonwealth Secretary'. Both the Foreign and Commonwealth Secretaries worked under the overall control of the Secretary-General—a post which was almost in continuous existence between 1947-64. with a short break in 1952. The post of the Secretary-General was abolished in 1964. After the reorganisation of MEA in 1965, the post of the 'Commonwealth Secretary' was also abolished. Under the new arrangement, the Foreign Secretary became the head of MEA ; below him there were two other secretaries—Secretary EA-1 and Secretary EA-II.

The re-organisation of the policy-making machinery has thus done away with the formal recognition of the 'Commonwealth' as a special area of interest for the foreign policy makers. For details of the changes, see, *Report of the Committee on Indian Foreign Service* (Ministry of External Affairs, Government of India, New Delhi 1968, pp. 1-2.

58. *Ibid.*

59. M. Brecher : *Nehru : A Political Biography* (abridged edition, O.U.P. London, 1961), p. 216,

60. See, M. Brecher ; *India and World Politics : Krishna Menon's View of the World*, pp. 249-51. Also see J. Bandyopadhyay : *The Making of India's Foreign Policy* (Allied Publishers, Bombay/Calcutta/New Delhi/Madras, 1970), pp. 140-44.

61. On this, see V. Sheean ; *Nehru : The Years of Power* (Victor Gollancz, London, 1960,) pp, 238-55.

Also see, M. Brecher : *Nehru : A Political Biography*, pp. 219-20.

62. M. Brecher : *India and World Politics : Krishna Menon's View of the World*, especially ch. 2.

63. *Ibid.*, p. 29.

64. Cited in Walter Crocker : *Nehru : A Contemporary's Estimate* (Allen & Unwin, London, 1966), p. 113.

65. For a discussion on the distinction between India's foreign *economic* policy and foreign *political* policy, see, Warren Illchman ; "Political Development and Foreign Policy : The Case of India" in *Journal of Commonwealth Political Studies,* vol. IV, No. 3, November, 1966.

66. H. Dayal : "The Organisation of Consular and Diplomatic Services with special reference to India" in *India Quarterly,* Vol. XII, No. 3, July-September, 1956, pp. 275-76. Mr Dayal, at the time of writing this article, was Joint Secretary and Foreign Service Inspector in MEA.

67. W. Illchman ; *op. cit.*, p. 223.

68. J. Bandyopadhyay ; *op. cit.*, p. 141.

69. For a discussion on the background and genesis of the Cotton Textile issue, see K.K. Sharma : 'Anti-British Pick on Cotton' in *Financial Times*, 9 July, 1971. Also see, Chapter 5.

70. See *The Guardian,* 3 July, 1971.

71. See, the text of the joint Indo-UK statement of 21 June, 1971, in *India News* (Indian High Commission, London) 26 June 1971, p.1. For expression of similar views by other officials in India, see *The Times*, 25 June, 1971.

72. For example, *Annual Report 1964-65* devoted 13 lines on Indo-UK relations, *Report 1965-66*, 20 lines, *Report 1966-67*, 29 lines, *Report 1967-68*, 17 lines and *Report 1968-69*, 19 lines. These, however, do not include the space devoted to the problems relating to the migration of Indians to Britain.

73. Winston Churchill, in his speech before the House of Commons on 30 July, 1948, said that Hyderabad had an indefeasible right to independence, and that it was fully entitled to membership of the U.N. if accepted by that body. Referring to a speech by Nehru in which he was reported to have said that the Indian Government were prepared for military action against Hyderabad, if necessary, Churchill commented : "It seems to me that this is the sort of language which really might have been used by Hitler before the devouring of Austria, but I think he was more careful in the choice of language...All these matters, these incidents, cannot be brushed aside as of no consequence, merely because they are committed one against another by Indians." For the full text of Churchill's speech see *Hansard* (Commons), 5 series, vol. 454, cols. 1726-33 ; also see Mr Selwyn Lloyd's speech on the same day in *Ibid.*, cols. 1722-26, and of Mr Butler, during a foreign affairs debate on 4 May, 1948 in *Ibid.*, vol. 450, cols. 1127-28.

74. See, for example, Attlee's speech during the debate on Hyderabad and Kashmir on 30 July, 1948 in *ibid* vol. 454, cols. 1737-40. Also see, Herbert Morrison's speech in reply to the debate on the King's speech on 28 October, 1948 ; *Ibid.*, vol 457, especially cols. 266-69.

75. Jennie Lee : "Socialists can be proud of India" in *Tribune*, 29 June,

1956 reproduced in E. Thomas (ed.) ; *Tribune 21* (Macgibbon & Kee, London, 1958), p. 272.

76. *Ibid.*

77. See, S.E. Finer, et al. : *Back-bench Opinion in the House of Commons 1955-59* (Pergamon Press, Oxford/London, 1961), p. 54.

78. *The Hindu*, 17 November, 1955.

79. Cited in S.E. Finer et al.; *op. cit.*, p. 39.

80. *The Times*, 17 November, 1955.

81. EDM 27/1956. See, House of Commons : *Notices of Motions : Questions and Orders of the Day*, vol. 1, November-December 1956, p, 703.

82. S.E. Finer, et. al. *op. cit.*, p. 37

83. The term refers to those within the Party who were 'hawks' on the Suez issue and were against the policy of withdrawal from Egypt. See, S.E. Finer et. al. ; *op. cit...*, p. 91.

84. Colin Jackson : 'Time to Remember India', in *Venture*, October, 1956, vol. 8, no. 5, p. 6.

85. See, The Labour Party : *Report of the 56th Annual Conference*, (Transport House, London, 1957,) p.181. Mr Bevan retorted by saying : "No. Nehru has no bomb, but he has got all other weapons he wants. Nehru has no bomb, but ask Nehru to disband the whole of his police force in relation to Pakistan, and see what Nehru will tell you." *Ibid.*

86. See S.E. Finer et al.; *op cit.*, pp. 104-106, 123-124.

87. *Ibid.*, p. 125. The Conservative 'Monday club' may be closely associated with this group.

88. A typical example of this attitude was the almost vituperative campaign launched against Nehru by the right-wing press in Britain during the Indo-Portuguese dispute over Goa in 1954-55, and again, in 1961, when Indian troops occupied Goa. See, for example, editorial comments in *The Daily Express* and *The Daily Telegraph*, for the relevant periods. On the attitude of the right-wing press towards India and Nehru also see, Maurice & Taya Zinkin ; *Britain and India : Requiem for Empire* (Chatto & Windus, London, 1964), p. 131 and D. Ingram : 'Commonwealth Communications—The Press', I.C.S. Seminar Paper, 14 November, 1967.

89. See comments by Francis Williams in the *New Statesman*, 24 December, 1961.

90. This refers to the Congress party as it was before its split in 1969. The party was split into two factions in 1969. The two new parties are now generally labelled as The Congress Party of India (Requisitionists) or the Ruling Congress, and the Congress Party of India (Organisation) or the Opposition Congress. The Congress (R) attracted nearly two-thirds of the membership of the original Congress party.

During the sixties, the Communist Party of India was also split into two halves, following the open split in the international communist movement—The Communist Party of India and The Communist Party of

India (Marxists), popularly dubbed as the pro-Moscow Communists and the pro-Peking Communists respectively. The distinction is misleading, particularly since 1967 when the hard-core militants of the Communist Party of India (Marxist) broke away to form The Communist Party of India (Marxist-Leninist), popularly known as the Naxalites.

91. See M.S. Rajan ; *India in World Affairs 1954*-56 (Asia Publishing House, London, 1964), p. 351. Also see K.R. Pillai ; *India's Foreign Policy : Basic Issues and Political Attitudes* (Meenakshi Prakasan, Meerut, 1968).

92. See footnote 90.

93. *Parliamentary Debates* (Lok Sabha) Vol. 3, No.8, pt. 11, 8th April 1953, col. 3929.

94. *Ibid.*, col. 3930.

95. *Ibid.*, vol. 9, No. 4, pt. 11, 19th November 1956, col. 398.

96. See, K.R. Pillai ; *op. cit.*, p. 162.

97. *Rajya Sabha Debates*, vol. XLVI, No.8, col. 1253. Speech by Mr. Ruthnaswamy.

98. For a general discussion on the foreign policy alternatives as proposed by the spokesmen of different political parties in India, see R. Bhatkal (ed) ; Political Alternatives in India (Popular Prakasan, Bombay, 1967). K.R. Pillai also presents a useful section containing excerpts from the election manifestos of the different political parties in India for the first four general elections. See, K.R. Pillai ; *op.cit.* pp. 205-36. Also see, Sisir Gupta : "Foreign Policy in the 1967 Election Manifestos". in *India Quarterly* (New Delhi), January-March 1967.

99. This would include, in the context of relations between two states, the senior diplomats accredited to each partner country by the other. For a brief discussion on the Indian and British High Commissioners accredited to London and New Delhi respectively.

100. In 1951, for example, of the 2 Secretaries in MEA, 1 was a member of ICS. Of the 34 senior officers in different departments of the central government in New Delhi, as listed in a CRO publication, 18 were members of ICS. See, CRO ; *List 1951*, p. 140.

In 1955, all the 3 Secretaries in MEA were members of ICS, as were all the 4 Secretaries in 1960, and all the 4 Secretaries in 1965. See, CRO ; *List 1953*, p. 160, *List, 1960*, p. 176 and *List 1965* p. 267.

101. As late as 1959-60, of the 16 senior officers in the Indian Army, listed in the Armed Forces Year Book, 13 were commissioned from Sandhurst and two had their education at the military academy at Woolwich. See J. Singh (ed) : *Indian Armed Forces Year Book 1959-60* (Bombay 1960). pp. 865-77.

* See, M. Brecher ; "India's Decision to Remain In the Commonwealth" in *Jonrmal of Commonwealth and Comparative Studies* (London), vol. XII. No. 1. March 1974, p. 65.

102. For example, of the 6 Permanent Under-Secretaries of State in CRO between 1947-65, 2 were formerly in the India Office, and 4 in the

Dominion Office. Of these 6, one had been to India as High Commissioner, and one to Pakistan. Of the rest, one, Sir Saville Garner (later Lord Garner) was Dy. High Commissioner to India (1951-53). See, CRO ; *List 1965* (H.M.S.O. London, 1967), pp. 10-16.

103. See footnote 46. Referring to this Mackenzie and Grove wrote : "It is quite easy for everyone in the Administrative Class in the CRO to know others personally, and to keep in touch with the general course of business throughout the Commonwealth." See, W.J.M. Mackenzie and J.W. Grove ; *op. cit.*, p. 227.

104. For example, in 1958-59, CRO had to deal only with 10 countries. See *Third Report from the Select Committee on Estimates*, 1958-59 session. Minutes of evidence submitted by CRO on 29 Jan. 1959, pp. 6-7.

105. See H. Wilson ; *The Labour Government 1964-70 : A Personal Record.* (Weidenfeld and Nicolson and M. Joseph, London, 1971), pp. 133-34.

106. W.P. Kirkman ; *Unscrambling An Empire : A Critique of British Colonial Policy 1956-66* (Chatto & Windus, London, 1966), p. 173.

107. D.C. Watt : "The Making of Foreign Policy" in *The Review of Politics* (Vol. 24, No. 4, October, 1962) p. 580. Italics original.

108. D.C. Watt ; *Personalities and Policies : Studies in the Formulation of British Foreign Policy in the Twentieth Century* (Longmans, London, 1965) Chap. 1.

109. J.M. Lee : *Colonial Development and Good Government* (Clarendon Press, Oxford, 1967), Chap. 1. The 'official class' here refers to the traditional governing class within and outside the governmental structure. The latter includes the ex-Colonial Administrators, and representatives of financial and trading groups having interest in the colonies and former colonial territories.

110. For a short biographical note on each one of them, see Ch. 3.

111. An example of this was the 'Kipping Loan' instituted in 1963 on the recommendation of Sir Norman Kipping, the then director of the Federation of British Industries. For further discussion on this, see Chap. 5.

112. This would include the Voluntary Committee on Overseas Aid and Development, and its political power-house, Action for World Development, the Overseas Development Institute (London) and the Institute for Development Studies (at the University of Sussex), the Ministry of Overseas Development, and politicians such as Reg Prentice, Frank Judd, Sir George Sinclair, academics such as Michael Lipton and John White, and the voluntary charitable organisations such as Oxfam and the Christian Aid. This list is by no means exhaustive.

113. The Indian Council of World Affairs and the Indian School of International Studies (renamed School of International Studies and now a part of the Jawaharlal Nehru University), both in New Delhi, are two exceptions. But none of them enjoyed the intellectual prestige of the

Royal Institute of International Affairs in Britain. The Institute for Defence Studies and Analyses (New Delhi) was set up in the 1960s.

114. See M. Brecher : *India and World Politics* : *Krishna Menon's View of the World*, pp. 257-8.

115. See M. Kidron : *Foreign Investments in India* (O.U.P., London, 1965), especially pp. 103-10.

116. R. Braibanti ; 'Elite Cadres in the Bureaucracies of India, Pakistan, Ceylon and Malaya since Independence' in W.B. Hamilton et al. (eds.) ; *op. cit.*, p. 279.

117. See *Civil List of the Indian Administrative Service* (Ministry of Home Affairs, Government of India, New Delhi, 1968), p. 287.

118. See Appendix—III.

119 N.B. Bonarjee : *Under Two Masters* (O.U.P., Calcutta, 1970), p. 103.

120. *Op. cit.*, p. 105.

121. In the case of Pakistan, British influence has been more enduring. There were two principal reasons for this : (a) immediately after independence, a large number of British ICS officers continued to serve in Pakistan and they constituted 34 per cent of the total cadre of Pakistan Civil Service, compared to only 7 per cent in India ; and, (b) down to 1960 Pakistan continued to send her Civil Service recruits to England for a year's training either at Oxford or at Cambridge, a practice which was discontinued in India long before that. In 1963, 70 per cent of the officers of Pakistan Civil Service had training in Britain, compared to only 7 per cent of IAS Officers in India. See, R. Braibanti : *op. cit.*, p. 279.

CHAPTER II

NETWORK OF COMMUNICATIONS

AN ESTABLISHED network of communication is a necessary though not sufficient condition "for amicable relations between "two nations which are affected by each other's actions."[1] This applies to Indo-British as to all diplomatic relationships. An analysis of the instrumentalities of Indo-British relations—especially the governmental machinery of co-operation and consultation, and the various channels for attention and communication between the non-governmental elites—is, therefore, necessary to show the multiplicity of the ranges of communication between Britain and India which make Indo-British relations so different from the stereotyped formal relations existing between, say, India and the Soviet Union.

I

THE DIPLOMATIC CHANNEL OF COMMUNICATION BETWEEN THE TWO STATES : THE HIGH COMMISSIONER AND THE HIGH COMMISSION

There are various channels for communication between the foreign policy elites in the two states, and at various levels—from the Commonwealth Prime Ministers' Conference at the apex, through the bi-lateral meetings between ministers and officials, to the regular meetings of Commonwealth Ambassadors which used to be held at UN or at the UK Embassy in Washington. Day-to-day problems in inter-governmental relations are dealt with "either by direct correspondence between Governments or through the representatives (High Commissioners) whom Commonwealth Governments maintain in other Commonwealth capitals."[2] Professor Mansergh noted that in the early 1950s, though Government-to-Government communications continued to be extensively used by members of the Commonwealth, India, Canada and Britain adopted the practice of routing all their communications through their High

Commission Offices.[3] By 1963, according to an official British account,[4] this practice had become common throughout the Commonwealth.

The High Commissioners have the same diplomatic status and rank as Ambassadors, and enjoy the same diplomatic privileges and immunities as those enjoyed by Ambassadors. But the special title of High Commissioner was maintained to preserve the myth that the Commonwealth relationship meant something more than the relationship existing between two foreign countries. In the case of India, however, where the *inter se* doctrine was never accepted with the same enthusiasm as in Britain, the terminological distinction between an Ambassador and a High Commissioner was largely irrelevant, especially, after she became a republic. Since 1950, India has accredited her High Commissioners in the same way as Ambassadors.[5]

But in theory, at least, there is one substantial difference between a High Commissioner and an Ambassador. Whereas an Ambassador must do all his business through the department of External Affairs, or the Foreign Office, the High Commissioner is entitled to deal directly with other departments of Government.

> "The result", concluded a C.R.O. memorandum, "is that the High Commissioner and his staff at appropriate levels have contacts of an informal sort throughout the machinery of government. A point of particular note is that the U.K. High Commissioner has closer and more frequent contact with the Prime Minister of the Commonwealth country in which he is serving than is the case with the foreign heads of missions."[6]

This claim may be true theoretically. In London, Commonwealth High Commissioners may, no doubt, have easier access to Whitehall, and perhaps, to No. 10 Downing Street, than that available to an Ambassador of a foreign country. Whether this is equally true of all other Commonwealth capitals is not certain. We do not know, for example, whether the Russian Ambassador in New Delhi and his American counterpart have got the same access to the Prime Minister as their British colleague. A lot depends on the personality of the men concerned and the countries they represent. One is inclined to think that a man with the intellectual reputation and political background of Professor Galbraith would have as easy access to Prime Minister Nehru as, say, his contemporary British colleague—a quiet and affable career diplomat Sir Paul Gore-Booth (later Lord Gore-Booth).

UK High Commissioners in India

The role of the successive British High Commissioners in New Delhi and of the Indian High Commissioners in London would itself provide an interesting subject for study, though this cannot be attempted here. Nevertheless, the differences in style and background of the different individuals must be noted briefly to indicate something of the character of relationships between the political elites in Britain and India. Of the first four British High Commissioners in India,[7] Lt. Genl. Sir Archibald Nye and Mr Malcolm Macdonald were the most prominent ; but their styles of diplomacy were very different. Sir Archibald Nye was a soldier with a keen insight into Asia and India. Before his appointment as the British High Commissioner, he was the Governor of Madras ; and as British HighCommissioner to India, he was quite popular in New Delhi.[8]

Mr Malcolm Macdonald was a man with a different background. The son of a former Primer Minister, and himself a former Secretary of State for Dominion Affairs,[9] Mr Macdonald was prominent in his own right long before he became the High Commissioner to India. As the Governor General for Malaya (1946-48) and later the Commissioner General for UK in South East Asia (1948-55), he acquired personal experience of Asian affairs before becoming the British High Commissioner to India. A former Labour MP, he had the rather unusual distinction of being chosen for the post by a Conservative Government in London. He succeeded in projecting a popular image of Britain in India which, though sullied by the traumatic experience of 1956, was revived by his efforts, as well as by the efforts of the British Government in London. This was clearly demonstrated during the British Prime Minister, Mr Harold Macmillan's visit to India in 1958. At the end of Mr Macmillan's visit, the High Commissioner wrote to him :

> "You and your wife's visit to Delhi was a huge success. You made a tremendous impression on Nehru, his Cabinet colleagues and various other personalities who met you...Many visits here by VIPs have only a short, transitory impression...the impression left by you is quite different."[10]

Mr Macdonald's successor, Sir Paul Gore-Booth, was a career diplomat from the Foreign Office, with little previous experience of Indian affairs.[11] His period of stay in New Delhi (1960-65) coincided with a number of developments affecting Indo-British relations—the British Government's decision in the summer of 1961 to apply for membership of the European Economic Community, Indian annexation of Goa in December of that year, the Sino-Indian armed conflict of 1962, and the pressure put by the British and American Governments to settle the Kashmir dispute as a *quid pro quo* for Western military aid to India. If relations between Britain and India suffered a set-back in December 1961 because of the British Government's criticism of Indian action in Goa, they reached a new peak during and immediately after the Sino-Indian war of 1962. At that time Sir Paul was one of the most popular diplomats in New Delhi. But he had his problems too ; on occasions the views of his political boss Mr Duncan Sandys were not particularly welcomed by Indians, nor, perhaps, by Sir Paul himself.[12] Nevertheless, he made his mark as a diplomat in New Delhi.

Mr John Freeman, who succeeded Sir Paul Gore-Booth as the British High Commissioner to India, had experience in politics and journalism, but not in diplomacy. He was one of the ablest junior Ministers in Attlee's two successive Administrations.[13] But it was as the editor of the *New Statesman* (1961-64) that he was best known in India. When his appointment was announced, it was greeted with enthusiasm in India. It was thought at the time that he would constitute 'a hot line to 10 Downing Street' in the same way as Ambassador Galbraith did to the White House.[14] To the Indian intellectuals he represented that tradition in British politics exemplified by the *New Statesman*, though by the time he arrived in New Delhi, it was no longer in the mainstream of Indian political thinking. With this favourable background, did he succeed in interpreting the policies and attitudes of London to New Delhi? Before he could settle down to his job, he found himself knee-deep in the intricacies of Indo-Pakistani conflicts. First there was the crisis over the Rann of Kutch which suddenly erupted into an armed conflict between India and Pakistan in April, 1965. It was the successful mediatory role played by the British Government which brought about a settlement between the two parties. The British High Commissioners in New Delhi and Rawalpindi played a very important role in preparing the diplomatic background for the Shastri-Ayub agreement in London. Paying tributes to their efforts, Mr Wilson said in the House of Commons, on 5 May, 1965 :

> "I should like to pay my tribute to the tremendous work of the two High Commissioners, who met for seven hours to try to sort out the difficulties. This may be a guide to further activity of that kind in future."[15]

But a few months later, when the Indo-Pakistani war broke out, British diplomacy reached the nadir of its influence in India, because of the ill-advised diplomatic intervention by the British Prime Minister. The role of the British High Commissioner in New Delhi in this diplomatic *faux pas* is not clear. We do not know, for example, what was the course of action advised by the High Commissioner.[16] But there was a feeling, by no means confined to the High Commissioner, that the Prime Minister acted in haste.[17] During the latter part of his stay in New Delhi, he was faced with another problem which could have developed into a major row in Indo-British relations. When the British Government introduced legislation in 1968, to curb the entry into Britain of Kenya Asians holding British passports it created considerable indignation in New Delhi. Thanks to efforts made by both the Governments to keep passions cool, the incident passed off without a major diplomatic row. No doubt, part of the credit for this goes to

Mr Freeman. It also fell on him, during the latter half of the 1960s, to convey to Indians the message of Britain's withdrawal from her post-imperial role in South and South East Asia.

Indian High Commissioners in London

The role and influence of the successive Indian High Commissioners to Britain,[18] similarly depended on the personality of the people concerned, and the issues with which they had to deal. None of the first six Indian High Commissioners to London was a career diplomat ; four of them had been partly educated in England, and two—Krishna Menon and Mrs Pandit—were first-rate political personalities, already known in London, before they took up their appointments. Krishna Menon had established himself in London as a campaigner for India's independence.[19] During the lean years of his struggle against British imperialism, he developed friendship with many left-wing intellectuals in Britain. But he had, in the process, antagonised many others. When Krishna Menon was named India's first High Commissioner to Britain, the British Government was not very pleased with this announcement, and Attlee informed Nehru of his displeasure.[20] Krishna Menon had criticised Attlee when the latter sat on the Simon Commission, and had been a source of embarrassment to the Attlee Government between 1945 and the transfer of power in 1947. Relations between him and Stafford Cripps had also cooled following his criticism of the Cripps Mission to India. Nevertheless, he succeeded in establishing a *rapproachement* with both Attlee and Cripps. The relationship which developed between Attlee and Krishna Menon in later years was certainly more intimate than that existing between the Prime Minister and the representatives of other countries. In a letter marked 'strictly personal and confidential' Krishna Menon wrote to Attlee on 1 September, 1948 :

> "In the last twelve months I have come to know you better than I did in the past and, if I may say so with respect, have developed a genuine affection and regard for you. This has enabled me in part to struggle

> with some of the trying situations which had to be faced."[21]

Towards the end of the same letter he wrote :

> "This is not the kind of letter that the representative of one country writes to the Prime Minister of another and of a great state, but I hope you will forgive me if I have presumed by implication the right to greater intimacy than I may claim."[22]

To what extent this intimacy with the Prime Minister helped him to argue his country's case with the British Government is difficult to ascertain. After all, he was not a very easy man to get on with and his tendency to correspond directly with the Prime Minister of India (and to some extent with the Prime Minister of Britain as well), by-passing the normal channels of communication did not endear him to the bureaucrats either in London or in New Delhi. In the letter referred to above, he gave vent to a personal feeling of frustration about this. Referring to his dealings with the British Government he wrote :

> "I have the uncomfortable feeling that I am letting my side down by not recognising that we are very much on the outside and will perhaps remain so."[23]

Perhaps his outstanding achievement as Indian High Commissioner was to pave the way for the continuation of India's membership of the Commonwealth.

His successor, B.G. Kher, stayed in his post for six months too short a time to make any mark. He was succeeded by Mrs V.L. Pandit, perhaps the most popular Indian diplomat to U.K. to date. She had long experience in politics and diplomacy.[24] Her previous appointments included Ambassadorships to Moscow (1947-49), and to Washington (1949-51). She was the first woman to become the President of the General Assembly (1953-54). Above all, she was the sister of the Indian Prime Minister, and had his confidence. But how successful was she in influencing the British Government's policy on such sensitive issues as the Indo-Portuguese dispute over Goa during 1954-55, or, say, the Indo-Pakistani dispute over Kashmir which came up for discussion in the Security Council in 1957 ? That she failed to influence the British Government's attitude to the Kashmir dispute becomes quite evident from the Security Council deliberations in February, 1957. What is more, she even failed to elicit the sympathy of the Labour Party on this issue. This was, partly, the result of the setback in Indian contacts with the Labour Party—a process that started with the departure of Krishna Menon, and became quite pronounced in Mrs Pandit's time. With the Labour Party out of power, shift towards the conservatives was, perhaps, inevitable. But considering the fact that there were many Labour leaders who were sympathetic to India, this neglect was unwise and short-sighted. Mrs Pandit, as her country's representative, shared some of the responsibility for this.[24a].

With the exception of Mr Apa B. Pant, none of Mrs Pandit's successors made any marked impact in London. Mr M.C. Chagla, a distinguished Indian lawyer,[25] became the Chief Justice of the Bombay High Court at the relatively early age of 47. Before his appointment as High Commissioner, he was the Indian Ambassador to USA (1958-61). He stayed in London for only a year and was, perhaps too willing to go back to India to start his political career. His successor Dr J.N. Mehta (1963-66) was a physician by profession, and rose to be the Director-General of Health Services, Government of India (1947-48). During the 1950s, he held various ministerial appointments in the then Government of Bombay.[26] Later he became the Chief Minister of Gujarat (1960-63). By the time he came to London, he was 76. He was not particularly known for his initiatives and to many observers he gave the impression of being a politician in retirement rather than a diplomat in earnest. His successor, Mr S.S. Dhawan, was formerly a judge of the Allahabad High Court,[27] and stayed in London for less than two years. Among his friends in London he was known for his scholarship. But according to one view, his early recall was due to his relative ineffectiveness as Indian High Commissioner. When the name of his successor, Mr Apa B. Pant was announced, it caused not a little surprise in Whitehall, as he was involved in a controversy—for allegedly supporting the Mau Mau rebels—during his tenure of office as the Indian High Commissioner to East Africa. With long experience in diplomacy,[28] he was perhaps, the ablest Indian representative sent to Britain in recent years.

The Functions of the High Commissions

What are the functions of the High Commissions ? Both Britain and India maintain large 'comprehensive' missions in each other's capitals. Of all the Commonwealth countries, Britain maintained the largest diplomatic mission in India.[29] The size of the mission does not, by itself, always indicate the importance attached by one country to another. Indeed, the large size of the British High Commission in India was at the initial years, a legacy of the past. As the number of staff employed by the British High Commission Offices in India and Pakistan was so much larger than in other Commonwealth capitals, in 1958-59 the matter came under the review of the Select Committee on Estimates. Referring to the size of the Indian establishment Sir Gilbert Laithwaite, the then Permanent Under Secretary in CRO, told the sub-Committee 'E' of the Select Committee that when the establishment was set up "a rather exaggerated idea of what was necessary prevailed."[30] According to the evidence given to the sub-Committee, the main reasons for the size of the staff in India and Pakistan were : (1) the size of the countries, (2) the low level of mechanisation, (3) the relative inefficiency of locally-recruited clerical staff who were not proficient in English, as it is not their first language, and (d) "the natural human tendency to take more staff precisely because labour is cheap. This may sometimes take the very understandable form of a wish to save one more person from starvation."[31]

According to CRO, the office of the UK High Commissioner

> "is in effect an offshoot in a miniature form of the United Kingdom Government with the primary responsibilities of representing United Kingdom policies and interests in the Commonwealth country concerned and of advising the United Kingdom Government of the trends of policy of the Commonwealth Government as well as of major developments in the country generally."[32]

This is a fairly general statement of the activities of the diplomatic missions. One particular task of the UK missions in India and Pakistan, which was not paralleled elsewhere, was to look after the interests of the British citizens scattered over the two countries. As Sir Gilbert pointed out :

> "Take Calcutta, which has, with the adjoining provinces, 13,000 United Kingdom citizens. This is quite a different position from Alberta in Canada or any Australian state, where United Kingdom citizens will be indistinguishable from the ordinary Canadian or Australian, and there would not be the same need to look after particular minor business interests..."[33]

The extent of influence exerted by the British Government, through the High Commission in promoting UK commercial interests in India is difficult to determine. But the importance of this aspect of the High Commission's function was emphasised by a number of witnesses in their evidence before the sub-Committee 'E' of the Select Committee on Estimates.[34]

The work of the High Commission offices may broadly be divided into (a) diplomatic or political, (b) trade promotion and (c) consular. Of these three only the first category of work was performed by Commonwealth Service Officers. In India the work of trade promotion and reporting on local economic conditions was entrusted to the Trade Commission headed by a Senior Trade Commissioner who was an officer of the Board of Trade. He had his own staff who were not members of the Commonwealth Service. But they worked in close contact with the staff of the High Commissioner who was responsible for matters of discipline within the High Commission. The Senior Trade Commissioner also acted as an Adviser to the High Commissioner on economic matters. Publicity work was handled by the Central Office of Information, and by the Information Officers of CRO. The CRO's Information Service concerned itself primarily with political, economic and commercial propaganda. According to a CRO memorandum, roughly one third of the work of UK Information Officers in the Overseas Commonwealth was in support of British trade interests.[35] "Relationships between the Information Services and Trade

Commissions are close and in India, for instance, offices are shared and there is regular consultation."[36]

But the division of political and economic work between two separate groups of officers with different departmental loyalties made co-ordination of work difficult, and was criticised by the Select Committee on Estimates. It was with an eye to remedying this defect that the Plowden Committee recommended in 1964 the establishment of a unified Diplomatic Service embracing the former Commonwealth, Foreign and the Trade Commission Services.[37]

However, this separation of functionaries doing 'political' and 'economic' work, had some advantages as well. One feature of this division of work was that changes in the political and economic aspects of relationship between Britain and India were not always parallel. For instance, even at a time of 'political' crisis in Indo-British relations, officers in the British High Commission who dealt with economic issues could maintain the 'dialogue' with the economic ministries in New Delhi.

Sending regular reports about the political developments in the host country is one of the important functions of the High Commission, as of any diplomatic mission. But the importance of the 'subjects' for reporting changes with time. For example, one British diplomat with long experience of Indian affairs said that in the early 1950s the Kashmir problem was one of the major preoccupations of the British High Commissioner in New Delhi.[38] Reports about political developments also included extensive coverage on state politics. With the passage of time, however, the need for such function came to be questioned, and the extent of reporting on state politics has declined. But the High Commission officials became involved in other activities. During the 1960s, an important part of the High Commission's function related to 'aid',[39] and, immigration, especially after the introduction of regulations in 1969, making entry certificates compulsory for the dependents of Commonwealth immigrants.[40] Thus, at a time when Britain's political and economic interests in India were on the decline, the British Government maintained a large 'comprehensive' mission in India, partly to deal with subjects which are not, strictly speaking, 'political'.

The Indian High Commission

The Indian High Commission in London is "a class by itself."[41] It is more than a 'diplomatic' mission, in the ordinary sense. In a way it is a microcosm of the whole Government of India, with representatives of nearly half the ministries of the Government in New Delhi. During the 1960s many of the personnel were not engaged in diplomatic work, but handling such matters as purchase and inspection of stores all over Europe, for which there was an Indian Supply Mission in London. Again, because of the large number of Indian students in Britain, there was a large Education Department in the High Commission.[42]

But these are, however, the peripheral functions. The core of the High Commission's functions may be divided into (a) political, (b) economic and (c) consular. Unlike the British practice prior to 1964, political-diplomatic and economic aspects of functions of the Indian diplomatic missions overseas have always been handled by members of a single service—the Indian Foreign Service. While this made co-ordination of work easier, there was a tendency among the Foreign Service Officers "to look askance at economic and commercial duties."[43] The Committee on the Indian Foreign Service therefore recommended that the Heads of Missions should play their full part in commercial work and be encouraged to take sustained interest in it.

The Information work in the Mission was originally handled by an Information Officer drawn from a separate group of officers who were specially recruited for publicity work abroad, with professional experience in journalism and public relations. The Information Officer tended to regard himself as being outside the fold, and corresponded with the External Publicity Division directly, often independent of the Head of the Mission. In 1959, it was decided by the Government of India that information function should be taken over by the Foreign Service and further recruitment of Information Officers was stopped.[44]

Both Britain and India maintained in each other's capital a large complement of Service Officers attached to their respective High Commissions.[45] The specialist officers within the High

Commission, while under the overall control of the Head of the Mission, are seconded from the different specialist Ministries in New Delhi, and as such can correspond with them directly. The size of the Indian High Commission has however been reduced following the recommendations of an IFS Inspection team that visited London in 1967.

The Multilateral Links

While day-to-day consultation between the two Governments is carried through their respective High Commissioners, there are various other channels of communication between them, both bilateral and multilateral. Most of these channels are, however, peculiar to the Commonwealth organisation, and cannot be used by India in the conduct of relations with, say, USA or USSR.

At the apex of the inter-Governmental machinery of co-operation are the Prime Ministers' Conferences which are in fact meetings attended by the heads of the Commonwealth Governments, or by persons designated by them. For example, since the adoption of a Presidential form of Government in Pakistan, she has generally been represented at these meetings by the President, as was Cyprus or Ghana after their independence. The meetings are held to discuss a wide range of subjects : international affairs, economic issues and intra-commonwealth constitutional problems ; and generally avoid discussion of intra-commonwealth disputes such as the Indo-Pakistani dispute over Kashmir. However, intra-Commonwealth disputes could be discussed informally, and outside the plenary sessions. Lord Attlee said later about the Commonwealth Prime Ministers' Conference :

> "There are generally some inter-Dominion difficulties, either unimportant or large, but it is not the practice to discuss these at formal meetings. In my time there was the very grave difficulty between India and Pakistan over Kashmir ; the matter was never raised at a formal meeting, but a vast amount of time was taken up, both by me and by other Commonwealth Prime Ministers, in endeavouring to reach a settlement."[46]

The Commonwealth Prime Ministers' Conference also provided excellent opportunities for bilateral informal contacts among the member states, and the successive British Governments have taken an active interest in promoting such contacts. In 1955, for example, Britain and India discussed the Formosan crisis, and with Canada, the crisis in Indo-China. During the 1956 Commonwealth Prime Ministers' Conference, the Indian and Pakistani Prime Ministers met at No. 10 Downing Street informally. Mr Macmillan wrote about this later in the following words :

> "Since the two men (Nehru and Suhrawardy) are on the worst of terms and never met—either in India or in London—this was rather a risk. But the talk—which lasted an hour—went off very well."[47]

A more significant meeting between the Indian Prime Minister and the Pakistani President took place in 1965, under the auspices of the British Prime Minister, when they came to London to attend the Commonwealth Prime Ministers' meeting.[48] The outcome of this meeting was an agreement between the Indian and Pakistani leaders to settle the Rann of Kutch dispute through international arbitration.

Apart from the Prime Ministers' meetings there have been regular ministerial meetings dealing with particular fields of activity. During the years 1947-54, there were meetings of Foreign Ministers (1950), Defence Ministers (1951) and of the Supply (1951) and Finance Ministers (1952 and 1954). Since 1954, meetings of Finance Ministers were regularly held almost annually, except in 1962.[49] In 1958 a Commonwealth Trade and Economic Conference was held in Montreal when it was decided to set up a Commonwealth Economic Consultative Council to co-ordinate the actions of the existing machineries in the field of trade and economic affairs.[50] Meetings of the Council, both at official and ministerial levels have been held annually between 1959-65, except in 1962.

A wide range of Inter-governmental agencies have been established within the Commonwealth to deal with specific subjects. Some of these functional organisations are concerned with the systematic supply of specialist information such as the

Executive Council of the Commonwealth Agricultural Bureaux and the Commonwealth Economic Committee ; others act in a purely advisory capacity, such as the Commonwealth Telecommunications Board and the British Commonwealth Scientific Committee. While the activities of these functional agencies may have little political bearing on Indo-British relations, they do illustrate the multiplicity of the avenues as well as of the ranges of communication between the elites of the two states and, as such, are important.[51]

Any account of the governmental machinery of co-operation remains incomplete without reference to the regular meetings of the Commonwealth High Commissioners wihch used to be held in London, with the British Commonwealth Secretary in the chair. Such meetings were usually attended by a Minister from the Foreign Office. Similar meetings of Commonwealth Ambassadors were held in Washington at the British Embassy, every fortnight, except during summer and—as a former British Ambassador to USA wrote—discussed 'everything...even difficulties between individual members like Kashmir,...with conviction but without heat."[52] During the sixties, these regular meetings in London and Washington were no longer held, although special meetings were arranged, such as the 1962 meeting of Commonwealth High Commissioners in London during the EEC negotiations or the 1971 meeting of the High Commissioners of the sugar producing countries, to discuss the future prospects of the Commonwealth Sugar Agreement, once Britain joined EEC.

The regular multilateral meetings apart, there were also occasions for bilateral contacts between the executive (including the Ministers) and the legislative elites in the two states when Ministers, officials or legislators from one state visited the other. So far as ministerial visits are concerned, the flow of traffic has been heavier from New Delhi to London than the other way round. This was not surprising. Prime Minister Nehru used to visit London almost regularly to attend the Commonwealth Prime Ministers' Conferences ; but during 1947-65, only one British Prime Minister visited India. Similarly, other ministers also visited each other's capitals to discuss specific problems such as Finance Minister Desai's visit to London in 1957 to discuss India's foreign exchange problems, or, Defence Minister Chavan's visit to Britain in 1964 to discuss India's long-term defence needs. From the British side, some of the more important visits were : foreign secretary, Mr Selwyn Lloyd's visit to India in 1956, Commonwealth Secretary Mr Duncan Sandys's visit to India in the summer of 1962 to explain the reasons for the British Government's decision to apply for the membership of EEC, and again in October, immediately after the cessation of hostilities between India and China, to assess India's defence needs and to press Nehru for a settlement of the Kashmir dispute, and Foreign Secretary Michael Stewart's visit to India in 1968. Similar visits were also undertaken by high-ranking officials of the Government or by envoys-extraordinary to discuss specific issues, such as the Bhoothalingam mission to Britain in 1964, preceding Mr Chavan's visit, to prepare the ground for the discussion of India's long term need for arms, or the Mountbatten mission to India in 1965, to explain the British Government's immigration policy.[53]

Thus the existing machineries provided channels for almost continuous consultation and co-operation between the two states.

II

Communication Among The Non-Governmental Elites

The official relationships between the two states, important as they are, by no means exhaust or even adequately reveal the richness and variety in Indo-British relations. There is a vast network of personal and business contacts among those engaged in trade and commerce, and close links have developed between professional men such as university teachers, doctors and lawyers. Valuable links have also developed through art, sport and other cultural activities. Though they do not form a major part of the present study, a brief mention of some of these unofficial channels for attention and communication is necessary as they add a new dimension to Indo-British relations.

A large number of Indian students study in British universities every year,[54] and some British students also go to Indian

5

universities for specialised studies. This gives them an opportunity to acquire intimate knowledge about the problems facing the country, and the views of the people on important issues. The impressions they carry with them are important as most of the overseas-trained students are likely to end up in positions of influence in their later life. This is particularly true of Indo-British relations as a high proportion of India's Western-educated elite—politicians, administrators, and professional men—were educated in British universities. In the initial years after independence, many of them constituted a pro-British lobby in the higher echelons of the civil service, the army and in the universities.

Migration of people from one country to another is also an important channel of communication between two states. The experience of the immigrants in their new 'home' and the reception accorded to them by the 'host' community are generally reported back to their country of origin. This is particularly important in the case of Indo-British relations, as a large number of Indian immigrants reside in Britain.[55] If they feel insecure and suffer discrimination, and if their feelings be communicated to India, they may become a positive source of irritation in Indo-British relations.[55a]

In UK as will as in India, there are numerous cultural and educational organisations (e.g. the British Council), clubs (e.g. the ex-Servicemens' clubs and the regimental clubs), professional associations (such as the British Medical Association and its counterpart the Indian Medical Association), learned societies (e.g. the Royal Institute of International Affairs in London and its counterpart the Indian Council of World Affairs in New Delhi), sports associations (e.g. MCC and its counterpart the Board of Cricket Control in India) which are the residual links from the days of empire and provide opportunities for co-operation in cultural, educational, scientific and professional matters.[56] The professional links are particularly strong in law,medicine and the allied disciplines, in accountancy, and extends to such fields as banking, commerce and industry.

Exchange of visits by members of the academic and business communities (apart from those by the executive and legislative elites mentioned above) constitutes an important channel for communication at the elite level. English language newspapers, journals and periodicals constitute another link at the elite level, as the reporting and analysis of events in one country by the newspapers and journals of another are an important source of information for what Professor Almond has called the 'attentive Public'.[57]

In the field of reporting and journalism, Reuters and the Commonwealth Press Union peovide professional links between the journalists. Even in the field of broadcasting, BBC had close link with India. The BBC television's South Asia correspondent was India-based. In 1970 following the controversy between the Government of India and the British Broadcasting Corporation over the screening of a series of films on India by the French director Louis Malle, the BBC's office in India was closed and there was a temporary imposition of censorship on television filming. Since 1972, links with BBC have been partially restored.

Thus, besides inter-governmental agencies, there are numerous other important channels for attention and communication between the elites in the two states.

III

In the preceding pages we have analysed the various agencies of inter-governmental consultation and cooperation. But how effectively have these channels been used for the promotion of cooperation and prevention of conflict or misunderstanding between the two states ? In many cases, these channels were used very effectively, as was demonstrated by the cooperation between the two Governments during the Prisoners-of-war negotiations in Korea in 1953, Indo-China Peace conference in Geneva in 1954, the Formosan crisis in 1955, the conference on Laos in 1962 ; or by the close cooperation between the two states in the immediate aftermath of the Sino-Indian war of 1962. The then Permanent Under Secretary to the Commonwealth Relations Office told the Estimates Committee of the Parliament in 1959 that so far as consultation with the Commonwealth colleagues was concerned the British Government were, broadly speaking, most anxious to pass on all the information that they could. "If we have information which we have only been given on certain understanding, we are naturally bound by these understandings,"

> 'but, it "is an implicit understanding that is well-known, that we are anxious to keep our Commonwealth colleagues as fully informed as possible."[58]

and to illustrate this point Mr Sandys wrote in 1962 that during the previous year the British Government were in 'frequent communication' with other Commonwealth Governments on such subjects as Laos, the control of nuclear tests and the problems of Congo and Berlin.[59] The flow was by no means onesided. As Mr Sandys pointed out, other Commonwealth Governments also kept Britain informed about these matters and about other matters which were of special concern to them.[60]

Despite the facile official claims, exchange of information, in defence matters, between Britain and the various members of the Commonwealth was not exactly similar. For example, in defence matters sharing of "classified" information between Britain and Australia, or between Britain and Canada, was likely to be more extensive than that between Britain and India ; because unlike Australia and Canada, who were allied to Britain through regional defence pacts, India was non-aligned. Even in the matter of diplomatic information, it is doubtful whether New Delhi received as much information from C.R.O. as was received by Washington from the Foreign Office.

There was another limit to such consultation. When decisions were made involving the nation's "vital interests"—as seen by the decision-makers—such consultations were avoided. During the Suez invasion, the British Government's failure to consult India as a fellow member of the Commonwealth was one of the causes of resentment voiced by more than one Member in the Indian Parliament.[61] Defending the decision of the British Government Sir Anthony Eden said at the time, in a broadcast on 3 November 1956 :

> "Our friends inside the Commonwealth, and outside, could not, in the very nature of things, be consulted in

time. You just cannot have immediate action and extensive consultation as well."[62]

But a few years later he was more candid in giving the real reason. In the first place, there was not enough time for consultation.

"Nor was there any chance that all concerned would take precisely the same view of what action must follow consultation. As a result there would be attempts to modify our proposals to reach some compromise between divergent points of view and before we knew where we were, we would be back at an eighteen-power conference once more. This was the last thing in the world we wanted, because we knew quite well that once palavers began, no effective action would be possible."[63]

Britain was not alone in her failure to consult the Commonwealth partners. The Government of India did not consult the British Government before deciding to send troops to Goa in December, 1961, although there was wide-spread speculation in the press about the possibility of such a move by the Indian Army. Indeed, some diplomatic pressure was brought to bear on the Indian government by UK and USA not to proceed with the contemplated move.[64] Furthermore, the British government did not consult its Commonwealth partners before the devaluation of the Pound Sterling in 1949, or in 1967, nor did the Government of India consult the British government before devaluation of the 'Rupee' in 1966.

These were, however, exceptional cases. Normally, the existing channels for communication between the two Governments have been used in matters affecting the interests of one or both of them, as, for instance, was shown by the decision of Prime Minister Macmillan to send Mr Duncan Sandys to India in the summer of 1962 to explain the British Government's policy regarding the Common Market. The continuous exchange of views did not necessarily lead to an identity of policies ; but it continued even on issues where the two Governments failed to agree. This was demonstrated in 1954 by Sir Anthony Eden's anxiousness to consult Indian opinion before taking any final decision on the system of security in South-East Asia.

So far as the non-official channels for elite communication are concerned, their main contribution has been in the strengthening of the links between the two states in cultural, economic and professional spheres. The role of the mass media has been rather dubious. The mass media, especially the press and the television, have been a powerful though rough strand of relations between Britain and India. There have been bad feelings in India over what is regarded as the consistently hostile attitude of the British press and the television to affairs in India.[64a] Implicit to this criticism is the idea that this hostility was born out of a feeling of malice or spite against India and the Indians. This might be true of a section of the press. Certainly this cannot be said to be true of all the British newspapers and journals. For one thing, the British press, by no means, presents a united front on all issues ; the spectrum of views varies widely from the *Tribune*, the *Daily Mirror*, the *New Statesman* and the *Venture* on the one hand, to the *Daily Express*, the *Daily Herald*, the *Daily Telegraph*, and the *Spectator* on the other, with *The Times*, *The Guardian*, the *Sunday Times*, *The Observer*, *The Financial Times* and *The Economists* holding a large and variable 'middle ground'. Some of these papers and journals have generally taken a sympathetic attitude to the problems faced by India and the policies evolved to solve them. If, therefore. any emphasis is to be placed on the general and rather vague criticisms voiced by Indians, one has to make a special study of the British press and television reports and comments on Indian affairs over a period of time. This is not intended here.[65] But from an impressionistic study of British press reporting on Indian affairs, it appears that on many international disputes involving India, she got more than the fair share of the blame. The Kashmir dispute, particularly the Indo-Pakistani war of 1965 ; and the Indo-Portuguese dispute over Goa (1947-61), especially, Indian military action in December, 1961, are some of the examples. With a few exceptions, the view of the British government on such issues tended to coincide with the views expressed in different sections of the press, though the tone of criticism varied. While this does not necessarily mean the existence of a collusion between Whitehall and Fleet Street to embarrass or malign India, it is only fair to point out that the attitude of the British press on the issues mentioned above has contributed to the worsening of relations between Britain and India.

NOTES AND REFERENCES

1. B.M. Russett ; *Community and Contention : Britain and America in the Twentieth Century* (M.I.T. Press, Cambridge, Mass. 1963), p. 97. Also See, K.W. Deutsch et al.; *Political Community in the North Atlantic Area* (Princeton, 1957), p. 8.

2. C.R.O. ; *List 1964*, p. 125.

3. N. Mansergh : *Survey of British Commonwealth Affairs : Problems of War-time Cooperation and Post-War Change 1939-52* (OUP for R.I.I.A., London, 1958), p. 409.

4. Central Office of Information ; *Cooperation and Consultation in the Commonwealth* (H.M.S.O., London, 1963), p. 3.

5. See, *Third Report from the Select Committee on Estimates : Commonwealth Relations Office*, 1958-59 session (H.M.S.O., London, 1956, p. 2.)

6. *Ibid.*, p. 56. Prior to the publication of the Plowden Report in 1964, an important feature of British diplomatic missions in the Commonwealth countries was that the work of trade promotion was entrusted not primarily to the High Commissioner, but to the senior Trade Commissioner, who was an Officer of the Board of Trade. This practice of separating commercial and economic functions from "political" functions was terminated in 1965.

7, For a list of thelr names, see, Appendix IV, Table IIa.

8. S ee, for example, one of his contemporary's estimate in Chester Bowles ; *Ambassador's Report* (Harper & Brothers, N. York, 1954), p. 29.

9. Malcolm Macdonald : Member of Parliament (1929-45), Parliamentary Under-Secretary of State for Dominion Affairs in First and Second National Governments, August and November 1931—June 1935 ; Secretary of State for Dominion Affairs & Colonies, October 1938—September 1939, Secretary of State for Colonies, September 1939—May 1940, Minister of Health. May 1940—February 1941, British H.C. to Canada 1941-46, Governor-General, Malayan Union and Singapore, May-July 1946, Governor General for Malaya, Singapore and Borneo 1946-48, Commissioner General for UK in South East Asia 1948-55, and H.C. to India 1955-60. After his tenure of office in New Delhi, he became Co-Chairman of the International Conference on Laos 1951-62,

Governor of Kenya, January-December 1963, and H.C. to Kenya, 1964-65.

10. Cited in Harold Macmillan : *Riding The Storm 1956-59* (Macmillan, London, 1971), p. 389.

11. After his tenure of office in New Delhi, he became the Permanent Under-Secretary of the Foreign Office (later Foreign & Commonwealth Office), February 1965-69, and concurrently Head of the Diplomatic Service, March 1968-February 1969. He was made a life peer in 1969.

12. For example, at the end of the Sino-Indian war in 1962, Mr Sandys apparently proposed that India should enter into a military alliance with the West and come under a NATO nuclear deterrent. This proposal was not liked in India. According to Professor Galbraith, this 'perturbed' Sir Paul, but he defended the Minister 'in the finest traditions of English Civil Service'. See J.K. Galbraith ; *Ambassador's Journal : A Personal Account of the Kennedy Years*, (Hamish Hamilton, London, 1969) p. 498. During a personal interview with Lord Gore-Booth when he was asked to comment on this, he remained evasive.

13. In 1951, he resigned as Parliamentary Secretary to the Ministry of Supply, along with Bevin, over Gaitskell's budget.

14. See *The Times*, 11 January, 1965.

15. *Hansard* (Commons), 5 series, 1964-65 session, vol. 711, col. 1361.

16. On this point, see Ch. 3.

17. Personal impression gained from interviews with a number of British observers.

18. For a list of their names, see Appendix V, Table 1a.

19. Mr V.K. Krishna Menon : Barrister (Middle Temple), Secretary, India League (1927-47), Borough Councillor, St. Pancras (1934-47), Chairman, Arts Council of St. Pancras, Labour Party candidate for Dundee (1939-42), H.C. for India in UK (1947-52), Member, Indian Delegation to UN (1946), Dy. Chairman, Indian Delegation to UN, (1952), and Chairman, (1953-62) ; Member of Lok Sabha (1952-67) and (1969-74), Minister without Portfolio (1956) ; Minister of Defence (1957-62) and Minister for Defence Production (1962).

20. T. J. S. George ; *Krishna Menon : A Biography* (Cape, London,) pp. 155-56.

21. *Private Papers of Attlee* (University College Library, Oxford, file No. 6), p.1.

22. Ibid., p.4.

23. Ibid,, p.2.

24. V.L. Pandit : Member of the Congress Party and sentenced to three terms of imprisonment in 1932, 1941 and 1942 ; Minister of Local Self-Government and Public Health, U.P. (1937-39 and 1946-47), leader of Indian delegation to the U.N. (1946-51), Ambassador to USSR (1947-

49), to the U.S.A. (1949-51), Member of Parliament (1952-54), and (1964-68), H.C. to U.K. (1952-1961), Governor of Maharastra (1962-64).

24a. See, *The Statesman*, 6.4.57.

25. M.C. Chagla : Educated at Oxford and Inner Temple, Puisne Judge, Bombay High Court (1941-47) and Chief Justice (1947-58) ; Judge I.C.J. (1957), Member, Law Commission (1955-56), Ambassador to U.S., Mexico and Cuba (1958-61), H.C. to U.K. 1962-63, and Ambassador to Ireland (1962-63), Minister of Education, Government of India (1963-66), and Minister for External Affairs (1966-67), Member of Rajya Sabha.

26. Dr J.N. Mehta : Joined Bombay Cabinet as Minister for Public Works, in 1949 ; Minister of Finance, Bombay (1952-60), Chief Minister, Gujarat (1960-63), H.C. to U.K. (1963-66).

27. S.S. Dhawan : Educated at Cambridge and Inner Temple, Puisne Judge, Allahabad High Court (1958-67), President, Indo-Soviet Cultural Society, U.P. Branch (1965-67), H.C. to U.K. (1968-69), Governor of West Bengal (1969-71).

28. Apa B.Pant : Educated at Oxford and Lincoln's Inn, Member, All-India Congress Committee (1948), Commissioner for India to British East Africa (1948-54) and concurrently Commissioner to Central Africa and Nyasaland, Political Officer, Sikkim and Bhutan, with control over Indian mission in Tibet (1955-61), Ambassador to Indonesia (1961-64), to Norway (1964-66), UAR (1966-69), H.C. to U.K. (1969-72), and currrently Ambassadar to Italy and H.C. to Malta.

29. In 1958-59 for example, the total staff employed in British diplomatic missions in India was 634. The home establishment of CRO was 737. The number of men employed in Australia was 96, in Canada 115, in New Zealand 26, in South Africa 75, in Pakistan 323, in Ceylon, 61, in Ghana 52 and in the Federation of Rhodesia and Nyasaland 39. See, *Third Report from the Select Committee on Estimates,* 1958-59, pp. 6-7, Minutes of evidence submitted by CRO on 29 January 1959.

30. Lipton and Firn wrote that the British High Commission in New Delhi and the subordinate consulates at Bombay, Calcutta and Madras "together make up Britan's 7th costliest diplomatic community, her fourth largest in terms of UK-based staff and her second largest in terms of total staff." See, M. Lipton and John Firn ; *op. cit.* p. 172.

30. *Ibid.* p. 57.

31. *Ibid.*, p. VI.

32. *Ibid.*, p. 56. Memorandum submitted by CRO on 5 March 1959.

33. See Sir Gilbert's evidence on 29 January, 1959, *Ibid.*, p. 14.

34. See, for example, evidence by Sir Archibald Nye, on 7 May, 1959, *Ibid*, p. 112 ; and the evidenee of Sir Percival Griffiths, a former ICS officer with business links in India, especially in Tea, on 23 April, 1959, *Ibid.*, pp. 91-93.

35. See, *Third Report from the Select Committee on Estimates*, C.R.O. memorandum of 11 June, 1959.

36. *Ibid.*, p. 160.

37. *Report of the Committee on Representational Service Overseas, Cmnd* 2276 (H.M.S.O., London, 1964), p. 13.

38. Personal interview.

39. In December 1967, for example, the number of men employed full time, on aid and development work, at the British High Commission in New Delhi, and at the Dy. High Commission Offices at Calcutta, Bombay and Madras, was 9. In addition, 37 officers were attending to this as a part of their functions. See, *Hansard*, (Commons) 5 series, 1967-68 session, vol. 755, col. *398*, written answer.

40. In May 1970, 33 persons were working at the British High Commission Office in New Delhi and in the three Dy. High Commission offices, in connection with the issue of entry certificates. See, *Select Committee on Race Relations and Immigration, session 1969-70* ; *Control of Immigration.* Minutes of evidence by the Foreign and Commonwealth Office and the Home Office, on 7 May 1970 (H.M.S.O., London, 1970) p. 758. H.C. 17-XXVI.

41. H. Dayal : "The organization of diplomatic and consular services, with special reference to India" in *India Quarterly*, July-September, 1956, p. 277.

42. In 1971, for instance, the Education Department was headed by a Minister, Education and Scientific Affairs. See, Foreign and Commonwealth Office ; *A Year Book of the Commonwealth 1971* (H.M.S.O., London, 1971). p. 22.

43. Ministry of External Affairs ; *Report of the Committee on the Indian Foreign Service* (New Delhi, 1968), p. 44.

44. *Ibid.*, pp. 45-46.

45. In 1965, for example, there were 14 Service Officers in the Indian High Commission of the rank of Adviser or Deputy Adviser ; in 1956, the number was 13. See C.R.O. ; *List 1965*, pp. 54-55, and C.R.O. ; *Year Book of the Commonwealth*, 1966, p. 217. Britain also maintained a large military mission in India.

46. Lord Attlee ; *Empire into Commonwealth* (OUP, London/New York, 1961), P, 25.

47. H. Macmillan ; *op. cit.*, p. 381.

48. H. Wilson : *The Labour Government 1964-70 :* A Personal Record, p. 112.

49. See C.R.O.; List 1962, pp. 143-49 and List 1964, p. 151.

50. See the Communique of the 1958 Meeting in N. Mansergh (ed) ; *Speeches and Documents in Commonwealth Affairs 1952-62*, (OUP for RIIA. London 1963) especially pp. 552-53.

51. For a list of the meetings of these associations, see CRO ; *List 1962*, pp. 143-49. and *List 1964*, p.151. These, however, include the names of many non-official organisations as well.

52. Oliver Franks : *Britain and the Tide of World Affairs* (B.B.C. Reith Lectures, 1954, O.U.P., London, 1955), p.17.

53. A list of such visits is to be found in the annual *Report* of the Ministry of External Affairs, Government of India, New Delhi.

54. An accurate estimate of the number of Indian students studying in Britain is difficult to get, as many of them study in private colleges or institutions, or in the Inns of Court. Many students also study for professional qualifications in accountancy, medicine or surgery. However, the number of full-time students in different universities is available and the number has declined in recent years. See Appendix V. The number of professional students, particularly those studying for professional qualifications in medicine or surgery is likely to be drastically reduced with the decision of the General Medical Council in Britain (in 1975) not to allow Indian (Medical) Graduates to pursue higher studies in UK without a qualifying test. This amounted to a virtual de-recognition of Indian degrees (in medicine) & created rancour and resentment in India.

55. For the number of Indian immigrants living in Britain, see Appendix-V, Tables I and II.

55a. See Ch, 4. Also see, A.K. Banerji ; "Unburdening an Imperial Legacy : Colour, Citizenship and British Immigration Policy" in *India Quarterly* Vol. XXXII No. 4, October-December 1976.

56. For a discussion on this, see John Chadwick ; 'Intra-Commonwealth Relations ; Non Governmental Associations' in W.B. Hamilton et al. (eds) ; *op. cit*. Also see Derek Ingram : *The Commonwealth at Work* (Pergamon Press, Oxford/London, 1969).

57. See G.A. Almond : *The American People and Foreign Policy* (Praeger, New York, 1960), Ch. 6, p. 138.

58. *Third Report from the Select Committee on Estimates*, p. 16, evidence before the sub-Committee 'E' of the Estimates Committee, on 29 January 1957.

59. Duncan Sandys : 'The Modern Commonwealth' in CRO ; *List 1963* p. 154. Mr. Sandys was the Secretary of State for Commonwealth Relations, at the time of writing this article.

60. *Ibid.*

61. See, fo r instance, A.K. Gopal an's speech in the Lok Sabha on 19 November, 1956 : "On such a grave matter as this India, which is the biggest country in the Commonwealth, was not even consulted or even informed of what the British Government were intending to do." Cf. *Parliamentary Debates* (Lok Sabha). vol. 9, No. 4, Pt. 11, cols.397-98.

62. Cited in James Eayrs (ed.) ; *The Commonwealth and Suez : A Documentary Survey* (O.U.P., London, 1954), p.214.

63. Anthony Eden : *Op. cit.*, p. 426.

64. On this point see M. Brecher : *India and World Politics : Krishna Menon's view of the World*, pp. 127-31.

64a. Whether such criticisms are valid or not, the force of such arguments is recognised by responsible journalists in UK, and in an attempt to right the balauce, *The Times* (London) even brought out a special supplement on India containing articles on various aspects of India's development, written by experts, mostly Indian. See, for example, *The Times—India : A Special Report*, 30 November, 1970. See, especially, the article by Richard Harris, *ibid.*, p.1.

65. Such an attempt was made, though on a much smaller scale, by the Press Institute of India who studied the attitude of the British press to the Indo-Pakistani war of 1965. See "The British Press on the India-Pakistan Conflict" reproduced in *Foreign Affairs Reports* (ICWA, New Delhi), vol. XLV, No. 12, December, 1965.

For discussions on the role of the mass media in influencing the "images" held by the British and the Indians about each other, see M. Lipton and John Firn, *op. cit.* Ch. 12.

CHAPTER III

BRITAIN AND INDIA-PAKISTAN CONFLICTS*

> "Pakistan really was the result of the Indian national struggle led by the Congress. She is like Northern Ireland, a remnant of imperialism. So far as the British are concerned, it's their classic imperial solution." —V.K. Krishna Menon to Michael Brecher.
>
> M. Brecher : *India and World Politics : Krishna Menon's view of the World* (1968), p. 197.

> "...it is a matter for deep regret to me that repeatedly when subjects which concern us greatly and about which we feel passionately almost, like Goa and Kashmir, are debated, it should be our misfortune that these two Great Powers, the United States and the United Kingdom should almost invariably be against us."
>
> —J. Nehru in the Rajya Sahha on 23 June, 1962.

THE HISTORY of discord in Indo-British relations in the post-independence era must to a considerable extent be explained by reference to the tragic enmity between India and Pakistan which has persisted ever since their emergence as sovereign states. In the arena of international politics there are few instances where relations between two states have been so influenced over such a long period of time by their attitudes towards a third state. The significance of Pakistan as an influence in Indo-British relations can be appreciated only in the context of the fact that Britain and India view Pakistan from two entirely different perspectives. A number of factors have contributed to the shaping of these attitudes, some of which have their origin in events during the period of the Raj.

Indians looked upon Pakistan as a theocratic state, as an arrogant neighbour that had failed to move forward to a constructive nationalism. Born in violence, so Indians believe, Pakistan had deliberately pursued an anti-Indian policy since independence. Hostility towards India played a major role in keeping together the two wings of Pakistan which were separated from each other by nearly a thousand miles of Indian

* Throughout this discussion, 'Pakistan' refers to the political unit as it was between August 1947—December, 1971.

territory, and divided by linguistic and cultural difference.[1] Disputes with Pakistan, therefore, influenced the general tenor of India's foreign policy, and relations with other states have in most cases been affected by their policies towards these disputes.

Britain had, and has, political and economic interests in India as well as in Pakistan. Because of Britain's friendly relations with both countries, successive British Governments sometimes failed to take an unequivocally neutral stand on many issues in which both the parties solicited her support. Ambivalence satisfied neither India nor Pakistan, and evoked criticisms from both states at some time or other. Indeed, many British observers having knowledge of political developments in the Indian sub-continent feel, and not without justification, that whenever relations between the two neighbours took a turn for the worse, Britain was made the first whipping boyby either or both of them.[2]

I

Partition and Independence

Indian attitudes towards Britain have been strongly influenced by the widely-held view that the partition of India (albeit British-administered India) was the parting blow of the British. According to this view, partition was the logical culmination of the British Government's policy of *divide et impera.* The Congress party repeated this charge against the British Government, both officially—through the resolutions of the Congress Working Committee—and unofficially, through the statements of leaders like Gandhi, during the negotiations with the British government in the late 1930s and early 1940s.[3] But even many politicians of independent India with articulate ideas on politics subscribe to this view. Krishna Menon's comment on the partition of India, cited at the beginning of this chapter, is a typical example. The suggestion that the partition of India was the result of a policy of 'divide and rule' has generally been resented by the 'official class' in Britain. It is held that the partition was a regrettable necessity which arose out of the failure of the Hindus and Muslims to compose their differences and to take over power from the British government on the basis of the unity of India. During the debate on the Indian Independence Bill, Lord Listowel, the Secretary of State for India, said in the House of Lords that when it became clear that the Cabinet Mission Plan for one Indian Union would never be accepted and that there was no alternative form of government to which Hindus and Muslims would consent, "we had either to agree to implement their separation, or to remain indefinitely in control of India."[4] It has even been argued that the political unity of India was a creation of the British which never struck deep roots in the sub-continent and, therefore, collapsed once the British left.[5]

Hindu-Muslim conflicts in India during the first half of the 20th century had their roots deeply in past history as well as in the composition of contemporary Indian society.[5a] Though the Muslims and the Hindus have lived together in the sub-continent for centuries, they maintained their separate identities. When the British came to India, they certainly did not *create* Hindu-Muslim differences. Religious differences were there along with such other divisive forces as caste, language and regional loyalties, to segment Indian societies both horizontally and vertically. What the British did was to encourage the differences among the two communities by favouring one against the other, as this would divide the subjects without impairing the territorial unity of India.[6] For example, after the mutiny of 1857, which was led mainly by the Muslim feudal lords, the British became suspicious of the Muslims and favoured the Hindus. It is significant to note that the original foundation of the Indian National Congress had the support of a section of the British officials. It is only when they realised that the Congress was trying to develop an all-India nationalism which would threaten British power in future, that they turned to the Muslims.[7] In 1905 Lord Curzon partitioned Bengal ostensibly for administrative convenience, but in reality dividing it (broadly) on communal lines. In 1906, when agitation against the partition had reached a cresendo of protest, most leading Muslims cooperated with the government. *The Times*, while commending the Muslims for their cooperation, warned the government that if it failed to retain the confidence of the minorities, they would join the Congress, or set up an organisation of their own.[8] Lord Minto encouraged the Muslims to seek official recognition of their community as a separate political entity, and accepted their demand for a separate electorate in 1909. In the language of Lady Minto, it was nothing less than the "pulling back of sixty-two millions of people from joining the ranks of seditious oposition."[9] The process was perfected by the Government of India Acts of 1919 and 1935. The grant of separate electorate to the Muslims in fact drove a deeper wedge between the two communities. Once the decision was taken by the British Government to classify the electorate by religion, for political purposes, the theory of two nations became the logical consequence to be followed by the demand for a separate homeland for the Muslims.[10]

Throughout the first half of the 20th century the Congress agitated against the British. At first, the demand was for limited participation in the affairs of the Government ; later it was for complete self-government. The Congress was dominated by the Hindus, even though there were some nationalist Muslims in its ranks. Thus the Hindus came to be identified in British eyes as the trouble-makers. This became particularly evident during the Second World War, especially in 1942, when the British forces suffered military reverses in South East Asia and the Japanese were edging towards India. While the Congress refused to support the government's war efforts, the Muslim League continued its policy of passive support. As a result, the Hindus in general, and the Congress in particular, became suspect in the eyes of the British. On 9 June 1942, Sir George Cunningham, the Governor of the North West Frontier Province, wrote to the Governor-General about the reaction of the people of his state towards the Japanese victories in the following words :

> "Muslim opinion is solidly anti-Japanese. Hindus apparently have a sort of brotherly feeling for them. This might be dangerous if the Japanese were strong enough to get a footing in India, but for the present our Hindus here would discount such a possibility.[11]

But Sir George was not alone in his assessment of the

Hindus. On 30 April, 1942, Sir H. Twynam, the Governor of the Central Provinces, wrote to the Viceroy, Lord Linlithgow, at the end of the Cripps Mission, that it was the opposition of Gandhi which was responsible for the failure of the Mission. Not many British people would have quarrelled then with this assessment. But Twynam's letter went on to describe the Congress leaders as the quislings (of the Japanese) and recommended that "in the event of an enemy landing attended with success,...we may have to be prepared for instant action against large number of Congressmen and possibly even the Congress as an organisation."[12] A few months later the British Government did precisely this when the Congress planned to start the 'quit India' movement. If the British government thought that the execution of war effort took precedence over all else, this policy to silence nationalist demands by 'pre-emptive action' is quite understandable. While this feeling was certainly there, this policy reflected another aspect of the British mind—that India was still primarily a British concern.[12a] Referring to the Congress plan for the 'Quit India' movement, Leo Amery wrote to Linlithgow on 15 July 1942,

> "If any law-breaking in action should result you will deal with Gandhi and the Working Committee and not merely punish the wretched villager...After all, we are dealing with people who are more and more advancing the claim to be considered as the alternative Government of India and ingeniously fortifying that claim step by step. At some point or other we have got to make it quite clear that we are the Government of India..."[13]

It was this claim of the Congress "to be considered as the alternative government of India" which made it, in British eyes, "the intelligentsia (sic) of non-fighting Hindu elements".[14] The correspondence between the Viceroy and his Governors during the first half of 1942, and his correspondence with the Secretary of State reveal many instances which show that the British government in India (or at least, many leading members of the government) developed an anti-Congress bias so much so that the Viceroy came to look upon the Congress as the "fascists".[15] Given the circumstances, perhaps, this was not

6

unnatural. They also deliberately allowed Muslim demands for separation to grow, as a counterpoise to the Congress party's demand for complete independence at the end of the war.

The Muslim League demanded a separate homeland for the Muslims, for the first time, in its Lahore Resolution in 1940. Fully realising that this demand for Pakistan was likely to grow irresistible in the future, the Viceroy in New Delhi allowed matters to drift. In a letter to Leo Amery on 8 January, 1942, he wrote :

> "I have not the least doubt that as you say the Muslims will in the long run press for Pakistan either as a bargaining asset, or as a genuine objective. But I am in no hurry to face up to this matter and I would propose to leave them alone and would not get into it too closely for some considerable time...I am not a bit fussed about the post-war period save where I judge that to be short-sighted or unwise, and I am prepared to leave it to the post-war men."[16]

This attitude of the Viceroy matched his preoccupation of the moment perfectly well, but had he been more imaginative, he would have taken steps to initiate a dialogue between the Congress and the League to lessen their differences. The Viceroy's attitude only strengthened the criticism of the Congress that the British government were deliberately using League-Congress differences to postpone serious negotiations on the transfer of power. Even when the Cripps Mission came to India for negotiations with the Indian leaders, the Secretary of State was hoping to use the League-Congress differences to curb the demands of the Congress. On 24 March, 1942, immediately after the arrival of the Cripps Mission to India, Leo Amery wrote, in a private letter to the Viceroy :

> "...It remains to be seen whether in the face of external danger any of the Congress leaders can be persuaded to realise that the half loaf, which is all that either we or the rest of India can give them, is better than no bread. Jinnah, I should have thought, will be content to realise that he has got Pakistan in essence, whether as something substantive, or as a bargaining point..."[17]

Lord Linlithgow's successor to the Viceroyalty was no more immune from the anti-Congress bias. His distrust of the Congress and sympathy for the Muslim League become apparent from his personal diary. By the end of 1946, the Labour Government in London had decided, in principle, to hand over power to the Indians, within 18 months. This decision was taken largely because of Wavell's insistence and was announced in 1947. But Wavell was not the man to carry this policy to a successful end. Being a soldier, he was straightforward and blunt and lacked the political finesse to deal with lawyer-politicians in New Delhi. He did not have the youthful charm and personal charisma of Lord Mountbatten ; and his attempted political initiatives were often hamstrung by a number of unfavourable factors. In the early years of his viceroyalty he had to deal with Churchill, who was hostile to the idea of Indian independence and was contemptuous of Indian politicians ; and after the Labour Party came to power at the end of the War, Wavell had to deal with a government in London whose trust he did not enjoy. In India, his main problem was that he never got on well with Gandhi. His idea of Gandhi as an unscrupulous "wrecker' bent on overthrowing British rule to establish a 'Hindu Raj' made it almost impossible for him to be neutral between the Congress and the Muslim League, and in his diary he made no efforts to conceal his partisan views.[17a] It must, however, be said to his credit that Wavell did not like the idea of partition, but realised at the end that it had become virtually inevitable.

It needs to be emphasised that as far as the British were concerned, not all the cards were staked in favour of the League. Lord Mountbatten has often been blamed by the supporters of Jinnah and the Muslim League for his pro-Congress bias ; and Lord Wavell complained that Cripps and his colleagues in the Labour Government were obviously bent on handing over India to their Congress friends as soon as possible.[18] Perhaps an exaggeration. But the fact remains that both the Congress and the Muslim League had their lobbyists in London.

A restatement of the events leading to the partition of India is not necessary here.[18a] It was, in the final analysis, the result of the attempts made by a section of the Muslim elites in India —represented by the Muslim League—to move out of a political and economic system dominated by an 'alien' Hindu elite, and to create for themselves opportunities for autonomy and self-assertiveness. The real criticism against the British Government is that they helped the League to sustain the demand. The rationale of this policy would have been impeccable, if the division of the sub-continent had put an end to Hindu-Muslim conflicts. Instead, the partition of India led to the 'externalisation' of Hindu-Muslim 'group' conflict with an increase in the scale and cost of conflict. It must, however, be said to the credit of the British that at the very end they tried to avoid partition, and regretted it when it became a necessity. For the first time in centuries, the British had succeeded in imparting administrative unity of India and it would have been a crowning achievement on their part if they could have transferred power to a united India, as indeed they proposed to do through their successive offers in 1942 and 1946.[19] But it was already too late. The League-Congress differences became deep-seated and that made cooperation between them almost impossible.

To say this is not to suggest that the Congress did not have its share of the blame. The leadership of the Congress party was, to some extent, responsible for the rapid growth in power and influence of the Muslim League during the 1940s. They underestimated the ability of the League to exploit Muslim fears about Hindu domination ; and refused to recognise the League as an organisation representing Muslim interests. It was this implicit psychological rejection which led the League to make extreme demands to justify its existence as an entity separate from the Congress. Tactically, the Congress made a series of mistakes—each of which strengthened the League—first, by resigning from the provincial ministries in 1939, and then by refusing the Cripps offer in 1942. The 'Quit India' movement of 1942, which landed all the prominent Congress leaders in jail, provided the greatest opportunity to the League to increase its influence among the Muslim masses. But perhaps the greatest blunder was made by Nehru, in 1946, when, on becoming Congress President, he denounced the grouping scheme of the Cabinet Mission plan, and declared that the Hindu majority provinces would oppose it.[20] This, in fact, implied considerable modification of the original plan, and provided Jinnah with an "incomparable wedge to press openly for Pakistan."[21] He withdrew the League's acceptance of the Plan and threatened to use violence to achieve his goal of an independent Pakistan.

The creation of Pakistan was a strategic victory for Jinnah and the Muslim League. He realised that if the Congress failed to come to terms with the League on the future constitution of India, all he had to do was to stick to his demand and to consolidate the position of the League to ensure that he obtained some kind of Pakistan. He followed this strategy with considerable skill.

But Pakistan was born out of negatives—the principal ethos of the League's demand was the opposition to Hindu domination. The new state was a geographical monstrosity. Once Pakistan was created, its leaders had to find some new ideology to ensure its continued existence as a nation. The pattern of 'integration' in the new state created an elite structure and ethos that defined Pakistan as an antithesis of Hinduism and of India.[22] The League-Congress conflict—which, by 1946, had become almost coterminous with Hindu-Muslim conflict—was 'internationalised', and emerged as the India-Pakistan conflict in the post-independence years. There was the same mutual distrust between India and Pakistan, similar feelings of animosity and even hostility, which had prevented the growth of a 'cooperative' relationship between the Congress and the Muslim League. So long as the British were the dominant power in the sub-continent, their role was to act as the 'mediator' in Hindu-Muslim 'group conflicts'; once the transfer of power was effected, their capacity to act as the 'regulator' or 'manager' of conflicts declined.

This decline in their capability did not, however, mean non-involvement in India-Pakistan conflicts. The British government could not view with equanimity any escalation of conflict in the sub-continent and thought it their responsibility—at least in the initial years after independence—to act as a 'crisis-manager' in India-Pakistan conflicts. Both India and Pakistan—Pakistan more persistently than India—have sought some sort of British support ; both have been disappointed as none could secure total British commitment. This illustrates the dilemmas of the British government in formulating a policy that would have satisfied both India and Pakistan.

In the following pages we shall analyse the role of the British Government : (1) in the Kashmir dispute, with particular reference to the years 1947-51, 1957 and 1962, (2) in the Rann of Kutch conflict in 1965, and (3) in the India-Pakistan war of 1965.

II

Britain And The Kashmir Dispute

Of all the India-Pakistan conflicts that have bedevilled relations between the two states, the dispute over the State of Jammu and Kashmir was by far the most important. Because of its geographical location and strategic position, Kashmir was, and is, important to both India and Pakistan. Both have also sought to justify their claims on economic grounds,[23] although, on economic considerations, Kashmir was perhaps more important to Pakistan than to India. But the dispute over Kashmir was not a mere territorial dispute ; it symbolised the genesis of the differences between the two states since their emergence as independent entities. Pakistanis think that because of its Muslim majority, Kashmir should properly belong to Pakistan ; it is a vindication of the Muslim League's 'two nation' theory. Without the inclusian of Kashmir, many Pakistanis argue, even the concept of 'Pakistan' remains incomplete.[24]

Indians, on the other hand, looked upon Kashmir as a symbol of India's secularism. As Nehru explained to his biographer in 1956, what made Kashmir so important to India was its implications for India's efforts to establish a secular state, and to maintain communal harmony in the country.[25] Mutual fear and suspicion between India and Pakistan also made an amicable settlement of the dispute very difficult, if not impossible. To the Pakistanis it appeared that the Indian 'occupation' of Kashmir was only the first step in a grand design to destroy the very existence of Pakistan as an independent state.[26] To the Indians, equally, the invasion of Kashmir by the tribal raiders from NWFP appeared to be a threat to the security and integrity of India. It reminded them of the Muslim raiders of the past who traditionally used this route for the invasion of India.[27] These fears might have been exaggerated ; the 'hostile image' of each state as seen by the other, and the projected insecurities following from this image were, perhaps, more important than the 'reality'. But such fears continued to exist, especially in Pakistan.

Although the British Government was not directly involved in the Kashmir dispute, it found it difficult to formulate a policy that would have satisfied both India and Pakistan.[28] Indians have resented Britain's pro-Pakistan bias in the Kashmir dispute,[29]—a bias which, they think, had its origin in the pro-Muslim League policies of the British Government in India. It has even been suggested that the continuation of the Kashmir dispute is the result of Anglo-American machinations, that "Britain, ably assisted by the United States, is, and always has been the villain of the piece."[30] The implication is that without British and American support, Pakistan would have been more amenable to a peaceful settlement of the Kashmir dispute. The fairness of such criticisms may be open to question, but it is important to take note of these as they shed some light on the attitudes of some members of the foreign policy-making elite who had the most influence in the shaping of India's relations with Britain.

Pakistan's frustration with the British Government's policy has been no less than that of India's. She expected that British influence and power would be invoked on her side in the same way as the pro-Muslim League sentiments of many British officials in the pre-independence days. Though Pakistan gained the sympathy and support of some of these men[31] even after independence, as well as of some Members of Parliament, belonging to the Conservative Party,[32] on the whole she failed to enlist Britain's *total* commitment to her side. Indeed, some Pakistani leaders had a feeling that Pakistan had been badly betrayed at the time of independence, and even after it.[33] It is widely believed in Pakistan that Lord Mountbatten helped the Indian government in securing the accession of Kashmir to India.[34] Even many British observers accept this suggestion.[35]

Lord Mountbatten has also been criticised for his failure to subordinate 'narrow' Indian interests, to the larger cause of inter-Dominion harmony and peace. This he could have done, point out his critics, by getting in touch with Jinnah before accepting Kashmir's accession to India.[36] According to some of these critics, he did not do this because of his wholly pro-Hindu inclinations, and his personal dislike for Jinnah.[37] Indians have, similarly, criticised the role of Field Marshal Sir Claude Auchinleck, and of some of his subordinates for their pro-Pakistan bias.[38] Such accustations and counter-accusations —whatever might have been their justification—made the role of the British suspect in the eyes of both the Indians and the Pakistanis.

Nevertheless, the presence of senior British officers in the armed forces of the two Dominions acted as a force for restraint limiting the armed conflict to the territory of Kashmir only, and averted the possibility of an indo-Pakistani war during 1947-49. For example, on 27 October 1947, when Jinnah ordered the acting Commander-in-Chief of the Pakistan Army, General Gracey, to send his troops to Kashmir, the latter refused to do so without the prior approval of the supreme Commander Field Marshal Claude Auchinleck. Auchinleck then flew to Lahore and explained to Jinnah that with the accession of Kashmir to India, the Government of India were perfectly justified to send troops to Kashmir in response to the Maharaja's request.[39] He informed Jinnah that if he were to persist with his order, all the British officers would immediately resign from the Pakistan army, as otherwise they would be involved in an inter-Dominion war. Jinnah was thus persuaded to cancel his order. Later on, however, Pakistani troops were sent to Kashmir. It has been claimed by Lord Birdwood[40] that the cease-fire in the first Kashmir war was the result of the initiative taken by the Commander-in-Chief of the Indian Army, General Bucher, who was supported by General Gracey, in Pakistan.

At the early stage of the Kashmir dispute, between October-December, 1947, the attitude of the British government was non-committal. Sympathy for Pakistan was quite natural, in view of the fact that she was the smaller of the two states. From the organisational point of view, both administrative and military, India had an advantage over Pakistan, as she had inherited a ready-made structure from the former British Indian empire. There was probably a feeling in Britain that a militarily stronger India might threaten the territorial security of Pakistan. This view was further strengthened by the declaratory views of some of the Congress leaders at the time of the partition of the country. On 28 September, 1947, Field Marshal Auchinleck sent a personal report to London 'for the eyes' of the Prime Minister, the Chief of the Imperial General Staff, as well as of the Chiefs of the Naval and Air Staff, giving his assessment of the existing situation in the Indo-Pakistani sub-continent. He wrote,

> "I have no hesitation whatever in affirming that the Present Indian Cabinet are implacably determined to do all in their power to prevent the establishment of Pakistan on a firm basis. In this I am supported by the unanimous opinion of my senior officers and indeed by all responsible British officers cognisant of the situation..."[41]

The credibility of this assertion is open to question. It is doubtful whether any serious threat to the security of Pakistan from India existed at that time. For, even if she wanted, India simply did not have the military capability to undo Pakistan. Moreover, whatever might have been the attitude of the Congress leaders to the question of partition, for a variety of reasons they came to look upon Pakistan as a good riddance, after independence.[42] Therefore, if some declaratory statements were still being made regarding the laudability of Indian unity, these should be looked upon as the normal attempts of politicians to make a vital change of policy look as consistent with the past as possible, by the expression of pious hopes and platitudes. Nevertheless, it seems likely that the opinion of men such as Sir Claude Auchinleck considerably influenced the attitude of the British government towards India and Pakistan. As a result, when the continuing uncertainty over Kashmir suddenly erupted into a crisis in October, 1947, the British government were reluctant to accept India's version of the situation.

An intriguing fact still remains. The British Government must have known the real position in Kashmir from Lord Mountbatten's personal report to the King, detailing the situation in Kashmir and the conditions under which the Maharajah had acceeded to India.[43] This clearly repudiated Pakistan's allegation that Kashmir's accession to India had been secured by "violence and fraud". But officials in Whitehall had a different view of the whole situation, as Lord Mountbatten, for obvious reasons, came to be identified too closely with the Indian leaders.[44]

Thus a suspicion about Indian motives and intentions had already developed among a section of influential British officials and there was a tendency to do justice to the infant dominion. Another, and probably more important factor influencing British attitude to the Kashmir conflict was the widely-held view in the West that it was a dispute having religious overtones. The communal killings in the Punjab in the wake of independence, the steady flow of refugees from both sides of the Indo-Pakistani border, the repressive policies followed by the Maharajah of Kashmir in suppressing the "Poonch rebellion"—all these events created a feeling in the West that the Kashmir dispute was basically a religious one, and that the people of Kashmir genuinely desired union with Pakistan. There was also a tendency, in UK, to draw a parallel between the conflict over Kashmir, and that over Hyderabad.[45]

During the first few months of the crisis, both India and Pakistan tried to win British sympathy and support and kept the British Prime Minister informed of the developments as seen from their respective sides.[46] At this stage, both the states were willing to accept some form of mediation by the British. On 24 November, Liaquat Ali Khan of Pakistan sent a telegram to the British Prime Minister, suggesting the introduction of an international force in Kashmir, and informed him of Pakistan's willingness to accept a force drawn from the Commonwealth countries. The purpose of this exercise was clearly to gain British sympathy, and some form of British/Commonwealth involvement. Similarly, towards the end of December, 1947, Lord Mountbatten, with Nehru's concurrence, telegraphed Attlee to fly out immediately to India and to try to resolve the dispute by personal mediation.[47] The British Prime Minister, however, turned down the request, preferring reliance on UN. The British government's attitude during this period was thus non-commital. Partly, this was because of the conflicting versions of the dispute presented by the two sides. But there was also a reluctance to get directly involved in an inter-Dominion dispute which might jeopardise Britain's interests in the sub-continent.

Britain's role in the Kashmir dispute had two aspects : (i) as a 'neutralist' in the Commonwealth Prime Ministers' Conference, ready to act as a 'mediator' if called upon by both parties to the dispute ; and (ii) as a partisan, in UN. As a permanent member of the Security Council, Britain was one of the principal protagonists in the cold war ; and as the Kashmir dispute became enmeshed in the cold war politics, Britain's policy was, more often than not, favourable to Pakistan.[48]

So far as the role of the Commonwealth in intra-Commonwealth disputes is concerned, the British government supported India's contention that the Commonwealth being a voluntary association of independent states, should not, formally, intervene in disputes involving two member-states, unless both the parties so desire.[49] The British Government, therefore, resisted Pakistan's efforts to raise Kashmir issue in the plenary sessions of the Commonwealth Prime Minister's Conference. This policy was influenced by the consideration that if intra-Commonwealth disputes were allowed to be discussed in these conferences, this might lead to the dismemberment of the Commonwealth as a voluntary association of independent states at a rather delicate moment in the Commonwealth's development. Pakistan's view was, however, different. She felt that if the Commonwealth "cannot guarantee one member against aggression by another, then its membership is of little importance."[50]

Pakistan's views were influenced by her desire to raise the Kashmir dispute in the Commonwealth Prime Ministers' Conference where she expected to get the support of the British Government and of other members of the Commonwealth. Several attempts were made to that end. In January 1951, for example, the Pakistani Prime Minister Liaquat Ali Khan refused to attend the Commonwealth Prime Ministers' Meeting, unless the Kashmir issue was put on the agenda of the Conference. However, a crisis was averted by the agreement among the Prime Ministers to have informal discussions on the Kashmir problem, outside the plenary sessions. A number of such meetings were held,[51] and on 15 January a communique was issued from Downing Street which said that the subject was discussed freely and fully by the Prime Ministers, suggestions were made for the solution of the dispute, though no agreement was reached.[52] It did not give the details of the proposals though the Pakistani Prime Minister, in a press conference, said that three alternative proposals were made for the demilitarisation of Kashmir. These proposals were: (a) that Kashmir should be administered by stationing troops from the Commonwealth, (b) that a combined force drawn from India and Pakistan should be stationed in Kashmir during the plebiscite, and (3) that the plebiscite administrator should be authorised to raise force locally. Liaquat Ali Khan said that all these proposals were accepted by Pakistan and rejected by India.[53] Prime Minister Nehru's version of the proposals was, however, different.[54]

Though India always objected to Pakistan's efforts to raise the Kashmir dispute in the plenary sessions of the Commonwealth Prime Ministers' Conferences, these conferences provided opportunities for bilateral discussion of the problem, and successive British Prime Ministers have encouraged such contacts.[55]

In 1964, during the Commonwealth Prime Ministers' Conference in London, President Ayub Khan had informal discussion with Mr Krishnamachari—who was leading the Indian delegation owing to the illness of Prime Minister Shastri—on the various aspects of Indo-Pakistan relations. Kashmir featured prominently in their discussions. The atmosphere of good-will created by these talks was soon changed by the wrangle over the final wording of the communique that was to be issued at the end of the Commonwealth Prime Ministers' Conference. President Ayub insisted that the communique should contain a reference to the Kashmir dispute—but Mr Krishnamachari opposed it on the ground that an intra-Commonwealth dispute could not be a subject of discussion in a Commonwealth Prime Ministers' meeting. Mr Krishnamachari was supported in this matter by the then British Prime Minister Sir Alec Douglas Home, who argued that the Principle on which Mr Krishnamachari relied was important.[56] The impasse was finally broken by a compromise formula, and the communique referred to Kashmir indirectly by noting the friendly public statements by Indian and Pakistani leaders. But even this was resented in India. As the correspondent of *The Times* reported from New Delhi, it was suggested in a section of the Indian press that President Ayub's move was made "in connivance if not in concert with the British".[57]

THE KASHMIR DISPUTE IN UN : BRITAIN'S ROLE (1948-51)

The Government of India referred the Kashmir dispute to UN on 1 January 1948. In their original letter,[58] addreseed to the President of the Security Council, the Indian government alleged that a situation existed between India and Pakistan which was likely to endanger international peace and security. Such a situation arose because of the aid that invaders, consisting of Pakistani nationals and tribesmen from NWFP, were receiving for operations against the State of Jammu and Kashmir, which, as a result of its accession to India by the Maharaja, became part of the Indian territory. The Government of India, therefore, requested the Security Council to ask the Government of Pakistan : (a) to prevent Pakistan government personnel, military and civil, from participating or assisting in the invasion of the State of Jammu and Kashmir ; (b) to call upon Pakistani nationals to desist from taking any part in the fighting which was taking place in the State, and (c) deny to the invaders : (1) any access to and use of its territory for operations against Kashmir, (2) military and other supplies, and (3) all other kinds of aid that might tend to prolong the present struggle. In order to avoid any possible suggestion that India had utilized the State's immediate peril for her own political advantage, the letter continued,

> "The Government of India made it clear that once the soil of the State had been cleared of the invader and normal conditions restored, its people would be free to decide their future by the recognised democratic method of a *free and impartial plebiscite or referendum* which, in order to ensure complete impartiality, might be held under *international auspices*."[59]

The Pakistan government, in a letter from their Foreign Minister,[60] addressed to the UN Secretary-General, denied that they had aided the tribal invaders, though conceding that a number of independent tribesmen and persons from Pakistan were helping the "Azad (Free) Kashmir Government" as volunteers. They denied that Pakistan territory was being used as a base for military operations against Kashmir, denied the legality of Kashmir's accession to India which was, in their view, secured by "violence and fraud". The Pakistan Government then brought to the attention of the Security Council, under Article 35 of the Charter, the existence of other disputes between India and Pakistan and requested that appropriate measures be taken to resolve these disputes, for the restoration of friendly relations between India and Pakistan.

The details of the complaints and counter-complaints made by India and Pakistan need not be repeated here. To the Government of India the issue was a simple one. There was no dispute about territory. "The territory is that of Kashmir, and it is this territory which has been invaded, its towns and villages sacked, its people massacred and its women abducted."[6] Secondly, it was emphasised that the subject matter of reference was limited to the dispute in Kashmir. Pakistan had committed an aggression in Kashmir by aiding the tribal invaders, and by encouraging its own nationals to take part in armed action in Kashmir, which had legally acceded to India. Pakistan must, therefore, be persuaded to stop this unfriendly act. Regarding the future status of the state, the Indian representative assured the Security Council that

> "The question of the future status of Kashmir *vis-a-vis* her neighbours and the world at large, and the further question, namely, whether she would withdraw from her accession to India, and either accede to Pakistan or remain independent, with a right to claim admission as a Member of the United Nations—all this we have recognised to be a matter for unfettered decision by the people of Kashmir, after normal life is restored to them."[62a]

The Government of Pakistan had, however, different views about the origin of the dispute. The Pakistani Foreign Minister, Sir Mohammad Zafrullah Khan, told the Security Council that the Kashmir problem could not be viewed in isolation from other problems pending between India and Pakistan. He said that fighting in Kashmir would not be stopped till the conditions for a fair and impartial plebiscite were agreed to, and the invaders were satisfied regarding their fairness.

The two sides agreed on only one thing, that the future of Kashmir should be decided by a plebiscite. But beyond that the agreement broke down. When the Government of India offered to hold a plebiscite in Kashmir, they had in mind a plebiscite which would be arranged by Kashmir's National Government (with Sheikh Abdullah as its head) ; in this matter UN would have only a limited supervisory role.[63] To the Government of Pakistan, however, this was unacceptable. They wanted to vest in UN the final authority for holding a fair and impartial plebiscite, preceded by the establishment of an impartial interim administration, and the withdrawal of all troops from Kashmir.[64]

These arguments have been repeated over and over with meticulous details by both sides, tons of pages have been written on them, endless deliberations have taken place in the Security Council, and a number of UN mediators have tried their hands to bring about an agreement between the two sides ;[65] but a solution of the Kashmir problem has eluded everyone.

It needs to be recorded at the outset that from an examination of the dispute as it has existed over the years, none of the parties emerge with an unblemished record. With the hindsight of events, it is now possible to argue that the Indian Government made a mistake, initially, by referring the dispute to the UN under Article 35 of the Charter. If they felt that they had a good case against Pakistan in Kashmir—and according to the present author, they had, in 1947-48—the dispute should have been referred to UN under Chapter VII of the Charter dealing with threats to peace and acts of aggression. There can be no denying the fact that the Government of India gave a *unilateral promise*—both before referring the dispute to UN, and after that—to hold a plebiscite in Kashmir, under international auspices to ensure impartiality ; but in the end they did not act up to it. India has often been blamed for her self-righteousness for the intransigent attitude she has taken towards the Kashmir dispute by refusing to accept the various solutions suggested by a number of UN mediators. All this may be true. At the same time, it needs to be emphasised that opportunities for solving the dispute were lost duriug the early months of 1948, because of the inept handling of the dispute by the Security Council. The Security Council refused to accept the fact that irrespective of the claims of the two sides to Kashmir—which might have been equally strong for both India and Pakistan —*it was Pakistan and not India that initiated the trouble in Kashmir in October, 1947.*[66]

Indians were particularly critical of the British Government's action as, of all the Security Council members, Britain was the only power with long experience of the affairs of the sub-continent. Mrs Pandit said later that British criticisms on Kashmir were like a stab in the back, because the British knew about the whole situation.[67]

It is at least arguable that at the initial stage of the dispute, had the Security Council attached more importance to the cessation of hostilities and the withdrawal of Pakistani nationals and tribal invaders from Kashmir, than to the procedure for holding the plebiscite, the Government of India would have been more willing to hold the plebiscite with some degree of international control, to ensure that there was no coercion or threats to the Kashmiris. For, with Sheikh Abdullah in power— at that time the most popular leader in Kashmir – and with the memories of tribal invasion still fresh in people's minds, the Government of India had a fair chance of winning a plebiscite in Kashmir.[68] But deliberations in the Security Council dragged on, with the war in Kashmir continuing, and with the direct intervention of the Pakistani troops in Kashmir, at least since May 1948. It took the Security Council six months before it could send a team to the subcontinent—the United Nations Commission for India and Pakistan[69]—for studying the situation and to offer mediation. Why the Commission could not be sent earlier is not known. However, when the Commission arrived in the subcontinent it found that it was confronted with a situation which was "different from that envisaged by the Security Council during the deliberations which preceded the formulation of its resolution, inasmuch as regular Pakistani troops were within the frontiers of the State of Jammu and Kashmir participating in the fighting."[70] With the disclosure of the presence of the Pakistani Army in Kashmir, India's attitude hardened, and the Government of India insisted, with increasing resoluteness that Pakistan must be condemend for aggression.[17]

Indians felt down by the British Government. Despite the serious charge that Pakistan had abetted the tribesmen who invaded Kashmir, and that she had sent her own troops to Kashmir—an act which was, to use Sir Owen's expression, "inconsistent with international law,"[72]—the British Government, along with the majority of members of the Security Council, supported a procedure more acceptable to Pakistan than to India. They associated themselves with Pakistan's insistence that the cessation of hostilities should be preceded by guarantees for a fair and impartial plebiscite. As Mr Noel-Baker said in the Council, whatever the Security Council did, "...must also seem fair to the Government of Pakistan, to the insurgents, to the tribesmen, to the Government of India, to the other inhabitants of Jammu and Kashmir and to the outside world."[73] This was lofty idealism ; but in Noel-Baker's scale of priorities, India's claim to be treated fairly came far below that of Pakistan, and even that of the invaders and of the insurgents. When the Kashmir question was referred to UN, India was the aggrieved party ; before the Security Council acted on the complaint, the title of the agenda had been changed from the 'Jammu and Kashmir Question' to 'India-Pakistan Question', to discuss all problems affecting India-Pakistan relations, as suggested by Pakistan. India protested against it at the time, and this protest was supported by the British delegate.

The proceedings in the Security Council greatly disappointed India. Expressing this feeling of disappointment, Nehru said at Jammu on 15 February 1948 : "Instead of discussing and deciding our reference in a straightforward manner, the nations of the world sitting in that body got lost in power politics."[74] He was not alone in voicing this disappointment. *The Times* (London) wrote on 14 February 1948 : "...a prolonged shock has been administered to Indian opinion by the course which the discussion at Lake Success has followed." According to Alan Campbell-Johnson, Lord Mountbatten also felt "that Attlee and Noel-Baker do not seem to be showing themselves sufficiently alive to the psychological influences of this dispute and that their attempt to deal out even-handed justice is producing heavy handed diplomacy."[75] He thought that the UK delegate to the Security Council could have taken a less unfriendly line towards India by calling upon Pakistan, as a first step towards solving the crisis, to stop helping the raiders. The question of supervising plebiscite without interfering with the legally constituted Government of Kashmir, he believed, should have received more sympathetic treatment.[76]

Perhaps as a reaction to such criticism in India, or perhaps at Nehru's request, passed on to him by Lord Mountbatten, it seems at this stage Prime Minister Attlee intervened in the Kashmir dispute in a way which was favourable to India. In later years, Sir Muhammad Zafrullah Khan, the former Foreign Minister of Pakistan, and one of the ablest defenders of Pakistan's case in the Security Council, complained to T.B. Millar about this.[77] The precise nature or the time of Prime

Minister Attlee's intervention is not clear. But that he intervened at some stage seems probable from the following letter of Krishna Menon, who was then the Indian High Commissioner in London. In a 'strictly personal and confidential' letter to Attlee he wrote :

> "The Kashmir business at New York was a great shock to us, perhaps far more than I have been able to convey to you. Thanks to *your intervention*, it has somewhat improved, but it is a running sore which has affected god relations between our two peoples."[78]

The British Government's policy towards the Kashmir dispute continued to be a running sore in Indo-British relations.

The basis for the settlement of the Kashmir dispute was laid down in the two resolutions of UNCIP—that of 13 August, 1948[79] and that of 5 January, 1949[80]—which said, inter alia, that the future of the State should be decided through a free and impartial plebiscite. The main criticism against India is that it was because of her obstinacy that the plebiscite could not be held in Kashmir. It needs some examination.

The Augnst 1948 resolution of the Security Council was divided into three parts ; Part-1 dealing with Cease-Fire, Part-II with the Truce Agreement, and part-III referred to Plebiscite.

Most attention has been focussed on the Part III of the resolution which states :

> "The Government of India and the Government of Pakistan reaffirm their wish that the future status of the State of Jammu and Kashmir shall be determined in accordance with the will of the people and to that end, upon acceptance of the Truce Agreement, both Governments agree to enter into consultations with the Commission to determine free and equitable conditions whereby such expressions will be assured."[81]

But it is clear from this part that the plebiscite could not be held, until the Truce Agreement was concluded.

Part II dealing with the Truce Agreement stated clearly:

> "As the presence of troops of Pakistan in the territory of the State of Jammu and Kashmir constitutes a

> material change in the situation since it was presented by the Government of Pakistan before the Security Council, the Government of Pakistan agrees to withdraw its troops from that State."[82]

It was regarding the implementation of this part that Pakistan started dragging her feet. The principles of demilitarisation were also enunciated in the same resolution. The Government of India was to begin to withdraw the *bulk* of its forces *after* the Commission had notified them that (a) the tribesmen and Pakistani nationals had withdrawn thereby terminating the situation referred to in India's complaint, and (b) the Pakistani forces were being withdrawn. The Government of India agreed "to withdraw the bulk of its forces from the State in stages to be agreed upon with the Commission." Pending the acceptance of conditions for a final settlement India was allowed to maintain within the cease-fire line, the minimum of forces "which in agreement with the Commission are considered necessary to assist local authorities in the observance of law and order."

Before accepting the terms of the resolution, Nehru sought some clarifications from the Commission on certain points. The Commission agreed on the following points: (a) that there could be no question of limiting the sovereignty of the State of Jammu and Kashmir to the Indian half of the cease-fire line; (b) that it did not recognise the Azad Kashmir Government; nor would it allow that part to be consolidated, during the Truce period, to the disadvantage of the State and that (c) should it be decided to seek a solution of the future of the State by means of a plebiscite, "Pakistan should have no part in the organisation and conduct of plebiscite or in any other matter of internal administration in the State."[83]

It was also recognised, that in view of the paramount need for security,

> "the time when the withdrawal of Indian troops was to begin, the stages in which it was to be carried out and the strength of Indian forces to be retained in the State, were matters of settlement between Commission and the Government of India."[84]

Two points should be noted. First, UNCIP clearly recognised the Indian position that the plebiscite in Kashmir was a matter between the Government of India and the Commission, where Pakistan would not have any say. Secondly, so far as holding plebiscite was concerned, it was to be preceded by demilitarisation in which Pakistani nationals, tribesmen and troops were to be withdrawn, followed by the withdrawal of the bulk of the Indian forces. The UNCIP resolution of January, 1949, while reiterating the wishes of the two parties to solve the dispute through a fair and impartial plebiscite, also emphasised these two points.

Both India and Pakistan accepted these two resolutions. But when it came to the question of implementing them, differences between the two parties began to grow wider. These differences related to the (a) disposal of the Azad forces, (b) withdrawal of the regular forces from the State and (c) the Northern Area. The Azad Forces posed a real problem. India insisted that the disbanding and disarming of the Azad forces on a large scale was an essential condition to be fulfilled before any plebiscite could be held. By the spring of 1948, they grew into 32 batallions of well-trained and well-armed forces, and in the opinion of the military adviser to the Commission, constituted a formidable force.

The Commision (UNCIP), faced with the problem of the deadlock on demilitarisation, proposed a joint meeting between the leaders of India and Pakistan—a suggestion accepted by both sides. However, the meeting was unilaterally cancelled by the Commission—to the surprise of both the Indian and Pakistani leaders. The Commission then proposed arbitration on the points of difference between India and Pakistan—a proposal accepted by Pakistan but rejected by India probably because of the fear that the concessions gained from UNCIP might slip out of hand once the whole issue was thrown open to the arbitrator.

One day after the arbitration proposal was made, President Truman and Prime Minister Attlee publicly appealed to the leaders of India and Pakistan to accept it. This might have been done with the best of intentions. But the circumstances leading to the appeal suggest that the Commission might not have been free from outside influence. As Dr Chyle later disclosed in his *Minority Report*, the Commission's letters to the two Governments, which were to be a secret memorandum, got into the hands of the British High Commissioners in New Delhi and Karachi, at the same time or earlier than they could be officially presented to the Government of India.[85]

The concern of the British and American Governments about the deteriorating situation in the sub-continent, and especially their awareness of the strategic importance of Kashmir, perhaps, explains the motive behind this dramatic move. Commenting on this, the *Time and Tide* (London) wrote on 17 September, 1949 : "Four main trade routes to Central Asia pass through Kashmir. A few miles beyond the northern border lies the Soviet Union...Both Great Britain and the United States are aware of this situation and that explains the Truman-Attlee demarche." It is likely that henceforth the question of Kashmir's strategic importance began to influence British and American attitudes towards the dispute. The appointment of Admiral Chester Nimitz as the Plebiscite Administrator in 1949 showed that America had some strategic interest in Kashmir.[86]

It is not possible, nor is it necessary, to trace the tangled and involved course of the Kashmir dispute in UN, within the space of this chapter.[87] An analysis of the principal features of the August 1948 Resolution of UNCIP has been necessary in order to show that in later years the British Government have either supported or initiated proposals in the Security Council which substantially modified the principles of demilitarisation envisaged in the resolution.[88]

Despite the denial by the British Government of any intention to intervene in the Indo-Pakistani dispute over Kashmir, in fact they intervened at various times in a way which favoured Pakistan. Two examples may be cited in support of this argument—the British Government's initiative in the Security Council in February, 1951, and their initiative in 1957, to press for the solution of the Kashmir dispute by a plebiscite.

In a letter to the Security Council on 14 December, 1950,[89] the Pakistani Foreign Minister drew the Council's attention to the proposal for convenning a Constituent Assembly in the State which would determine its future. He expressed regret at the failure of the Dixon Mission, and called for urgent action by the Council. In January of the following year, Liaquat Ali Khan unsuccessfully tried to raise the Kashmir issue in the Commonwealth Prime Ministers' Conference. He even threatened that Pakistan would withdraw from the Commonwealth if it failed to resolve the Kashmir dispute.[90] On 21 February, the Kashmir issue came up for discussion in the Security Council. The British representative, Gladwyn Jebb, while introducing a draft resolution[91] said that though Sir Owen Dixon had recommended in his report to leave the disposition of the State of Jammu and Kashmir to the parties themselves his Government, on reflection, "could not agree that it should now, as it were, wash its hands of the problem."[92] The draft resolution, jointly sponsored by Britain and the United States reiterated that the future of the State of Jammu and Kashmir should be decided by holding a free and impartial plebiscite. Referring to the proposed Constituent Assembly, the resolution said, inter alia, that "any action that the Assembly might attempt to take" would not constitute a disposition of the State in accordance with the principles enumerated in the previous resolutions of the Security Council. The draft resolution also authorised the new UN mediator—who was to succeed Sir Owen—to consider the possibility of raising a force from among the UN members or locally, to be stationed in Kashmir to facilitate demilitarisation, and called upon the parties, in the event of their failure to reach an agreement, to accept arbitration on all points of disagreement. Introducing the draft resolution the British delegate explained that a neutral force was essential for a fair plebiscite in Kashmir, and that arbitration which India had rejected earlier, was the only solution.[93] The resolution which was finally adopted by the Security Council on 30 March, 1951[94] dropped the reference to the UN forces, to accommodate Indian objections. Both the British and and the American delegates emphasised in their speech that the Security Council could not propose a solution which was not acceptable to the parties in dispute; but they were in fact pressing for a solution which was not acceptable to one of them—in this case India.

Indians were, no doubt, proving more intransigent than the Pakistanis over the question of demilitarisation. Perhaps, for domestic political reasons,[95] by 1950 the Government of India had become reluctant to agree to a 'fair and impartial' plebiscite which might lead to Kashmir's secession from India. The insistence that Pakistan—being the aggressor—could not have equal rights with India in the matter of holding plebiscite was based on a legal point on which the United Nations never gave its verdict. It ignored the fact that once the Government of India had conceded that the status of Kashmir was a matter of dispute between India and Pakistan, they could not deny that the Pakistan Government had also the right to be assured that the plebiscite was fair and impartial. In 1950, Sir Owen had concluded that "India's agreement would never be obtained for demilitarisation in any such form, or to provisions governing the period of the plebiscite of any such character as would··· permit of the plebiscite being conducted in conditions sufficiently guarding against intimidation and other forms of influence and abuse by which freedom and fairness of plebiscite might be imperilled."[96]

It should, however, be emphasised that Sir Owen had also pointed out the immense practical difficulties in the way of holding an overall plebiscite in the State. The State of Jammu and Kashmir is not a homogeneous unit geographically, demographically or economically. It is an agglomeration of territories. The rule by the Maharaja was the only element of unity it possessed. If, therefore, as a result of an overall plebiscite, the whole of the State as an entity passed to either India or Pakistan there would have been a large movement of people and a new refugees problem. Sir Owen thought, therefore, that

> "if there is any chance of settling the dispute over Kashmir by agreement between India and Pakistan, it now lies in partition and in some means of allocating the valley rather than an overall plebiscite."[97]

While India agreed to this plan for partition and partial plebiscite, in principle, Pakistan was reluctant to consider any such plan. In the end, he recommended that the initiative for the final disposition of the State should be left to the parties themselves.

Therefore, in 1951, when the British and American delegates reiterated the Security Council's earlier stand on overall plebiscite in Kashmir, they seemed to ignore the realities of the situation, and supported a position that was acceptable to Pakistan.

The external factors : the effect of super-power conflict and rivalry on the South Asian sub-system.

Political developments in Asia and the Middle East during 1950-51 considerably influenced the policy of the British and the American governments towards the Kashmir dispute.

The Korean war started in June 1950 and with China's involvement in the war since October of that year, there was a growing estrangement between India and USA. India's opposition to the crossing of the 38th parallel by the UN forces in Korea, and her advocacy for Communist China's entry to UN, had alienated the US Government. The story of the growing warmth in Pakistan-American relationship during this period is too well-known to need repetition. However, there were two important factors which influenced the American government's policy towards India and Pakistan : (1) Washington's disillusionment with Nehru and neutralism, and (2) Pakistan's alleged importance in any Western-backed scheme of defence in Asia. The role of geo-political thinkers such as Sir Olaf Caroe in this new policy orientation was considerable.[98] In March 1949 Sir Olaf wrote that the stability in the Persian Gulf region could be preserved "by the closest accord between the States which surround this Muslim Lake, an accord underwritten by the Great Powers whose interests are engaged..."[99] He was, at this point, not sure of the motives of the Indian government and wrote that any concept of defence in this region should take account of India as the geographical centre of South Asia. But by 1951 he had lost faith in Nehru's foreign policy and wrote, elaborating his earlier views, that India was no longer an obvious base for Middle Eastern defence ; "it stands on the fringe of the defence periphery. Pakistan, on the other hand, lies well within the grouping of Southern Asia as seen from the air."[100] Sir Olaf envisaged a grand design for the defence of the Persian Gulf region, and wrote that any scheme of defence would remain incomplete without Pakistan.

There is evidence to suggest that by the beginning of the 1950s Pakistan had been assigned to the Middle East, in the US strategic map, under the strangely compounded influence of 'British Tory geopolitical fancies' and the single-minded commitment of the Americans to collective security.[101] In September 1951, the late General Vandenburgh, the then chief of the US Air Force, disclosed to the American Ambassador-designate to India, Mr Chester Bowles, US interest in the possibility of securing military bases in Pakistan.[102]

The degree of congruence between British and American policies regarding Kashmir, during this period, suggests substantial agreement between the two Governments in respect of their policies towards the Indo-Pakistani conflict.[102a] The United States looked upon Pakistan as a potential member of the anti-communist club, and, therefore, a valuable ally in her strategy to prevent the expansion of communist influence in the Middle East and in Asia. It was also the policy of the Republican administration in the 1950s to maintain a military balance between India and Pakistan, to prevent India's emergence as the dominant power in South Asia. For, the sort of military equipment Pakistan asked for and received from US, since 1954, could be of little use in the mountain passes through which a Soviet or Chinese invasion might, conceivably, have come.[103] These could only be used in a war with India, on the plains of the Punjab. But Dulles carried to its logical extreme a policy which was allowed to go far within the Pentagon and the State Department, before he took office. Britain, also, came to look upon Pakistan as an extension of what Sir Olaf called, 'the Muslim Lake', in the Middle East. To prevent Russian penetration in the region, British policy after the Second World War was to organise a defence line along the 'northern tier' frontier between the Middle East states and the Soviet Union.[103a] Pakistan thus came to acquire importance in the Anglo-American scheme for the maintenance of Western hegemony in the Middle East, from the beginning of the 1950s, if not from earlier years. It is impossible to say to what extent Sir Olaf's thinking influenced British foreign policy ; but the conclusion of the Baghdad Pact (later CENTO) in 1955 was certainly a partial fulfilment of his dream.[104] Both the British and the American governments were reluctant to adopt any posture towards the Kashmir dispute that was likely to offend Pakistan's sensitivities, or that of other Arab states. Reflecting this attitude, one of the most influential English dailies wrote, on the eve of the Commnwealth Prime Ministers' Conference in 1951, that a settlement of the Kashmir dispute was essential. Without this settlement the people of Kashmir were beginning to despair which was

> "turning into resentment not only against India, but also against the British Government, against the Commonwealth and against the United Nations."

A country in this mood, it continued,

> "cannot pull its weight on the side of international security ; yet...it is not only in South-East Asia that Pakistan has as indispensable part to play at this time. Her strategic situation, her close ties with Persia, Turkey and the Arab world, her reputation as the *leading Islamic State* combine to make her *an essential factor in the security of the Middle East*."[105]

This attitude explains the background to the Commonwealth Prime Ministers' attempts in 1951, to find a settlement between India and Pakistan. This was followed by the Anglo-American resolution in the Security Council to 'impose' a settlement of the Kashmir dispute which was acceptable to Pakistan. It should also be remembered that during this period bitterness against Indian policy on the Korean war reached its height in USA.[106] Frequent reference in the press to India's double standards in Korea and Kashmir is symbolic of this attitude.

British and American policy towards the Kashmir dispute came increasingly to be determined by factors which were extraneous to the problems of the sub-continent. In May 1954, Pakistan became an ally of the West when she signed the Mutual Defence Assistance Agreement with the United States ; later that year she joined SEATO and, the following year, the

Baghdad Pact. Whatever might have been the objectives of the Western powers, Pakistan joined these military alliances to strengthen her position vis-a-vis India.[107] During the middle of the 1950s the Kashmir dispute became overtly involved in the so-called 'East-West' coldwar, with the Soviet Union endorsing India's stand on Kashmir,[108] and Britain and the United States calling for an early settlement of the Kashmir dispute.[109] As one former British diplomat with personal experience of Indo-Pakistani affairs pointed out, the British government, "in determining its policy towards India and Pakistan was *bound to take some account* of the fact that, especially during the fifties, Pakistan was allied to certain Western countries, while India chose to be non-aligned and, after death of Stalin, developed close relations with the Soviet Union."[110]

Britain's role in the United Nations (1957-64)

In 1957, Indo-British relations reached a new low because of what most Indians considered to be the anti-Indian posture of the British government in the Security Council debates on Kashmir. After a period of direct negotiation between India and Pakistan which ended in failure, the Kashmir dispute was brought back to the Security Council by Pakistan, in January 1957. This was done following a declaration by the Indian Government that a new Constitution adopted by the Constituent Assembly of Jammu and Kashmir would come into force from 26 January 1957. In the Security Council, Britain, along with U.S., sponsored a resolution,[111] which reaffirmed that the final disposition of the State of Jammu and Kashmir could be effected only through a free and impartial plebiscite held under UN auspices and that the convening of the Constituent Assembly or its resolution would not alter the status of the State. She also supported the Pakistani suggestion for the introduction of a temporary UN force in Kashmir for facilitating demilitarisation.[112]

Two points which emerged from the arguments of the Indian delegate deserve our attention, as they underlined far-reaching changes in the attitude of the Indian government. In the first place, Krishna Menon told the Council that Kashmir's accession to India was final, as there was no provision in the Indian Constitution for conditional accession. This was the first time that India made such a claim officially, regarding the status of Kashmir ; and this was repeated, with emphasis, during the subsequent debates in the Security Council in 1962 and 1964. Secondly, it was pointed out that because of some vital changes in the circumstances,[113] a plebiscite had become an impracticable solution for the Kashmir dispute. Any attempt at ascertaining the will of the people by holding a plebiscite would jeopardise the political stability of the State, and by releasing communal tensions, would stir up violence and instability in the whole of the sub-continent. This would jeopardise the security of the minorities on both sides of the Indo-Pakistani border. This argument was based on sound political reasoning, and in fact, such fears were expressed by Sir Owen Dixon as early as 1950. Even Dr Gunnar Jarring in his report[114] submitted in April, 1957, took note of the changes in the strategic, economic and political forces surrounding the Kashmir dispute, and of the power relations in South Asia. He also expressed doubts about the possibility of implementing international agreements of an *ad hoc* character where situation with which they were to deal had tended to change. The British and the American governments did not seem to appreciate these facts. Referring to Britain's support to Pakistan in the Security Council, Aneurin Bevan said in a B.B.C. interview in May 1957 :

> "Our action in the UN over Kashmir was foolish. This is because the British Government knew it perfectly well that the course proposed, a plebiscite, was impracticable. The British Government should have been equally well aware of the fact that a plebiscite based on religious premises must inevitably cause untold upheaval both in India, where there are at least 40 million Muslims, and in Pakistan, where there is a large number of Hindus."[115]

Indian resentment against Britain ran high. Speaking in the Rajya Sabha on 9 September, 1957 Nehru said :

> "The kind of speeches delivered and arguments used by the representatives of great powers like the U.S.A., Britain and other countries who are supposed to know about this matter, were so far from truth, and even from a fair appraisal of the situation, that we were astonished."[116]

Perhaps, the British Government's stand on the Kashmir dispute in 1957 was influenced by the policy of the Indian government during the Suez crisis in the previous year, when Indians were far more criticial of the British Government's action than the Pakistanis. In the House of Commons there were many members of Parliament, particularly among the Conservatives, who made no secret of their depth of feeling against Nehru and his Government.[117] Nonetheless, the essential core of the British Government's policy towards the Kashmir dispute—settlement through plebiscite—remained unchanged throughout the 1950s.

During the 1960's, there was a shift of emphasis in British policy. The British government, no doubt, refused to accept New Delhi's claim that Kashmir was an integral part of India ; but their emphasis now shifted from the insistence on plebiscite for determining the future of the state, to a negotiated settlement between the two parties. This was quite clear from Britain's role during the Security Council debates on Kashmir in 1962 and again in 1964. On both these occasions, while supporting the idea of direct negotiations between India and Pakistan, the British government maintained that some outside assistance in the form of good offices or mediation by a third party might still be necessary for a satisfactory settlement of the dispute. The British government's policy towards the Kashmir dispute thus remained a recurrent cause of friction in Indo-British relations. Most Indians felt, and not unjustly, that it was because of the support she received in London and Washington that Pakistan could act as a diplomatic irritant to India.

III

Britain as a Mediator in Indo-Pakistani Conflicts : Two Contrasting Case Studies

(a) *The Anglo-American attempt at mediation in the Kashmir dispute in the aftermath of the Sino-Indian war (1962-63)*

Towards the end of 1962, the British Government made an abortive attempt to initiate bilateral talks between India and Pakistan on the Kashmir dispute. During the Sino-Indian border conflict of that year, Britain promptly came to India's aid. This was highly appreciated in India and created a favourable attitude towards Britain. At the political level, relations between the two countries had not been so good in recent years. But the goodwill created by the British gesture was soon vitiated by the re-introduction of the Kashmir problem. Within a week of the announcement of a unilateral ceasefire by China, and withdrawal of her forces, two parallel missions from Britain and USA arrived in India, led by Mr Duncan Sandys and Mr Averell Harriman respectively. These missions came ostensibly to study India's long-term military needs, but also sought to persuade Nehru to start a dialogue with Pakistan over Kashmir. Mr Sandys informed the House of Commons later that in an emergency when a fellow member of the Commonwealth was attacked and asked for aid, it was the policy of the British Government to give as much aid and as quickly as possible. But, he added,

> "...both Harriman and I pointed out (to Nehru) that when we came to consider long-term military aid, the British and American people would be unhappy to see that an appreciable part of the Indian Army was being employed not for defence against China, but for defence against Pakistan. We, therefore, expressed to Mr Nehru our *strong hope* that in the face of the Chinese threat to the whole of the sub-continent, a new attempt would be made to settle the differences between India and Pakistan."[118]

There was logic in this argument. For India and Pakistan together could constitute a strong single unit of defence against any attak from the north. Any solution of the Kashmir dispute might have increased the chances of co-operation between the two states. But there is ample evidence to suggest that the policy of the British and American governments was influenced by diplomatic pressures from Pakistan.[119] The Pakistani leaders chose to reactivate the Kashmir issue at a time when, they thought, India would be more amenable to Western pressures, as she needed arms to re-equip and reorganise her defence forces. There was also an element of fear in Pakistan's reactionto the proposals for long-term military aid to India which were then being considered in London and Washington. President Ayub thought that India was deliberately exaggerating the threat from China, to secure arms from US and the UK, which would strengthen India's position vis-a-vis Pakistan. On 5 November, 1962, in a letter to the late President Kennedy, Ayub Khan wrote that China had limited aims in the war—"to occupy the territory which they believe belongs to them and over which there has been a dispute between her and India."[120] Therefore, the long-term plans for the supply of arms to India seemed to Rawalpindi to be unjustifiable. The differences with China were not insurmountable, wrote Mr Bhutto later. Once China and India had settled their differences, "All the strength and might of India will then be turned against Pakistan, for in India's eyes Pakistan alone is a heresy."[121]

But the timing of the Anglo-American initiative for a settlement of the Kashmir dispute, was not appropriate ; because the Indians were yet to recover from the shock of their recent military defeat. Any attempt to put pressure on India on a sensitive issue like Kashmir at such a time was likely to be counterproductive.

Mr Sandys arrived in India on 25 November, and two days later, he flew to Rawalpindi to meet Ayub Khan for discussions on Kashmir. The draft of an agreement had been drawn up in Rawalpindi between President Ayub, and Mr Sandys and Mr Harriman ; and with that Mr Sandys returned to New Delhi. On 29 November, he met Nehru with the draft and suggested that a joint statement should be issued by the Governments of India and Pakistan. Nehru agreed, but suggested some variations in the wording of the draft. On the same day a joint statement was issued simultaneously by the Governments of India and Pakistan, with the signatures of President Ayub and Prime Minister Nehru. The joint declaration stated :

> "The President of Pakistan and the Prime Minister of India have agreed that a renewed effort should be made to resolve the outstanding differences between their two countries on Kashmir and other related matters so as to enable India and Pakistan to live side by side in peace and friendship.
>
> In consequence, they have decided to start discussions at an early date with the object of reaching an honourable and equitable settlement.
>
> These will be conducted initially at the ministerial level. At the appropriate stage direct talks will be held between Mr Nehru and President Ayub Khan."[122]

On the following day, Nehru made a statement in the Lok Sabha which evoked grave concern in Pakistan and caused Mr Sandys to return to New Delhi. In view of the controversy which later developed regarding the statement, it is necessary to quote the relevant section.

Nehru informed the House of his meetings with Mr Sandys and Mr Harriman, and thanked the British and the American governments for their help in India's crisis. In the course of these talks, he said,

> "The question of our relations with Pakistan was raised...The question of Kashmir was referred to and we explained to them our position in regard to it and pointed out that anything that involved an upset of the present arrangement would be very harmful to the people of Kashmir as well as to the future relations of India and Pakistan. We were, however, always ready to discuss this, as other matters, with representatives of the Pakistan Government at any level desired..."
>
> Mr Sandys and Mr Harriman appreciated our position but still suggested that a friendly discussion

> about these matters might be helpful. I was agreeable to this...I explained to them, again, however, our basic principles and how it was not possible for us to bypass or ignore them...."[123]

Later on, in reply to a question by Mr H.V. Kamath, he said : "It was not for Mr Sandys or any one else to suggest what kind of talk we should have or what manner of talk we should have."[124]

It is quite clear from the last sentence that Nehru was not pleased with Mr Sandys's personal diplomacy. So far as the substantive part of the statement is concerned, it seems that he was merely reiterating the Government of India's stand that they were quite prepared to talk with Pakistan on Kashmir on the basis of the existing *status quo*. India has long maintained that a settlement on the cease-fire line, with adjustments on the boundary favouring Pakistan, especially in the Poonch area, would in itself be a concession. What was agreed between Nehru and Mr Sandys in their meeting is not known to us. It would be surprising if Nehru had been willing to concede anything more, if only because any such move would be interpreted in India as a 'surrender' to Western pressure and Pakistani 'blackmail'. It should be noted that when the Prime Minister made the statement in the Indian Parliament, the government was under fierce attack for weakness and indecision.

However, in Karachi the statement was interpreted differently. This might have been because PTI extracted the 'worst' part of the statement and sent it over the wire for publication in the press. President Ayub wrote later that Nehru's statement created doubts in Pakistan about India's intention to enter into any "meaningful and constructive talks about the Kashmir dispute."[125] Mr Sandys arrived in Karachi from New Delhi on his way back to London. On being shown the text of Nehru's statement he was

> "so surprised that he decided to fly back to Delhi to clear the matter up. From the airport he drove straight to the Prime Minister's house and caught Nehru as he was going to bed."[126]

Mr Sandys pressed Nehru to issue a statement which, without involving any eating of words, would put a more favourable construction on what he said, and would allay some of the doubts which his statement had created. Nehru at first declined and suggested that it was wrong to attach too much importance to particular phrases, especially because he made the observations without a prepared text. However, later on he agreed to issue the following statement, on 1 December 1962 :

> "There has never been any question of pre-conditions or of any restrictions on the scope of the talks which the two governments are initiating. As I indicated yesterday in the Lok Sabha, the problem of Kashmir is complicated and difficult. But I am sure that with goodwill on both sides it would be possible to work out an honourable and equitable solution of this as of other problems."[127]

It may reasonably be argued that here Nehru was retracting from what he had said in the Indian Parliament, and that this was done under Western pressure. In the meantime, Pakistan had been requested to make some gestures which would enable India to withdraw some part of her troops from Kashmir, if needed elsewhere. Pakistan said that it would agree not to advance in Kashmir if Indian troops were replaced there by UN troops. Even Mr Sandys realized that this would be unacceptable to New Delhi, and the proposal was dropped.[128] On the face of Pakistan's inflexibility, the style of Mr Sandys's personal diplomacy appeared to be sheer diplomatic arm-twisting even to the most moderate Indian. The Anglo-American effort to 'impose' a settlement in this fashion on an India still nursing her wounds from a military defeat was one of the "most ham-handed diplomatic moves ever attempted", wrote Evan Charlton, a former editor of the *Statesman* (Calcutta and New Delhi); and goodwill for Britain changed "overnight into resentment."[129] Whether this change occurred 'overnight' may be a matter of argument, but even senior British diplomats agree that the good effects of Britain's gesture during the war were depreciated by the introduction of the Kashmir issue.[130] The correspondent of *The Times* (London) wrote from New Delhi that Mr Sandys had been "misled by a mirage effect of India's mood of 'nothing matters but repelling the Chinese' and had misread as willingness to make concessions to Pakistan over Kashmir what was in fact a readiness to settle with Pakistan on the basis of the existing status quo—something which the Pakistanis were bound to reject."[131]

These negotiations also revealed differences between Professor J. K. Galbraith, who was then the US Ambassador to India, and Mr Duncan Sandys.[132] While both UK and US were pressing India for a settlement of the Kashmir dispute, Britain was pressing harder—at least this was the prevalent impression in India.[133] Professor Galbraith's view was that while a settlement of the Kashmir problem was desirable, India should not have been pressed too far to make concessions which would not be politically acceptable. Mr Sandys perhaps thought that because of Britain's past involvement in the affairs of the sub-continent, he was in a better position to influence the attitudes of the two Governments in New Delhi and Rawalpindi. While he failed to get any meaningful concession from Rawalpindi, [134] the style of his diplomacy did not contribute to any improvement in Anglo-Indian relations either.

Six rounds of talks were held between India and Pakistan at ministerial level.[135] In a sense, as G.W. Choudhury wrote later, these talks "were a quadripartite affair because Britain and the United States—while maintaining, of course, a correct aloofness from the matter of issue—were deeply committed to promoting a successful outcome."[136] The talks got off to a bad start. On the eve of the first meeting at Karachi, Pakistan announced the conclusion of a border agreement with China. "On any reckoning", wrote Gore-Booth, "this was an intolerable discourtesy."[136a] To Indians it was even worse, as the border agreement included agreement on the frontier of Pakistan-occupied Kashmir—a territory which India claimed to belong to her.

When negotiations began, Indian and Pakistani views were wide apart. The British and the US governments, as friends of both, could hardly do anything unless the negotiating parties agreed to a solution. American thinking ultimately developed in the direction of persuading India to make concessions in the valley of Kashmir. The British High Commissioner in New Delhi, on the other hand, realised that a plan for the division of the valley would not be acceptable to either India or Pakistan. Although no formal proposal was made by the British, when the talks reached deadlock Sir Paul (later Lord Gore-Booth) did suggest to Nehru the idea of a "mixed regime for the Vale, either under or without United Nations auspices."[137]

By the time of the fourth meeting in Calcutta, the steam had gone out of the negotiations. As far as India was concerned, as the threat from China receded, she lost some of the urgency that was forced on her by the British and the US Governments. Nevertheless, it seems India offered terms for a political settlement of the dispute which constituted a substantial advance on her former proposals.[137a] But Pakistan demanded even more. Eventually the talks ended in failure; and bitterness between the two states increased.

Shortly before the conclusion of the six rounds of talks, Lord Mountbatten visited India, along with Mr Sandys, to study India's long-term need for arms. A parallel mission came from US, led by the Secretary of State Dean Rusk. The occasion was used to make a final bid for a settlement of the impasse and the emphasis now shifted to mediation, and Lord Mountbatten had persuaded Nehru to accept the idea, which had also the support of the Americans. But the idea had to be given up when the Pakistanis demanded impossible terms. Both the British and the American governments had decided by the middle of 1963 that arms to India would not be conditional upon a successful settlement of the Kashmir dispute.[138] The correspondent of *The Times* reported from New Delhi: "Misunderstanding between Britain and India had been nipped in the bud by the intervention of Lord Mountbatten and an attempt to use the Sino-Indian border war as a lever to force a settlement of the Kashmir dispute has been written off.[139] Thus ended one of the unsuccessful attempts at mediation by the British and American Governments.

(b) *The Rann of Kutch War and Britain's mediatory role*

British diplomacy failed in 1962-63, to effect a settlement of the Kashmir dispute between India and Pakistan ; two years later, however, the British Government's mediatory efforts in the Rann of Kutch conflict were successful.

The crux of the dispute over the Rann of Kutch, from the Indian point of view, was not a territorial one—since the border was well-defined in pre-partition maps. It was rather the linear demarcation of the boundaries that was in question. Indians claimed that the boundary was roughly along the northern edge of the Rann, as shown in the pre-partition maps. Pakistan claimed, on the other hand, that there was a jurisdictional dispute ; that the Rann as a "maritime feature" should be treated as an inland lake, and, therefore, should be divided equally between the two states.

Pakistan first raised the issue in 1956 in relation to certain landmarks ; it featured in the talks between the two Prime Ministers in 1958. But it never constituted a serious problem in the relations between the two states. In 1960, both sides agreed to consider the matter on the basis of documentary evidence, after which the dispute lay dormant.

Fighting accidentally broke out in January 1965. But until the end of March, the conflict was confined mainly to clashes between probing patrols. On 9 April units of regular Pakistani army attacked Indian posts near Kanjarkot and initially drove back the Indian guards. India then despatched a force from her regular army. On 24 April, 1965 Pakistan escalated the conflict by launching fresh attacks on four Indian posts with American-supplied armour. India then also brought up some armour but apparently could not make use of it because of logistical difficulties. The peace proposals made by the two sides ended in a diplomatic stalemate.

Britain's role

Further escalation of the conflict was avoided by the timely diplomatic intervention of the British and American governments. But in India, American influence proved to be less effective than that of Britain as Indians resented the use of

American arms by the Pakistanis. The two British High Commissioners in New Delhi and Rawalpindi worked for the de-escalation of the conflict, and for finding common grounds on which negotiations could be started between India and Pakistan.[140] These efforts were later followed by the personal intervention of the British Prime Minister. During the Commonwealth Prime Ministers' Conference in London in June 1965, Mr Harold Wilson, along with the Commonwealth Secretary Mr Arthur Bottomley, succeeded in securing a basis for the settlement of the Indo-Pakistani conflict. Mr Wilson described this succinctly in later years. While entertaining some of the Commonwealth leaders at Chequers, he took the chance of sounding out the Indian Prime Minister, informally, about the dispute and soon they were looking at maps.

> "Gradually the sticking points became clearer. Meanwhile, a similar process was going on at Dorneywood. Each tentative advance or embryo concession was passed through private secretaries from one house to the other and we began to make progress."[141]

On the next day, the process was reversed, with Mr Wilson engaging President Ayub, and Mr Bottomley playing host to Shastri. "By midnight", Mr Wilson wrote,

> "taking together the moves in both houses, we were moving towards a political settlement. Both our guests accepted my proposal, that, with the Queen's permission, we might retire for a few minutes from the Royal dinner for the Commonwealth prime ministers to see if an agreement could be worked out."[142]

On the night of 22 June, the basis for a settlement was reached, which was followed up by the two British High Commissioners with their host Governments. A cease-fire agreement was signed by the two Governments on 30 June. The officials at CRO, and the British High Commissioners in New Delhi and Rawalpindi contributed a great deal towards the settlement, both before and after the Chequers/Dorneywood meetings.[143]

The two parties agreed to withdraw their troops from the disputed area, while maintaining police posts which were there before the troubles began. In effect, this meant the restoration of the *status quo ante*, as on 1 January, 1965. They also decided that in case they failed to reach any agreement on the border, within a period of two months from the conclusion of the cease-fire, they would refer the matter to an independent tribunal whose decision would be obligatory on both sides.[144]

The Rann of Kutch Agreement is an example of the successful mediatory role played by the British Government in an Indo-Pakistani conflict. There were a number of reasons for this success. In the first place, none of the parties to the dispute wanted it to escalate. For Pakistan, it was a low-cost test of India's will and military capability.[145] In India also, despite political pressures to the contrary, the government wanted to de-escalate the political tension and the conflict with Pakistan. Any Indian offensive in the Rann of Kutch would be difficult because of the problems faced by the Indian Army in the inhospitable terrain ; and above all, the onset of the monsoon would submerge the entire area thereby making the movement of armour from the Indian side well-nigh impossible. There was also the willingness to accept British mediation. The Labour Party won the General Elections in 1964, and the new Prime Minister had a favourable image in India. None of these factors was present a few months later, when the Indo-Pakistani war broke out.

IV

The Indo-Pakistani War of 1965 : Failure of Britain as a Mediator

During the two years 1964 and 1965 (till the outbreak of war in that year) tensions in India-Pakistan relations increased and compulsions of domestic politics led to hardening of attitudes on both sides.[146]

The year 1965 opened with India and Pakistan complaining against each other for violations of the cease-fire line, in Kashmir—in fact there were several violations by both sides. But a change could be seen in Pakistan's public posture.[147] The first signs of Pakistan's militancy were seen in the Rann of Kutch. Events were moving fast driving the two states towards a collision course.

The results of the limited offensive in the Rann of Kutch encouraged the Pakistanis to proceed towards their ultimate aim which was to have a military solution of the Kashmir problem. The Pakistani newspapers began to write of the 'easy victories'. In London, President Ayub boasted of the performance of the Pakistani Army. "We had to shake off the Indians somehow", he remarked, "because Pakistan did not want a widening of the conflict." He declared Pakistan's willingness to live in peace with India ; but added ; "if war is forced on us, it will have to be one that seeks a decision."[148] This clearly reflected Pakistan's belligerent mood.

In India, on the other hand, the Rann of Kutch Agreement was criticised by the right-wing political parties. The Jan Sangh described this as a sell-out to Pakistan ; and there was a feeling in the country, by no means confined to the Jan Sangh, that the attackers were allowed to run away with impunity. This ruled out the possibility of a benign or conciliatory gesture towards Pakistan.

Before the ink on the Kutch Agreement had dried Pakistan started sending armed men, not in uniform, to the Indian side of the state of Jammu and Kashmir, to act as saboteurs, for the disruption of law and order in the state. This movement of armed infiltrators from the Pakistani side of the border began on 5 August, a fact which was clearly revealed in the report submitted by the UN Secretary General to the Security Council on 23 September, 1965.[149] Secretary-General stated in his report :

> "General Nimmo had indicated to me that the series of violations that began on August 5, were to a considerable extent in subsequent days in the form of armed men, generally not in uniform, crossing the CFL from the Pakistan side for the purpose of armed action on the Indian side..."

The press and radio in Pakistan began to propagate the news of a rebellion in Kashmir which was strongly denied by the Indian and Kashmir Governments. Independent foreign observers of the situation in Kashmir at the time also cofirmed the absence of any revolutionary situation in the state.[150] With the security of the state thus threatened, Indian forces began 'mopping up' the armed infiltrators. By the end of August, the regular forces of both the states were involved in fighting all along the cease-fire line in Kashmir, and Indian forces occupied some important positions in Azad Kashmir.

On 1 September, the Pakistani forces launched a major assault in the Chhamb-Jaurian sector of Jammu in an attempt to cut off the Indian supply line to Kashmir, with a column of tanks, estimated between 70 and 90 in number. The fighting in the previous month had been of a limited character, and along the cease-fire line in Kashmir in which no armour had been used. It is difficult to determine what prompted Pakistan to switch the conflict from a limited offensive to a full-scale conventional war. The elaborate arrangements with which the attack was launched make it clear that the whole operation, code named 'grand slam', was pre-planned. Even the UN military observers in the area warned the Indian authorities about the possible attack.[151] If the Pakistani attack of 1 September had been successful, it could completely cut off the supply line to the Indian forces in the north-western fronts, and isolate the Indian garrison in Kashmir. While Indian forces contained the Pakistani attack with difficulty, they failed to dislodge the Pakistani forces from the area occupied by them about 6 to 10 miles within the Indian border. On 6 September India retaliated launching a three-pronged attack across the international boundary in the Punjab, towards Lahore. From the Indian point of view, this was a defensive military strategy. According to Indian officials, the offensive had two major aims (a) to relieve the Pakistani pressure in Jammu and (2) to prevent a Pakistani attack, across the Punjab border, on India. For the next 15 days, the armies of the two states were locked in a see-saw battle, with limited air offensives, until a cease-fire was effected by the UN Security Council on 23 September, 1964.

The details of the senseless war[152] which failed to deliver any gains to either of the parties, are outside the scope of the present study. One of the first casualties of the Indo-Pakistani war, however, was India's relations with Britain. Indians complained that the attitude of the British Government was not impartial, and that India had a very bad press in Britain. Both these complaints had some justification.

To take the role of the British press first, while the Pakistani attack of 1 September passed almost uncondemned, and reports of advance by the Pakistani Army featured well in the press, the Indian counter-offensive of 6 September—with the solitary exception of the *Financial Times*[153]—was described as invasion and aggression. One aspect of the reporting was the continuous emphasis on the numerical superiority of the Indian forces compared to the qualitative superiority of the Pakistani armour and weaponry. But this picture was not correct. Though India had the larger army, and a larger industrial base which would be of definite advantage to her in a long-drawn conflict, in the quick shattering campaigns of the Indo-Pakistani war, the last factor proved to be of little use. Even the numerical superiority of the army could not be brought to bear on Pakistan, as a substantial part of it was deployed on the Himalayan border.

For the bad press India got in Britain (as well as in other Western countries), the Government of India's policy was partly responsible. Pakistan allowed foreign correspondents to go to the battle-fronts, particularly in areas where the Pakistan Army was doing well, but imposed severe restrictions on the transmission of the news. As a result, nothing critical about Pakistan could come out of reports sent by correspondents from the Pakistan side. The Indian Defence Ministry, on the other hand, adopted the alternative method of pre-censoring the news, as all news about the war was being released through official spokesmen ; but there was no restriction on the transmission of news by foreign correspondents. The result was less effective as the foreign correspondents were rather sceptical about the claims made by the Government of India. When they were finally allowed to go to the forward areas, there was no action reporting, as the theatre of war had already moved. The reports they sent were, therefore, based on official communiques and announcements, which were no match for the reports sent from the Pakistani side, based on first-hand accounts of war.

It should be noted that taken as a whole, the British press was by no means fully committed to Pakistan. There was a fair amount of reporting which may be classified as unfavourable to Pakistan and some was objective. For a proper assessment of the role of the press during the Indo-Pakistani war we should distinguish between (1) news reports of the fighting and (2) editorial opinion. By further subdividing each category under the headings of 'pro-Pakistan', 'pro-India', 'anti-Pakistan' 'anti-India' and 'objective', it has been found in a study by the Press Institute of India that 'the volume of anti-India reports outweighed the volume of 'anti-Pakistan' reports.'[153a]

As far as the reports were concerned, anti-India reports emanated mostly from correspondents in Pakistan who presented the Pakistan Government's claims as their own. They were also easily gullible, because most of the full-time British correspondents in the sub-continent were India-based, whereas most of the British correspondents in Pakistan came 'fresh', when the war broke out. Therefore they had little knowledge of the intricacies of the dispute ; nor did they do enough 'home work'. As a result, even *The Guardian* published reports from its man in Rawalpindi which were, to say the least, irresponsible. For example, Peter Preston of *The Guardian* wrote : 'The limited military situation now seems overwhelmingly stacked in favour of Pakistan' and, "...Pakistan hopes to bring down the rickety (Indian) federal house of cards and this may not be an idle planning."[154] It seems that the writers of such reports had taken leave of their critical faculties, and were unable to distinguish between fact and fiction.[155] There was more of this from the Pakistani side.

Regarding editorial opinion, most of the British papers took the view—with the notable exception of the *Financial Times*—that the war began when the Indians crossed the international boundary in the Punjab on 6 September. The *Financial Times*, however, wrote on 7 September,

> "The Indian thrust towards Lahore is explicable as the opening of a major campaign. But it may also have been planned with more immediate aims of relieving the

> pressure in Kashmir, where the Indian position is highly vulnerable."

As regards the long-term cause of the dispute, most of the leader-writers blamed India for the continuance of the impasse over Kashmir. For, despite the Government of India's declared policy of treating Kashmir as an internal part of India, most leader-writers in Britain continued to mention that there was a genuine dispute about Kashmir, and that it was not closed merely because one side in the dispute unilaterally claimed it to be so.[156] These views were, no doubt sincerely held ; but there was a feeling, not merely confined to Indians, that the British press was far from impartial in the Indo-Pakistani conflict. When the dust of the battle had settled down, there was considerable soul-searching among British commentators and journalists. One commentator wrote in the left-wing *Tribune* that there 'has been blatant partiality for Pakistanis, not based on their case, but on anti-Indian feelings. When Indian troops won battles, papers wrote editorials about India's "military" feelings and recalling Gandhi's teachings. Even the BBC got mixed up in its emotions'.[157] The Delhi correspondent of *The Times* (London) wrote :

> "...there nevertheless remains in such British comment on this war a thin but persistent note of malice, against India. The simplest explanation of this lies in the world's tendency to rejoice in the downfall of the preacher...English gibes about non-violence reveal ignorance as well as spite."[158]

If the role of the British press during the Indo-Pakistani war gave rise to much resentment in India, greater damage had been done to Indo-British relations by the statement issued by the then British Prime Minister Mr Harold (now Sir Harold) Wilson on 6 September 1965. Britain's primary concern was, no doubt, to bring about an early end to the hostilities. In the month of August the British government had advised the Pakistan government through diplomatic channels, not to send armed infiltrators to the Indian side of the state of Jammu and Kashmir.[159] To this the Government of Pakistan did not, apparently, pay any attention. On 3 September, two days after the outbreak of the war, the British Prime Minister sent personal messages to Prime Minister Shastri and President Ayub[160] expressing concern about the deteriorating situation. These messages were identically worded, balanced and non-condemnatory.[161] But after the Indian forces crossed the international boundary in the Punjab on 6 September, 1965, Mr Wilson issued a statement which caused widespread anger and resentment in India. He said:

> "I am deeply concerned at the increasingly serious fighting now taking place between India and Pakistan and *especially at the news that Indian forces have attacked Pakistan territory across the Indian frontier* in the Punjab. This is a distressing response to the resolution adopted by the Security Council on September 4, calling for a ceasefire.
>
> "The dangerous situation now created may have the gravest of consequences not only for India and Pakistan but also for the peace of the world...No lasting solution of the Kashmir problem can possibly be reached by force. I have therefore appealed in the most urgent terms to both President Ayub and Mr Shastri to respond to the Security Council resolution and to bring the present fighting to an immediate end."[162]

Taken by itself, the statement was definitely anti-Indian, as there was no reference to the origin of the conflict. The current flare-up in the sub-continent was, by all evidence, the result of the infiltration of armed men into the Indian side of the territory of Kashmir from the Pakistani side.[163] There was also ample evidence to show that the infiltrators were being armed by the Pakistani army. Mr Wilson's statement ignored these facts. Moreover, it means that India alone was responsible for the escalation of the conflict, whereas in reality Pakistan first escalated the conflict by launching a major attack on 1 September. Implicit in the statement was the criticism that India had committed an aggression by attacking Pakistani territory "across the international frontier" in the Punjab. However, if India was guilty of violating an international boundary, so was Pakistan, when she launched the offensive on

1 September in the Chhamb-Jaurion sector of Jammu. The attack had occurred just west of the Chhamb where the international boundary between India and Pakistan meets the Kashmir ceasefire line. After the Pakistani attack in the Chhamb, a spokesman of the Government of India said : "...it is our understanding that the attackers have crossed the international border."[164] So fairness and impartiality would require that if India was to be criticised for the violation of the international boundary, Pakistan should also have been criticised for the same offence.

Mr Wilson wrote a few years later that he had been "taken for a ride by a pro-Pakistani faction in the C.R.O." who had "inveigled him into issuing on 6th September, a statement—justified as they said by cast-iron evidence—condemning India for an act of aggression." And Mr Wilson added, in his memoirs, "I was wrong in this ; all the facts were too much in dispute."[165] The Commonwealth Secretary Mr Arthur Bottomley was in Scotland for a brief holiday at the time ; but before he could unpack, he was recalled to London. When he arrived the following morning, he told Mr Wilson that if he had been in London, no statement would have been issued from No. 10.[166]

Mr Wilson's reference in 1971 to the alleged influence of a "pro-Pakistan faction" in the CRO, brought a sharp rejoinder from some of the former senior members of the Office, both in private and also in their public pronouncements. Sir Algernon Rumbold, who was the Deputy Under-Secretary in the Commonwealth Relations Office at the time, wrote a letter to *The Times*, refuting Mr Wilson's allegations. He wrote :

> "There were powerful international reasons why it was particularly important in September, 1965, to bring the fighting quickly to an end. These reasons were well-known to Mr Wilson, even if he has now forgotten them....The best contribution we could make to shortening the war in 1965 was to shake both contestants to a reluctant realisation of the possibility that they might be wrong, and to make it clear that neither could expect material assistance or moral support from Britain in

their quarrel. The forthright actions of the British Government, to that end, of which the statement issued on September 6, 1965, was part, *were impartial as between the two parties*."[167]

This was a brilliant piece of diplomatic understatement. No one would deny Sir Algernon's assertion that ending the hostilities was the most important thing ; but his claim that the statement of 6 September, was 'impartial between the two parties' is not accepted even by some of his former colleagues who then and later were critical of Mr Wilson's allegations about the pro-Pakistan bias of some of the officials in the CRO.[168]

One thing which does not emerge either from the account by Mr Wilson or from that of Sir Algernon, is the role of the British High Commissioner in New Delhi. Sir Algernon has referred to the "powerful" international reasons, which influenced the British government's policy, but has not defined them. Nor is it clear whether the initiative for the 6 September statement came from CRO, or from No. 10 Downing Street.[169] However, from the strong words used by Mr Wilson in criticising his CRO advisers both in his memoirs, and later on, in private, it seems highly likely that there *was* a pro-Pakistan faction among the senior officials in CRO,[170] and that they had advised the Prime Minister to issue a statement which, on Mr Wilson's own account, would not have been recommended to him by the Commonwealth Secretary.[171] Perhaps the action of these officials was precipitated by the wide publicity given in the press to the Indian attack of 6 September ; surely there was also concern at the possibility of the Indo-Pakistani war escalating into a bigger international conflict. But what was not sufficiently realised at the time was that even the Pakistani attack of 1 September, 1965, involved a violation of the international boundary, as distinguished from the cease-fire line in Kashmir. *It appears that even the British High Commissioner in New Delhi was not certain, as late as the morning of 6 September, whether the Pakistani forces had in fact violated the international boundary*,[172] though at the end he was not very pleased with the statement issued by the Prime Minister.[172a] Later on Mr Wilson himself admitted in a television interview on 1 August, 1971, that the statement was far too pro-Pakistani and far too anti-Indian. "Anglo-Indian relations were in consequence embittered for many months to come."[173] In April, 1966, Mr Wilson met the Indian Prime Minister Mrs Indira Gandhi at the airport, when she stopped in London, on her way back to India from New York. They talked for two hours. These discussions, in Mr Wilson's own words, "were able to do something to repair the harm done by the statement of the previous September. I explained what had happened and made clear what I felt about the mistake."[174]

V

India's disputes with Pakistan, and British attitudes to these disputes have powerfully affected Indo-British relations during the first two decades of India's existence as an independent state. In the context of Indo-Pakistani disputes Indians have taken towards Britain much the same stance that shaped the Congress party's view of the role of the British government in the League-Congress struggle for power. In this sense, the image of Britain as perceived in India is really a continuation of the image that was formed in the pre-partition days. The most important factor that has contributed to the crystalisation of this image was the British government's attitude towards the Kashmir dispute.

Most India-Pakistan conflicts during the period under discussion were initiated by Pakistan. Being the weaker and territorially unsatisfied power, she has followed what Boulding has called, a policy of 'rational aggression'[175]—which means a policy of deliberately planned conflicts, or 'a game of ruin'—against India, in the calculated hope of a limited benefit, or 'pay-off'.

Britain, along with the United States as the 'crisis managers' in the sub-continent, at least till the Indo-Pakistani war of 1965, had always sought to maintain a balance between the two sides. While the British government refrained from giving military assistance to either of the parties during armed conflicts—say, during 1947-48, or in 1965—they have generally supported Pakistan's efforts in UN to change the *status quo* in

Kashmir in a way favourable to her. The introduction of external factors—the involvement of the Great Powers in support of either of the parties—led to the perpetuation of the conflict. "The West", wrote Walter Crocker, "on more than one occasions increased the tension between the two countries by well-meaning but ill-informed efforts to mediate instead of letting the two countries feel their own way to a solution."[176] It is difficult not to agree with this observation.

Since the reference of the Kashmir dispute to the United Nations in January 1948, the British Government had taken an active interest, and at times had been rather over-zealous, in securing a settlement of the Kashmir dispute either through UN, or through direct negotiations between India and Pakistan, But their inability to influence the policies of either of the disputants became quite clear on a number of occasions, and particularly from the failure of India-Pakistan negotiations in 1962-63, and again, during the Indo-Pakistani war of 1965.

By the middle of the 1960s there were signs that the British were growing weary of the Kashmir problem. This was reflected in the re-organisation of the policy-making machinery at Whitehall. Between the years 1951-64, the South Asia Department within CRO always treated 'Kashmir' as a separate subject along with India and Pakistan, Ceylon, Burma and other countries in South Asia.[177] This ceased to be the practice after 1964. At least, 'Kashmir' ceased to appear in the list of subjects dealt with by the South Asia Department.[178] This may be interpreted as a mere departmental reorganisation for administrative convenience.[179] But perhaps there was something more to it. Kashmir was and still is a matter of dispute between India and Pakistan. If that was the reason for treating it independently of India and Pakistan, the practice should have continued after 1964. The real reason for changing the system, therefore, seems to be a deliberate decision by the British government to abstain from their previous role. The success of Britain's mediatory role in the Rann of Kutch dispute, in the summer of 1965, was atypical ; it was an unusual example of Britain playing a successful role as a mediator in India-Pakistan conflicts, and might have influenced the policy of (diplomatic) intervention during the war of September, 1965. In marked contrast, the Tashkhent conference in January 1966, not only meant a diplomatic victory for the Soviet Union in its attempt to act as a 'peace-maker' in the sub-continent, it also signalised the decline of British influence in the region.

During his visit to India and Pakistan in December 1968, the then Foreign and Commonwealth Secretary Mr Michael Stewart said that in future Britain would not intervene in the Kashmir dispute, unless both the parties asked for such intervention. This declaration of deliberate abstention and neutrality was well-received in India at that time.

NOTES AND REFERENCES

1. Arif Hussain ; *Pakistan : Its Ideology and Foreign Policy* (Frank Cass, London, 1966), p, XV.

2. This theme was stressed to me by a number of British observers I have talked to.

3. Later on, however, Gandhi changed his view. See, for example, his statement on 4 June, 1947 : "The British Government *is not responsible* for partition. The Viceroy had no hand in it. In fact he is as opposed to partition as the Congress itself. But if both of us, Hindus and Muslims, cannot agree on anything else, the Viceroy is left with no choice." Cited in V.P. Menon : *Transfer of Power in India* (Princeton University Press, Princeton, 1957, p. 382). Italics added. The rank and file in India regard such statements as being declaratory in intent.

4. *Hansard* (Lords), 5 series, Vol. CL. Cols. 808-09.

5. See, H.V. Hodson : *The Great Divide : Britain-India-Pakistan* (Hutchinson, London, 1969), p. 524. Also see, Olaf Caroe : 'The End of British India : Storms Which Still Blow' in *The Round Table*, January, 1970.

5a. For further discussions on this see, A.K. Banerji : "The Great Divide And the British Raj" in *Socialist Perspective* (Council for Political Studies, Calcutta), Vol. I, No. I, p. 56.

6. See, Sisir Gupta : *Kashmir : A Study In India-Pakistan Relations* (Asia Publishing House, Bombay, 1966), p. 1.

7. K.M. Panikkar : *The Foundations of New India* (Allen & Unwin, London, 1963), pp, 69-70.

8. *The Times*, 26 September, 1906.

9. Cited in V.P. Menon : *op. cit.*, p. 10.

10. See H.N. Brailsford ; 'India's Two Nations' in the *New Statesman and Nation*, March, 1946.

11. See N. Mansergh, (ed) : *The Transfer of Power 1942-47,* Vol. 1, The Cripps Mission, January-March (H.M.S.O., London, 1970), p. 19.

12. *Ibid.*, p. 873.

12a. See, P.D. Reeves ; "Quit India : The Response of the Raj" in *South Asian Review*, Vol. 5, No. 1, October, 1971.

13. See N. Mansergh (ed) ; *op. cit.*, vol. II, 'Quit India' (H.M.S.O., London, 1971), pp. 390-91, Italics original.

14. *Ibid.*, vol. II. See Prime Minister Churchill's telegram to President Roosevelt on 31 July, 1942 (p. 533) ; also see p. 830.

15. *Ibid.*, vol. II, p. 509. For further evidence of the anti-Congress bias of the British Government, also see, Sudhir Ghosh : *Gandhi's Emissary* (Cresset Press, London, 1969), and Pyarelal : *Mahatma Gandhi : The Last Phase* (Navajivan Publishing House, Ahmedabad, 1958), esp. pp. 260-62.

16. N. Mansergh ; *op. cit.*, Vol. I, pp. 16-17.

17. *ibid.*, p. 468.

17a. Take, for example, the following entry in his diary on 30 October, 1946, musing over the causes of the failure of the Cabinet Mission : "I am sorry for the Muslims ; they have more honesty, courage and dignity than the Hindus, but cannot stand up to the power of the rupee and the superior education and chicanery of the Congress. Up to a point Jinnah played his cards well, but I think he has been too unyielding": Penderel Moon (ed.), *Wavell : The Viceroy's Journal*, (O.U.P., London, Delhi, Karachi, 1973, p. 368.)

18. *ibid.*, pp. 169-70.

18a. A mountain of literature exists on the subject. On the Indian side, the different aspects of the story has been narrated by some of the participants. Among them, A.K. Azad : *India Wins Freedom* (Orient Longman, Calcutta, 1959), V.P. Menon ; *op. cit.*, R. Prasad : *India Divided* (Hind Kitab, Bombay, 1946), Pyarelal ; *op. cit.*, and Sudhir Ghosh : *op. cit.* are important. M. Brecher : *Nehru : A Political Biography* (abridged edition, OUP, London. 1961) contains an assessment of the role of the Congress party and of Nehru in the events leading to the partition of India, while R.P. Masani : *Britain in India : An Account of British Rule in the Indian Sub-continent* (OUP, Bombay, 1960) is an account of some of these events as seen by an Indian Liberal. Durga Das (ed) : *Sarder Patel's Correspondence 1945-50* (Navajivan Publishing House, Ahmedabad) particularly vols. 2-4 are important.

On the British side, the story has been told by a number of observers, some of whom had the privilege of observing the developments from 'inside'. Among them, Alan Campbell-Johnson : *Mission With Mountbatten* (Robert Hale, London, 1951), H.V. Hodson ; *op. cit.*, F.W. Tuker : *While Memory Serves* (Cassell, London, 1950), and P. Moon (ed) : *op. cit.*, and P. Moon : *Divide and Quit* (Chatto & Windus, London, 1961) are important, while Hugh Tinker : *Experiment With Freedom : India and Pakistan 1947* (OUP for RIIA, 1967), Leonard Mosley : *The Last Days of the British Raj*

(Weidenfeld & Nicolson, 1961), M. Edwardes : *The Last Years of British India* (Cassell, London, 1963) are useful reconstruction of events during the last years of British rule. C.H. Philips and M.D. Wainwright (eds) ; *The Partition of India : Policies & Perspectives* (Allen & Unwin, London, 1970) is an attempt to present the different aspects of partition as seen by scholars, journalists and some of the participants, in Britain, India and Pakistan. For collection of documents, M. Gwyer and A. Appadorai (eds) : *Speeches and Documents on the Indian Constitutions 1921-47*, vol. II, (OUP, London, 1957), N. Mansergh (ed.) : *Documents And Speeches On British Commonwealth Affairs 1931-52,* Vols. I & II, (OUP, London, for RIIA, 1953) and N. Mansergh (ed) : *The Transfer of Power 1942-47* vol. I, *The Cripps Mission* and vol. II, *Quit India* (H.M.S.O., London, 1970 & 71), vol. III, *Reassertion of Authority (1971)*.

19. *Cmd.* 6350. The Cripps Mission Proposals and *Cmd.* 6829. The Cabinet Mission Plan.

20. This argument is, of course, based on the assumption that the Congress was still working for the maintenance of Indian unity ; whether that, in itself, was a feasible goal under the circumstances, is a different question. Indeed, many Congress leaders came to think that the creation of Pakistan was a 'good riddance'.

21. M. Brecher : *Nehru : A Political Biography*, p. 121.

22. See, Wayne Wilcox ; 'India and Pakistan' in Steven L. Spiegel and K. N. Waltz (eds) ; *Conflict In World Politics* (Winthrop, Cambridge, Mass. 1971), p. 260.

23. On 15 January, 1948, G. Ayyangar told the Security Council : "Kashmir, because of its geographical position, with its frontiers contiguous with those of the countries like the Union of Soviet Socialist Republics and China, is of vital importance to the security and international contacts of India. Economically also Kashmir is intimately associated with India. The caravan trade routes from Central Asia to India pass through Kashmir State." See, *S.C.O.R.*, 3rd year, Nos. 1-15, p. 13.

24. The letter 'K' in the word 'Pakistan' is supposed to stand for Kashmir. As late as 1964, Mr Z. A. Bhutto, the then Foreign Minister of Pakistan said : "Kashmir must be liberated if Pakistan is to have its full meaning." See Z. A. Bhutto, *Foreign Policy of Pakistan : A Compendium of Speeches made in the National Assembly of Pakistan 1962-64* (Pakistan Institute of International Affairs, Karachi, 1964), p. 13.

25. See Michael Brecher's 'Talks with Nehru' in M. Brecher : *New States of Asia* (O.U.P., London, 1963) especially, pp. 207-9.

26. See, Pakistan's letter to the Secretary General of UN, on 15 January, 1948, S/646, Doc. II.

27. As V.P. Menon, the then Secretary to the States Ministry, wrote later : "Personally, when I recommended to the Government of India, the acceptance of the accession of the Maharaja of Kashmir, I had in

mind one consideration and one consideration alone, viz, that the invasion of Kashmir by the raiders was a grave threat to the integrity of India. Ever since the time of Mahmud of Ghazni...India had been subjected to periodical invasions from the north-west. And within less than ten weeks from the establishment of the new Pakistan, its very first act was to let loose invasion. Srinagar today, Delhi tomorrow. A nation that forgets its history or its geography does so at its peril." V.P. Menon : *The Story of the Integration of the Indian States*, (Longmans, Green, London/ New York/Toronto, 1956). p. 413.

28. For a variety of reasons, Kashmir has been less important a factor in determining India's foreign policy, than it was in the determination of Pakistan's foreign policy. India being a territorially satisfied power in Kashmir was quite prepared to bury the issue, whereas Pakistan always had to take the initiative in keeping the issue alive. When the British Prime Minister Mr Harold Macmillan visited India and Pakistan in 1958, he clearly discerned this difference in the attitudes of the two states. He wrote about it later : "Whereas in India the difficulty had been to induce the leading figures, including Nehru, to discuss Indo-Pakistani differences, in Pakistan both the President and the Ministers seemed able to think or talk of little else. Of course, this reflected Pakistan's acute sense of being at a disadvantage." Consequently, apart from some discussion about cotton imports and plans for economic aid, the whole discussion in Pakistan was taken up with questions of Kashmir, the Indus Water and the supply of arms. See, H. Macmillan : *Riding The Storm 1956-59* (Macmillan, London, 1971). pp. 391-93.

29. See, for example, Nehru's statement in the Rajya Sabha on 23 June, 1962, cited at the beginning of this chapter. While there is no evidence to show that at the time of independence the British Government in London wanted Kashmir's accession to Pakistan, in the Indian sub-continent many of Jinnah's British advisers and admirers were working to get Kashmir for Pakistan. See, Durga Das : *India : Curzon to Nehru and After* (Rupa & Co., Calcutta/Bombay/Delhi, 1973). p. 270,

30. Krishna Menon to Michael Brecher in M. Brecher : *India and World Politics : Krishna Menon's View of the World*. p. 195.

31. This pro-Pakistani attitude may broadly be discerned in the writings of Sir Olaf Caroe, Sir William Barton, Mr Ian Stephens, and Lord Birdwood. Sir Olaf was the Governor of NWFP before India's independence ; in later years he became a frequent writer on Indian affairs. Known for his extensive knowledge of Soviet Central Asia and the Middle-East, Sir Olaf became a leading ideologue of sophisticated Conservative thinking in foreign affairs. In Britain, he was the champion of the idea that Pakistan, being a Muslim state was an extension of the 'Muslim lake' in the Middle-East ; and that the UK and the USA, because of their oil interests in the area around the Persian Gulf, should organise an alliance extending from Turkey to Pakistan, embracing all

the northern tier states. Sir Olaf had also his critics, and in Britain Sir Archibald Nye was one of the critics of his thesis.

Sir William was a member of the Indian Civil Service, and British resident in three Indian States. For his pro-Pakistani views, see, W. Barton ; "Pakistan's Claims to Kashmir" in *Foreign Affairs* , January, 1950.

For a biographical note on Ian Stephens, see f.n. 35 below.

Lord Birdwood, a former officer in the British Indian Army and a frequent writer on Indo-Pakistani affairs, has generally supported Pakistani views in the Kashmir dispute. See, for example, Lord Birdwood : *Two Nations and Kashmir* (Robert Hale, London, 1956).

32. For example, Sir Frederick Bennett and Mr Biggs-Davison, who have consistently supported Pakistan's case in the House of Commons. The list of names is by no means exhaustive.

33. For a discussion on this point, see R. Symonds : *The Making of Pakistan,* (Faber and Faber, London, n.d.).

34. To take one example, see G.W. Choudhury : *Pakistan's Relations with India* 1947-1966 (Pall Mall, London, 1968), pp. 97-98.

35. For example, Ian Stephens wrote later : "At a Hindu Maharajah's choice, but with a British Governor-General's backing, three million Muslims, in a region always considered to be of vital importance to Pakistan if she were created, were legally to be made Indian citizens." See Ian Stephens : *Pakistan* (Benn, London, 1963), p. 204. Ian Stephens was the editor of *The Statesman*, Calcutta and Delhi (1942-51) and the Historian to the Pakistani Army between 1957 and 1960.

36. See, for example, Sir Muhammad Zafrullah Khan's speech in the Security Council, *S.C.O.R.* 3rd year, Nos. 1-15. 228 mtg., pp. 53-4.

37. Ian Stephens ; *op. cit.*, p. 203.

38. John Connell (Pseud.) ; *Auchinleck : A Biography of Field Marshal Sir Claude Auchinleck* (Cassell, London, 1959, pp. 920-21). It is interesting to note how some of the old 'India Hands' in Britain have carried on among themselves this Indo-Pakistani cold war. See, for example, the role of Lord Mountbatten at the initial stage of the Kashmir dispute as depicted by his Press Attache, Alan Campbell-Johnson ; *op. cit.*, ch. 19 and by H.V. Hodson ; *op. cit.*, ch. 25. For a contrary view, Ian Stephens : *op.cit.*, pp. 2-3-4, This makes it almost impossible for them to be non-partisan in Indo-Pakistani disputes.

39. Alan Campbell-Johnson ; *op. cit.*, p. 226.

40. See, Lord Birdwood ; *op. cit.*, p. 73.

41. John Connell (pseud.) ; *op. cit.* pp. 920-21.

42. For a discussion on this, see Sisir Gupta ; 'India's Policy towards Pakistan' in *International Studies*, Vol. 8, Nos. 1 & 2, July-October, 1966.

43. *Governor-General's Personal Report,* No. 5, 7 November, 1947. See H. V. Hodson ; *op. cit.*, especially pp. 452-53 and 459.

44. On 17 February, 1948, Campbell-Johnson recorded in his diary : "Mountbatten finds his present constitutional position of friendly

adviser (to the Government of India) irksome at times. He can no longer step in between London and New Delhi, and his only link now is with the King, who strictly separates his various sovereignties." See Alan Cambell-Johnson, *op. cit.*, p. 287.

45. For example, Churchill said in the House of Commons on 30 July 1948 : "In Kashmir, four-fifths of the people are Muslim and the ruler is a Hindu. His accession to the Dominion of India is accepted without any reference to the vast majority of his people. In regard to Hyderabad, the case, as a communal problem, is the other way round. The ruler is a Muslim and the bulk of the people are non-Muslims. The India Government—the Nehru Government—take the line that in one case it is the will of the people and in the other case it is the decision of the ruler. In either case, however we work it, they get them both." *Hansard* (Commons) 5th series, vol. 454, 1947-48, session, col. 1731.

46. For the details of the exchange of letters and telegrams between London and Karachi, and London and New Delhi, see *SCOR*, 3rd year, Nos. 1-15, 228 and 229 mtgs,

47. See Alan Campbell-Johnson ; *op. cit.*, p. 257.

48. See the later part of this Chapter.

49. On 26 January, 1948, Mr Patrick Gordon Walker, the then Under-Secretary of State, Commonwealth Relations Office, told the House of Commons : "It is, of course, always open to members of the British Commonwealth to seek the assistance of other members in the settlement of their differences. In the dispute between India and Pakistan as regards Kashmir, no such suggestion was made by either Government. As regards the suggestion for setting up a permanent consultative body of representatives from British Commonwealth countries, this is a matter which would require the consent of all the Commonwealth countries, and the United Kingdom Government do not believe that, in the present conditions, it would be practicable to obtain such agreement." See *Hansard* (Commons), Fifth series, 1947-48 session, vol. 446, col. 108, written answer.

50. See R. Symonds ; *op. cit.* p. 172.

51. See *The Times*, 16 January, 1951.

52. For the text of the Communique, *Ibid*.

53. See *The Times*, 17 January 1951.

54. Nehru made a note of these proposals which was later read out by Krishna Menon at the Security Council, on 24 January, 1957. See *SCOR*, 12th year, 764 mtg.

55. See above.

56. See *The Times*, 17 July, 1964. Sir Alec's stand was quite consistent with the policy of the British Government in earlier years. Reporting to the House of Commons at the end of the Conference he said: "...while we maintained the convention that we do not discuss among ourselves the substance of differences between members of the Common-

wealth—unless Commonwealth countries ask that be done—we felt that we should note with satisfaction the friendly public statements which have been made by the President of Pakistan and the Prime Minister of India ; and we expressed our hope that the problem between their two countries will be solved in the same friendly spirit." See *Hansard,* (Commons), 5 series, 1963-64 session, vol. 698 col. 1424. 17 July, 1964.

57. *The Times*, 17 July, 1964.

58. S/628.

59. *Ibid.*, para. 6 (Italics added).

60. S/464, of 15 January, 1948.

61. For India's complaints, see S/628, and also *SCOR*, 3rd year, Nos. 1-15, especially 227th mtg., pp. 10-30.

For Pakistan's reply and counter-complaint, S/646 and also *SCOR*, 3rd Year, Nos. 1-15, 228th mtg, pp. 35-88 and 229th mtg. pp. 90-120. These arguments were repeated again, with further evidence, by both India and Pakistan, in the subsequent meetings of the Security Council.

62. *SCOR*, 3rd year, Nos. 1-15, p. 28. Also see, V. P. Menon : *The Story of the Integration of the Indian States.* He wrote : "We had no territorial ambition in Kashmir. If the invasion by the raiders had not taken place, I can say in the face of any contradiction that the Government of India would have left Kashmir alone." *op. cit.* p. 413.

62a. *SCOR*, 3rd year, Nos. 1-15, p. 29.

63. *SCOR*, 3rd year, Nos. 1-15, pp. 266-67.

64. *ibid.*, p. 267-68.

65. Altogether there were five attempts at mediation, sponsored by the UN. The reports of these mediators reveal the sad story of complete lack of good-will or trust between these two countries, which made any attempt at successful mediation impossible. The reports of the UN mediators were, in chronological order : S/1453 (McNaughton Report, 1950), S/1791 (Dixon Report, 1950), S/2375, S/2448, S/2611, S/2783 and S/2967 (all five submitted by Dr. Frank Graham between 1951-53), S/3821 (Jarring Report 1957) and S/3894 (Graham Report. 1958). All these Reports were later published in a single volume by the Government of Pakistan. See *Reports on Kashmir by United Nations Representatives* (Government of Pakistan, Karachi, 1962).

66. For evidence on this, See, *SCOR*, 3rd year, Nos. 1-15, especially, pp. 10-30, and *Ibid.* 12th year, 762 mtg. ; *White Paper on Jammu and Kashmir* (Ministry of External Affairs, Government of India, Delhi, 1948), V. P. Menon : *The Story of the Integration of the Indian States*, Ch. 20, Alan Campbell-Johnson : *op. cit.* , Ch. 19, and H. V. Hodson ; *op. cit.*, Ch. 25.

67. *Lok Sabha Debates*, 3rd series, Vol. XLVI, No. 29, Cols. 7528-30.

68. This was one of the reasons why Pakistan gave lukewarm support to the idea of a plebiscite, during the first few months. On 1 November, 1947, Jinnah had turned down a suggestion by Lord Mountbatten that the future of the State should be decided by a plebis-

cite under *international auspices*. He proposed instead that a plebiscite should be held under the authority of the two Governors-General. Jinnah being the head of the state as well as the head of the Muslim League, obviously hoped that he could win the vote of the Kashmiris in favour of Pakistan. See, Alan Campbell-Johnson ; *op. cit.* p. 230.

69. Set up, originally, under the resolution No. 39 (1948) on 20th January, 1948, with three members ; but later on, the membership was raised to five, by the resolution No. 47 (1948) of 21st April, 1948. For the texts of the two resolutions, see *SCOR : Resolutions and Decisions*, 3rd year, 1948, pp. 2-8.

70. S/1100, First Interim Report of the UNCIP. The UNCIP submitted three Reports all of which were later published by the Ministry of External Affairs, Government of India, in a single volume, *Kashmir Papers*. See, especially, p. 1.

71. As Nehru told a member of the UNCIP, "...Pakistan must be condemned. I do not require any solemn formal verdict, but a declaration about Pakistan Army's presence in Kashmir and its withdrawal." See, J. Korbel ; *Danger in Kashmir* (Princeton University Press, Princeton, rev. edn., 1966), p. 129.

72. See S/1791, *Dixon Report*. Sir Owen wrote that though the Security Council had not pronounced on the legality of Kashmir's accession, without going into their causes he was prepared to take the view that "when the frontier of the State of Jammu and Kashmir was crossed, on, ..., 20 October 1947, by hostile elements, it was contrary to international law, and that when, in May 1948, ...units of the regular Pakistan forces moved into the territory of the State that too was inconsistent with international law." See *Reports on Kashmir by United Nations Mediators*, p. 20.

73. *SCOR*, 3rd year, Nos. 16-35, p. 8.

74. *The Hindu*, 14 February, 1948. Nehru returned to the same theme a few days later. On 5 March, 1948, he said in the Constituent Assembly (Legislative) : "I must confess that I have been surprised and distressed at the fact that the reference we made has not even been properly considered thus far and other matters have been given precedence." See, S. L. Poplai (ed.) *Select Documents on Asian Affairs : India 1947-50*, vol. II (O.U.P. for I.C.W.A., Bombay 1959), p. 438.

75. Alan Campbell-Johnson ; *op. cit.*, p. 287.

76. *ibid.*

77. According to Sir Muhammad Zafrullah Khan, there was only one occasion when a solution of the Kashmir dispute seemed within the reach of the Security Council. This was during the first two weeks in February, 1948, after the submission of a draft-resolution (S/667) by the President of the Security Council, General McNaughton of Canada, and Van Iangenhove of Belgium. The proposals contained in the draft resolution, Zafrullah Khan said, had the support of the majority of the

Council members. Impressed by the weight of opinion behind them, Indians were also receptive to these ideas. But on 11 February, the Indian delegate sought the adjournment of the proceedings to enable him to return to India for consultations with his Government. During the intervening period, Zafrullah Khan complained, Nehru successfuly influenced Attlee, through Lord Mountbatten, to withdraw British support from the scheme, which led to its failure. See, T. B. Millar ; "Kashmir, The Commonwealth and the United Nations," in *Australian Outlook* (Vol. 17, No. 1, April, 1963). p. 63. Also see, C. W. Choudhury ; *op. cit.*, pp. 109-10.

78. *Private Papers of Attlee,* File No. 6, University College Library, Oxford. See Krishna Menon's letter of 1 September, 1948 (Italics added).

79. For the text of the resolution, see S/1100, First Interim Report of UNCIP, in *Kashmir Papers,* pt. 1, pp. 12-14.

80. S/1196, Second Interim Report of UNCIP in *ibid.* Pt. II, pp. 119-20.

81. S/1100, First Interim Report of UNCIP in *Kashmir Papers*, Pt. I, p. 14.

82. *ibid.*, p. 13. In the language of a former Member of the Commission, "This was the slap on the wrist the Commission delivered to Pakistan. It could hardly be labeled denunciation ; but though Nehru described it later as at best 'feeble', he accepted it as at least an admission of the illegal presence of the Pakistan Army in Kashmir." See J. Korbel ; *op. cit.*, p. 141.

83. S/1100, paras, 78-80, and Annexure-12, in *Kashmir Papers*, Pt I, pp. 15-17 and 79-84.

84. *Ibid.*

85. See Addendum to the Third Interim Report of the UNCIP, in *Kashmir Papers*, Pt. IV, p. 332.

86. See L. K. Rosinger ; *India and the United States : Political and Economic Relations* (Macmillan, New York, for the American Institute of Pacific Relations, 1950, pp. 104-11).

87. A number of books of varying qualities exist on the subject. Some of the good ones are : M. Brecher : *The Struggle for Kashmir* (Ryerson Press, Toronto, 1953 for the Canadian Institute of International Affairs, and the Institute for Pacific Relations) ; Lord Birdwood : *Two Nations and Kashmir* (Robert Hale, London, 1956), J. Korbal, *op. cit.*, A. Lamb : *Crisis in Kashmir* (Routledge & Kegan Paul, London, 1966), Sisir Gupta : *Kashmir : A Study in India-Pakistan Relations*, and B. L. Sharma : *The Kashmir Story* (Asia Publishing House, London, 1967).

88. An example of the British attitude was the support given to the proposals for demilitarisation submitted by General McNaughton of Canada (S/1433). One of the distinctive features of the Plan was that it drew a distinction between the regular forces of Pakistan and the Azad forces thus legitimising the concept of Azad Kashmir. It also envisaged

simultaneous withdrawal of forces by India and Pakistan. While rejecting the McNaughton Plan the Indian representative Sir B. N. Rau told the Security Council that......these proposals were substantially the same as the UNCIF proposals "minus certain parts which were intended to meet India's point of view, plus certain additions favourable to Pakistan." See *SCOR*, 6th year, 1951, 463 mtg.

89. S/1942.

90. See earlier portion of this Chapter.

91. S/2017.

92. *SCOR*, 6th year, 21 February, 1951, p. 3.

93. *Ibid*,, pp. 7-8.

94. Res. No. 91 (1951). For the text of the resolution, *S.C.O.R. Resolutions and Decisions*, 6th year, 1951, pp. 1-4.

95. First, there was the fear that any plebiscite based on an appeal to religion would disturb the communal peace not only in Kashmir, but also in the rest of India and Pakistan. See, Nehru's Press Conference in London on 16 January, 1951, as reported in *The Times*, 17 Jan., 1951. There was also another consideration. On the Kashmir issue, there was near-unanimity among the political parties in India. In the First General Election in 1951, Kashmir figured prominently in the election manifestos of some of the major political parties. The main criticism against the Government was that it was not firm enough in dealing with Pakistan. This considerably narrowed options left to the Government in formulating a policy which would be politically acceptable to the country.

96. S/1791 (Dixon Report). See *Reports on Kashmir by United Nations Representatives*, pp. 25-26.

97. *Ibid.*, p. 33. Josef Korbel, also, wrote that the mere technicality of carrying out the plebiscite seemed beyond the scope of reality. See, J. Korbel ; *op. cit.*, p. 136.

98. For an excellent analysis depicting this phase of American policy towards India and Pakistan, see Selig. S. Harrison ; "India, Pakistan and the U.S. : The Case History of a Mistake" in *The New Republic*, (10 August, 1959).

99. See, Sir Olaf's unsigned article 'The Persian Gulf : A Romance' in *The Round Table*, March 1949, p. 137.

100. Qlaf Caroe : *Wells of Power* (Macmillan, London, 1951), p. 180.

101. See S. S. Harrison ; *op. cit.*

102. *ibid*.

102a. As early as 6 March, 1948, the *New York Times* published a report that US would like to take a more active part, along with UK, in finding a settlement for the Kashmir dispute. Officials in Washington acknowledged Britain's special knowledge and experience about the subcontinent and thought that the United States could work closely with Britain.

103. This point has been developed in Chester Bowles : 'American Roulette' in *The Guardian*, 24th August, 1971.

103a. Patrick Gordon Walker : *The Commonwealth* (Mercury Books, London, 1965), p. 319.

Occasional references to the 'Russian bear' during the discussion of Indo-Pakistani affairs in the British Parliament is also revealing. On 4 May 1948, Mr R. A. Butler (later Lord Butler) told the House of Commons : "Kashmir is not the only frontier trouble with which we are concerned...We must remember that the Imperialist dagger of the Soviet Union aided by the microbes of communist subterranean influences are ready to be used when the body is sick. If there is no solution to the Kashmir problem it might well develop into a much larger international blaze than it is at present." *Handsard* (Commons), 5 series, 1947-48 session, col. 1128. Again on 7 March, 1950, speaking on the Indo-Pakistani conflict Mr Gammans said in the House of Commons, "These two countries cannot go very much further before war does break out...if that tragedy happens, its only result will be that hammer and sickle will be flying from the flag points on the Cape Comorin, from which the Union Jack was pulled down only two years ago. Have we to admit that our influence today is so negligible with the two Dominions that we have to sit still and do nothing ?" See, *Hansard*, (Commons), 5 series, 1950 session, Vol. 472, col. 227. Also see, *ibid.*, col. 221, for speech by Mr Price.

104. The Baghdad Pact was only a partial fulfilment of the British scheme as Britain failed to persuade the Arab countries (except Iraq) to join it. As to its success, it is doubtful whether it could gain anything of permanent value, except importing international tensions in the region by dividing the Arab countries.

105. *The Times*, January, 1951 (Italics added).

106. On 27 June, 1950, both India and Pakistan voted in UN branding North Korea as the aggressor. However, on 1 February, 1951, Pakistan abstained while India voted with the Communist block, against a resolution censuring China as the aggressor on the ground that such condemnation would make a settlement more difficult.

107. Ayub Khan wrote later : "I have a feeling that the reason why we joined these Pacts are not always fully understood, even in Pakistan. The crux of the problem from the very beginning was the Indian attitude of hostility towards us : we had to look for allies to secure our position." See, Mohammed Ayub Khan ; *Friends Not Masters : A Political Autobiography* (O.U.P. London, 1967), p. 154.

108. In 1955, during an official visit to India the Soviet Prime Minister firmly declared Kashmir to be a part of the Indian Union.

109. The SEATO Council, in its communique of 8 March 1956 "affirmed the need for an early settlement of the Kashmir question through the U.N. or by direct negotiation." For the text of the communique, see,

Documents on International Affairs 1956 (O.U.P., for RIIA, London. 1959, p. 757). Nehru criticised this statement and said in the *Lok Sabha* on 20 March 1956 that this statement implied that a military alliance was backing one country, namely Pakistan, in its dispute with India. See *Ibid.*, p. 761.

110. Personal interview. Italics added. This was also the view of some other officials in the Foreign and Commonwealth Office in UK, who were interviewed by me.

111. Res. 122 (1957) of 24 January 1957. For the text, see *SCOR : Resolutions and Decisions of the Security Council*, 1957, pp. 1-2. The draft of the resolution was circulated even before the Indian representative Mr Krishna Menon had finished his speech. Krishna Menon told the Council, "...I want the people of my country to appreciate that this resolution has been put forward by its five sponsors before hearing the statement of the representative of India." See *S.C.O.R* 12th year, 764 mtg. p. 2. The British delegate Pierson Dixon, as one of the five sponsors, said in reply that the draft resolution dealt with the constitutional aspect of the issue which had already been dealt with by the Indian representative. In addition to this there was a special reason "for expedition in connexion with this particular point, since the other party to the dispute, the Government of Pakistan, had expressed concern lest some step be taken in the very near future." See ibid., 765 mtg.. p. 4.

112. Draft resolution S/3787 of 14 February, 1957, sponsored by the UK, the US and three other Powers. This was vetoed by the Soviet Union.

113. These changes were : (a) The US-Pakistan arms deal of 1954 ; (b) Pakistan's membership of the military alliances, and (c) the adoption of a new constitution by the Kashmir Constituent Assembly. As early as 8 July, 1955, the then Indian Home Minister G.B. Pant said in Srinagar that though India had originally agreed to a plebiscite in Kashmir, it could no longer be a solution for the Kashmir problem because of the changed circumstances. See *The Hindu*, 9 July, 1955. About almost a year later on 2 April, 1956, Nehru said the same thing at a press conference in New Delhi, though he did not claim that the Kashmir dispute had been finally settled for all. In fact, he pleaded for a new approach to the problem. See *Asian Recorder*, (New Delhi, 31 March-6 April, 1956, p. 761).

114. S/3821 (the Jarring Report), See *Reports on Kashmir by United Nations Representatives*, pp, 281-83.

115. See, The Information Service of India : *Kashmir : Foreign Press Comments* vol. II (New Delhi. n.d.) p. 17. The *Manchester Guardian* wrote editorially on 15 January, 1957, on the eve of the Security Council debates : "The Indian Case must be studied sympathetically ; and it is a strong one. The proposal for a plebiscite dates from eight years ago and time changes many things. Stability has come to Indian-occupied

Kashmir...If the existing settlement should be altered there would probably be an influx of Hindu refugees from Kashmir into India. This would almost certainly inflame opinion and start off new communal riots between Hindus and Muslims."

116. J. Nehru : *India's Foreign Policy* : *Selected Speeches, September 1946-April 1961.* (Publications Division, Ministry of Information and Broadcasting, Government of India, New Delhi, 1961), p. 487.

117. For example, on 20 December 1956, Mr Frederic Bennett (later Sir Frederic Bennett) said that at a time when Britain had been criticised rightly or wrongly, for not complying with UN resolutions, "it would not be a bad idea if one of the chief protagonists were to set an example and practise just a little of what he preaches...is it not a fact which no one in any quarter of this House can deny this moment. Mr. Nehru stands in default of precisely six United Nations Resolutions ?" See, *Hansard*, (Commons) 5 series, 1956-57 sessions, col. 1448. For expression of similar views by others, see *Ibid.*, cols. 1447-48.

118. *Hansard*, (Commons), 5 series, vol. 668, vol. 935, 3 December, 1962. (Italics added).

119. See Mohammad Ayub Khan ; *op. cit.*, Ch. 9. Also *The Times*, 27 November, 1962. The correspondent of the paper reported from Rawalpindi on 26 November, 1962 that strong indignation was expressed by members of the National Assembly against Pakistan's continuing alliance with the American bloc, and her dependence on aid. Calling for all possible steps for the solution of the Kashmir dispute, members accused Britain and America of letting Pakistan down. Mahbubul Haq charged Britain of anti-Pakistan bias. Countries which created Israel at the cost of influence in the Arab world, he said, would never be friendly to Pakistan.

120. Ayub Khan ; *op. cit.*, p. 142.

121. Z.A. Bhutto ; *op, cit.*, p.9.

122. For the text of the joint statement, see *The Times*, 30 November, 1962. Also see *Lok Sabha Debates*, 3 series, vol. X, col. 3975, statement by Nehru on 30 November, 1962.

123. *Ibid.*, cols. 3973-75.

124. *Ibid.*, col. 3978.

125. Ayub Khan ; *op. cit.*, p. 149.

126. *Ibid.*

127. For the text, see Z.A. Bhutto's speech in the Pakistan National Assembly on 1 Dec. 1962, reproduced in Z.A. Bhutto ; *Foreign Policy of Pakistan*, pp. 50-51. Also see Ayub Khan ; *op. cit.*, p. 149.

128. See, Evan Charlton ; "Some Sort of Relationship" in *Asian Review*, vol. 1, no. I, November 1967. Also see, President Ayub's reply to President Kennedy's letter of 28 October 1962, making a similar request. President Ayub wrote : "...I am surprised that such a request is being made to us. After all, what we have been doing is nothing but to

contain the threat that was continuously posed by India to us. Is it in conformity with human nature that we should cease to take such steps as are necessary for our self preservation ?...No, Mr. President, the answer to this problem lies elsewhere, It lies in creating a situation whereby we are free from the Indian threat, and the Indians are free from any apprehensions about us. This can only be done if there is a settlement of the question of Kashmir..." See, Ayub Khan ; *op. cit.*, pp. 124-43.

129. Evan Charlton ; *op. cit.*, p. 41.

130. Personal interview.

131. See, 'The Times Diary' in *The Times*, 5 September, 1969.

132. See, J. K. Galbraith : *Ambassador's Journal : A Personal Account of the Kennedy Years* (Hamish Hamilton, London, 1969), pp. 495-503. It was pointed out to me by Lord Gore-Booth who was the British High Commissioner in India at the time that the differences between Professor Galbraith and Mr Sandys related mainly to the procedure of action, not to the basic principles of policy. These differences were accentuated by the differences in the personalities of the two men, Gore-Booth's memoir does not shed any further light on this. See, Paul Gore-Booth ; *With Great Truth and Respect* (Constable, London, 1974, pp. 304-5).

133. Ayub Khan wrote later : "It was obvious that the United States had decided to give long-term arms assistance to India, apart from providing emergency relief...while the United States wanted to see an amicable settlement of the Kashmir dispute between India and Pakistan, they were not prepared to use their full influence directly lest India should feel that she was being subjected to pressure." See, Ayub Khan, *op. cit.*, p. 146.

134. This seems to be the view of a number of observers of the Indian scene. See, e.g. Evan Charlton ; *op. cit.*, J. K. Galbraith ; *op. cit.*, Walter Crocker : *Nehru : A Contemporary's Estimate* (Allen & Unwin, London, 1966). Mr Crocker wrote : "By 1963, when India, under the stress of her fears of China, and of Anglo-American pressures, was offering concessions unimaginable a little earlier, Pakistan refused to compromise." See, *op. cit.*, pp. 93-94. Walter Crocker was High Commissioner for Australia in New Delhi (1952-55 and 1959-62). Similar views were expressed to me by one of the former senior British diplomats with personal knowledge of the events in the sub-continent during 1962-63.

135. For a discussion on these 'talks', see G. W. Choudhury ; *op.cit.*, pp. 131-40, Sisir Gupta ; *Kashmir : A Study in India-Pakistan Relations*, pp. 352-55, Peter Lyon ; 'Kashmir' in *International Relations*, Vol. III, No. 2, October, 1966 and Paul Gore-Booth ; *op. cit.*, pp. 302-3.

136. *Op. cit.*, p. 134.

136a. *Op. cit.*, p. 302.

137. *ibid.*, p. 303.

137a. Indian proposals for a political settlement included an agreed repartition of Kashmir—with the transfer to Pakistan of the Pakistan-held part of Kashmir together with areas north and south of the valley —military disengagement, and a 'no war' declaration by both sides. See Sisir Gupta ; *op.cit.* pp. 353-4 ; Peter Lyon ; *op.cit.*

138. Nehru told the Lok Sabha on 7 May, 1963 that both Mr Sandys and the US Secretary of State, Mr Dean Rusk had assured him that the arms aid to India against China would not be conditional upon a settlement of the Kashmir dispute. See *Lok Sabha Debates,* 2 series 4 session, vol. XVIII, cols. 14197-8.

139. *The Times*, 4 May, 1963.

140. For details see Mr Wilson's statement in the House of Commons on 5 May, 1965 in *Hansard*, (Commons), 5 series, 1964-65 session, vol. 711, cols. 1359-61.

141. Harold Wilson : *The Labour Government* 1964-1970 : *A Personal Record*, p. 112. Chequers is the official country residence of the Prime Minister, and Dorneywood, that of the Foreign Secretary.

142. *ibid.*

143. Personal information.

144. The dispute was referred to an International Tribunal constituted of three members, and by a two-to-one majority it decided (on 19 February 1968) that nine-tenths of the disputed territory should be regarded as belonging to India, and that the remainder, in the north, should go to Pakistan. Announcing the Tribunal's award the Chairman, Judge Gunnar Lagergan of Sweden said that the dispute was of a complicated character, because the evidence could be interpreted either way. His findings were concerned with what had been the true extent of sovereignty on the eve of independence, as there had not been any subsequent alteration in the situation. His main conclusion was : "In respect of those sectors of the Rann in relation to which no specific evidence in the way of display of Sind authority, or merely trivial or isolated evidence of such a character supports Pakistan's claims, I pronounce in favour of India. These sectors comprise about 90 per cent of the disputed territory. However in respect of sectors where a continuous and for the region intensive Sind activity, meeting with no effective opposition from the Kutch side, is established, I am of the opinion that Pakistan has made out a better and superior title." However the Indian nominee to the Tribunal, Judge Ales Bebler of Yugoslavia, in his dissenting opinion maintained that the whole of the disputed territory should go to India. See, *The Times*, (London), 20 February, 1968. For the dissenting opinion of Judge Ales Bebler see his two articles "Indo Pakistani Western Boundary—I and II" in *India Quarterly* (New Delhi), April-June 1968 and July-September, 1968.

145. See R. Brines : *The Indo-Pakistani Conflict* (Pall Mall, London, 1968), p. 288.

146. See, R. Brines, *op. cit.* Also see, Selig S. Harrison ; 'Troubled India and her Neighbours' in *Foreign Affairs,* January, 1965.

147. This was evident from the statements of different Pakistani leaders. For example, Mr Abdur Rab, Parliamentary Secretary in the Pakistani Foreign Office, told the National Assembly, on 22 January 1965 : "The Government of Pakistan was trying to create circumstances which would *compel* India to come to a peaceful settlement with Pakistan on the Kashmir issue." See *The Dawn*, 23 January, 1965. (Italics added).

148. R. Brines : *op. cit.*, p. 290.

149. S/6651.

150. R. Brines ; *op. cit.*, pp. 307-09.

151. D.R. Mankekar : *Twenty Two Fateful Days* (Manaktalas, Bombay, 1966) p. 94.

152. For the details, *ibid*. Also, see R. Brines ; *op. cit.* Ch. 13.

153. See, *The Financial Times*, 7 September, 1965.

153a. See, 'The British Press on the India-Pakistan Conflict' reprinted in *Foreign Affairs Reports* (ICWA, New Delhi), vol. XLV, No. 12, December, 1965.

154. *The Guardian*, 5 September, 1965, and 9 September, 1965.

155. This was also the view of a leading British journalist. See, e.g. Stephen Hugh-Jones ; "British Attitude to the Indo-Pakistan war" in *Economic Weekly* (Bombay, October 16, 1965).

156. Stephen Hugh-Jones ; *op. cit.*, p. 1589.

157. See, *The Tribune* (London), 1 October, 1965.

158. *The Times*, 28 September 1965.

159. Related to me, in an interview, by one of the senior British diplomats who was in the sub-continent at that time.

160. H. Wilson ; *op. cit.*, p. 133.

161. Information received from one of the former senior officials of the CRO who was personally involved in the shaping of British policy during the India-Pakistan War of 1965.

162. *The Times*, 7 September, 1965. (Italics added).

163. See the report of the UN Secretary-General, quoted above.

164. See report by Anthony Lukas in the *New York Times*, 2 September, 1965.

165. H. Wilson ; *op. cit* . pp. 133-34.

166. *ibid.*

167. *The Times*, 5 August, 1971 (Italics added).

168. See foot note 161.

169. Whereas Mr. Wilson claimed, later, that the initiative for an early statement came from CRO, some former senior CRO officials maintain that the initiative actually came from No. 10 Downing St. (Personal information).

170. This is, of course, denied by the officers who were responsible for advising the Prime Minister in September 1965. But I had the opportunity to talk to some others, with personal knowledge about

CRO, and later about FCO, who seems to share Mr Wilson's views about the existence of a pro-Pakistan' faction in the Office.

171. H. Wilson : *op. cit.*, p. 134.

172. In his telegram to CRO, the then British High Commissioner in India reported : "I have no firm evidence that Pakistan Army had themselves crossed international boundary up to last night". The telegram was received in London at 11.28 a.m. on 6 September, 1965. Later researchers my be able to establish whether the 6 September statement of Mr Wilson was made on the basis of this telegram.

172a. Personal interview.

173. H. Wilson ; *op. cit.* p, 134.

174. H. Wilson ; *op. cit.*, p. 221. Also see, Ministry of External Affairs : *Report, 1966-67*, p. 52 (New Delhi). Another aspect of British Policy which affected Indo-British relations, was the decision of the British Government to place a total embargo on arms supplied to India, which included arms purchased commercially. This point has been discussed in Ch. 6.

175. See, K.E. Boulding ; *Conflict and Defense : A General Theory* (Harper, New York, 1962,) pp. 88-89. Also see, Wayne Wilcox ; *op. cit.* p. 257.

176. Walter Crocker ; *op. cit.* pp. 93-94.

177. See, CRO ; *List* 1951-64 issues.

178. See, CRO ; *List 1965*, p. 37 and *Year Book 1966*, p. 182.

179. The Foreign, Commonwealth and Trade Commission Services were merged in 1965, to form H. M. Diplomatic Service. See. above.

CHAPTER IV

COLONIAL AND RACIAL ISSUES IN INDO-BRITISH RELATIONS

"We in Asia, who have ourselves suffered all the evils of colonialism and of imperial domination, have committed ourselves to the freedom of every other colonial country."

—J. Nehru to the 3rd session of the General Assembly. *GAOR*, 3rd session, 1948, p. 376.

"Indians tend to regard themselves as champions of under-developed countries and are opposed to 'colonialism', and in pursuing this line seem to lecture other countries rather than offer constructive criticisms."

—Alan Burns ; *In Defence of Colonies* (Allen & Unwin, London, 1957, p. 453).

OF ALL the revolutionary changes that have characterised the development of international politics after the Second World War, the ending of West European overseas colonial empire is perhaps the most important. India, as one of the first states to achieve independence and by far the largest of the newly independent states, naturally saw herself and was cast in the role of the leader of the non-aligned anti-colonial movement. Indeed, India's role as a principal champion of anti-colonialism and anti-racialism often brought her into open disagreement with UK in international forums such as the United Nations, thus embittering relations between the two states. Lord Alport conveyed a characteristic British feeling of indignation as early as 1953 when he wrote that India's policy of anti-colonialism was a potential—and even growing—threat to British colonial system in Asia and Africa.[1] He had, probably, exaggerated the real impact of Indian policy on Britain's colonial interests ; but the substance of his criticism had the support of many others in Britain, especially of the right-wing of the Tory Party, and of the members of what J. M. Lee calls the "official class".[2]

The point, however, should not be stretched too far. So far

as the question of independence for the colonies was concerned, there was no basic difference between the views of the British and the Indian governments. This was recognised in India. One, therefore, has to make a distinction between the formal declaratory policy of the Government of India, and its actual implementation. Though the Indian government were opposed to colonial domination in all its forms, and were critical of the colonial policies of the West European states, their criticism of British colonial policy in Malaya, Kenya or Cyprus was more restrained, than for example, their criticism of French policy in Indo-China, or of Dutch policy in Indonesia. Perhaps, this was due to the fact that the British were more humane in the treatment of their colonies ; but it was also the result of India's membership of the Commonwealth. Where the progress towards self-government was obvious, as in Gold Coast or in Nigeria, the Government of India praised British policy. But differences arose mainly regarding those colonies where there was a conflict betwen the interests of the white settlers, and those of the natives. In the multi-racial colonies in Africa the British generally tended to identify their interests with those of the white settlers, while Indians supported the natives.[3]

With the development of the anti-colonial movement, and the consequent emergence of many newly independent states, questions of race and colour assumed increasing importance in international politics. Racial issues became particularly important in Britain's relations with her Commonwealth partners, because of the British Government's policy towards South Africa, and since 1965, to the white minority regime in Rhodesia. Introduction of legislation designed to restrict immigration to UK from the new Commonwealth, and the incidence of racial violence within Britain, contributed to the aggravation of tensions in Anglo-Indian relations.

I

Elite Attitudes Towards Colonialism

The term 'colonialism' meant different things to the people in Britain and in India. To the official classes in Britain, and to the majority of the British people born before the second World

War, it was not a word of abuse ; colonies were associated with the memories of Britain's past pride and glory, and for some, with a romantic idealism. Feelings of racial superiority, as expressed in the concept of 'white man's burden', and a sense of paternalistic responsibility for the welfare of the colonised people, as symbolised in the concept of 'trusteeship', were also important ingredients in British attitude.[4] The Leninist theory of imperialism which influenced the thoughts of many leaders in Africa and Asia had little influence in Britain outside the circle of the communists, and the left-wing intellectuals. The conscientious colonial administrators looked upon themselves as the 'guardians' of the interests of the subject people.

In independent India the term 'colonialism' had a different connotation. It was essentially derogatory in meaning, and symbolised a system of unequal relationship which undermined the human dignity of the peole in the colonies. Indians could not fully appreciate the paternalistic philosophy of colonialism expounded by men such as Milner or Lugard and followed in later years by the colonial administrators in Asia and Africa. They were opposed to colonialism, and criticised many aspects of the British government's colonial policy. Few of them could visualise that by the end of the 1960s the British empire would be virtually non-existent.

Criticism of British colonial policy gave rise to much resentment in Britain. But to state that India's preoccupation with anti-colonialism contributed only to tensions in Indo-British relations, would be an over-simplification. Though differences between the two governments on colonial issues were frequent, and even deep-seated, there were occasions when their views were almost similar.[5] Above all, India's anti-colonialism, in spite of all its emotion and rhetoric, had an important effect on British policy in that it predisposed British statesmento re-think their attitude towards the dependent empire.[6]

The underlying purpose of British colonial policy was to prepare the colonies for self-government, within the Commonwealth ;[7] but prior to 1939 there was no sense of urgency in helping the colonies towards that goal. A tentative step was taken in 1940 in the form of the Second Colonial Development and Welfare Act which made explicit the British government's responsibility to provide public funds for the development of colonies, but even then there was no fixed timetable for the eventual transfer of power. Throughout the inter-war years the British government tacitly assumed that outside the Indian subcontinent British control over the colonial empire was going to stay for an indefinite period.[8] The Labour Party which came to power in 1945, had long campaigned for Indian independence; and between 1947-48, the Labour government transferred power to India, Pakistan, Ceylon, and Burma. Two years later the Secretary of State for Colonies, James Griffiths, reiterated that the object of the Government's policy was self-government for the colonies.[9]

The attitude of the Conservative Party towards the question of colonial independence was not so clear. In 1947 Churchill criticised the transfer of power to India. When the Conservatives came to power in 1951, the declaratory policy of the Government was "the careful, and if possible, the gradual and orderly progress of the colonies towards self-government within the Commonwealth".[10] On this theme, therefore, there was no basic difference between the two principal political parties in Britain. But this bi-partisanship broke down on the question of the Central African Federation.

The idea behind the formation of the federation was to strengthen the concept of empire on a basis called 'partnership'. At least this was one of the ostensible political reasons influencing the policy of the Conservative government. Oliver Lyttleton wrote in later years that the purpose behind the creation of the federation was to check the spread of Afrikaaner elements to the north of the Union of South Africa, as the Afrikaaner attitude to the natives ran counter to British policy and interests.[11] However, the meaning of 'partnership' was never clearly defined, and as became quite evident in the Central African Federation, the whites would be the dominant partner. From the administrative point of view, it might have been a sound decision to group the colonies together into powerful federal units;[12] but the scheme could succeed only on the assumption that nationalism did not matter.

During the second phase of their colonial policy, the Conservative government made a defensive attempt to stand up against nationalist revolts, and the Suez expedition of 1956 was an aspect of this policy. It was only in the post-Suez years, notably after the appointment of Iain Macleod to the Colonial Office in 1959, that the decision was made in favour of speedy liquidation of the empire—a decision which later came to be associated with Prime Minister Mr Macmillan's 'Wind of Change' speech in Capetown in 1960.[13]

Thanks to the existence of an anti-colonial movement within the country, the process of withdrawal from the empire was relatively less painful for Britain. The existence of the Commonwealth, enlarged since 1947 by the accession of three Asian states, also made renunciation easier. For those in Britain who felt unhappy at the dissolution of the empire, the emergence of the Commonwealth as a multi-racial association of independent states provided a new source of political identity. The possibility that the colonial territories would join the Commonwealth after the attainment of independence had softened the sharp edge of finality and thus made decolonisation less painful.[14]

India made a valuable contribution towards this development. If she decided in 1947, or in 1949, to withdraw from the Commonwealth its future development might have been different. During 1947-49, one of the objections to India's continued membership of the Commonwealth was the apprehension that it would compromise India's stand on colonial and racial issues. The uncertainties regarding the future of Indo-British relationship were resolved in 1949 by the decision of the Government of India to continue India's membership of the Commonwealth even after the adoption of a republican constitution—a decision which was welcomed by Britain and by other members of the Commonwealth, including South Africa. The political implications of this decision were significant.[15] By demonstrating that national independence was compatible with membership of the Commonwealth the Indian decision had set a precedent for the British colonies in Asia and Africa which became independent in later years, and joined the Commonwealth.

One new aspect of the empire which had become increasingly important in the post-war years was the colonial contribution to the British economy.[16] Apart from their value as privileged markets for export of British goods, and potential fields for overseas investments, the colonies were contributors to the dollar earnings of Britain. In the first place, during the dollar shortage after the War, Britain could always draw on the dollar earnings of the colonies like Ghana and Malaya—which had an export surplus with US—and thus pay for her own exports. Secondly, the dollar and sterling balances of the colonies were allowed to accumulate in London, and became available to British investors who could put them into long-term securities overseas, carrying higher rates of return.[17] The economic benefits accruing to Britain from the colonies were considerable. Many people in Britain—especially those having economic interests in the colonial territories[18]—were critical of the Government of India's policy of anti-colonialism, possibly because they thought that it constituted a threat to British economic interests in the colonies.

But there were also other causes for disagreement between the British and the Indian governments. The Government of India's approach to the problem of colonial development and self-government was different from that of the British government. According to the Indian view, colonialism was an evil in itself and should, therefore, be terminated without delay ; the British Government, on the other hand, insisted that the transfer of power should be preceded by economic and social developments within the Colonial territories. Differences thus arose on the question of priorities—whether economic and social development should precede the grant of the right to self-determination, or whether it should be the other way round. Even within Britain, the intra-party debates on colonial issues divided the leading ideologues in both the Labour and the Conservative parties along these lines.[19] By 1956, the Labour party had nailed political rights at the top of its masthead ; and by the end of the 1950s, particularly after the appointment of Iain Macleod to Colonial Secretaryship, the Conservative Party also came to accept this. The pressure of events in the colonial territories, and the mounting pressure from the anti-colonial states probably accounted for this change.

The members of the official class in Britain had their own conception of good government in the colonies, and wanted to leave behind them in each country an indigenous political elite —a governing class—who shared with their rulers their concept of good government.[20] There was an apprehension that succumbing to the anti-colonial pressure at the UN—at which India had often taken the lead—would mean proceeding faster with decolonisation than was deemed practical and wise in each case. There was also a sense of national pride in Britain's past greatness and glory, and once the process of decolonisation was set in, it caused considerable soul-searching even among the professed anti-imperialists.[21] The relative decline in Britain's international status after the Second World War, and the reluctance of the people to accept this made them sensitive to any criticism of British policy by a country which had been a part of the empire so recently. It was thought that India was criticising British policy in order to try to enhance her own international prestige at the expense of Britain. India's anti-colonial pressure at the United Nations often alienated Britain, and gave rise to acute resentment in the country.[22]

British critics of India's policy of anti-colonialism may be divided into three distinct, though by no means exclusive, groups —the right-wing press,[23] persons having economic interest in the colonies,[24] and the members of the official class.[25] The right-wing press in Britain, especially the Beaverbrook newspapers, have generally been hostile to Nehru and his policies. Partly, this may be explained by the fact that the right-wing forces in British policies, represented by the right-wing of the Conservative party, were traditionally opposed to the nationalist movements in the colonies, whether these were led by Nehru in India, Nkrumah in Ghana, or Kenyatta in Kenya. But criticism of Nehru's policies was also meant for domestic consumption. It was designed to discredit the Labour party, particulary the left-wing of the Labour party who supported Nehru's policy of anti-colonialism and advocated a policy for an early withdrawal from the empire.[26]

So far as the official classes in Britain were concerned, criticism of Indian policy of anti-colonialism usually took the following forms. It was said, in the first place, that Indians did not appreciate the efforts made by the British Government in advancing the colonies towards the path of independence; and that in criticising British policy they often ignored the problems existing in multi-racial societies. There were many people who thought that Indian policy of anti-colonialism had a sinister motive behind it, that Nehru was indulging in a Machiavellian tactic for expansion in Africa. More generous critics, while dismissing this theory, maintained that Indian policy constituted an interference in the internal affairs of colonies in Africa, primarily to gain some advantage for the Indians living in these states. The role of the Indian High Commission during the Mau Mau revolt in Kenya was sharply criticised by a former Colonial Secretary, who had personal experience of the events in Kenya at the time. It was alleged that large sums of money came from the Congress party in India and that "the activities of the Indian High Commission went beyond the bounds of diplomatic propriety."[27]

The Government of India, on their part, always denied any intention of interfering in the affairs of British colonies to advance the interests of overseas Indians. The declaratory policy of the Indian Government was to encourage Indians to identify their interests with those of the state in which they lived. Replying to a Foreign Affairs debate in the Lok Sabha, on 17 December, 1957, Mr Nehru said:

> "Indian settlers should associate themselves as closely as possible with the interests of the people of the country they have adopted, and never make it appear or to (sic) function in a way that they become an exploiting agency there."[28]

Another criticism usually levelled against India was that her policy of anti-colonialism was directed against the European nations—that it was a policy of racialism against the whites. It was suggested that while India herself continued her 'colonial' domination over the Nagas or the backward classes, she should not have, in fairness, criticised other powers.[29]

Finally, India was criticised for applying double standards of morality in dealing with the Western powers and the Soviet Union. The crux of this criticism was that whereas India was quick to condemn the imperial and colonial policies of the Western powers, she tended to ignore the imperialist policy of the Soviet Union, as was typically demonstrated by the Government of India's policy towards the Suez and Hungarian crises respectively, in 1956. This was the most widespread criticism of Indian policy voiced not only by the official classes, but also by many scholars in the West.

Anti-colonialism as a policy had a deeper significance for India which was not always recognised in Britain. It stemmed from her own experience as a colony, and was closely associated with a sense of having been exploited. Imperialism, colonialism, and exploitative capitalism are almost synonymous in the political vocabulary of Indians and India's support to the movements for the liberation of the colonies was based on a genuine concern for the condition of the colonised people. It was not at all unnatural for Nehru to demand an end to the domination of the East by the West, or to think in terms of an adjustment of realtions between Asia and Europe on the basis of friendship and equality. Behind such pronouncements one could trace a concealed aim to project India's image abroad—especially among the Afro-Asians. Although he persistently denied any claim to Asian leadership, Nehru was aware of the 'special position' which made India so well qualified for this role.[30]

Distrust of capitalist West and anti-colonialism were neatly interwoven in the minds of India's foreign policy-making elite. The Leninist theory of imperialism might have influenced this attitude towards colonialism. It certainly influenced Nehru's thinking during the early years of his political career. Though his honeymoon with the Leauge of Anti-Imperialists was short-lived, his exposure to communism at the Anti-Imperialist Conference at Brussels (in 1927), and his experience during the brief visit to Moscow (in November, 1927), considerably influenced his attitude towards colonialism, which he readily came to associate with capitalism. This could be seen from his speeches and writings during the late 1920s early 1930s.[31]

Krishna Menon, like Nehru, was also influenced by the Leninist theory of imperialism, though he was not a blind adherent to the Marxist creed. It was rather the neo-Marxism of Laski which attracted him more. The long years of his stay in British campaigning against British rule in India had bred in him a hostility against Western imperialism, but his attitude to Britain as a colonial power was tempered by his good personal relationship with many of those who were to lead Britain during the crucial phase of the withdrawal from empire.[32]

However, not only Nehru and Menon, but also a generation of Indian leaders were influenccd by the Leninist view of imperialism. This was chiefly because contemporary colonialism in Asia and Africa was the result of the expansionist policies of the European states ; and these colonial Powers benefited from their economic domination over the colonies. Indians were less critical of the Soviet Union's policy in Eastern Europe because the Soviet Union never ruled India, as the British did for nearly two centuries. This explains the ambivalence in Indian attitude towards Soviet domination of Eastern Europe.

India's policy of anti-colonialism was closely associated with the resurgence of nationalism in Asia, and since independence she took the lead on many occasions to voice Asian protest against the continuance of European colonialism. Anti-colonialism was the dominant theme of the un-official Asian Relations Conference held in New Delhi in 1947 ; and in early 1949, the Government of India sponsored the Second Asian Relations Conference in New Delhi to support the nationalist movement in Indonesia. Anti-colonialism was also the dominant theme of the Afro-Asian Conference at Bandung (in 1955) in which India played a leading role.

Cold war, military alliances and colonialism

India's opposition to military alliances was considerably influenced by her anti-colonialist views. The Government of India were critical of SEATO (1954) and of thc Baghdad Pact (1955), of both of which Britain was a member, not least because these were thought to be the instruments of Western colonial Powers to continue their hold over the Asian states. Speaking before the Political Committee of the Bandung Conference, Nehru criticised NATO as being one of the most powerful protectors of colonialism, and rebuked Portugal's allies for supporting her claims to Goa, which was considered to be the last vestige of colonialism in India.[33]

Discussion of colonial issues by UN members became invariably involved in the politics of cold war. Both US and USSR were anti-colonial powers in their different ways. During the Second World war US supported India's demand for independence, and during the San Francisco Conference in 1945 assumed an anti-colonial posture. But with the onset of the cold war in the late 1940s this policy changed, and during the fifties, USA sided with the European colonial powers—her NATO allies—on most important colonial issues. Similarly, UK supported the colonial powers on many issues where she had no interest at stake, or even some reservations about the policy of the particular colonial power. This was mainly because the Soviet Union and her communist allies often used the colonial issues in UN as an instrument of propaganda against the West. Communist propaganda attacks against Western colonialism and the movement against colonialism thus got mixed up. It was by accident rather than by design that India often found herself on the same side with the Soviet bloc of countries whenever colonial issues were discussed in UN.

Suez, Hungary, Goa and (Congo)

The Government of India's attitude to the Suez and Hungarian crises of 1956, and their decision to send troops to Goa in December 1961 reveal important aspects of India's policy of anti-colonialism.

India's sharp criticism of the Anglo-French invasion of Egypt, and the rather mild reaction to the Soviet armed intervention for the suppression of the nationalist uprising in Hungary, in 1956, occasioned much adverse comments in UK, and strained Indo-British relations. To be able to explain the apparent inconsistency in Indian action, we should note the differences in India's attitude towards these two crises.

To New Delhi, the Anglo-French invasion of Egypt appeared

to be the revival of gun-boat diplomacy, as an attempt by these two imperialist powers to coerce Egypt to submission. It was viewed as an imperialist war, and condemnation was therefore, spontaneous. Probably there was also a feeling that such criticisms would have some effect in the West.[34] But when the Soviet Union invaded Hungary, the initial response of the Government of India was halting. Sir Anthony Eden (later Lord Avon) retrospectively laid emphasis on this defect. "The Indian reaction", he wrote, "was remarkable. Mr Nehru declared in a speech that whereas in Egypt 'every single thing that happened was as clear as daylight, he could not follow the very confusing situation in Hungary'."[35] The initial ambivalence in the Indian Government's attitude to the Hungarian crisis might have been the result of the lack of proper information, as no information from the Indian embassy in Budapest was immediately available.[36] However, there were other reasons as well. India expressed regrets at Soviet Union's action and criticised the atrocities in Hungary ; but was inclined to treat the Hungarian crisis as a cold war issue. Nehru told the Indian Parliament that the majority of the people in Hungary wanted a change and actually rose in insurrection, but they were suppressed. Foreign influences were also at work in Hungary at that time. However, he hastened to add that unlike the Anglo-French invasion of Egypt, the presence of Soviet troops in Hungary was really a matter of 'continuing intervention' based on Warsaw Pact.[37]

In the United Nations India supported the demand for the withdrawal of foreign troops from Hungary, but did not support the call for free elections in Hungary under UN auspices on the ground that this would violate Hungary's domestic jurisdiction. The Indian Government's view was that Hungary could not be treated as a colony of the Soviet Union, as long as she was represented in the United Nations as an independent state.

This stand of the Government of India was legally correct, as Huugary was not a colony in the traditional sense of the term ; but it could not easily be reconciled with the content of Nehru's own statement in the Parliament that the Hungarian

Government was not a free Government, but an imposed one.[38]

The Anglo-French attack on Egypt put severe strains on relationship with Britain. Termination of India's membership of the Commonwealth was strongly urged by the spokesmen of different political parties in the Parliament. Though Nehru declined to accept this demand, he admitted that for the first time in many years, he felt that India's membership of the Commonwealth 'may some time or other require further consideration.'[39] But the breach was soon repaired. It was appreciated in India that the policies of the British Government were opposed by millions of British citizens, and particularly by the Labour Party, whose spokesman appealed to India not to judge a nation by what so many of its own people regarded as a mistaken and wicked adventure.[40] Five years later when Indian troops occupied Goa, she did not get this support in UK, even from the professed anti-imperialists, who had earlier supported India's claim to Goa.

The British Government's attitude to the Indo-Portuguese dispute over Goa, Daman and Diu, was far from being favourable to India, or even one of neutrality. India regarded the small Portuguese territories in India as the palpable vestiges of colonialism, and wanted their termination. The Government of India tried to settle the matter peacefully, by negotiations with the Portuguese Government. But Lisbon was adamant in its claim that Goa was a part of metropolitan Portugal. Because of her special relationship with India as a member of the Commonwealth, and with Portugal as a member of NATO as well as an ally of long standing, Britain could have played a useful mediatory role in the Indo-Portuguese dispute. But the partisan role of the Foreign Office in 1954 ruled out this possibility.

During the summer of 1954 relations between Portugal and India reached a new low. Tensions were increasing along the India-Goa border as unarmed Goan satyagrahis (freedom fighters) planned to march into the Portuguese territory from the Indian side of the border. The Portuguese authorities in Goa threatened to shoot down the demonstrators if they crossed the

Goan border. The Government of India repeatedly declared that they would seek a solution of the dispute through peaceful means, but refused to prevent Goan nationals from entering Portuguese territories from the Indian side. They warned Portugal that if force was used against the "peaceful volunteers" who had occupied parts of the Portuguese territories in India, there would be incalculable repercussions among the Indian people.[41] The Delhi correspondent of *The Times* wrote that India's reputation would suffer from such demonstrations, and that instead of applying indirect pressure on Portugal, the Indian government should have adopted methods recognised under international law.[42]

At the height of tensions in Indo-Portuguese relations the British Foreign Office issued a statement by Mr Selwyn Lloyd, the then Minister of State in the Foreign Office, which gave rise to indignation in India. At a meeting with the Portuguese Ambassador in London Mr Lloyd told him that Britain very much regretted the state of tension "now existing between a member of the Commonwealth and an ally of such long standing as Portugal." The British Government, therefore, "expressed to the Government of India their earnest hope that there will be no resort to force or to methods bound to lead to the use of force."[43] The text of the statement was conveyed to the Government of India with a note. This diplomatic intervention by the British government was featured in the press as a warning to India not to use force. India's handling of the dispute, it was thought in London, was inconsistent with her professed philsophy of settling international disputes by peaceful means ; nor, it was believed, had she exhausted all the diplomatic possibilities.[44] The political wisdom of the British move was, however, open to question. Though the Foreign Office statement did not constitute a protest in the diplomatic sense, most commentators agreed that it was unprecedented for Britain to send such a strongly worded message, and with such publicity, to a fellow member of the Commonwealth.[45] Despite New Delhi's assertion that India would seek a peaceful solution of the dispute the British government cautioned the Government of India against the use of force, but did not advise similar moderation on the part of Portugal, at least nothing was said in public. Portugal, therefore, secured the diplomatic support she wanted from Britain. The Portuguese Foreign Minister expressed his government's appreciation of "this demonstration of solidarity and cooperation of the British nation."[46]

This partisan policy of the British government is difficult to explain, as Britain herself had liquidated the vast empire in South Asia during 1947-48 and was committed, in principle, to grant independence to the rest of the colonies. Two considera-tion might have influenced this policy. In the first place, if the British government supported Indian claims to Goa, she might have faced similar demands from Spain over Gibraltar. Secondly, Portugal was an ally of Britain. Because of Portugal's membership of NATO, the Portuguese Prime Minister claimed the right to invoke the consultative clauses of the treaty in the face of a threat to Goa's security which, according to Portuguese law, was a part of Portugal. India made soundings in Ottawa, Washington and London, which supported Dr Salazar's view. However, it was pointed out that as these territories were outside the NATO area, the defensive obligations of the treaty would not apply to them.[47]

In India the reaction against the Foreign Office statement was sharp. The Indian government, in a note to the British government emphatically repudiated the 'unwarranted implications' of the statement.[48] Indo-British relations, which seemed to be particularly cordial after the Geneva Conference (in 1954) suffered a set-back as a result of the note sent by the British Government.[49] This had occurred at an awkward time when Britain was seeking Indian support in South East Asia.[50]

Perhaps, in response to criticisms in India the British government adopted a neutralist attitude to the dispute later. On 25 October, 1954, Mr Dodds-Parker, the then Under-Secretary of State for Commonwealth Relations, explained the British Government's policy in a written reply to a Member of Parliament.

> "Her Majesty's Government have" he wrote, "naturally been in touch with the Governments of India and Portugal in this matter. There has, of course, been no

question of Her Majesty's Government intervening in the merits of the case."

"The object of our representation to the Government of India in August", he continued "was to let them know as between friends, our concern lest the much advertised activities of some unofficial movements in India should lead to violence and bloodshed. The Government of India responded with assurances that they were determined to pursue a peaceful and conciliatory approach."[51]

Despite occasional press reports that Britain was willing to offer her good offices to bring about a settlement in Goa,[52] no such offer was made. In fact, by the middle of the 1950s, the Goa issue became overtly involved in cold war politics. During his visit to India in 1955, the Russian Prime Minister Bulganin condemned European colonialism, especially Portuguese colonialism in India. He said in a speech at Madras, "there is no justification for the Portuguese colony of Goa to exist still on the ancient territory of India." This was followed, a few days later, by the US Secretary of State's assertion, in a joint communique with the Portuguese Foreign Minister Dr Cunha, that Goa was a province of Portugal.[53]

India's claim to Goa was buttressed by geographical, political and economic arguments. It is surprising that the Western powers, especially Britain and the United States, supported Portugal in her dispute with India. But by 1961 there was a change in the attitudes of these governments, particularly of the US government, probably under the influence of the then American Ambassador to India, who strongly urged his government to reconsider their policy towards this dispute.[54] The US government appreciated the depth of Indian feeling on the Goa issue, and might have succeeded in persuading Portugal to be reasonable, and to settle the dispute with India. But the US government's initiatives towards this end came too late ;[55] whether any such effort would have been successful is a different question. By December 1961, the Government of India seemed to have made up their mind that the Portuguese could not be thrown out of Goa without the use of force, and contingency plans for such an emergency were already afoot.[56] A combination of circumstances had virtually forced the government's hands. Popular pressure within the country was mounting for military action against the Portuguese in Goa ; and nearly all the major political parties in India—with exception of the Swatantra Party—had some sort of a Goa plan in their election manifestos. The political implications of such popular pressure in a pre-election year were not lost on the government. Their options were further limited by reports that the Goan revolutionaries had set up a 'provisional Government' for Goa, adjoining the Maharasthra border. Outside the country, India's prestige as an anti-colonial power was at a low ebb among the Afro-Asian states. At the Belgrade summit conference of the non-aligned states in September, 1961, Nehru advocated a policy of moderation which failed to satisfy the "militant" anti-colonialists from Africa. In October of the same year, a seminar on Portuguese colonialism was held in New Delhi. It was made clear to the Indian participants that so long India tolerated Portuguese colonialism in Goa, her commitments to anti-colonialism would be regarded as superficial.[57] Later Nehru said in a press conference that this seminar left the Indian leaders in a receptive mood, searching for something to do about Goa.[58]

Indian troops entered Goa on 18 December, 1961. But Nehru was in two minds till the last day ; he was concerned about the probable consequences of Indian action. In deference to Western pressure, the D-Day had been postponed twice as both the British and the American governments had advised the Government of India against the use of force.[59] But Nehru's Chief of General Staff had warned him that the decision to call off the military action would lower the morale of the armed forces.[60] The Government would also lose its credibility to the people at large. Probably these considerations finally clinched Nehru's decision in favour of military action.

In UK the condemnation of India's action was all but unanimous, though the tone of disapproval varied. To the right-wing critics of Nehru's policy, his fall from grace was a cause for jubilation ; but to the Labour-left, and to most of those who supported India's claim to Goa, the Government of India's action came as a shock. During the debate in the House of Commons only one member, Mr Woodrow Wyatt, supported India's action. The Secretary of State for Commonwealth Relations, Mr Duncan Sandys, told the House that though Britain appreciated the feelings of Indians on this issue, "...Her Majesty's Government *deeply deplore* the decision of the Government of India to use military force to achieve its political objective."[61] In UN, the British representative Patrick Dean expressed the shock and regret of his Government at the news of the outbreak of hostilities in the 'Portuguese territories' in India.[62] He submitted a draft resolution calling for an immediate cease-fire, the withdrawal of Indian troops, the working out of a permanent solution by peaceful means in accordance with the Charter, and to that end, the assistance of the Secretary General where appropriate.[63]

The spate of criticisms in the West, especially in UK and US, created anger and resentment in India. So far as the British Government was concerned, there was some apprehension that the Indian action might encourage others, who had similar grievances against colonial powers, to resort to force. There was also disillusionment with India and scepticism about Nehru's protestation of peaceful intents for settlement of international disputes. Indo-British relations were strained.

The seizure of Goa damaged India's prestige in the West, where there was a disposition to brand Nehru as an aggressor ; but it was applauded by most of the states in Africa and Asia, as well as by the Communist countries. It seems the criticisms of the Western Powers were inspired by a high moral principle—that the use of force could not be justified as a means of settling international disputes. Neither UK nor US had an unblemished record in these matters. But their criticisms were poignant, as Nehru himself was one of the persistent advocates of this principle. It was not, however, sufficiently recognised that between 1947-61, India tried to settle the dispute with Portugal through peaceful negotiation, but without much success. During these years the Western powers did not take any initiative to persuade Lisbon to give up what was, by all accounts, an anachronism in the Indian sub-continent. If they did, probably the dispute could have been settled without the use of force.

Another political issue which suddenly ran Indo-British relations to near disaster during 1960-61, was the Congo problem. Congo, which was a Belgian colony, was declared independent in June 1960. It was followed by the secession of the mineral-rich province of Katanga from the newly-independent Republic of Congo, and a bloody civil war ensued. The Nationalist Congo Government blamed the Belgians, having substantial stakes in mining, for the troubles. Both because of local personalities and Britain's intimate relations with Belgium her role in the Congo crisis aroused deep suspicions in Indian minds.

As the fighting continued, especially in the Katanga province the Government of India decided, in February 1961, to send an Indian contingent to join the UN Peace Keeping Forces in Congo. British reservations about UN involvement ln hostilities in the Katanga province were interpreted in India as giving covert assistance to the "unregenerate Belgians" and Britain was criticised for letting down the United Nations.[63a] When fighting broke out in Katanga between the United Nations forces (including Indian) and the mercenary elements, relations between Britain and India deteriorated following a BBC report on the fighting which complained of the 'brutality of Indian troops'. On 17 September Prime Minister Nehru held a formal press conference, a large part of which was devoted to explaining events in the Congo. He spoke of 'foreign mercenaries' who escaped removal by UN forces and 'to some extent with the permission of the United Nations...took refuge in various consulates, notably the Belgian consulate. In course of the same spech he added : "It is apparent that some of these people, foreign officials, organized resistance to the United Nations...I cannot go into details, but the main or surprising thing is that the United Nations is being criticized and condemned by countries, notably the United Kingdom and, of course, Sir Roy Welensky of Rhodesia for the action it took...I think the whole thing is perfectly amazing and scandalous in its extreme."[64]

The way Nehru bracketed the United Kingdom with Rhodesia and Belgium shows the depth of feeling in India against Britain on this issue. Without belabouring the point one could draw a parallel between British support to Belgium in the Congo conflict and the British government's support to Portugal in the Indo-Portuguese dispute over Goa—at least this is how many Indians viewed it. Nevertheless, Nehru used rather strong words in his press conference in criticising British policy, and that was enough to create a diplomatic row in the relations between the two governments. On top of it came the news of the death of Dag Hammarskjold in an air crash at Ndola in Northern Rhodesia, and Indians suspected British foul play in it. On the 19th of September the *Indian Express*, a paper which was not normally given to anti-British hysteria, wrote. "Never, even during Suez, have Britain's hands been so blood-stained as they are now". Similar views were expressed in many other vernacular dailies. The current of anti-British feeling in India was running high. However, it subsided rather quickly, and in it the personal diplomacy of the then British High Commissioner—who repudiated the allegations against the British Government in a press conference—played no mean a part.

Colonial Issues and the United Nations: British and Indian Views

It was in the United Nations that British and Indian delegates often crossed swords when colonial issues were raised for discussion. So far as the role of the UN in colonial matters was concerned, there was a fundamental difference in the attitudes of the two Governments. India placed high hopes on the United Nations as the principal agency for speeding up the process of decolonisation,[64a] and as such would like to see more powers vested in this organisation (1) to put pressure on the colonial Powers to speed up the process of de-colonisation, and (2) to oversee the acts of the Administering Powers in relation to the Non-Self-Governing and Trust territories.

The British government's view, on the other hand, was that as British sovereignty extended to overseas territories, events in the overseas colonies were a matter for Britain alone, so long as they did not constitute a threat to international peace.[65] This was a strictly legalistic interpretation of the Charter. Within Britain there was a felling that so far as the British colonies were concerned, the role of UN was essentially negative, as it had encouraged much irresponsible and even scurrilous criticism by states whose main interest was not in the welfare of the colonies, but in stirring up as much mischief as possible.[66]

So far as the Trust and Non-Self-Governing territories were concerned, the British government's view was that Britain was prepared to co-operate with the United Nations, but would not be pushed around by the anti-colonial Powers. Sir Anthony Eden (later Lord Avon), addressing the General Assembly, said on November 11, 1952 :

> "Either these lands can continue, with the help of countries like my own, their orderly progress towards self-government. Or they can be prematurely abandoned by us and exposed to anarchy or despotism, so that all liberal tendencies are smothered, perhaps for generations. There is no question in my mind as to which of these courses most closely suits the purpose of the Charter of the United Nations."[67]

Differences arose between Britain and India with regard to the interpretation of the scope of Chapters XI and XII of the Charter—the provisions regarding the Non-Self-Governing and Trust territories. India played a vigorous and imaginative role in trying to extend, as far as possible, UN supervision and control over the remaining colonial territories.[68] In this matter the policy of the Government of India was often at variance with that of the British government. To take the case of the Trust Territories first, India regarded the Trusteeship system as a 'collective proprietorship' and would, therefore, like to extend the control of the General Assembly over every aspect of it, to which Britain, as an Administering Power, objected.

Differences also appeared between the two governments over the interpretations of the provisions of the Charter relating to the Non-Self-Governing territories. Britain, along with other colonial powers, contended that a distinction should be made between the provisions of the Charter relating to the Non-Self-Governing territories, and those relating to the Trust territories. According to this view, the United Nations is not authorised by the Charter to exercise any supervision or control over the administration of Non-Self-Governing territories ; therefore, the Administering Powers are not accountable to UN for their action.[70]

Under the provisions of the Charter (Article 73e), the Administering Powers are required to transmit regularly to the Secretary General statistical and other information of a 'technical nature'—relating to the territories, for the administration of which they are responsible—for 'information purposes', and 'subject to such limitations as security and constitutional considerations may require.' Britain, therefore, argued[71] that she was under no obligation to supply political information regarding the Non-Self-Governing territories, nor would she support any move by other non-Administering states to empower the General Assembly to exercise supervisory control over the Non-self-Governing territories. On this ground the British government objected to the right of UN to pass resolutions on Rhodesia, between the years 1961-65.

India's efforts, on the other hand, were concentrated on two matters : first, to extend the control of the General Assembly over the administration of the Non-Self-Governing territories by insisting that the Assembly has the right to examine the 'information' supplied by the Administering Powers to the Secretary General ; and secondly, to make it more or less obligatory for the Administering Powers to supply information of a political nature. A 'Committee on Information' was set up by the General Assembly in 1947, with Indian support, and in the face of objections from the Colonial powers, to examine the information supplied by the Administering states. It remained in being till 1963, when it was dissolved by the Assembly and its powers were taken over by the Committee of Twenty-Four.[72] A rivalry developed between Britain and India since the former refused to accept any mandatory obligation for the transmission of information of a political nature, though she was supplying some such information voluntarily. In a sense the December

1950 resolution of the General Assembly[73], and the subsequent establishment of the Committee to act as a watchdog on its implementation marked the success of the efforts of the anti-colonialists to narrow the gap between the Trusteeship system and the provisions of the Charter relating to the Non-Self-Governing territories.[74]

The General Assembly resolution of 1960 summed up what India and other anti-colonial powers had been working for from the beginning. This declaration, which was unanimously adopted by the General Assembly (with Britain, France, the United States and six other states abstaining) proclaimed the 'necessity of bringing to a speedy and unconditional end of colonialism in all its forms and manifestations.' It unambiguously removed the justification of colonialism on grounds of tutelage, and thus demolished one of the important moral and theoretical bulwarks of colonialism.[75] Britain did not accept the new standard which had been laid down, nor did she accept the injunction that colonial powers should take immediate steps to grant independence to the colonies and dependent territories; but the anti-colonial pressure at the United Nations was partly responsible for the speed with which the British empire in Africa was liquidated.

Therefore, so far as the role of the United Nations in colonial issues was concerned, the differences between Britain and India related mainly to the interpretations of the provisions of the charter regarding the Non-Self-Governing and Trust territories. India's efforts were concentrated in giving to UN certain prerogatives which the colonial Powers never thought of at San Francisco, or for a decade or more thereafter. Britain has generally taken her stand on a strictly legalistic interpretation of the charter and thus has tried to limit the role of the United Nations in dealing with colonial issues. But she did not hesitate to deviate from this strict legalism when it suited her purpose.[76] Nor has India, for that matter, been consistent in her interpretation of the Charter. For example, while she criticised the strictly legalistic interpretation of the Charter, she herself has tended to take that position in cases involving the Soviet Union.

II

Racial Issues In Indo-British Relations

Racial issues were a recurrent cause of conflict between Britain and India since the beginning of this century. There were two aspects of the racial question. The first related to the treatment of the Indian minorities in overseas territories, especially in South Africa. During the 1960s, the presence of large Indian communities in the former British colonial territories in East Africa created a new problem for Britain, as many of these East African Asians held British passports. The treatment accorded to them by the British government became a potentially explosive issue in Indo-British relations during the late 1960s because although New Delhi disclaimed any responsibility for the Indians settled abroad, their status and welfare were always a matter of concern for the Government of India.

Racial issues had also a broader aspect, and related to the question of discrimination on the basis of colour or racial origin. In principle, both Britain and India were opposed to racial discrimination, and worked for the development of multiracialism within the framework of the Commonwealth. Their differences related, chiefly, to the policy to be adopted towards South Africa, and since 1965, to the white-minority regime in Rhodesia. However, this was not an exclusively Indo-British problem and affected Britain's relations with the majority of her Commonwealth partners.

The British Government's responsibility for the situation in South Africa was vicarious. Though they did not support the policy of apartheid, racial discrimination was writ large of the time of the foundation of the South African state.[77] The British Government also refused to support any move in UN, at least till the beginning of the 1960s, to put organised international pressure on the Union Government as they maintained that racial discrimination in South Africa could not be brought to an end by such a policy. London was, therefore opposed to any policy that would reduce South Africa to the status of an international pariah.

Many Western commentators think that the Indian policy

of anti-racialism itself revealed a hatred towards the white man. This is a wrong interpretation of the Indian attitude. This attitude of mind had its origin in India's colonial experience which brought Indians into direct and personal contact with racial discrimination by foreigners, mainly British, in their own soil. It was, therefore, quite natural that on attaining independence India led the campaign against any manifestation of racial discrimination ; opposition to racialism became one of the corner-stones of Indian foreign policy.

An important consideration influencing this policy was, no doubt, the concern for the status of Indian communities living in the British colonies or former colonial territories. If, as a result of the policy of racial discrimination, overseas Indians were to return to India, new problems would be created for the government to rehabilitate them. One of the aims of Indian foreign policy was, therefore, to see that the overseas Indians living in British colonies were not subjected to difficulties. In fact, during 1948-49, one of the arguments in favour of the Government of India's decision to continue India's membership of the Commonwealth was the belief that this might do some good to the Indians living in the various British colonies.[78]

Organised emigration of Indian labour to British colonies began in the 19th century, under the active encouragement and direction of the British rulers in India.[79] Indian labourers were indentured to work in the plantations, and later, in the construction of the railways in the British colonies. In the distant colonies they were encouraged by their European masters to settle permanently, as this would reduce the cost of bringing new men from India. But before the First World War, the successive British Governments in India did little to protect the interests of the migrant Indians, who were subjected to various disabilities in the hands of their settlement.[80] In the colonies of European settlement, the aim of the colonists was to prevent the rise of a free Indian class who might compete with the Europeans or, in certain cases, with the indigenous communities.[81]

One of the worst cases of discrimination against Indians was in South Africa, where Lord Salisbury's earlier promise[82] of equality of treatment for the Indian and European subjects of Her Majesty's Government had been honoured more by its breaches than by its observance. Under the pressure of Indian opinion the Government of India raised the matter in the Imperial Conference towards the end of the First World War, and on several occasions later.[83] Some sort of compromise was reached between the Governments of India and South Africa regarding the future status of Indians living in the Union, which was embodied in the Capetown Agreement of 1927 and in the joint communique issued by the two Governments in 1932.

So long as India remained within the British empire, London could act as a restraining influence in the Indo-South African dispute. As Secretary of State for India, Leopold Amery passed on to Smuts, sometimes with his own emphatic comments about the treatment of the people of Indian origin in South Africa. One curious aspect of the Indian-South African conflict was the friendly personal relationship that developed between Gandhi and Smuts.[84] During the constitutional negotiations between the British and Indian Governments in the 1930s, South African statesman played an important role in promoting an Anglo-Indian accord, and he cautioned his British friends not to delay the grant of independence to India. "Dominion status in its full implications", he wrote to Lord Linlithgow in August 1941, "should not be denied them, but should be given them freely and graciously, as it is in any case inevitable."[85] Whether Smuts's favourable attitude to India's demand for independence influenced Indian-South African relationship is difficult to determine ; what, however, was surprising was that even at the height of tensions in Indo-South African relations, Gandhi's personal respects for the South African statesman remained apparently undiminished.[86]

The Capetown Agreement between the Indian and South African Governments did not lead to any improvement in the status of Indians living in South Africa ; with the passage of the Pegging Act in Natal (in 1943) and the Asiatic Land Tenure & Indian Representations Act in 1946, by the Union Parliament, the condition of Indians became even worse. As India moved towards independence, conflict with the South African Government became almost inevitable.

In 1946, the Provisional Government of India imposed an economic boycott against South Africa, and recalled the Indian High Commissioner. In the same year the question of the treatment of the people of Indian origin in South Africa was included in the provisional agenda of the Second part of the first session of the General Assembly of UN, on a request from the Government of India. The details of the Indo-South African dispute are beyond the scope of the present study. Between the years 1946-61 the issue was discussed almost annually by the General Assembly, but since 1952 it was relegated to the background by the larger issue of apartheid in South Africa.[87] One point, however, should be noted. In 1946, and in successive years the South African Government took their stand on the domestic jurisdiction clause (Article 2.7) of the Charter, and claimed that UN had no right to discuss the racial policies of the South African government, as these were essentially within the domestic jurisdiction of the South African Government. In this matter the British government supported South Africa.

In 1946, Britain's dilemma was voiced by the British representative to the United Nations, Sir Hartly Shawcross, who said that he would have preferred "...to take no part in this dispute between members of the British Commonwealth."[88] Despite this desire to remain neutral, the British Government's views on the Indo-South African dispute, as expressed between the years 1946-61, tended to support South Africa's stand based on a right interpretation of the domestic jurisdiction clause of the UN Charter.

The same was also true of the British government's attitude to the larger issue of apartheid in South Africa. In 1952, 13 Arab-Asian states (including India and Pakistan) requested that the South African policy of apartheid be included in the agenda of the General Assembly.[89] In their opinion, South Africa's policy of racial discrimination constituted a threat to international peace, and was based on a violation of the basic principles of human rights and fundamental freedoms enshrined in the Charter. The South African government, again, challenged the competence of the United Nations to discuss South Africa's race policies by invoking the domestic jurisdiction clause of the Charter. Though they had little support in this matter from the majority of the member-states, the British Government supported them.

By 1960 it became clear to the British government that supporting the South African contention in the name of domestic jurisdiction was an embarrassment. With the increase in the number of Afro-Asian members in the General Assembly, pressure of opinion for some action against South Africa began to increase. After the Sharpeville disturbances of 1960, resulting in the death of several Africans, the Afro-Asian members of the United Nations called for an urgent meeting of the Security Council to consider the situation in South Africa. Though Britain abstained from voting in the mildly-worded resolution of the Security Council[90] deploring the racial policies of the South African Government, a change in the attitude of the British Government was quite evident from the 'Wind of change' speech delivered by Prime Minister Macmillan a few months earlier, in February 1960.

Within the Commonwealth the disappreval of South Africa's racialist policies began to grow with the increase in the number of non-white members. Because of the long tradition of Commonwealth Conference not to discuss the domestic policies of member-states, South African affairs were not discussed in the Commonwealth Prime Ministers' Conference. But strong resentments were voiced against the racialist policies of the Union Government in the Commonwealth Prime Ministers' conference in 1960 and 1961. In 1961, South Africa became a republic. The Canadian Prime Minister, with the support of Afro-Asian members, asserted that a multi-racial association such as the Commonwealth should be based on the principle of racial non-discrimination. As South Africa refused to accept this, she ceased to be a member of the Commonwealth.

South Africa's departure from the Commonwealth made it easier for Britain to modify her policies in the United Nations to some extent.[91] However, she was opposed to sanctions against South Africa, and was unwilling to see South Africa diplomatically isolated. In 1962, Britain voted against the General Assembly resolution[92] which called upon the member-states to take such measures jointly and severally as would cut off diplomatic and economic ties with South Africa. But in the following year the British Government voted for the Security Council resolution[93] which called for, inter alia, a ban on the shipment of arms to South Africa.

Since both the British and Indian Governments were opposed to the policy of racial discrimination in South Africa, Indo-British differences arose mainly out of the divergence in their views regarding the role of UN. The British Government adhered to a strictly legalistic interpretation of the domestic jurisdiction clause of the Charter and held, at least till 1960, that the discussion of South Africa's racial policies in the United Nations constituted an intervention in the domestic affairs of the South African Government. India, on the other hand, thought that the racial policies of the South African Government constituted a threat to international peace, and violated the basic principles of human rights embodied in the Charter ; the United Nations, therefore, was entitled to deal with Africa's racial policies. Neither Britain nor India was, however, consistent in the interpretation of the 'domestic jurisdiction' clause (Article 2.7) of the Charter. Britain, for example, deviated from a rigid interpretation of this article during the Anglo-Iranian oil dispute (1951), during the debates on forced labour in the Soviet Union, or during the debates on the complaint against the Russian policy of preventing foreigners from taking their Russian wives out of the Soviet Union.[94] India, on the other hand, moved towards a rigid interpretation of Article 2.7 during the debates on the Hungarian crisis in 1956.

Behind the facade of this legalism there were more important causes for the differences between the policies of the British and the Indian governments. Once India had broken off her diplomatic and economic relations with South Africa, she had nothing to lose by advocating a policy of increasing international pressure on South Africa. But for the British government the matter was not so simple.

Because of the historical association between the two states a mutually advantageous economic relationship was established between Britain and South Africa. British investments in South Africa stood at £909m. at the end of 1962,[95] constituting nearly 60 per cent of the total foreign investment in the country. Britain was also the most important trading partner of South Africa, accounting for nearly a third of South Africa's total foreign trade.[96] For the United Kingdom, with a larger volume of trade, the importance of trade with South Africa was much less, in percentage terms ; but it was still an important element in Britain's foreign trade, especially at a time of her own balance of payments difficulties.[97] According to the Committee of Experts set up by the United Nations to study the implications of sanctions against South Africa a general embargo on trade with South Africa could create serious dislocations in UK.[98] Therefore, because of these economic links between Britain and South Africa, and also because of the operation of a powerful and effective pro-South African lobby within Britain,[99] the British government have always been reluctant to adopt any hostile policy towards the South African regime, despite the widespread disappoval of apartheid within the country.

There were other reasons as well which influenced the British government's policy towards South Africa. Within Britain, especially among the Conservatives, there was a sentimental attachment to the traditional view of the Commonwealth. The departure of a large number of British immigrants to the Union between 1948-61, the memory of South Africa's contribution to the allied war efforts, particularly the memory of Field Marshal Smuts, who was held in high esteem in Britain, contributed to the desire to avoid any break with South Africa.[100]

Finally, there was the strategic argument which favoured the strengthening of links between Britain and South Africa. Successive Conservative governments in Britain worked on the assumption that the retention of the naval base at Simonstown was a vital British interest. Although the strategic importance of the Cape route has declined considerably after the liquidation of the British empire in the East, especially since the rundown of British military bases east of Suez, it remains a politically potent idea which may be worked up by any British Prime Minister backed by a group of his influential colleagues.[101] The last Conservative government revived the idea of the strategic importance of the Cape route, and therefore, of the Naval base at Simonstown, to justify their policy of selling arms to South Africa. There was, however, considerable doubt about the wisdom of such a policy, among strategic experts as well as among Britain's allies, especially in the context of the declared opposition of the African states and of other members of the Commonwealth.

Because of Britain's considerable economic stakes in South Africa, and also because of the political and strategic reasons explained above, it was difficult for the British government to accept the policy advocated by India and other Afro-Asian members of the Commonwealth.

Immigration and colour in British politics : their impact on Indo-British relations

During the 1960's, questions of race and colour assumed a new dimension in Britain's relations with the Commonwealth countries. Before 1962, citizens from the Commonwealth countries had the right of entry to Britain without any statutory restriction. Because of shortage of labour in post-War Britain, there had been a steady influx of immigrants into UK from the new Commonwealth countries, and from the British colonies in Africa and the Caribbean. Though the British government was aware of the problems that might arise in future in respect of housing and other welfare services, there was no meaningful discussion of the problem of immigration on its own merit.[102] There was a small group within the Parliament vigorously advocating the case for controlling immigration. Conservative Members of Parliament such as Sir Cyril Osborne and Mr Norman Pannell were long-term campaigners against immigration on grounds which bordered on racism. There were also a group of Labour Members, some of whom represented constituencies affected by immigration, and a number of Trade Unionists outside Parliament who displayed some anxiety about the consequences of an uncontrolled flow of immigration. The

Trade Unionists were mainly concerned about the possible effect of immigration on the status and bargaining power of workers, and therefore, came out in favour of some form of control over immigration.[103] But neither the Government, nor the major political parties were in favour of controlling immigration from the Commonwealth countries and the British colonies. However, with the presence of a sizeable minority of coloured population in Britain, questions of race and colour moved from the periphery to the centre of political discussions during the 1960s. Indians watched these developments with suspicion and alarm, not only because these would affect many Indians living in UK, and many more intending to migrate, but also because the question of colour revived old memories of discrimination by the British in India and generated sympathies in favour of the people from the new Commonwealth.

In the summer of 1961 the British Government decided, for the first time, to enact statutory laws to curb immigration from the Commonwealth, and the Commonwealth Immigrants Bill was introduced in the Parliament in October.[104] The intention of the British Government was conveyed to the Government of India in an Aide Memoire on 14 October, 1961.[105] In their reply the Government of India stressed that there was no previous consultation 'before taking the decision to impose very drastic curbs which would affect considerable traffic of persons between the UK and India'; and that the intended restrictions might lead to discrimination between various members of the Commonwealth on the basis of colour.[106] Though the British government had given assurances that the proposed restrictions would not operate on the basis of colour, apprehensions about racial discrimination were voiced by various members of the Indian Parliament. Mr Nath Pai, an Opposition spokesman, said in the Lok Sabha that the Bill 'smacks of colour discrimination on the part of what is called the mother of the Commonwealth' and another member described it as a 'British brand of apartheid'.[107] There was also the feeling that the proposed law would make the position of the Commonwealth citizens even worse than that of the aliens.

Within Britain, there was fierce opposition to the Bill from the Labour Party. Mr Patrick Gordon Walker, a former Minister for Commonwealth Relations, criticised the Bill as being based on 'bare-faced, open race discrimination'; and added that the Bill was ill-conceived, and had been hurried through without prior consultations with the Commonwealth.[108] The Leader of the Opposition dismissed it as 'a plain anti-Commonwealth Measure in theory and...a plain anti-colour Measure in practice'.[109] In fact, this was one of the most hard-fought Bills and gave rise to much bitterness and recrimination during the debates in both the Houses of Parliament. But to what extent these words were meant for public consumption at home and abroad is difficult to determine. After all, in 1963, with prospects of electoral victory, the Labour Party had considerably watered down its opposition to the principle of controlling Commonwealth immigration, and a few years later, in 1968, the Labour government had enacted a law that was far more discriminatory in content as well as practice.

Outside the Parliament, opposition to the Bill came from a section of the 'metropolitan elite'.[110] A Committee was formed with distinguished men from various walks of life, to oppose the Bill. The Archbishop of Canterbury, a prominent member of the group, criticised the Bill in the House of Lords as 'lamentable', and *The Times* pointed out in an editorial:

> 'The damage, emotional, economic, and political which it is likely to do to the already fragile fabric of the Commonwealth can hardly be exaggerated.'[111]

Part I of the Commonwealth Immigrants Act (1962), which provided for control of immigration, required annual renewal by the Parliament. Shortly after taking office in October, 1964, the Labour Government obtained Parliamentary renewal of the Act for one year, pending consultation with other Commonwealth governments on the whole question of immigration. On 4 February, 1965, the Home Secretary informed the House of Commons that the Government had taken steps "to initiate Commonwealth discussions to review the whole question of Commonwealth immigration."[112] He said that under the existing control evasion on a considerable scale was taking place. Though no accurate estimate of the number of evasions was available, the Home Secretary emphasised that their number during the two previous years could not be less than 10, 000.[113] To check the problem of evasions, the Government proposed to take two measures : (a) to tighten the control by 'stricter use of the existing powers of control',[114] and (b) to send a high level Mission to certain Commonwealth countries to examine with their respective governments "what can be done to stamp out evasion at source, and to discuss whether new methods are needed to regulate the flow of migrants to the United Kingdom."[115]

A Mission led by Lord Mountbatten visited a number of countries, including India,[116]and submitted its report to the Prime Minister in June 1965. On 15 June Mr Wilson said in the Parliament that the Mission had been "immensely valuable in securing real understanding" about the nature of the problems between the countries visited and the British Government.[117] In India, Lord Mountbatten had discussions with the Prime Minister, the Foreign Minister, and the Ministers of Law and Labour, as well as with the senior officials of the Ministries concerned. According to an official publication, the discussions were held "in a cordial atmosphere."[118] The substance of these discussions was not revealed either in London or in New Delhi. Mr Wilson said in the House of Commons that the Report of the Mountbatten Mission could not be published as the discussions were held "on a strictly cofidential basis."[119]

Whether the Mission had been successful in its aim is, however, difficult to assess. It was an attempt by the Labour government to try to negotiate reciprocal arrangements with the Commonwealth Governments. But, pointed out one critic, Lord Mountbatten was "politely told by the Commonwealth Governments that it was the business of a sovereign state to tackle its own immigration problems rather than try to shuffle off the responsibility and odium to others."[120]

As the Report was being studied by the government, a number of problems remained to be solved ; and whatever was done, Mr Wilson assured the Parliament, would be done in consultation with the Commonwealth governments.[121] He hoped to discuss some of these problems, on a bilateral basis, with the Commonwealth Prime Ministers concerned, who were due to arrive in London within the next few days to attend the Commonwealth Prime Ministers' Conference.

On 2 August 1965, the British government issued a white paper elaborating its future policy on Commonwealth immigration.[122] This policy had two aspects. In the first place, it aimed at securing tighter controls on the entry of immigrants, "so that it does not outrun Britain's capacity to absorb them."[123] Secondly, it envisaged some positive measures to secure for the immigrants and their childern their 'rightful place' in British society.[124]

The new regulations introduced by the government in 1965 further restricted the entry of Indian and other Commonwealth citizens, to UK.[125] The new measures, however, failed to control evasion which continued on a considerable scale from India and Pakistan. This created new problems for the immigration authorities in Britain, and in many cases led to harassment and refusal of entry to Indian nationals. The treatment meted out even to many respected Indians created popular indignation in India, and became a source of embarrassment to the government in New Delhi.[126] The Indian Government made diplomatic representations to the British Government "about the difficulties experienced at British ports by Indian immigrants and visitors and impressed on them the need to complete formalities in India."[127]

Towards the end of 1967, a large exodus of people (of Indian origin) started from Kenya to Britain. This was the result of the drive for Africanisation of trade and services in Kenya and other East African countries. The people affected by this move were the Asians, who had settled in these territories when these were British colonies. At the time of Kenya's independence, they were given a choice either to apply for Kenyan citizenship within two years, or to retain their British citizenship ; and many of them opted for the latter. Denied of their trade licences and work permits, these Asians, who had opted for British passports, now wanted to migrate to Britain.[128] This alarmed the British government and in February 1968, they hurriedly introduced a Bill in the Parliament seeking to curb the right of these Asians (with British passport) to enter Britain.

A detailed analysis of the political background to the Commonwealth Immigrants Act (1968) is not intended here.[129] Two points should, however, be noted. In the first place, the law was based on discrimination on ground of colour because it created, in effect, two classes of British citizens on the basis of the colour of skin. There was a difference between the 1962 and the 1968 Acts. The former aimed at controlling immigration from the Commonwealth countries, especially from the new Commonwealth. That in itself could have been justified on the ground that the British government was under no obligation to allow citizens from these countries to migrate to UK. But the 1968 Act denied the right of entry to persons who were British citizens. It was a breach of commitment entered into at the time of Kenya's independence negotiations—and a breach of great significance, as it affected one of the basic human rights, that of citizenship. Secondly, as the available evidence showed, the British government acted in haste. The fears of an endless flow of migrants pouring into Britain were exaggerated. As an investigation by *The Sunday Times* (London) showed, out of a total of 192,000 Kenya Asians, only 100,000 enjoyed the right of unrestricted entry to Britain.[130] Taking into account the number of Asians who were unable or unwilling to make the journey, "It is improbable", concluded the same enquiry, "that the total number of potential immigrants who will enjoy unrestricted entry into Britain will exceed 65,000". This was approximately the same as the number of labour vouchers issued to non-Commonwealth aliens in 1966.[131] Reports from London about further restrictions on entry caused panic among the Asians in Kenya ; and increased the rush for beating the barrier before it was erected.[132] The fear among the Kenya Asians, which started the exodus to Britain for more than 10,000 in February 1968 alone, subsided as quickly as it started. As *The Guardian* reported, during the two months after the enactment of the Act, only 350 applications for entry vouchers had been made.[133]

Within Britain, as in 1961-62, opinion was divided; and the

differences cut across party lines. When the Act was passed, a pro-Labour weekly characterised it as 'the first incontestably racialist law to be placed on the statute book'.[134] It showed the alacrity with which Britain was prepared to shake-off her post-colonial responsibilities.

In New Delhi the introduction of the restrictive measures caused dismay, especially because they were being introduced by a Labour Government ; and there was a feeling that these measures constituted a 'blatant piece of racial legislation' and were designed to force the Kenya Asians back to India.[135] A senior member of the government reflected the mood of the country when he said that if the Bill was passed on the proposed basis, "we visualise a rift in Indo-British relations far more serious than anything experienced in the past, including the strains witnessed during the Indo-Pakistani war."[136]

The British government might not have wanted to 'force' the Kenya Asians back to India ; but that they would have liked to see a large number of them resettled in India became quite clear later on. In his evidence before the Select Committee on Race Relations and Immigration, the then Home Secretary Mr James Callaghan said :

> "A lot of 175,000 (Kenya Asians) were born in India, over half of them to my knowledge went to Kenya and Uganda in the late 1940s and early 1950s, when there was the upsurge of economic prosperity in these countries..."

Having been born in India, worked in Kenya or Uganda, he continued,

> "they now wish to make their home and their way in a third country. But if they are really in difficulties, as undoubtedly many of them are, I ask the question, why should they not go back to India where they were born, and make their way there until such time as in the queue their turn comes up and they are absorbed ?..."
>
> "We have a legal obligation to them. As to the moral obligation we have, that is a matter of opinion and judgement on which I do not wish to offer a view to this Committee."[137]

Whatever might have been the view of the British Government regarding their responsibility to the Kenya Asians holding British passports, the Government of India made it quite clear that they had no responsibility towards them. Nevertheless, the Indian government showed considerable moderation in dealing with the problem. At a meeting of the Executive Committee of the Congress Parliamentary Party both the Prime Minister and the then Minister of State for External Affairs, Mr B.R. Bhagat urged moderation in dealing with Britain's new law, in the face of demands for India's withdrawal from the Commonwealth, and, the nationalisation of British assets in India.[138] Mrs Gandhi appreciated Britain's difficulties in dealing with the sudden influx of Asians from Kenya ; but was anxious about the fate of thousands of people of Indian origin who might become stateless.[139] However, it was recognised in New Delhi that the Government could do little more than offer sympathy to fellow Indians.

The Government was, however, anxious not to be faced with the prospect of a sudden influx of people from Kenya, and introduced regulations to prevent it. Mr B.R. Bhagat informed the Lok Sabha that the Kenya Asians holding British passports would not be allowed to enter India for permanent residence. The Indian government had introduced new regulations, he said, "not as a retaliatory measure but to emphasise the urgent necessity of establishing the citizenship of Kenya Asians, irrespective of their country of origin."[140] He added that the Kenya Asians would be allowed to enter India on humanitarian and compassionate grounds, but only for a temporary period. It was emphasised, however, that the Government of India was not prepared "to acquiesce even indirectly in any attempt to hinder the right of these people to enter the country of their nationality."[141] He concluded by saying that unless Britain liberalized the quota system, India would 'seriously consider' the question of withdrawal from the Commonwealth.

The oft-repeated threat to quit the Commonwealth was meant for public consumption at home, and to put pressure on the British Government to liberalize the terms of entry for the Kenya Asians. Despite the possibility of a diplomatic row developing between New Delhi and London, the two governments handled the matter with considerable diplomatic skill. The Government of India had already made it known to the British Government through their High Commissioner, Mr John Freeman, that India would be prepared to act as a 'clearing house', until the problem was solved, if the entry quota for the Kenya Asians had been raised (to 15,000 per year).[142] Confidential negotiations therefore started between the two Governments. By the middle of June, Mr Praful Patel, the Secretary of the Committee on UK Citizenship, claimed on returning from a fact-finding tour of East Africa and India, that nearly 75 per cent of the Kenya Asians holding British passports, who were still in Kenya, were willing to return to India.[143] In July 1968, Britain and India agreed to a formula which would give the Kenya Asians the right to enter India, if they were expelled from Kenya.[144] The British government agreed to endorse their passports, giving the immigrants the right to enter Britain at any time in future. This face-saving compromise formula considerably eased the immigration deadlock created by Britain's Immigration Act, and India's subsequent entry restrictions on Kenya Asians.[144a]

III

Colonial and racial questions often gave rise to differences between the British and the Indian governments, and on occasions strained their relations. Given their different historical backgrounds, this was quite natural and even inevitable ; but the maintenance of close links between them through India's membership of the Commonwealth considerably influenced British attitudes and policies towards colonial and racial problems.

So far as colonial issues were concerned, the differences between the two governments related not to the question of independence for the colonies, but to the method and timing of particular acts of decolonisation. Disagreements between them were more frequent during the early phase of Britain's withdrawal from empire, particularly between 1951-56, than during the late fifties and sixties. There were two principal reasons for this. In the first place, in the post-Suez years, particularly after 1959, the British government adopted a policy of withdrawal from empire which increased the speed of decolonisation in Africa and the Middle East. In fact, one of the criticisms of British colonial policy in later years was that the transfer of power became an exercise in Lancaster House conferences.[145] Secondly, because of her preoccupation with events nearer home —mounting pressure of economic problems coupled with the deterioration in relations with China—and also because of the emergence of new states in Africa with a militant anti-colonial posture, India's policy on liquidation of colonialism became more realistic and less rhetorical in the post-Suez years. This trend continued in the sixties, with the single but notable exception of Indian military action in Goa in December 1961. During the Belgrade conference of non-aligned states in September 1961, Nehru appealed to his fellow neutralists not to rush through the process of decolonisation too fast. This call for moderation did not, however, satisfy the Africans ; for in 1961, though colonialism was a dying force in Asia, it was still lingering on in Africa. New Delhi's later decision to send troops to Goa may be seen as an attempt to restore India's credentials as an anti-colonial Power among the Afro-Asian states.

With the liquidation of most of the overseas empire by the European powers, and with the increasing rivalry among the super-powers for the extension of economic, political and strategic domination of the new states, colonialism assumed a new form in the post-War world. This neo-colonialism was influeneed by two factors : doctrinal antagonism between the super-powers, and the political and economic weaknesses among the new states.

The response of the British and the Indian governments to such new forms of imperialism at once revealed the differences between them as well as the extent to which their freedom of action in international affairs has been lost due to excessive dependence—in their different ways—on the two super-powers. The Government of India have been mildly critical of Soviet interventionist policy in Eastern Europe as was evident from their action (or inaction) during the Hungarian crisis of 1956 and the Czechoslovakian crisis of 1968. In 1956, one of the factors limiting India's freedom of action was the dependence on the Soviet Union for diplomatic support against Pakistan in the Kashmir dispute. In 1968, India's policy was further compromised by her dependence on the Soviet Union for economic aid and trade, and, as a major supplier of arms for the defence forces. Moreover, India looked for Russian neutrality, if not support, in her quarrels with China and Pakistan.

India was more critical of US imperialism in Asia, and this was largely due to the fact that after the Second World War the United States assumed the role of the policeman of the world and thus got *directly* involved in local conflicts, far away from the American continent in a way which the Soviet Union tried to avoid. American involvement in Korea and Vietnam are examples. In both these cases, the British Government supported American policy. In the Korean war the British Government did not take any initiative—despite China's warnings conveyed through Ambassador Panikkar[146]—to persuade USA not to extend the war by crossing the 38th parallel. Again, while the British Government were quick to condemn the Soviet Union for violating the independence of such states as Hungary and Czechoslovakia, they either remained silent or gave open support to the United States for similar action in South-East Asia and Latin America.[147] The British government's failure to register any public protest against US action in Vietnam was conspicuous.

With the virtual liquidation of traditional colonial empires in the sixties, racial issues became a more important cause of tension in international relations. India's policy of opposition to racial discrimination—especially discrimination against the Indians overseas—was a cause of conflict in Indo-British relations since the beginning of this century. This was closely linked with the policy of anticolonialism ; for the two evils of colonialism and racialism were thought to be the result of European expansion and settlement in non-European lands. India was fiercely critical of South Africa's policy of apartheid, but the treatment accorded to the Indian minorities in Ceylon (renamed

Sri Lanka) met with tempered criticism. Similarly, Kenya Government's policy of Africanisation of the economy, which led to hardship and harassment for many non-citizen Asians living in Kenya gave rise to relatively muted criticism in India. Probably this was due to the desire not to aggravate an already unhappy situation. But resentment against UK ran high when the British Government introduced, in 1968, entry restrictions on the East African Asians holding British passport. Similarly Britain's refusal to use force to overthrow the rebel minority regime in Rhodesia has invariably been associated, in India, with the reluctance of the British Government to use force against the 'whites' who are, after all, the kith and kin of the British.

A significant aspect of the racial question which became particularly evident in the 1960s was the extent to which it led to the polarisation of attitudes. In the continuing psychological war between different races in Southern Africa, leading in many cases to violence and suppression, there was little hope for a neutralist posture. For the British Government this posed a new problem. Britain was at the centre of a multi-racial Commonwealth, was opposed to the policy of racial discrimination, but claimed at the same time that this should not stand in the way of her bilateral trade, cultural or military links with South Africa. This dual role of the British government was already under severe pressure during the late 1960s ; whether Britain can maintain this dual role without damaging her relations with the non-white Commonwealth countries, especially her relations with black Africa, remains to be seen. Racial discrimination in South Africa is no longer a problem between New Delhi and Pretoria, with London acting as the mediator ; that relationship ended in 1947. Racial discrimination in South Africa and Rhodesia has become a matter of international concern. What became particularly significant in the 1960s was that in the campaign against the racialist regimes, New Delhi was overtaken by Lusaka and Dar-es-Salaam. To that extent racial issues have become less a cause of tension in Indo-British relations as such, than a cause of conflict in Britain's relations with the non-white members of the Commonwealth.

NOTES AND REFERENCES

1. C.J.M. Alport ; 'Indian Policy and the Colonies', in the *New Commonwealth,* 12 October, 1953.

2. J.M. Lee : *Colonial Development and Good Government* (Clarendon Press, Oxford, 1967), Chap. I.

3. See, Maurice and Taya Zinkin ; *Letters from India* (Conservative Political Centre, London, 1958), p.23. On the central issue of the settler colonies, support for the interests of the white minority came principally from the Conservative Party, especially its "settler lobby". The leadership's awareness of the latent strength of this group was high among the factors that prevented the successive Conservative Governments between 1951-1959 from taking initiatives which would have tipped the balance of power away from Europeans towards Africans. It was only after 1959 that the composition and attitudes of the intra-party majority changed sufficiently to allow new bounds to be set for policies towards these settler colonies. See D. Goldsworthy : *Colonial Issues in British Politics 1945-61,* (Clarendon Press, Oxford, 1971) especially pp. 34-35, 384-85.

4. For a brief discussion on British attitudes towards colonies, see, Rita Hinden : *The Colonies and Us* (Fabian Society Socialist Propaganda Committee, London, n.d., Pamphlet No. 4). For a discussion of the attitudes of the Labour Party and the Conservative Party see D. Goldsworthy, *op. cit.*, especially, Chaps. IV and V.

5. For example, in 1948-49, the views of the two governments were almost similar on the question of Indonesian independence ; again, during the Geneva Conference of 1954, there was considerable agreement between the two Governments regarding the policies to be followed for bringing an end to the French colonial war in Indo-China.

6. Nicholas Mansergh : *The Commonwealth Experience* p. 401.

7. For a selection of representative statements on British colonial policy see *Problems of Parliamentary Government in Colonies* (The Hansard Society, London, 1953), Appdx-C.

8. See K. Robinson ; 'World Opinion and Colonial Status' in *International Organisation,* vol. 8, No. 4., November 1954, p. 468. Mr Robinson was formerly an Assistant Secretary in the Colonial Office.

9. He said in the House of Commons on 13 December, 1950 : "As has been repeatedly stated by His Majesty's Government with the assent of all parties, our object is self-government within the Commonwealth." *Hansard* (Commons), Fifth series, vol. 482, Col. 1165.

10, See, Oliver Lyttleton : *Memoirs of Lord Chandos* (Bodley Head, London, 1962), p. 352. Oliver Lyttleton was the Secretary of State for Colonies between 1951 and 1954.

11. *ibid.*, p. 387.

12. There were, in fact, proposals for three such federations, two in Africa—the proposed East African Federation, comprising of Kenya,

Uganda, Tanganyika and Zanzibar which never materialised, and the Central African Federation including Southern Rhodesia, Northern Rhodesia and Nayasaland, which was formed in 1953 to be broken up in 1963—and one in the Caribbean, the West Indies Federation, established in 1956.

13. As it happens, Mr. Macmillan never intended this phrase to be symbolic in quite the same way. See, Anthony Sampson : *Macmillan : A Study in Ambiguity* (Allen Lane, the Penguin Press, 1967), pp. 189-90.

14. N. Mansergh ; *op. cit.*, p. 402.

15. See M. S. Rajan ; *The Post-War Transformation of the Commonwealth : Reflections on the Asian-African Contribution* (Asia Publishing House, London, for the ISIS, 1963), and especially pp. 17-19. Also see Chap. I, pp. 20-21 above.

16. The Conservatives were particularly aware of this. The fervour with which imperial preferences were advocated during the European debates of the annual conference of the Conservative Party, between 1945 and 1950, is perhaps an example of this. See, for example, the assertion of Ju ian Amery at the 1948 Conference. "We have got to be quite clear about it," he said. "Empire preference is a foundation of our whole economic life." *Conference Report*, 1948 (National Union of Conservative and Unionist Association), p. 67. Also see, D. Goldsworthy ; *op. cit.*, pp. 169-173.

17. Colonial holdings of sterling in London rose from 12% to 32% of total holdings between 1945 and 1955. "London was borrowing short and lend ng long, and doing well on it," was the sharp comment of a British Marxist author. See, M. B. Brown : *After Imperialism* (Heinemann, London, 1963). p. 218. Also see W.A. Lewis ; 'The Colonies and the Sterling' in the *Financial Times*, January 16, 1952.

18. See below,

19. See, John Hatch ; 'The Opposition's Part In Colonial Policy', a B.B.C. lecture reprinted in *The Listener*, 25 April, 1963. Mr Hatch was the Labour Party's Commonwealth Officer, 1954-61, director, Commonwealth Department, 1958-61, Member, Fabian Colonial Bureau (FCB) Advisory Committee, 1954-58, and Member, FCB. 1958-62 ; Commonwealth Correspondent of the *New Statesman*. He is the author of several books and articles on colonial affairs.

20. J.M. Lee, *op.cit.*, p. 195.

21. See. N. Mansergh ; *op. cit.*, p. 402.

22. See G.L. Goodwin ; 'The Commonwealth and the United Nations' in *International Organisation* (Summer, 1965, vol. XIX, No.3, p. 687).

23. This was represented in its extreme form by such papers as the *Daily Express*, the *Daily Mail* and *The Daily Telegraph*. See, for example, the reports and editorial comments on the Indo-Portuguese dispute over Goa in *The Daily Telegraph* (7 August 1954), the *Daily Express* (7 August

1954), the *Daily Mail* (18 August, 1955) and in all of these, during December, 1961, at the time of India's annexation of Goa. Even an elite newspaper like *The Times* (London) adopted a posture towards the Goa dispute which was far from being favourable to India. See, for example, the two articles, 'India's Designs on Goa', in *The Times*, 25 and 26 August, 1955, by the Special Correspondent of the paper.

24. See, e.g., C.J M. Alport ; *op. cit.* Lord Alport was the Chairman of the Joint Central African Board, at the time of writing the article. He was Under-Secretary of State for Commonwealth Relations between 1957-59 ; Minister of State, CRO, between 1959-61, and later became British High Commissioner (1961-63) to the Federation of Rhodesia and Nyasaland.

25. Alan Burns : *In Defence of Colonies* (Allen & Unwin, London, 1957), pp. 143-155. Ser Alan was a colonial administrator, and for 9 years he was Britain's representative to the Trusteeship Council. The list of names is not intended to be exhaustive.

26. See Chap. 1, Sec. II, a (ii).

27. Oliver Lyttleton ; *op. cit.*, p. 339. Also see, Alan Burns, *op. cit.* p. 149. The then Indian High Commissioner to East Africa explained to me in an interview, in later years, that the policy of the Government of India was to support the movement for liberation in all the colonial countries. The fact that the Mau Mau rebellion was violent seemed to be irrelevant in the general context of anticolonialism ! He, however, strongly denied the allegation that the activities of the Indian High Commission went beyond the bounds of diplomatic propriety.

28. J. Nehru : *India's Foreign Policy : Selected Speeches, Sept. 1946-April, 1961.* (Publications Division, Ministry of Information and Broadcasting, Government of India, New Delhi, 1961), p. 131.

29. Alan Burns, *op. cit.*, p. 143.

30. Speaking before the Constituent Assembly (Legislative) on March 8, 1949, Nehru said that India, as a meeting ground between the East and the West, and 'because of geography, because of history, and because of many other things' was destined to play a very important role in Asia. J. Nehru : *Independence And After* ; a collection of the most importont speeches of Nehru from September 1946 to May 1949 (Publications Division, Government of India, New Delhi, 1949), p. 231.

31. Nehru's attitude to communism was, however, ambivalent and remained so throughout the rest of his life. He was attracted by tde idea of a classless egalitarian society, but did not like the violent anh authoritarian methods of communism.

32. See, M. Brecher : *India and World Politics : Krishna Menon's View of the World*, p. 301.

33. Mr. Nehru said : "...do Honourable Members of the Conference realise that the NATO today is one of the most powerful protectors of colonialism ?...I am not saying that indirectly, but directly and explicity,

Here is the little territory of Goa, India, which Portugal holds. We get letters from the NATO Powers...telling us 'you should not do anything in regard to Goa, you should not do this and that.' I will not mention these Powers; they are some of the so-called Big Powers. It does not matter what Powers they are, but it is gross impertinence". See R.I.I.A.; *Documents on International Affairs 1955.* (OUP, London, 1958). p. 417. Among others, Nehru surely had Britain in mind.

34. M. Brecher; 'Neutralism: An Analysis' in M. Brecher: *New States of Asia: A Political Analysis* (O.U.P., London, 1963), p. 119.

35. Anthony Eden: *Full Circle: Memoirs of Sir Anthony Eden* (Cassell, London, 1960), p. 545.

36. This becomes evident from the account of the events given in later years by the then Indian Ambassador to Moscow and Budapest. See, K.P.S. Menon: *The Lamp and the Lampstand* (O.U.P., Bombay, 1967), pp. 100-06.

37. *Lok Sabha Debates*, pt. 11, Vol. IX, No. 4, 1956, cols. 378-84.

38. *ibid*, col. 388.

39. Quoted in James Eayrs; *The Commonwealth and Suez*, (OUP, London, 1964), p. 399.

40. *ibid.*

41. *The Sunday Times*, 1 August, 1954.

42. *The Times*, 3 August, 1954. On 5 August, 1954, the *Manchester Guardian* while supporting India's claim to Goa, warned that attempts to pass off demonstrators with arms as being non-violent would not win respect.

43. For the text of the Foreign Office statement, see *The Times*, 7 August, 1954.

44. See report by the Diplomatic correspondent of *The Sunday Times*, 8 August, 1954.

45. See the report by the London correspondent of *The Hindu*, 8 August, 1954.

46. Cited in *ibid.*

47. *The Times*, 10 September, 1954.

One British journal pointed out that a clue to Portugal's obstinacy and British support for it could be found in Dr Salazar's reference to NATO. This 'little Portugal' in Asia 'provided a strategic trouble-spot in India's flank which could be turned into a NATO supply and trooping base at the time of a crisis. France used both Pondicherry and Pakistan airfields for reinforcements in Indo-China. See, the *New Statesman and Nation*, 14 August, 1954.

48. *The Hindu*, 10 August, 1954.

49. See the *Manchester Guardian*, 10 August, 1954.

50. See, Chap. 1, Sec. II, a (i).

51. See *Hansard* (Commons), 5 series, vol. 531, col. 242, written answer. It is significant to note that this conciliatory statement was

made by a minister in CRO, though the earlier statement on the dispute was made by Mr Selwyn Lloyd, the Minister of State in the Foreign Office. This might have been simply a matter of division of responsibility. Relations with India, as a member of the Commonwealth. were dealt with by CRO, whereas relations with Portugal were dealt with by FO. But perhaps the difference in the nature of the two statements also indicates that there was some difference between FO and CRO regarding the policy to be adopted towards the Indo-Portuguese dispute over Goa. On the theme of differences between FO and CRO, see Chap. 1, Sec. II, a(i).

52. See *The Times*, 22 September, 1955. In a letter to *The Times*, on 7 November, 1955, a group of Labour MPs, also, called for mediatory efforts by the British Government in the Indo-Portuguese dispute.

53. For the report on Bulganin's speech, see *The Hindu*, 29 November, 1955 ; for the Dulles-Cunha communique, *ibid.*, 4 December, 1955.

54. See J.K. Galbraith : *Ambassador's Journal : A Personal Account of the Kennedy Years* (Hamish Hamilton, London, 1969), pp. 274-75 and 282-83. Also see, Arthur A. Schlesinger (Jr.) ; *A Thousand Days : John F. Kennedy in the White House* (Houghton A. Mifflin, Boston, 1965), pp. 526-30.

55. The Ball-Mcghee Proposal urging the Government of India to announce a six months' suspension of any possible military action against Portugal in Goa. It was proposed that by that time the United States would make a major effort with Portugal. The nature of the effort was, not, however, disclosed. See J.K. Galbraith, *op.cit.*, pp. 284-85.

56. See, Krishna Menon's interview with Prof. Brecher in M. Brecher : *India and World Politics ; Krishna Menon's View of the World*, pp. 126-28.

57. See N. Maxwell : *India's China War* (Jonathan Cape, London, 1970) pp. 227-32.

58. *ibid.* The Government of India's action might also have been intended as a measure to divert public attention from the more serious confrontation between the Chinese and Indian forces along the Sino-Indian border in Ladakh.

59. See *The Hindu*, 10 Dec. 1961, *The Times*, 14 Dec. 1961 and the *New York Times*, 14 Dec. 1961.

60. See B.M. Kaul : *The Untold Story* (Allied Publishers, Bombay, 1967) p. 300.

61. *Hansard* (Commons). Fifth series, vol. 651, col. 948 (Italics added).

62. SCOR, 16th year, 987th. mtg., 18 December, 1961, p. 18.

63. S/5033, sponsored by the UK, the US, France and Turkey.

63a. See, Paul Gore-Booth : *With Great Truth and Respect*, p. 277.

64. Cited in *ibid.*, p. 278.

64a. See Mrs Pandit's observations during the first session of the General Assembly, *GAOR*, 1st session, Pt. 11, Plenary mtg., pp. 732-33.

65. For a discussion on this point, see G. L. Goodwin : *Britain and the United Nations* (Manhattan Publishing Co., N. York, 1957), pp. 261-68.

66. See G. L. Goodwin ; 'The Political Role of the UN. Some British Views' in *International Organisation*, Autumn 1961, vol. XV, no. 4.

67. *GAOR*, 7th session, 393rd plenary mtg., p. 210.

68. For details see, R. N. Barkes and M. S. Bedi : *The Diplomacy of India : Indian Foreign Policy in the United Nations* (Stanford University Press California, and OUP, London, 1958), pp. 158-196. Also, see T. R. Reddy : *India's Policy in the United Nations*. (Fairleigh Dickinson University Press, Rutherford, 1968), Chap. 3.

69. R. N. Barkes and M. S. Bedi ; *op. cit.*, p. 178.

70. See the statement by the British representative to the Fourth Committee of the General Assembly, on October 3, 1947. *GAOR*, 4th Committee, 2nd session, p. 33.

71. For an interpretation of the Britlsh view, see G. L. Goodwin : *Britain and the United Nations*, pp. 353-59.

72. A de-colonisation committee set up by the General Assembly in 1961 with 17 members. In 1962 the Committee was expanded with the addition of 7 more members.

73. Res. 1514 (XV). Declaration on the granting of independence to colonial countries and peoples. (14 December, 1960). For the text of the resolution, see, *GAOR, Resolutions*, 15th session, Vol. I, Suppl. No. 16, pp. 66-67.

74. See, K.J. Twitchett ; "The Colonial Powers and the United Nations" in *Journal of Contemporary History*, Vol. 4, no. 1, Jan. 1969, p. 184.

75. Rupert Emerson : 'Colonialism' in *ibid.*, pp. 6-7.

76. For further discussion on this point, see sec. II. below.

77. The Union of South Africa came into existence by an Act of the British Parliament in 1909, and the constitution which that Act provided established franchise in three out of the four provinces, foı the white population only.

78. See, N.V. Gadgil : *Government From Inside* (Meenakshi Prakasan, Meerut, 1968), p. 55. N.V. Gadgil was a member of the cabinet between 1947 and 1952. Also see Jawaharlal Nehru's statement in the Lok Sabha on 3 February, 1950, as reproduced in *Jawaharlal Nehru's Speeches 1949-53* (Publications Division, Ministry of Information & Broadcasting, Govt. of India), 2nd impression, New Delhi, p. 273.

79. See, C. Kondapi : *Indians Overseas* (O.U.P. for ICWA, Bombay, 1952), p.5.

80. This point has been developed in A.T.Yarwood : 'The Overseas Indians as a Problem in Indian and Imperial Politcs at the end of World War One' in *The Australian Journal of Politics and History* (Vol. XIV, No. 2, August, 1968).

81. C. Kondapi ; *op. cit.* p. 7.

82. This promise was made in Lord Salisbury's despatch of 24 March 1875, which stated that Indian settlers, upon the completion of their terms of service, 'will be in all respects free men, with privileges no

what inferior to those of any other class of Her Majesty's subjects resident in the colonies.' Cited in A.T. Yarwood ; *op.cit.* p. 205.

83. The Government of India raised the question at the Imperial War Conferences of 1917 and 1918, and at the Imperial Conferences of 1921 and 1923.

84. W.K. Hancock : *Smuts* : *The Fields of Force* (*1919-50*), (Cambridge University Press, Cambridge, 1968), Ch. 26.

85. Cited in Hancock ; *op.cit.*, p. 453.

86. *ibid.*, p. 473.

87. For a detailed discussion on the Indo-South African dispute in the United Nations and Britain's attitude to it, and also for a discussion on the larger issue of apartheid, see, T.B. Millar : *The Commonwealth and the United Nations* (Sydney University Press, Sydney, 1967, Ch. IV). Also see, R.H. Wagenberg ; *Commonwealth Reaction to South Africa's Racial Policy* (*1947-61*), London, Ph.D. thesis, 1966.

88. *GAOR*, Ist Session, pt. 11, joint Ist and 6th Committees, 2nd mtg ; 25 November, 1946, p. 14.

89. A/*2183*.

90. Res. 134 (1960), of 1 April, 1960, for the text of the resolution see, *SCOR*, *Resolutions and Decisions*, 1960, 15th yr., pp. 1-2.

91. Speaking before the Special Political Committee of the General Assembly on 5 April, 1961, the British delegate said that while the importance attached by the British Government to Article 2.(7) of the Charter remained undiminished, it now regarded apartheid so exceptional as to be "sui generis". See, *GOAR*, 15th session, Spl. Political Committee, 242 mtg , 5 April 1961, p. 77.

92. Res. 1761 (XVII), adopted on 6 November, 1962. This was the first occasion when the United Nations endorsed for sanctions, against a member-state. For the text of the resolution, see *GAOR*. *Resolution*, 17th session, Suppl. 17, pp. 9-10.

93. Res. 182 (1963) adopted on 4 December, 1963 ; for the text, *SCOR*, *Resolutions and Decisions*, 1963, 18th yr., pp. 8-10.

94. See, G.L. Goodwin ; *Britain and the United Nations*, p. 264.

95. Colin and Margaret Legum : *South Africa* : *Crisis for the West* (Pall Mall, London, 1964), P. 124.

96. G.D.N. Worswick ; "The Impact of Sanctions on British Economy" in R. Segal (ed) : *Sanctions against South Africa* (Penguin Special, Harmondsworth, 1964), P. 185.

97. In 1961, 1962, 1963, British imports from South Africa as a % of total British imports were 2.4%, 2.3%, and 2.4% respectively ; and exports to South Africa constituted 4.0%, 3.9 % and 4.8% respectively of total British exports. See G.D.N. Worswick, *op.cit.*, p. 180. To Britain South Africa was, therefore, more important than India, from the economic point. British investments in South Africa far exceeded their investments in India ; trade with South Africa was also more profitable, as

Britain had always a trading surplus with South Africa. For figures on British investment in India and on Indo-British trade, see Appendix II.

98. U.N, Doc. S/6210, February, 1965. Prof. Worswick, however, thought that a trade embargo. if imposed by UN, would have marginal effects on the British economy, See, G.D.N. Worswick ; *op.cit*, p. 185.

99. See, Colin & Margaret Legum, *op.cit*,, pp, 246-51.

100. See R.H. Wagenberg, *op,cit.*, pp. 65-66.

101. See P. Calvocoressi ; "The Politics of Sanction ; The League and the United Nations" in R. Segal (ed) ; *op.cit.*, p, 59.

102. For a discussion on this see E.J.B. Rose et. al. ; *Colour and Citizenship* (O.U.P. For the Institute of Race Relations, London, 1969). Also see, N. Deakin ; "The Politics of the Commonwealth Immigrants Bill" in *Political Quarterly*, January-March 1968.

103. See, N. Deakin, *op.cit.*, p. 29.

104. The Bill became an Act of Parliament in 1962. For the political background to the Act, see N. Deakin ; *op.cit*.

105. See the statement by Mrs Lakshmi Menon, Dy. Minister for External Affairs, in the Lok Sabha on 4 December, 1961. *Lok Sabha Debates*, Second series, vol. LX, Col. 2927.

106. *ibid.*, col. 2928.

107. *ibid.*, col. 2929.

108. *Hansard* (Commons) fifth series, vol. 649, col. 709.

109. *ibid*, col. 799.

110. See N. Deakin, *op.cit.*, p. 38.

111. *The Times*. 14 November, 1961.

112. *Hansard* (Commons) 5 series, 1964-65 session, vol. 705, col. 1284.

113. *ibid.*, col. 1285.

114. *ibid.*

115. See statement by Prime Minister Mr Wilson on 9 March 1965, in the Commons : *Hansard* (Commons), 5 series, 1964-65 session, vol. 708 col. 249.

116. Other countries visited by the delegation were Canada, Nigeria, Jamaica, Trinidad, Malta, Cyprus and Pakistan. In the last named country, the team was led by the deputy leader, Sir Charles Cunningham the then Permanent Under-Secretary in the Home Office, as Lord Mountbatten was *persona non grata* in Pakistan.

117. *Hansard* (Commons), 5 series 1964-65 session, vol. 714, col. 247.

118. Ministry of External Affairs : *Report 1965-66* (Government of India, New Delhi), p. 94.

119. *Hansard* (Commons), 5 series 1964-65 session, vol. 714, cols. 247-48.

120. Angus Maude : "Immigration and the Eaten words" in *Daily Telegraph*, 18 July, 1968.

121. *Hansard* (Commons), 5 series, 1964-65 session. vol. 714, cols. 248-49.

122. *Cmnd.* 2739, *Immigration from the Commonwealth* (H.M.S.O., London, 1965).

123. *ibid.*, p.2.

124. *ibid.*, p.2, and pt. III.

125. For the details of the new restrictions, *ibid.*, pp. 6-9. A useful summary of these regulations may also be found in Ministry of External Affairs ; *Report 1965-66*, p. 94.

126. During 1964 and '65, respectively 61 and 167 Indian nationals were refused entry by the immigration authorities in Britain, mostly on the ground that they would seek employment, but did not have employment vouchers. See, M.E.A. ; *Report 1965-66* (New Delhi), p. 95. In 1966 and '67, respectively 173 and 612 Indian nationals were refused entry. See *Report 1966-67*, p. 74, and *Report 1967-68*. p. 82.

127. M.E.A. ; *Report 1967-68*, p. 82.

128. The new trade licencing laws did not affect those Asians who had taken up Kenyan citizenship.

129. For such a discussion, see David Steel : *No Entry : the Background and Implications of the Commonwealth Immigrants Act, 1968*. (Hurst, London, 1969). Mr Steel is a member of Parliament, and was one of the leading opponents of the Act.

130. See INSIGHT : 'The Great Immigration Scare' in *The Sunday Times*, 18 February, 1968.

131. *ibid.*

132. See, R. Kershaw ; 'How London Panicked Nairobi' in the *New Statesman*, 1 March, 1968.

133. *The Guardian*, 28 April, 1968.

134. *The New Statesman*, 1 March, 1968.

135. See, report by Peter Hazelhurst in *The Times*, 26 February, 1968.

136. *ibid.*

137. *Select Committee on Race Relations and Immigration : Minutes of Evidence : The Home Secretary* (1969-70 session), 13 May, 1970. (H.M.S.O., London, 1970), H.C. 17-XXVII.

138. See, *The Times*, 5 March 1968.

139. *The Daily Telegraph*, 27 February, 1968.

140. See *The Times*, 7 March, 1968.

141. *The Guardian*, 7 March, 1968.

142. *The Times*, 5 March, 1968.

143. *The Times*, 13 June, 1968.

144. *The Times*, 27 July, 1968.

144a. For further discussion on British immigration laws and their implications for Indo-British relations, see, A.K. Banerji ; "Unburdening an Imperial Legacy : Colour, Citizenship and British Immigration Policy" in *India Quarterly* (New Delhi), October-December, 1976 : Also, A.K. Banerji ; "British Immigration Laws : A Surrender to the Extremist Lobby" in *The Statesman*, 23 Aug. 1972.

145. W.P. Kirkman : *Unscrambling an Empire* (Chatto & Windus. London, 1966).

146. David S. K. McLellan ; "Dean Acheson and the Korean War" in *Political Science Quarterly,* March 1968, pp. 20-21.

147. See, E.F. Penrose ; 'Britain's Place in the Changing Structure of International Relations' in E.F. Penrose et al. ; *New Orientations : Essays in International Relations* (Frank Cass, London, 1970), p. 58.

CHAPTER VI

INDO-BRITISH ECONOMIC RELATIONS : 1947-68

THE MAIN theme of this chapter is an analysis of Indo-British economic relations since India's independence. The foundation of this relationship was laid during the period of colonial rule;[1] and independence of India did not mean a complete break with the past.

At the time of the transfer of power, India's dependence on Britain, in economic matters, was overwhelming. British investments constituted nearly 80 per cent of the total foreign investments in India, and in 1948-49, Indo-British trade accounted for more than a quarter of India's total foreign trade. The trade links were strengthened by India's membership of the Sterling area, and by a system of preferential trading arrangement with the Commonwealth countries, evolved under the Ottawa Agreement of 1932.

The dependence on UK, however, declined over the years. In the first place, this was the result of a deliberate policy of the Indian Government to try to reduce dependence on any one state by developing new channels of trade, and by attracting foreign aid and investment from various sources. Secondly, the relative decline in Britain's international position as the supplier of economic aid also accounted for the decline of Britain's importance to India.

The main trends in economic relations between Britain and India can be depicted in outline in terms of : (a) the changing pattern of trade between the two countries, and, Britain's involvement in India's economic development as (b) a supplier of foreign investment and (c) as a donor of economic aid.

I

INDEPENDENCE AND AFTER : THE EVOLUTION OF POST-COLONIAL RELATIONSHIP

(a) *The Changing Pattern of India's Trade with Britain*

No other single factor can more pertinently reveal the loosening of economic links between Britain and India than the changing pattern of their bilateral trade. In 1948-49, UK accounted for nearly 26 per cent of India's total foreign trade ; in 1964-65 Indo-British trade constituted no more than 15.28 per cent of India's total foreign trade. This becomes clear from the following table.

TABLE-1[2]

Direction of India's trade with Britain
(Value of Merchandise in Rs. Lakhs)[3]

Year	India's total foreign trade (1)	Trade with Britain (2)	(2) as a % of (1)
1948-49	966,23	250,64	25.93
1953-54	1,102,72	296,33	26.87
1958-59	1,425,14	322,86	22.65
1963-64	2,016,09	335,13	16.62
1964-65	2,165,33	330,95	15.28

Since independence there has been a two-fold change in India's foreign trade, viz. in volume and in direction. Imports more than doubled between the years 1948-49 and 1964-65. This was due to large imports of capital goods and machineries to meet the needs of planned economic development, as well as the import of large quantities of food-grains from abroad specially from US to meet food shortages. Britain's share in this increase in imports was less than proportional. In 1948-49 she accounted for nearly 28.6 per cent of total imports to India ; her share fell to 12.1 per cent in 1964-65.[4] Since 1960-61, imports from Britain declined in value as well as a percentage of total imports to India.[5] This was the result of a number of causes ; (a) rapid import substitution, (b) deliberate diversification of India's trade links to reduce dependence on any one state, and (c) the influence of tied aid in changing the suppliers' share in India's imports.

Import substitution has been effected both to conserve the scarce foreign exchange. and to encourage indigenous production of the imported commodities. As a result, some of the traditional items of imports from UK have been hit. It has also been the policy of the Government of India to diversify India's international trade to reduce dependence on any one state. During the Third Five-Year Plan the direction of India's international trade changed in such a way that it considerably undermined the importance of UK as the predominant trading partner. Another factor accounting for the decline in Britain's share of the Indian market was her relatively small contribution to the total aid received by India from various sources. Commenting on this the authors of a report on India wrote in 1963 that Britain's export supremacy in India was being undermined by the latter's dependence on foreign aid in which Britain could not lead, and that the outstanding fact for the British exporter was that his share in the growing imports of India depended almost entirely on Britain's share in the growing aid to India.[6]

India's exports to Britain also declined as a percentage of total exports, but the rate of decline was less than that of imports from Britain. At the time of India's independence Britain was India's largest customer, and remained so till the end of the period under review. India's exports to Britain rose steadily from 23.2 per cent of total exports in 1948-49 to a peak of 31.9 per cent in 1954-55 ; and from then with the exception of the year 1958-59 showed a continuous downward trend.[7] However, looking to the value of exports, it becomes evident that exports to Britain were more or less stagnant between the years 1958-59 and 1964-65, with a minor boom during the year 1960. One of the reasons for this is that nearly 70 per cent of India's export earnings from U.K. was accounted for by five commodities, viz. tea, cotton-textiles, jute manufactures, oil-cakes and tobaccos, and demands for all of them except oil cakes have been either stagnant or on the decline.

The commodity composition of India's export trade changed significantly during the Third Plan. Although tea, cotton-textiles, and jute manufactures continued to be the principal export-earners, their share in the total exports declined from 48 per cent in 1960-61, to 43 per cent in 1965-66.[8] At the same time, there was increase in the export of a number of non-traditional goods in the engineering and chemical fields.

The decline of India's tea exports to UK was the result of stagnation in total consumption in the importing country which may be seen from the actual decline in total imports of tea in Britain between 1957-69.[9] It was also the result of competition from other producers in the Commonwealth, notably Ceylon (Sri Lanka), and the countries in East Africa.[10]

Cotton textiles have also been an important item of India's export to UK. In the post-War years, India's cotton manufactures had a ready market in Britain. But difficulties arose during the late 1950s, because of increasing competition from other developing countries, and also because of increasing demands for protection made by the Lancashire producers. Because of the Indo-British Trade Agreement of 1939, Indian cotton textiles enjoyed duty-free entry in UK market, and the British Government could not unilaterally impose quota restrictions on imports from India. In 1957, the Cotton Board in UK initiated discussions with the producers in India and Pakistan for 'voluntary limitation' on their exports to Britain, and after protracted negotiations, such an agreement was announced in 1959. The agreement was to come into force from 1960.

However, even with the system of general quotas, import of cotton textiles in Britain reached 53 per cent of total consumption by 1969.[11] The greater part of these imports entered duty-free ; in 1969 the Government decided to introduce, as from 1 January 1972, a tariff of 15 per cent on imports from the Commonwealth preference area, and to terminate the existing system of general quotas. Announcing this in the Parliament, the President of the Board of Trade said :

> "There is no reason to think that, with the possible exception of India, the developing countries of the Commonwealth generally will be able to send less to Britain over a tariff of this amount than they would under a continuation of the quota system."

So far as India was concerned, he assured the House

> "the Government will, when the time comes to determine the level of aid to India after 1972, take into account, against the background of India's general aid

requirements at the time, any adverse effects on her exports arising from the tariff."[12]

The decision of the British Government caused concern in India. Matters came to a head in the summer of 1971, when the Indian Trade Minister refused to grant a waiver to the British government, and even hinted at the possibility of retaliatory measures against British interests in india.[13] The British Government, in turn, gave notice for the termination of the Indo-British Trade Agreement of 1939. Indo-British relations were strained at a time when India needed Britain's diplomatic support over the Bangladesh crisis. It seemed to many observers that the Indian Trade Minister, the late Mr L.N. Mishra, was partly to be blamed for the situation. India's cotton textile exports to Britain were around £ 11.7 m. a year, and as a result of the British government's decision, India was to lose about £ 1.8 m. annually.[14] To offset this the British Government offered a compensatory aid of £ 10 m. Even the estimated loss was likely to taper off, after Britain's entry to EEC with its system of duty-free quotas for cotton textiles. But Mr Mishra's refusal to grant the waiver to the British Government, and the latter's hint at the possibility of terminating the Indo-British Trade Agreement (1939), in fact exposed Indian goods to the risk of British duties all along the line. As an Indian commentator put it, "Mr Mishra has cheerfully thrown the baby out with the bath water."[15]

India, though not a major supplier of sugar, sells part of her exportable surplus to UK. She acceeded to the Commonwealth Sugar Agreement (CSA) in 1965 which provided that each exporting territory shall receive the price settled by negotiation as being reasonably remunerative for a specified quantity of sugar sold to Britain. Under this agreement India sold 25,000 long tons of sugar to Britain every year at an agreed price ;[16] the rest of the exportable surplus was sold at 'free' world price. Originally, the Agreement was for 8 years. In 1968, it was amended for an indefinite duration, with a provision for review every three years beginning in 1971.

This arrangement was changed after Britain joined EEC. According to the British Government's White Paper, "The

Government's contractual obligations to buy agreed quantities of sugar under the CSA from all participants, including Australia, until the end of 1974, will be fulfiilled";[17] after that, there was only a declaration of intent that the enlarged community will have as its 'firm objective' the safeguarding of interests of the developing countries. At a meeting of the Commonwealth sugar producing countries, held in London in June, 1971, this arrangement was accepted as satisfactory.

During the 3rd Five Year Plan, there were notable changes in the geographical distribution of India's export trade. While the value of exports to the Western European countries recorded a small decline, exports to USA increased. But the most important development was the increase in India's exports to the East European countries whose share in India's exports rose from 7.7 per cent to 19.6 per cent in 1965-66 (see Table II below).

TABLE II[18]

Geographical distribution of India's Export during the Third Plan (as % of total exports)

Region	1960-61	61-62	62-63	63-64	64-65	65-66
I. W. Europe	37.3	34.3	34.4	31.7	29.6	27.2
of which						
(a) E.E.C.	8.1	8.2	7.9	7.8	7.0	6.8
(b) U.K.	26.8	23.7	23.1	20.6	20.5	18.1
II. Asia & Oceania	25.8	25.9	23.5	27.1	25.0	23.2
of which ECAFE countries	22.1	22.4	20.3	23.3	21.7	19.6
III. Africa	7.6	8.3	7.0	5.8	5.7	7.6
IV. Americas	21.5	22.0	22.1	21.7	22.1	22.3
of which USA	16.0	17.0	16.2	16.4	18.0	18.3
V. East Europe	7.7	9.5	13.0	13.7	17.6	19.3
of which USSR	4.5	4.7	5.4	5.6	9.5	11.5

With the demand for tea remaining stagnant, heavy competition from other Commonwealth countries in cotton-textiles, and with the availability of substitutes for jute-bags and hessians; and above all, with the imposition of quota restrictions on the import of jute and cotton-textiles in Britain—the most important items of India's manufactures sold to Britain—this shift of emphasis reflected an economic rationale as well as deliberate reorientation of policy.[19]

India's importance to Britain, economically, has been much less than Britain's importance to India. In 1948, Britain's exports to India constituted 6 per cent of total British exports overseas; in 1966 India's share of British exports fell to 1.8 per cent, and it declined further afterwards.

One of the reasons for the decline in Britain's exports to India was no doubt, the realtive decline in her position vis-a-vis the United States as the donor of economic aid. The amount of British aid to India was much less than that given by the United States. Not all of this aid was tied to purchase from UK. Another cause for the fall in British exports to India seems to be the deliberate redirection of Britain's trade and salesmanship towards the high-income countries of West Europe and North America. By taking a look at the top ten items of British exports during the last decade it can be seen that there was a remarkable increase in the export of such commodities as non-electrical complexes of different kinds, chemical and petrochemical products, cars and aeroplanes—products more in demand in the developed economies of the world. No wonder, therefore, that Britain became sceptical of the value of the Indian market, and the then Foreign Secretary, Michael Stewart during his visit to India in December, 1968, characteristically explained this by his remark that 'the economic advantages to Britain from past relations were fast dwindling.'[20] The decline in Anglo-Indian trade may, therefore, be explained by India's import-substitution, the influence of tied aid in changing the suppliers' share in India's imports, and by the deliberate policy of redirection of trade by Britain.*

*Lack of officially guaranteed medium-to-long term credits for exports to India, delay in delivery, and Britain's worsening price competitiveness, at least until the 1967 devaluation of the Pound-Sterling also seem to have adversely affected British exports to India. See, M. Lipton and J. Firn; *op. cit.* p. 39.

(b) *Britain as a source of foreign investment* :

The flow of foreign capital in a country may take two forms : the form of loans and grants from foreign governments or international institutions (which we shall call aid) ;[21] and the form of investment by private individuals or corporations which we shall describe as foreign private investment.

India has for long been a field for foreign investment—and before independence this meant chiefly British Investment. The opening of the Suez Canal in 1869 gave a fillip to British investors who now increasingly turned their eyes to the East. The years between 1870 and 1914 probably saw the peak of foreign investment in India which was, for all practical purposes, British investment.[22] After 1919 British investment continued to flow in, but the rate had slowed down till the curve had taken a backward turn in 1942 following the political turmoils of the period.

When India became independent she was desperately short of capital investment that was needed to lay the foundations of a modern industrial economy. The leaders of India were apprehensive of the role of foreign capital as it was identified with foreign domination, and therefore, at the initial stage they were rather hesitant about it. There was an atmosphere of uncertainty about the future of the private sector in India ; added to this were the periodic outbursts by Indian leaders against foreign capital, which discouraged the flow of foreign private capital in the country. The Industrial Policy Resolution of 1948, though welcoming the participation of foreign capital and enterprise in the rapid industrialisation of the country, did not go far enough to encourage foreign investors. Foreign investment policy was further elaborated by Nehru in his statement to the Constituent Assembly on 6 April, 1949. Foreign Capital was recognised as an important supplement to domestic savings, and foreign enterprises were assured equal treatment with domestic enterprises.[23] But for the first few years the response of the foreign investors was very poor.

At the time of independence, Britain was the chief source of foreign capital. According to a survey by the Reserve Bank of India, in 1953, British investments in India stood at Rs. 347

crores and constituted more than 80 per cent of the total foreign investments in the country.[24] Britain had some advantage over other foreign competitors. Because of their long association with the country, British investors were better acquainted with the conditions in India than their American or West German counterparts. Secondly, though the Government of India followed an open-door policy towards foreign capital and, in theory, offered equal opportunities to all foreign investors, in practice the officials would in many instances favour the British. This was the feeling among many American observers of the Indian economic scene.[25]

Throughout the period under study, Britain was the principal supplier of foreign capital to the Indian private sector although its share in total foreign investment was declining. Thus in 1962, British investments in India (Rs. 482.8 crores) accounted for nearly two-thirds of total foreign investments in the country, but its share declined to 57 per cent in 1964, to 41 per cent in 1968, and further to 36 per cent in 1972.[26] This is because Britain's share of the total capital inflow has been declining over the years. Between 1948-53, British share in the total capital inflow had been 90 per cent, it came down 70 per cent in 1953-54, and to 65 per cent in 1956 and fell further to 57 per cent between the years 1956-61.[27] The decline becomes even more precipitous if the flow of public funds into the private sector is taken into account (largely because of the flow of capital from the Soviet bloc). Therefore in India, "British and foreign investments are no longer the near-synonymous once they were."[28]

There have also been changes in the pattern, nature and the field of British investments in India. In the past, most of the investments were in branches or in wholly-owned subsidiaries of British Companies ; in recent years, on the other hand, joint ventures with Indian companies are on the increase. Moreover, in the past, investments were mostly in plantations, mining, and in services related to international trade. The picture in the sixties was different.[29] No doubt, British investors had a large stake in tea, and in shipping ; but the trend of investment in the post-independence years has been in the direction of manufacturing industries, with a large British stake also in petroleum.

British investments in India cover a wide variety of industries such as iron and steel, automobiles, agricultural machinery, radio equipment and cables, transport equipment, chemicals and fertilisers, sugar and textile machineries. Among the British investors in India are some of the giants of the British industries.

The ICI, with their subsidiary the Alkali and Chemical Corporation of India Ltd. hold the key position in explosives, paints and chemicals ; in dyestuff (in collaboration with the Atul products) and in plastics and insecticides. They have played an important role in the development of the nitrogenous fertiliser industry in India ; they acted as the consultants to the Government of India for the Sindri Fertilizer Factory—the country's first public sector factory in fertilisers. In 1967, they themselves entered the field by setting up a fertiliser factory in Kanpur. Another famous British firm Fisons, have long been associated with the Tatas (Tata-Fison) for the manufacture of pesticides. Tata-Fisons have recently acquired an interest in Rallis (India), who are manufacturing phosphatic fertilisers in Kanpur.[30] Bakelite Ltd. (of the De La Rue group) are collaborating with two Indian firms, the Hyderabad Laminated Products and the Bombay Burmah Corporation respectively, for the manufacture of finished plastic products.

Apart from the public sector steel plant at Durgapur, British firms have made a valuable contribution to the development of the iron and steel industry in India. Since 1945, the Indian Iron and Steel Co. at Kulti (West Bengal), have been collaborating with a British firm in the production of spun iron pipes ; F.H. Lloyd & Co. of Staffordshire have been associated with the Chittaranjan Locomotive Works, for the manufacture of cast iron. Stewarts & Lloyds of Glasgow have collaboration agreement with Indian Tubes (Jameshedpore) for the manufacture of steel tubes. Guest, Keen and Nettlefords of Birmingham and their Indian associates Guest, Keen and Williams have a major stake in the production of a wide range of screws, nuts and bolts.

In the field of electrical machinery and equipment almost all the important British firms are represented. One of the pioneers in the field were Crompton Parkinson of London, who first started the production of electric fans in India. Greaves Cotton and Crompton Parkinson now produce a wide range of electrical equipment in India, and offer general consultancy services. Three of the leading British firms, the Associated Electrical Industries (AEI), the English Electric Co and the General Electric Co. produce a wide range of electrical equipment in India ; and the AEI—now merged with GEC—are acting as consultants to the Heavy Electricals factory at Bhopal – a Government of India undertaking. Another public sector project, the Indian Telephone Industries, are collaborating with the Automatic Telephone and Electric Co. Ltd. of London.

A large number of British firms have collaboration agreements with Indian firms in the general engineering industries, including shipbuilding, boiler-making, machine tools, textile machinery, stationary engines, and mining and agricultural machinery. One of the biggest collaborating enterprises ACC-Vickers-Babcock, a combination of Associated Cement Companies of Bombay, Vickers Ltd. of London, and Babcock and Wilcox Ltd. of London are engaged in the manufacture of a wide range of engineering equipment. Besides John Thompson of London and Cochrane and Co. of Scotland are collaborating with Indian Sugar and General Corporation at Yamnanagar, and the Structural Engineering Works at Bombay, respectively, for manufacturing boilers.

During the period under review jute mill machinery manufacture was British-controlled. All the three firms, which between themselves supplied almost the entire world demand, were operating in India either through their subsidiaries, or in collaboration with other Indian firms.[31]

Ship-building and aircraft manufacturing industries are in the public sector, but in both these industries collaboration agreements have been concluded with some leading British firms. Thus in the ship-building industry, Simons-Labnitz of Glasgow concluded an agreement in 1964 with Indian Government Shipyards at Mazagaon and in Calcutta for the construction of three Leander class vessels in India. The Government of India also concluded agreement with the British firms (Folland Aircraft for the air-frame and the Bristol-Siddeley for the aero-engines) for the production of Gnat fighters in India under licence. In July 1959 the Government of India concluded an agreement with the British firm Hawker Siddeley for the manufacture of a military version of the Avro-748 transport planes in India.

Two of the three types of commercial vehicles now being produced in India are manufactured in collaboration with British firms. The Birla firm, Hindustan Motors Ltd., is producing Ambassadors in collaboration with the British Motor Co. Ltd. of Birmingham and the Triumph Herald is being produced in India by the Standard Motor Products of India Ltd. in collaboration with the Standard Motors, Coventry (now a part of the Leyland group) ; Leyland buses are being produced in India by Ashok-Leyland. Tube Investments of India Ltd., a British subsidiary, along with their two associates, T.I. Cycles of India Ltd. and the Sen-Raleigh Industries of India Ltd. control the bicycle industry. Motor cycles and scootars are being produced by Enfield India Ltd. In the production of electrical accessories Messrs Joseph Lucas (Industries) Ltd. of Birmingham are collaborating with three Indian firms, while in the production of non-electrical accessories, the Dunlops have a dominant position. They produce tyres of all kinds, including rubber hoses for industries, and the earth-moving and construction equipment, transmission and rayon cord etc.

In some branches of the glass and ceramics industry also the British firms had a dominant position. Production of plate glass was under the monopoly control of the Hindustan Pilkington Glass Works Ltd.[32] Hindustan Pilkington are also a major producer of sheet glass, an important branch of the glass industry in India. Messrs Doulton & Co. of London are collaborating with the Parrys of Madras for the production of high-quality sanitary ware.

British capital had an important share of the oil industry in India. The Government of India had, no doubt, exclusive rights in the matter of prospecting, and in the production of crude oil. But the Burma Oil Co. through its 50 per cent share in the Government-owned Oil India Ltd., was active in prospecting oil. In oil refining, Burmah-Shell was the biggest producer in the private sector, producing nearly half the total production by private sector refineries.[33] Burma Oil also branched out in other business. Besides running the largest refinery and marketing organisation in the private sector, they were the sole producer of tinplates in the private sector and a major producer of cans,[34] as well as being shippers and contractors.

The drugs and pharmaceuticals industries in India are dominated by foreign firms, British, American and Swiss. Among the British firms are some of the household names such as the Boots Pure Drug Co. Ltd., the Glaxo Group, the Burroughs Welcome and Co. Ltd., the British Drug House and the Beecham Group Laboratories (India) Ltd.

The British firm Hindustan Lever Ltd. has a controlling position in the production of detergents and toiletries ; they are also a leading producer of food articles, specially those with a high proportion of manufactured content. The British along with the Americans control nearly two-thirds of the tobacco industries in India, and the British firm Imperial Tobacco Co. (India) Ltd. (now named as Indian Tobacco Co. Ltd.) is the largest producer in the country.

Since independence British capital has thus been firmly entrenched in the manufacturing industries in India in the private sector ; and down to the end of the 1960s continued to hold the dominant position in some of the industries. Other areas where British capital had been concentrated were the traditional areas of investment—plantation, mining and international trade. So far as plantations are concerned, most of the British capital had gone in the production of tea—India's most important foreign exchange earner. As late as 1960-61, of the 12 biggest tea plantations (by total crop) not one was Indian.[35] All processing factories were foreign-controlled as late as 1960, and two British firms handled nearly 85 per cent of the retail distribution within India.[36] The export trade was a British monopoly, and the tea machinery manufacturing industry was virtually British-controlled.

In the mining industry, the influence of foreign capital is on the wane. But some British managing agencies controlled coal-mining.[37] In the production and smelting of copper, the Indian Copper Corporation Ltd., a British-controlled firm, were the only producer till the mid-sixties.[38] In the production of lead, The Rio Tinto International Metal Co. Ltd. is operating in India through its financial control over the Metal Corporation of India Private Ltd.

It follows from the facts mentioned above that India's foreign private sector is still very much dominated by the British. Others are, no doubt, taking interest, the chief among them being the United States in the field of finance capital, and USA, W. Germany and Japan, in the field of technical collaboration.

However, though British investors remained the biggest suppliers of foreign investment in the private sector, Britain's share of the total foreign investment in India was declining. In the case of subsidiaries, Britain's share of the foreign paid-up capital in manufacturing industries declined from 75.8 per cent in 1960-61, to 68.6 per cent in 1963-64 ; in the case of minority capital participation firms, Britain's share went down from 57.2 per cent in 1960-61 to 44.5 per cent in 1963-64.[39]

The same trend becomes evident if one looks to India's foreign collaboration agreements. Between 1948 and March 1964, the Government of India granted approvals for about 2,200 foreign collaboration agreements, of which about four-fifths were by companies. The agreements were divided into three categories ; (1) minority foreign capital participation, (2) subsidiaries, and (3) pure technical collaboration. The country-wise classification of agreements indicated that the United Kingdom accounted for 40 per cent of the total, the United States for about 19 per cent, and West Germany for 14 per cent.[40] The United Kingdom accounted for 56 per cent of the agreements by subsidiaries, but for only 38 per cent of the agreements in other groups. The share of the UK in newer agreements was declining and the higher proportion of agreements by subsidiaries with the UK was explained by fewer new agreements in subsidiaries.[41]

Between the years 1060 and 1966, there was a sharp decline in the flow of net UK direct investment in India. In 1960 investment in India constituted 14.1 per cent of net British overseas direct investment, the figure came down to 2.0 per cent in 1966.[42] The sharp decline in UK investment in 1966 might have been due to the political uncertainties in the aftermath of the Indo-Pakistan war of 1965, and the wave of anti-British feelings which had swept through the country during the period. But to be able to explain the declining trend of British investments in India, we must look to other causes.

Low rate of return has not been a major factor affecting the flow of British investments in India. According to a survey by the Reserve Bank of India, the return on investment for the British firms in India was 11.9 per cent, and 9.5 per cent for the years 1953 and 1955 respectively ; the average earning of the British firms at home for the two years were between 8-9 per cent.[43] Profits were thus higher in India than at home. There is no particular connection between profitability of an industry's overseas operation and the rate of its expansion there. This becomes clear from the following table.

TABLE III[44]

UK direct overseas investment in selected countries

Country	Addition to net operating UK assets during the years 1955-64 £ million	Average pre-tax profitability (%) (1955-64)
India	70.4	21.2
South Africa	34.9	14.6
Australia	170.6	13.8
USA	101.9	13.6
Canada	201.8	8.9

In the above table we have taken the cases of five countries which were the first five recipients of UK investments during the period 1955-64. It shows that though the average pre-tax profit on UK investments in India has been higher than the rates in all other countries under consideration, the flow of net direct investment has been highest in Canada, followed by Australia and the United States in that order. This is because the most powerful force making for additional investment is not necessarily the rate of profit ; a high rate of return on existing capital does not necessarily mean that a high rate would be earned on substantial additional investment. What is more important as an incentive for additional investment is, possibly the growth of the market for the company's products.[45] The rates of growth of the economies of Canada, Australia and the United States were higher than the rate of growth of the Indian economy. This explains one of the reasons for the decline in the rate of British investment in India.

Secondly, the pattern of British investment in India for the period 1960-66 reflects the general trend of British investments in the states east of Suez. In all these states except Japan and Hong Kong—a British Colony—British investment declined between 1960-66, though the rate of decline has not been the same in all cases. This might have been due to the absence of the political guarantees which the *Pax Britannica* once gave to the whole of South and South-East Asia. But "Duncanism" in investment and trade diplomacy was in operation even before the Duncan report[46] was published.

Finally, the additional flow of British investment in India during the middle sixties was arrested by the measures adopted by the British government to discourage investments overseas. In 1965 faced with a large balance of payments deficit, the Chancellor of the Exchequer, Callaghan, introduced in his budget fiscal measures that would discourage the companies investing abroad. The various taxes which the Government proposed, on top of the Corporation Tax, particularly affected companies whose major interests were abroad, especially the overseas trading corporations—mainly rubber, tin and tea-planting companies—that did not pay any profits tax so long.[47]

These measures were perfectly sensible ; for, given Britain's balance of payments problem and the size of the gold reserves, which was then at half the size of West Germany's, the government was overstretching the state's reserves by trying to police a major part of the world, by maintaining the role of the pound sterling as a world currency, and by allowing British investors to invest overseas on a considerable scale. However, the fiscal measures introduced by the Labour Government to check the flow of investments abroad, were likely to affect the flow of investment to the developing countries. As the *Financial Times* pointed out, "...a company thinking of operating in India will have to see a profit rate 70 per cent above that of the stay-at-home counterpart, to make the game worth the candle."[48]

(c) *British official economic aid to India's economic develpoment*

For a country such as India, with a low rate of growth and dearth of capital necessary for rapid industrialisation, foreign aid can play an important role, provided it is utilised with the right priorities.[49] This was realised by the policy-makers in India at an early stage of economic development.

It should, however, be recognised at the outset that the philosophy of foreign aid is based on considerations of mutual benefit, that it is beneficial to the state at the receiving end as well as to the state giving aid. The donor may, no doubt, be moved by moral considerations, that it is a moral responsibility for the developed nations of the world to help the under-developed in achieving the 'break-through' in the process of economic development. But the decision to give aid is also influenced by considerations of the donor's self interests. By giving aid it expects to gain some benefits in the form of increased trade, and in the long run, political influence on the decision-making process of the recipient. Considerations influencing the policy of foreign aid, therefore, are not only economic and humanitarian, but also political.

It is necessary, therefore, to make a distinction between aid and charity, as the term 'aid' has come to acquire, in common parlance, the odium of charity which—in the context of inter-state relations—it is not. When we talk of foreign aid, it means, principally, two things ; (a) loans, given by the donor states or international institutions at rates below the opportunity cost, and (b) grants in the form of technical assistance and training.[50] Most of the aid is used by the recipient for purchasing goods from the donor. Aid, therefore, is one way of increasing trade. In 1969, UK provided about 7.5 per cent of the total flow of aid, but received nearly 12 per cent of the orders for goods imported by the developing countries of the world from the developed ones.[51]

It is natural, therefore, to contend that by giving aid to India Britain has not only helped in the process of her economic development, but also expected a greater share of the increased activities induced by this development. Whether she has achieved it is, however, a different question. The then British Foreign Secretary, Mr Michael Stewart, during his visit to India in December 1968 said that though British aid to India had doubled during the last seven years, her exports to India declined over the same period.[52] Apparently the situation might seem to be paradoxical ; but in fact this was related to Britain's position as a donor of aid. As the authors of the F.B.I. report on India put it : "The new development imports into India are in effect a trade created by aid, and only on proportion that Britain is able to supply the aid, can she secure the trade."[53]

TABLE IV[54]

External assistance received by India from all sources till March 1966 (in Rs. Crores)

Country/ Institution	loans	grants	P.L.480/665 & third country currency assistance	Total aid authorised upto March 1966	Total aid utilised upto March 1966
	1	2	3	4	5
IBRD/IDA	741.5	—	—	741.5	581.5
USA	1284.1	166.4	1598.2	3048.7	2605.2
USSR	484.3	1.2	—	485.5	283.3
W. Germany	442.3	2.1	—	444.4	341.7
UK	364.6	1.4	—	366.0	293.1
Others	546.7	168.7	—	715.4	377.0
Total	3863.5	339.8	1598.2	5801.5	4481.8

It is quite evident from the above table that so far as economic aid is concerned, India was more dependent on the United States than on Britain. This was largely because of the paucity of Britain's own resources ; India's needs were out of proportion to Britain's capacities. If one looks to the total authorisation of aid till the end of March 1966, it becomes evident that the list of donors was dominated by the United States. Countrywise, Britain was the fourth largest donor of economic assistance to India, the second and third places being taken by USSR and West Germany respectively. However, if one considers the amount of aid utilised as distinguished from the amount of aid authorised, Britain's position was above that of the Soviet Union. (See Table IV)

But Britain's role in the economic development of India can not be properly assessed by looking at the aid figures in absolute terms. What is more important in this connection is the total mobilisation of resources in the form of aid and investment. The total of authorised British aid to India during the three Five-Year Plans amounted to Rs. 3664.3mn (approximately £263.35mn) of which nearly 99.5 per cent (Rs. 3493mn) was in the form of loans through Aid-India Consortium. The rest (Rs. 18mn) was technical assistance provided in the form of grants under the Technical Cooperation Scheme of the Colombo Plan. In addition to these, Lazard Brothers, a syndicate of British banks, extended a credit of £11.5 mn for the Durgapur Steel project.[55]

The amount of aid given under the general heading of technical assistance covers a wide range of activities both in Britain and India. The most important of these are : (a) education and training, (b) supply of experts and consultants, and (c) the supply of equipment for training and research. Much of the work in the field of education and training is undertaken by the British Council. An example of the largest single item of technical assistance is the Indian Institute of Technology at New Delhi.[55a]

What is the impact of British aid on the Indian economy ? It is important to note that unlike loans from the United States or IBRD/IDA, British aid has generally avoided fields like the railways, transport and communications, power etc. which may be said to constitute the industrial infrastructure. It had a set pattern, and most of the aid has gone to the industrial and manufacturing sectors. The chief beneficiaries are : steel (of which the Durgapur Steel complex has received the largest share), industrial development, and technical assistance and training. In a sense, the bulk of British aid can be identified with certain projects. Besides Durgapur, other major industrial projects assisted by Britain are : (a) an oil pipe-line in Assam, (b) the Heavy Electricals Plant at Bhopal, (c) a fertiliser plant at Naharkotiya in Assam, and (d) the Hindustan Cables Ltd. at Rupnarayanpur, in West Bengal. There can be little doubt that this concentration of British aid on certain havy industrial projects was motivated by political considerations ; and this suspicion is confirmed by the fact that British loan for the largest of these plants (at Durgapur) was not forthcoming till the Russians came out with their offer to build the steel mill at Bhilai.[56] And if one looks to the performance of these projects, it has certainly been far from satisfactory. To take the example of Durgapur, again, when one compares the performance of the three public sector steel plants at Bhilai, Durgapur and Rourkella built with Russian, British and German aid respectively, the position of Durgapur is at the middle.[57] Of course, this unsatisfactory performance reflects more the inefficiency of Indians than the fault of the aid-givers. It is also true that stringent conditions attached to selection of projects by the donor is liable to be misunderstood at the receiving end. But as most of British aid has been identified with some prestige projects, their failures are quickly associated with that of the donor country. It was with this possibility in mind that the Estimates Committee of the House of Commons recommended in its report on overseas aid, that in future in countries like India and Pakistan the emphasis of British aid should be on the agricultural sector.[58] The government also decided in the latter half of the 1960s that in giving aid to the developing countries more attention should be given to such projects as rural development, employment opportunities and family planning. Mr Albert Oram, Parliamentary Secretary in the

Ministry of Overseas Development told the House of Commons on 24 October, 1964 "we have increased our support for the International Parenthood Federation in developing countries from £6,000 to £50,000 a year and we have announced our readiness to contribute to the UN Trust Fund for population control activities. We are ourselves giving priority to all requests for aid in this field, and a Population Bureau, attached to the Ministry, will be set up shortly to increase our ability to give expert assistance on these matters. As a result, we shall be spending four times as much in 1967-68 on assistance to family planning overseas as we did a year ago."[59]

The character of aid is as important as the quantum of aid, and in this respect Britain has been one of the path-setters. She was one of the first countries to recognise the importance of non-project aid for the developing countries. During the Second Plan, slightly over three-fourths of British aid (nearly 77.4 per cent) was non-project aid, and during the Third Plan more than half of British aid was in the nature of non-project aid. During 1966-67 and 1967-68, all British aid was non-project aid.[60]

There is a further type of aid known as the 'Kipping aid', which takes the form of loans for the supply of spares and components for British-oriented industries. It was originally suggested by Sir Norman Kipping, the then Chairman of the Federation of British Industries, during his visit to India in 1963, as it was felt that for a comparatively small expenditure there could be a vast increase in industrial production by the fuller utilisation of capacity.

Britain has also progressively softened the terms of loans over the years. The loans granted during the Second Plan were to be repaid over periods varying between 6½ to 20 years. Terms were further liberalised during the Third Plan period, and loans granted during the Plan were to be repaid over a period of 25 years, with the provision of a grace period of 4-7 years during which no payments were to be made. The interest rate was similarly linked with the British Government's borrowing rates for a comparable period, while no payments were to be made during the first seven years for the loans granted during the last two years of the Third Plan. The credits authorised by UK since October 1966 were wholly interest free.

India received the highest amount of bilateral aid given by Britain to any state, and this was on the increase at a time of Britain's own financial difficulties. A large portion of this aid could be utilised by India for supporting her own balance of payments. But if one looks to aid in relation to population, net British aid to India was one-tenth of the total British aid to all Commonwealth countries in Africa (excepting Rhodesia), and about one-fiftieth of British aid to countries in Central and South Africa.[61] The usual official explanation is that whereas countries like India can look to other sources, countries of Central and South Africa are entirely dependent on Britain.

The most disquieting feature about British aid to India was that about half of Britain's assistance went back as re-payments of past loans and in the form of interest. The British Government tried to ease the situation by giving part of the aid as 'refinancing' loans, i.e. as loans to cover the cost of old ones. But so long as British aid was pegged to a constant figure, 'refinancing' loans would have to come from a fixed allocation, leading to reductions in other forms of aid.

What is the effect of British aid on the UK balance of payments ? If loans are considered as overseas assets, Britain's long-term-external position is actually strengthened by aid. Even in the short-run, a considerable portion of British aid to India returns direct to the donor country by way of repayment of debts, and to this extent represents no loss to the balance of payments. Further, taking into account the substantial indirect benefits and orders Britain gains from other countries' aid programme, it can be argued that Britain actually stands to gain from her overseas aid policy. Indeed, this has been one of the arguments put forward by the aid lobby in Britain in support of their assertion that by giving aid to the developing countries, Britain ultimately stands to gain.[62]

Private Transfer Payments

If we think of aid and investments as transfer of resources, and consider their impact on the balance of payments, one newly important element should also be considered. This is the substantial remittance made by Indian immigrants in Britain back to India. Any assessment of the quantum and importance of this factor can be no more than tentative, as no definitive record of such remittances is available. From the evidence to the House of Commons' Select Committee on Race Relations, it was estimated that Indians send £10m annually to India.[63] This figure must be treated with caution, as a large part of such remittances is made through unofficial channels. Indian official sources do not publish, separately, details of annul remittances by Indians living in Britain. However, it is possible to get some idea of relative magnitudes and flows by looking at India's Regional Balance of Payments on Current Account. Assuming that a large portion of private transfer payment to India from the sterling area countries is actually made from Britain, the annual average for such payments may be estimated between £10m-£20m, during the years 1962-63 and 1966-67, with substantially higher figures, in rupees, for the year 1965-66.[64]

Such remittances are a gain to India's balance of payments, and they partly offset the traditional flow of resources from India to Britain. It was estimated, in 1970, that "£20m is being annually sent to Britain from India by way of dividends."[65]

II

The Traditional Links : (A) The Imperial Preferences and (B) The Sterling Area

In the preceding section we have seen that India's economic dependence on Britain has gradually declined because of the diversification of India's foreign trade, and the sources of foreign investment, and above all, because of the greater reliance on the United States and on other donors for aid. In this section the theme will be further developed by analysing the declining importance of two of the traditional economic links between Britain and India : (a) the Imperial Preferences and (b) India's membership of the sterling area.

In the thirties, the Imperial Preferences were important for both Britain and India. They gave the British an edge over the Japanese competitors in the Indian market : Indian primary products also had a guaranteed entry to the British market at a price which was above the rock-bottom level. This was specially valuable at a time of collapsing prices for products like edible oils and oil seeds, which constituted important items in India's export list. But the value of preferences had been much less for either of the two countries than has usually been recognised. Preferences were of little importance for two-thirds of Indian exports. There was no competition for jute textiles, which was one of the chief items of Indian exports ; and competition for tea came from within the empire. On the British side, similarly, the real threat to British exports came less from "other foreign countries than from India's own growing industries."[66]

The value of the preferences has declined further since the War. The traditional items of exports on which India had enjoyed large margin of preferences even in the fifties (e.g. items like edible oils and oilseeds) no longer bulk large in India's trade ; jute-goods and jute-bags are facing competition from substitutes ; and in addition, Dundee's textiles are getting protection from Indian competition. The decision of the British government to impose a 15 per cent tariff on cotton-textile exports from the Commonwealth countries, from 1972, was viewed with disquiet in India, as Indian exporters were already hardpressed to compete in the international market. With the gradual industrialisation of India what became more important to her in the post-independence years was the quota-free entry of her manufactured products in the British market, assured by the Ottawa Agreement of 1932. But even in this matter, the imposition of voluntary quota restrictions by the Government of India had taken away most of the benefits.

Indeed, many of the advantages of preferential treatment enjoyed by the British exporters in India had been greatly reduced because of the imposition of import restrictions by the Government of India. In fact, the margin of preferences became much less for both the countries due to the operation of such factors as tariff revisions, changes in the trade patterns, and the effects of price inflation on particular commodities.[67]

The value of India's membership of the sterling area has also declined. The sterling area may be described "as an association of the United Kingdom with certain other countries whose trade is financed mainly in Sterling and whose reserves are held in Sterling."[68] When India became independent she had piled up large war-time sterling balances with the Bank of England, and decided to stay within the Sterling Area. In the pre-war days, the sterling area referred to the group of countries who had their exchange rates tied to the pound-sterling, because London was their banker, financier and chief trading partner. During the Second World War the British Government imposed stringent restrictions over the spending of dollar by the member-states. In the post-War years the situation changed, especially after the independence of the colonies. Membership of the sterling area was never exactly coterminus with the membership of the Commonwealth.[69] But it was, with a few notable exceptions, roughly the same as the Commonwealth, and this constituted an important link between and among the members of the Commonwealth. Indeed most of Britain's former colonies decided to stay within the sterling area as well as the Commonwealth after gaining independence. Thus the sterling area was a sort of loose financial-cum-currency association where the member-states agreed to hold their principal foreign exchanges in sterling. The gold and dollar earnings of the member states were kept in a common fund, and there was agreement among member-states to leave their management to the Bank of England.[70] Member-states could draw upon the reserves for non-sterling purchases.

The essential merit of the system was the sort of security it provided for member-states against temporary dollar shortages. But the advanced industrialised nations benefited more than the underdeveloped ones from this system, especially during the period of the dollar gap in the late 1940s, as the colonies earned more dollars than they spent. A severe blow to the system came with the decision to embark on the plan for sterling convertibility. The easing of discriminatory exchange control against dollar purchases by the sterling area countries in 1953-54, followed by the decision taken at the Montreal Conference in 1958 to further liberalise dollar purchases had really taken away much of the special benefits of staying in the sterling area.

In the sixties, India's membership of the sterling area became simply a matter of convenience. The Bank of England had little control over India's currency rates; the decision to devalue the rupee in 1966 was taken without prior consultation with the Bank of England, nor was the decision to devalue the pound sterling in 1967 preceded by consultations among the member-states of the sterling area.[71] India now turns to IMF to tide over temporary foreign exchange difficulties, and not to the Bank of England. Similarly, when the British Pound is under pressure, the British Government looks to Washington, and to the Central Banks of the Group of Ten, rather than to the Sterling area countries. It has long been argued by informed observers that Britain can no longer afford to have the pound-sterling as an international currency, however prestigious it may appear to be politically.[72] The benefits which she used to enjoy previously by using the sterling as an international currency can no longer be realised, as most of the sterling-area member-states now run large current account deficits in their balance of payments. Moreover, the sterling area has changed its essential character. The old banker-customer relationship no longer exists; and most of the member-states now look upon it as an investment fund. As a result, the British people have to take the strain "of both a big outflow of British investment funds and a run on the bank at the same time."[73]

The banker-customer relationship between the Bank of England and the different member-states had become weak even during the fifties; this could be seen from the fact that the Bank had no power to force its clients to live within their means. Faced with a severe foreign exchange crisis in 1957, the Government of India asked Britain for a loan of £200m. This would have avoided the need to reduce the sterling balances below the minimum level which had been fixed in agreement with the British government. When the loan was refused, India continued to draw on the sterling balances, which had called for a change in the law reducing the minimum reserves to be held. The fact is that membership of the sterling area no longer forged an important link between Britain and India, and India's membership of the club during the 1960s was a matter of convenience. After the United Kingdom joined EEC, even this tenuous link was severed.[74]

The discussion may be concluded with a brief reference to Britain's membership of EEC, and the effects of British entry on Indo-British economic relations. When Britain first applied for membership of the Community in 1962, a hue and cry was raised in India about the adverse effects of the British move on the Indian economy.[75] By contrast, Britain's second attempt to join the Common Market in 1967 passed almost unnoticed in India. There were a number of reasons for this change in attitude. It was recognised in India that sooner or later Britain would join the Community as the intra-Commonwealth economic links were gradually becoming less important. It was also realised that India might get better terms from the Community by direct negotiations with the EEC authorities, rather than approaching Brussels via London. (It is significant that the size of the Indian diplomatic mission in Brussels was expanded in 1971-72, which coincided with Britain's third attempt to join EEC, and, the reduction in size of the Indian High Commission in London.) Perhaps the most important factor accounting for the change in Indian attitude was the realisation that the effects of British entry would not, after all, be catastrophic for India.

Britain joined the Community in 1973. By July 1977, when Britain becomes full member of the Community at the end of the transitional period, Indian exports to UK will lose their preferences, and will be subject to a Common External Tariff (CET) or import levies under common agricultural policy. Imports to UK from other states within the Community will, on the other hand, be duty-free. Indian goods will thus be discriminated against. Nevertheless, trade will be little affected in those commodities—primary products and raw materials—on which CET rates are very low or nil. Almost three-fourths of India's exports to the EEC member-states fall in the category of raw-materials and primary products, and many of these items already figured in the zeo-tariff list of the Rome Treaty. As a result, all these items would enjoy duty-free entry, "even after Britain and the Six work out their tie-up or exchange of tariff concession."[75a]

On the basis of 1964-65 figures Dr Dharma Kumar had calculated that India's exports to UK might fall by 10 per cent, if Britain joined the Community.[76] But since then India's exports to UK have declined as a share of India's total exports, from over 20 per cent to 11.7 per cent. The British Government also decided to impose a tariff on the import of cotton textiles from India and other Commonwealth countries in Asia from January, 1972. The Community has, on the other hand, introduced the generalised scheme of preference. Therefore the fall in India's exports to UK "will be a smaller share of a smaller total."[77]

III

Since independence the traditional economic links between the two states have thus become less important and there has been a decline in India's economic dependence on Britain, as a result of the diversification of India's international economic connections. Indo-British trade has declined as a percentage of India's total foreign trade, with imports from Britain declining at a faster rate than that of exports to that country. Secondly, British investments in India have declined as a percentage of total foreign investments in the country. Moreover, for foreign assistance India became more dependent on US than on UK, during the period under review.

The reasons for all these trends have been discussed above and need not be repeated here. What is important to note is that in spite of these changes Britain still remained an important factor in India's economic links with the outside world. Even in 1965, Britain was India's largest buyer and the principal source of private foreign investment. Moreover, Britain played a very active and helpful role in the Aid-India Consortium ; if she decided to reduce her concern for India, this might encourage similar policies by other donors to India's disadvantage.

India's importance to Britain declined too, particularly in trade. British exports to India never constituted a high proportion of total British exports ; during the last few years under review, exports to India declined both in absolute terms and as a percentage of total UK exports. As Britain has a fairly high

Trade-GNP ratio, it is not unnatural that she gave relatively less attention to a country like India to which exports in 1966 constituted less than 2 per cent of total British exports.

One significant aspect of Indo-British trade in recent years has been India's favourable balance of trade with UK, which has led to renewed efforts by the British Government to find out ways of increasing exports to India. When Mr Michael Foot, the Leader of the House of Commons, visited India in October 1976, problems of Indo-British trade were discussed with the Minister for Trade, Mr D.P. Chattopadhyay. The latter suggested during these discussions that joint ventures in third countries, particularly in West Asia, would be an excellent means for balanced growth of trade.[78] A similar suggestion was also made by the British Industrial Delegation which visited India in November, 1976.[79] This would, no doubt, involve micro-level planning by individual firms, but the task of identifying the projects in which collaboration could take place may be given to the Indo-British joint Commission.

NOTES AND REFERENCES

1. For a discussion of the various aspects of the British Government's economic policy in India, prior to independence, see, V. Anstey : *The Economic Development Of India* (Longmans Green, London, 1952, 4th edn.), and 'Economic Development' in L.S.S.O. 'Malley (ed) ; *Modern India and the West* (O.U.P., London for R.I.I.A, 1941),...D.H. Buchanan : *The Development Of Capitalistic Enterprise in India* (Frank Cass, London, 1966), M. Kidron ; *Foreign Investments in India* (O.U P., London, 1965), Ch. 1., D. Naoraji ; *Poverty and Un-British Rule in India* (London, 1901), presents the Indian nationalist view.
2. Source : Appendix II. Table 1.
3. 1 lakh = one hundred thousand. One significant aspect of Indo-British trade in recent years has been India's favourable balance of, trade with UK. For example, during 1973-74, India's imports from Britain amounted to Rs. 24,481 lakhs and exports to that country amounted to Rs. 25,839 lakhs. See, *India : A Reference Annnal 1976* (Publications Division, Ministry of Information and Broadcasting, New Delhi 1976) pp. 297-99 : Tables—19.6 and 19.7.
4. See Appendix II, Table 1.
5. *ibid.*

6. Federation of British Industries ; *India, 1963* : a report by Norman, Kipping and M. Donelan, London, 1963, pp. 6-8.

7. Appendix II, Table 1.

8. *Fourth Five Year Plan—A Draft Outline* (Planning Commission, Government of India, New Delhi, 1966), p. 93.

9. See K. Mandavawalla ; 'Problems and Prospects for Indian Tea Exports During the Fourth Five Year Plan' in *Reserve Bank of India Bulletin*, March, 1971, p. 334.

10. *ibid.*

11. See, Anthony Croslsnd's statement in the House of Commons on 22 July. 1969. *Hansard* (Commons), 5 series, vol, 787, col. 1508.

12. *ibid.*, cols. 1508-09.

13. See, K.K. Sharma ; 'Anti-British Pick on Cotton' in *The Financial Times*, 9 July, 1971.

14. *ibid.*

15. Cited in K.K. Sharma ; *op.cit.*

16. See, Foreign and Commonwealth Office ; *A Year Book of the Commonwealth* 1971 (H.M.S.O., London, 1971), p. 776.

17. *Cmnd.* 4715, *The United Kingdom and the European Community* (H.M.S.O., London, 1971), p. 281.

18. Source : *Fourth Five Year Plan—A Draft Outline*, p. 94.

19. Michael Lipton and Clive Bell ; 'The Fall in Commonwealth Trade' in *The Round Table* (No. 237, January, 1970). p. 47.

20. As reported in *The Times*, London, 9 December, 1968.

21. For a definition of the term aid, see pp. 216-17.

22. G. Tyson ; 'Foreign Investment in India' in *International Affairs*, (vol. XXXI, No. 2, April, 1955), p. 174.

23. R B.I. ; *Foreign Collaboration in Indian Industry* : *Survey Report*, (Bombay, 1968), p. 2.

24. R.B.I. ; *Report on the Survey of India's Foreign Liabilities and Assets as at the end of 1953*. (Bombay, 1955), p. 86.

25. J.B. Cohen, for example, wrote : "...the Indian Government appears to have granted more favourable terms of entry to some foreign investors than its general policy statement would lead one to expect." See J.B. Cohen ; 'India's Foreign Economic Policies' in *World Politics* (July 1953), p. 56.

26. See Appendix II, Table III ; and *Reserve Bank of India Bulletin*, July 1975, p. 425.

27. *Reserve Bank of India Bulletin*, September 1958, p. 1012, and R.B.I. ; *India's Foreign Liabilities and Assets, 1961*, *Survey Report* (Bombay, 1964), p. 38.

28. M. Kidron, *op. cit.*, p. 241.

29. See, Appendix II, Table VI.

30. Materials for this paragraph and the following few paragraphs, if not otherwise mentioned, are from : J.N. Gupta et al. ; *Directory of*

Foreign Collaboration in India (de Indiana Overseas Publications, New Delhi, 1968), Vol. I. and M. Kirdon, *cp. cit.*, pp. 187-222.

31. M. Kidron ; *op, cit.*, p. 196.

32. M. Kidron : *op. cit.*, p. 217.

33. Three others in the private sector being the Esso-Standard, the Caltex and the Assam Oil Co. In 1976, the Burmah-Shell was taken over by the Government of India.

34. M. Kidron, *op. cit.*, p. 222.

35. These and several other small estates were being managed by a group of British managing agency houses : Jardine Henderson, Shaw Wallace, Duncan Bros., Davenport, Octavius Steel, Brooke Bond etc.. See, H. Venkatasubbiah ; *Indion Economy since Independencc* (Asia Publishing House, London. 2nd edition, 1961), p. 134.

36. M. Kidron : *op.cit.*, p. 189.

37. The biggest of the coal-mines, producing more than 2 million tons a year, was managed by Andrew Yule. Others producing between 1-2 million tons were managed by Jardine Henderson, Macneill and Barry, and Bird. See, H. Venkatasubbiah, *op.cit.*, p. 154. The Government of India nationalised the coal-mines in 1974.

38. M. Kidron : *op. cit.*, p. 190.

39. R.B I. ; *Foreign Collaboration in Indian Industry—Survey Report.* Statement—1, p. 114, and Statement X, p. 121.

40. *ibid.*, p. 101.

41. *ibid.*, p. 102.

42. See, *The Times* (London, East of Suez Supplement, 7 January, 1969, p. IV).

43. See, 'Returns on Foreign Investments in India 1953/55' in *Reserve Bank of India Bulletin*, May 1958, pp. 536-37.

44. Source : W.B. Reddaway et al ; *Effects of Direct UK Investments Overseas : an Interim Report* (Cambridge University Press, 1967), p. 44, Table IV. 6.

45. W.B., Reddaway et al ; *op. cit.*, p. 42.

46. *Cmnd.* 4107.

47. See *The Economic Weekly* (Bombay), 17 April 1965, pp. 662-663.

48. Cited in *The Economic Weekly, ibid* Regarding the future of British investments in India, Sir Michael Walker, the British High Commissioner said on 9 Nov. 1976 : "the amount of new British investment was going to be fairly limited" until the British investors were certain of the foreign exchange regulations in future. See *The Statesman* (Calcutta) 20 Nov. 1975. This was also emphasised by Sir Ralph Bateman, the leader of the British industrial cooperation mission that visited Indiain November 1976. See, *The Sunday Statesman* 21.11.76.

49. For an opposite and a highly critical view of the role of foreign aid in India's economic development, see B.R. Shenoy : *Indian Planning and Economic Development* (Asia Publishing House, London, 1963), p. 44-50 and 86-118.

50. Throughout the present discussion we shall use the term 'aid' in this sense. As aid is not a form of charity, the role of voluntary organisations is beyond the scope of the present study. Moreover, the contributions of voluntary organisations such as Oxfam or Christian Aid, however well-intentioned these might be, touch only the fringe of the problems in a state like India. Secondly, for our present discussions we will not include military aid within the definition of the term aid, as it is not 'economic aid' in the strict sense of the term, though this semantic difference may disappear in the case of a State which gets military assistance without paying for it. For a different definition of aid, see H.J.P, Arnold ; *Aid for Development* (Bodley Head, London, 1966).

51. Reg Prentice ; 'Aid : The Elusive 1 per cent' in *New Statesman*, 17 October, 1969.

52. *The Times*, 9 December, 1968.

53. F.B.I. : *India—1963*. A Report by Norman Kipping & M. Donelan, p.8.

54. R.B.I. : *Report on Currency and Finance* (1965-66), Bombay, 1966, p. 28.

55. *External Assistance 1965-66* (annual) Ministry of Finance, Department of Economic Affairs, Government of India, New Delhi, 1966. See, the chapter on British aid. There has, however, been a shift in emphasis as far as composition of aid is concerned. Britain's new aid strategy in relation to countries most affected by the world economic crisis and with a per capita income of less than $200 was twofold : to give all aid as outright grant and to put more emphasis on the rural sector. In pursuance of this policy Britain gave £100m aid to India during 1975 all of which was in the form of grant. See *The Statesman* (Calcutta), 20. 11. 1975, and 3.12.1975.

55a. It should, however, be recognised that India is also providing technical assistance to UK by supplying doctors and other skilled manpower, trained in India. Lipton and Firn calculated that by taking doctors from India Britain is a net receiver of £6m TA each year ; and over the 1960s, India contributed something like £60m (gross) of extra trained manpower to Britain. See, M. Lipton and J. Firn ; *op. cit.* pp. 135-37.

56. This has also been pointed out by the Estimates Committee. See Overseas Aid ; *Seventh Report from the Estimates Committee* (Session 1967-68), H,M.S.O. London, 1968, p. XXIII. Commencing with the year 1968-69 the loans for specific projects (e.g. Durgapur, Bhopal etc) have been replaced by a continuing yearly series of capital investment loans and mixed project loans, the former for importing large and small capital equipment from Britain for new or expanding projects and also for industries getting assistance through NSI, ICICI or IFC ; the latter for large projects such as Fertiliser plants on partial funding basis. See *External Assistance 1970-71.*, p. 16.

57. For a comparative study of these projects on the basis of limited

but valuable data, see, P.J. Eldridge ; *The Politics of Foreign Aid in India* (Weidenfeld & Nicolson, London, 1699), pp. 140-143.

58. *Overseas Aid* : *Seventh Report From the Estimates Committee*, (Session 1967-68), p. XXIV.

59. *Hansard* (Commons), Fifth series, vol. 751, 1966-67 session, Col. *447*, Written Answer.

60. See Appendix II, Table VIII.

61. John White ; 'Fact and Fiction in Aid Statistics', review article in *Asian Review* (April, 1968).

62. See Reg Prentice ; "Aid—What Went Wrong" in *New Statesman*, 13 August, 1971. Also see, *British Aid-2* : *Government Finance*, (Overseas Development Institute London, 1964), p. 127.

63. See *The Times*, 7 July 1970.

64. See Appendix II, Table IX. The higher figure, in rupees, for 1965-66 may be explained, partly, by the devaluation of the Rupee in 1966. It may also be due to larger remittances by individuals during 1965 and 1966 when Indian economy was experiencing a recession as a result of (a) the war with Pakistan in Sept. 1965 ; and (b) long droughts leading to drastic fall in food grains production.

65. Evidence before the Select Committee on Race Relations, as reported in *The Times*, 7 July, 1970.

66. Maurice and Taya Zinkin ; *op. cit.* p. 161.

67. See, *Economic Survey of Asia and the Far East, 1962* ; (The ECAFE Secretariat, Bangkok), p. 101.

68. A.R. Conan ; *Sterling Area* (Macmillan, London, 1952), p. VIII.

69. Canada is a member of the Commonwealth, though she is not a member of the Sterling area ; Sout Africa ceased to be a member of the Commonwealth from 1961, but continued to be in the Sterling area.

70. South Africa, though a member of the Sterling area, did not agree to the pooling of dollar resources ; but UK earned more gold and dol'ar through South Africa, than through any other member-state.

71. Unlike in 1967, the devaluation of the Pound Sterling in September 1949 was followed by the devaluation of the national currencies in the member countries of the Sterling area, with the exception of Pakistan. However, as the British Government's decision was taken without prior consultation with the Commonwealth countries, this created misgivings in New Delhi. The possibility of devaluation was not discussed even at the Commonwealth Finance Ministers' Conference in July 1949, though resolutions were framed representing the views of the Finance Ministers regarding the measures to be taken by the Sterling area countries, to increase dollar reserves. The British Government's contention, justifiably, was that any previous consultation on devaluation would defeat its very purpose. See N. Mansergh ; *Survey of British Commonwealth Affairs : Problems of Wartime Cooperation and Post-war Change* (O.U.P. for RIIA, London, 1960), pp. 344-45.

72. See, for example, Andrew Shonfield ; *Britain's Economic Policy since the War* (Penguin Special, Harmondsworth, 1958).

73. Andrew Shonfield ; *op. cit.*, p. 131.

74. Forty-four years after it was established, the rupee-sterling link was severed on 24 September, 1975.

75. See, for example, Mr Nehru's speech at the Commonwealth Prime Ministers' Conference in London on 11 Sept. 1962 in *Jawaharlal Nehru's Speeches* Vol. 4 (Publications Division, Ministry of Information & Broadcasting, Government of India, N. Delhi, 1964). pp. 397-401.

75a. D.K. Rangnekar ; *India, Britain and the European Common Market* (R.&. K Publishing House, New Delhi, for the Institute Of Public Affairs, 1963). p. 134.

76. See, D. Kumar , *India and the European Communnity* (Asia Publishing House, 1966, Chap. VIII.)

77. D. Kumar ; 'The New Community and the Developing Commonwealth' in *Round Table*, October, 1971. Also see, A. K. Banerji ; "UK's ECM entry and India : An opportunity or a challenge" in *The Hindusthan Standard* (Calcutta), 6 July, 1972.

In 1973 India and EEC concluded an agreement which, though falling short of a conprehensive treaty India had been urging since 1970, may provide a framework for expansion of trade.

78. *The Statesman*, 7. 10. '76.

79. See, *The Statesman*, 7. 11, 76 and 12. 11. 76.

Chapter VI

DEFENCE OF INDIA AND THE DECLINING IMPORTANCE OF BRITAIN

"An Integrated conception of the defence of India, and a doctrine of Indian defence supported by a consistent foreign policy are among the two major contributions of Britain to Indian people." This claim was made by one of the most perceptive Indian students of his country's defence and strategy.[1] The conception of the defence of India as an integrated unit on which the strategic thinking of independent India is based is very largely a legacy from the days of the Raj, as well as being conditioned by the geopolitical character and position of the state.

Britain made a valuable contribution to the reorganisation and modernisation of the defence forces of India, during the initial years of independence. Independent India constantly refused to join any military alliance as a matter of policy, nor has she entered into any mutual security agreement with Britain. Nevertheless, she has maintained close links with UK. After 1947 India depended on Britain as the major supplier of arms and weapons, and although she always paid for them—at least till the Sino-Indian conflict of 1962—excessive dependence on UK could, and in some cases did, affect India's freedom of action. This was quite evident from the diplomatic row preceding the Indo-Soviet MIG deal in 1962, and from the Anglo-American political pressure on India to reopen negotiations with Pakistan on the Kashmir issue, immediately after the cessation of hostilities with China in 1962. The Sino-Indian war and the reorganisation of India's armed forces, however, marked the beginning of decline in Britain's importance to Indian defence.

I

Defence And Security Of India : The Trend Of Thinking During And Immediately After The Second World War

The few books and articles on India's defence which were published during and immediately after the Second World War are of considerable importance to us as they throw some light on the current trends of thinking, in knowledgeable circles, about the future defence of India. The central point of all these discussions was whether independent India, left to herself, would be able to contain a major threat to her security posed by a first-class military power. The consensus of opinion among these writers was that India's defence could best be organised on the basis of some sort of cooperation with Britain. Sardar K.M. Panikkar, one of the high priests of this view, was convinced of the need for a long-term agreement between Britain and India for the maintenance of peace in the Indian Ocean region,[2] and thought that for India there could be no better alternative than this. In an article published in 1946 he wrote that in future peace in Asia, and perhaps in the whole world, would depend on the "organisation of an integral relation between Britain and India."[3] India's situation on the mainland of Asia and in relation to the whole Indian Ocean region creates for her problems of security of a great magnitude. Panikkar repeatedly pointed out that India must play a vital role in the maintenance of peace and security in this region. But it was impossible for her to undertake this task alone as she had neither the well-organised army to meet a first-class military power, nor the industrial base to sustain it. Under the circumstances, cooperation with Britain was an impending necessity, if India was to avoid falling into the Russian orbit. Writing with Haushofer-like views he contended that from the point of view of Great Britain, an essentially maritime power, the necessity of an Indo-British treaty was patently clear. Her strategic and economic interests in the region of South and South East Asia, and the safety of her trade routes to India, China and Australia—all these called for close cooperation with India. He even went to the length of suggesting that without such cooperation, Britain's position in the world would be untenable.[4]

But Panikkar was not alone in advocating Indo-British cooperation in the field of defence.[5] Similar wiews were held by many British officers of the Indian Army. Lt. Col. C.B. Birdwood (later Lord Birdwood) suggested on the eve of independence that if India chose to remain a willing member of the Commonwealth (as an independent Dominion), Britain could provide India with many facilities in respect of training and equipment for the new army.[6] Moreover, he pointed out that in view of the inadequacy of the Royal Indian Navy, it would be difficult for independent India to guard her coastlines without British help. India could, no doubt, develop closer relations with the Soviet Union. But as long as she depended on foreign states for technical equipment for the air forces and the army, and as long as Britain retained her supremacy in the seas, cooperation between them—argued Birdwood—would be a practical necessity. Maintenance of British interests in South and South East Asia would also be facilitated by such cooperation.

There were many British officers who thought that the problem of Indian defence could not be viewed separately from that of the empire. According to this view, the defence of India was certainly an empire problem whether she was a part of the empire, or allied to Britain by some treaty. British interests would also be promoted by cooperation with India, as she held a position of strategic importance on the great lifeline of the British Commonwealth.[7] To what extent such views reflected official thinking is difficult to ascertain. What is certain, however, is that before the transfer of power a section of informed opinion in Britain as well as in India was in favour of some sort of Indo-British cooperation in the field of defence. The experience of the Second World War also demonstrated beyond doubt that without external help India had relatively limited military capability to deal with a major threat to her security.

Against this background we should note the views of the Indian National Congress, and of its chief spokesman on foreign affairs, Nehru. During the thirties, Nehru maintained that because of India's geostrategic position, her size, and also because of a balance of power among the major states, independent India would be secure against any threat to her territorial integrity.[8] He contemplated the possibility of aggressive action by Afghanistan or by the tribal people in the North West Frontier ; but thought that these could be dealt with by India herself. The war brought to Indians the realisation of India's strategic importance, and of her potential strength, in the Indian Ocean region, between Australia and the West Coast of Africa. In a number of speeches during 1945-46 Nehru said that in future India would play a vital role in the defence of the Indian Ocean region and called for cooperation among the states in South and South East Asia. The All India Congress Committee declared in September 1945 that a free India would maintain friendly relations with the neighbours and would "especially seek to develop common policies for defence, trade and economic and cultural development with China, Burma, Malaya, Indonesia and Ceylon as well as the countries of the Middle East."[9]

However, the international scene was fast changing and the Indian leaders had, as yet, no clear vision of the nature of the defence problems that might arise in future. Pakistan was not yet born, and the Congress could not envisage the possibility of any threat to India's security from the Soviet Union or China. Though the Congress party was favourably inclined to the idea of regional cooperation in the field of defence, trade, economic and cultural development, it was opposed to any system of 'entangling alliances' that might involve India in an imperialists' war. On 7 September, 1946, Nehru said in a broadcast from New Delhi that independent India would keep away, so far as possible, from the power-politics of the groups of states, aligned against one another.[10] It is important to remember that Nehru was at this time the head of the Interim government and, therefore, his statement reflected not only the views of the Congress party, but also of the man who was to become the Prime Minister of independent India. To the extent that Nehru was projecting the policy of the successor Government of India, his statement ruled out the possibility of any military alliance with UK. But he was also aware of the fact that the defence apparatus of India was closely linked with Britain, and that any sudden rupture in that relationship would be damaging to Indian interests. This consideration was one of the factors that ultimately influenced his decision, and the decision of his Government to continue India's association with the Commonwealth.

Nehru told the Constituent Assembly on 16 May, 1949, moving a resolution for the ratification of the Government of India's decision to remain in the Commonwealth: "Largely our military apparatus has been influenced by these considerations and we have grown up naturally as something rather like the British Army...If we break away completely, the result is that without making sufficient provision for carrying on in a different way, we have a period of gap."[11] Membership of the Commonwealth paved the way for the continuation of the link between Britain and India, in the field of defence. But even if India decided to leave the Commonwealth, probably some sort of link between the two countries would have been maintained, in defence matters.[12]

II

Cooperation After Independence

During the years immediately after independence cooperation with Britain became a practical necessity for India's armed forces. In the army, most of the British officers who held all the important positions of the Armed Forces' Headquarters and in the Commands, either resigned or opted for service in UK, at the time of the transfer of power. This created a void in the higher echelons of the Indian Army. This was a situation for which the British government was largely to be blamed. For, in spite of repeated Indian demands, Indianisation of the officer cadre of the Indian Army proceeded at a very slow pace till the outbreak of the Second World War. During the war, however, considerable progress was made in that direction under the pressure of events. Even then no Indian had risen above the rank of a Brigadier in the field, nor was there any Indian holding important staff appointments in the Armed Forces' Headquarters. Not a single Indian officer had the experience of commanding an independent corps in a battle. Reorganisation of the army and its proper training, therefore, posed considerable problems for the defence-planners in India. In the absence of adequate training facilities within the country, cooperation with Britain in the matter of training officers was of considerable benefit to the Indian forces. A number of selected officers of the Indian Army attended the Imperial Defence College every year. With the improvement of training facilities in India, especially since the establishment of the Defence Services Staff College at Wellington, and the National Defence College at New Delhi, the need for sending men to Britain declined.

Cooperation with Britain for training officers was even more important for the Air Force and the Navy. For, there was an acute shortage of officers. Moreover, most of the training institutions were lost to Pakistan, as most of them were situated in areas which were now within the newly-created state of Pakistan. The British government's readiness to assist India in setting up training institutions within the country, and the facilities which were offered for the training of a number of selected officers in UK, were of considerable help during the first few years, after independence. Shortage of officers was partly overcome by retaining British personnel in key positions in the Navy and the Air Force. But with the development of training facilities in India fewer men were sent to UK for training.[13]

Besides the facilities for training, India's membership of the Commonwealth provided opportunities for cooperation and consultation at other levels as well. The Chiefs of Staff of the Commonwealth countries could attend the annual conference held by the Chief of Staff in UK for the senior officers of the British Army. The Royal Navy and the Royal Air Force also held such conferences from time to time, to which the Commonwealth Service Chiefs were invited to attend. Similarly, valuable information on scientific developments and their use in the field of defence could be exchanged through the Commonwealth Advisory Committee on Defence Science, conferences of which were held in Australia and London, in 1958 and 1961 respectively.[14] As part of the Commonwealth scheme of cooperation, permanent military liaison is maintained between London and New Delhi through the posting of senior Service officers in the Deplomatic Missions of the two countries as advisers to their respective High Commissoners.[15]

Britain as the Source of Arms Supply (1947-62)

But it was in the field of military hardware that Indian dependence on Britain was more obvious. In 1947, all the equipment of the Indian Army were of British origin, or produced in India on British designs (though there were some lend-lease equipment of American origin). The policy of the Government of India, especially since 1957, was to produce within the country the "basic items of military equipment which we were likely to require in large enough quantity to make production economically feasible, and secondly, the production of items of which the overall requirement, though small, was essential."[16] This policy was adopted for two principal reasons: (1) to conserve valuable foreign exchange, and (2) to reduce dependence on foreign powers for the supply of essential equipment for the army. Such items as were not produced in India were purchased from abroad.

Most of the artillery pieces of the Indian Army were of British origin, and it also relied on Britain for its heavy armour. At the time of independence, it had obsolete Stuart and obsolescent Sherman (American) tanks. The first Kashmir war clearly revealed the need for modern equipment. In 1953, some 30 Sherman tanks were purchased from the United States as a stop-gap measure.[17] In the meantime enquiries were being made about the possibility of manufacturing tanks of foreign design in India, under licence. But in view of India's technological backwardness, these plans were shelved as being too early. During 1956-57, the Indian Army purchased nearly 200 Centurion heavy tanks from Britain—which still remain in the frontline of Indian heavy armour—and in 1957-58 about 150 AMX light tanks from France.[18] Interest renewed in the proposal for manufacturing tanks within the country during the Third Five-Year Plan. In 1961, a team of experts assessed the possibility of manufacturing a light tank of the French AMX or German Panzer variety. But ultimately an agreement was reached with the British firm Vickers-Armstrong for the manufacture of a modified version of the Chieftain medium tank in India. In the field of military hardware for the Army, though Britain had ceased to be the sole supplier, she continued to be the dominant one till 1962. Above all, the Army, with its emphasis on regimental tradition, remained a thoroughly British institution in organisation, training and outlook.

The Navy

The particular wing of the defence forces in India which was most dependent on Britain even after the attainment of independence was the Indian Navy. Referring to this Mr Y.D. Gundevia said on 10 November 1955 : "In the first years after independence we passed through what may be called a formative period in many things. One infant we have nursed is the Indian Navy. We could not have nursed this infant efficiently if it had not been for the enormous assistance we received from the Admiralty in Great Britain."[19]

This was not an exaggeration. At the time of partition, the Indian Navy had to start virtually from scratch. It consisted of a few destroyers, frigates, and minesweepers, tankers and some auxiliary vessels. Most of the modernisation programmes of the Indian Navy in the years after independence were conceived and implemented by a few British officers of the Indian Navy.[20] Reference has already been made to the facilities for training provided by the Royal Navy, as part of the Commonwealth pattern of cooperation. Joint exercises were also held annually by the British and Indian navies (in which other Commonwealth countries also took part). This created a feeling of camaraderie between the officers of the two navies.

At the time of India's independence, the Indian Navy was the weakest of the three wings of the defence forces. Indian leaders thought that because of India's strategic position in the Indian Ocean region, she should have a strong and powerful navy with preponderence over the navies of her Asian neighbours, and with an offensive-defensive capability.[21] Under this plan of expansion drawn up in 1947, the navy acquired from Britain one light cruiser (renamed *INS-Delhi*) in 1948, and three destroyers in 1949 which reached Indian waters in January 1950.

By 1950, due to financial difficulties the Government of India had to revise the original plan of expansion, and decided on a less ambitious programme of development for the Indian Navy. During the second phase of expansion (1956-61), large purchases were made in UK. The Government of India acquired a second cruiser from the Royal Navy in 1954 (renamed *INS-Mysore*) which was delivered in August 1957. The first aircraft carrier for the Indian Navy, *INS-Vikrant* (ex-*H.M.S.* Hercules) was acquired in 1957, which was delivered in 1961 after necessary modifications to suit Indian needs. Three '*Leopard*' class anti-submarine frigates launched in Britain in 1957, 1958 and 1959, were completed between 1958-60. Two '*Whitby*' class anti-submarine frigates launched in 1958 and 1959, were commissioned in 1960 ; and three '*Blackwood*' class anti-submarine frigates launched during 1956-58, were completed by 1959.[22] The fleet air-arm consisted of *Sea Hawk* fighters purchased from Britain between 1959-61, and *Alize* turbo-prop aircraft and *Aloutte* helicopters purchased from France between 1960-62.

On the eve of the conflict with China in 1962, the Indian Navy was almost entirely of British origin. There were only a fleet-replenishment ship of Italian origin, a few seaward defence patrol boats of mixed Yugoslav and Dutch origin, one Portuguese frigate *Alfonso de Albuequerque* captured during the Goa operations in 1961, and some minor vessels built in Indian ship-yards. The Indian Navy was essentially an anti-submarine force, and though it was capable of dealing with the navies of Pakistan and Indonesia, in the event of a major threat to India's maritime communications, she would have to depend on the British-US naval forces.

The Indian Air Force

Like the army and the navy, the air force also depended on Britain as the principal source of supply for aircraft. Before independence the British Government in India did not develop a first class air-arm for the country's defence ; the role of the air force was subsidiary to that of the army and its main function was to give tactical and strategic support to the ground forces. It continued to be so for a few years after independence, but it gradually came to develop a role and an identity of its own.

As one of the principal suppliers of aircraft and related equipment, Britain made a valuable contribution to the development of the Indian Air Force. So far as purchase of arms and equipment was concerned, the policy of the Government of India was definitely slanted towards the West, particularly towards UK. Whether this was the result of familiarity with British equipment, or, of the application of subtle political pressure, or of both, is difficult to determine. However, by following this policy the Government of India at times incurred losses, in strictly financial terms. The negotiations which ultimately led to the purchase of British Canberras for the Indian Air Force, in preference to the Russian Illyushins, in 1957, exemplify this.[23]

Between 1945-55, India acquired 120 military jet aircraft from foreign countries of which nearly half (50) were of British origin, and the rest were of French origin.[24] Most of these planes were, however, of the Second World War generation. The Indian Air Force launched an ambitious plan for expansion and development in 1953-54, and it was during the implementation of this programme between 1953-62, that a large number of aircraft was purchased in UK.

In 1954 the Government of India started negotiations with the English Electric Company for the purchase of Canberra bombers for the Indian Air Force ; these negotiations dragged on for the next three years, before any final agreement was reached. In the meantime, the Soviet Union offered to sell Illyushin-28 bombers at less than half the price of the Canberras ;[25] and it also reportedly offered to sell tanks and other equipment for the army. After a period of strenuous Western lobbying, the Government of India reportedly rejected the Russian offer, and decided in principle to buy Canberras (as well as Centurion tanks, negotiations for which were also progressing). However, at a press conference, Nehru strongly repudiated the suggestion of any Western pressure, and deprecated press reports from London that his Government had rejected a Russian offer.[26] He stated that the Government of India was not committed to any particular country for the purchase of arms. He disclosed that the Soviet Union had made no offer of arms, though his government had made enquiries in Russia about the availability of certain types of military and civil equipment.

Firm orders for the delivery of 68 Canberras were placed towards the end of January, 1957.[27] Subsequent orders for more planes were placed in September of the same year, and in 1961, deliveries for which continued till the middle of 1962.[28]

So far as the fighter squadrons were concerned the Government of India purchased 25 Folland Gnat aircraft from Britain in September 1956 ; and decided to enter into an agreement with two British firms for the manufacture of Gnats in India.[29] In the following year the Hawker Aircraft Ltd. concluded an agreement with the Indian Government for the supply of between 100—200 Hunter fighter aircraft costing between £20m.-£30m.[30]

At the time of the Sino-Indian war of 1962, most of the frontline aircraft of the IAF were of Western origin, mostly British, and some French.[31] The transport and communications squadrons were, however, of mixed origin. There were high-altitude Russian An-12 heavy transport planes, and Mi-4 and Illyushin-14 helicopters, American C-119 transport planes and some Bell helicopters, as well as Indian-built transport planes of British origin. The Indian Air Force therefore lacked standardisation of equipment, and this robbed it of one of the original characteristics of air power flexibility.

The British had also a dominant position in India's aircraft industry, till 1961-62. The Hindustan Aircraft Ltd. (HAL) which provided the nucleus around which the aircraft industry was developed in later years, was originally set up in December 1940 as a Private Limited Co. The Government of India joined the company as a partner in 1941, and took over its control in

July 1942, to use its facilities for overhaul and repair of tactical aircraft and related accessories. In 1946, a British technical mission came to India on the invitation of the Interim Indian Government, to advise on the establishment of an aircraft industry. The HAL plant at Bangalore was recommended as the most suitable centre for the development of the industry. Since independence the factory had undertaken the task of assembling various types of aircraft required by IAF. In 1955 negotiations started with two British firms (Folland aircraft for the airframe and the Bristol-Siddeley for the aeroengines) for the manufacture of Gnat fighters in India, under licence. The licences were acquired in 1956. In July 1959, the Government of India concluded an agreement with the British firm Hawker Siddeley for the production of the military version of the Avro-748 transport planes in India, and in December of the same year licence was secured for the production of the Rolls-Royce Dart RD a7 engines for the Avro series.

Since 1956 Indian engineers and designers had been working on a project under a German designer Dr Kurt Tank for designing a fighter plane (HF-24) to be produced in India. It was the first plane, the airframe of which was to be designed and manufactured in India ; but it was to be powered by the Bristol Orpheus 703 engines. The aircraft (HF-24 Mk. 1) took its maiden flight in June, 1961, and is operational with the Indian Air Force. Thus manufacture of aircraft of foreign designs in India virtually meant manufacturing under licence planes of British origin, or aircraft designed in India and powered by British engines.

Britain has, however, lost the position of preeminence in the Indian Air Force as well as in the Indian aircraft industry, with the slow but steady penetration in the field by the Soviet Union. This is a situation for which the Western Powers themselves are to blame. To be able to appreciate this we should briefly look at the MIG deal.

The MIG Deal

The diplomatic row over the MIG deal is an example of a situation where even a commercial transaction can become the subject of a political controversy in relations between two states.

Indian interest in acquiring supersonic fighters had increased with the delivery of a squadron of F-104 Starfighters to Pakistan by the United States in 1961-62. In the spring of 1962 press reports suggested that India was willing to buy supersonic MIG-21 planes from the Soviet Union.[32] It produced immediate reaction in Western capitals, and a flurry of diplomatic activities. The reported deal was interpreted as a calculated move by the Indian Government to outwit the Western Powers for supplying supersonic planes to Pakistan. But the real story was different.

It had long been the policy of the Government of India to manufacture a supersonic fighter plane for the IAF within the country. The HF-24 Mk 1 transonic fighter was the first step in this direction. By early 1962, the manufacture of the HF-24 Mk. 1 project was progressing slowly when the supply of supersonic planes to Pakistan seemed to alter the military balance in the sub-continent. Around this time the British firm Bristol-Siddeley, which was developing an aeroengine for the HF-24 Mk. 11 supersonic planes, reported its inability to proceed further with the project, unless the Government of India was prepared to bear the entire cost of it, estimated at £5m. The Indian government was unwilling to give this undertaking, and turned to other sources for the procurement of the engine. It is possible that the Government became interested at this time in the purchase of some supersonic fighters for their immediate operational use, and for their manufacture in India under licence.

The Russian RD 9 engines attracted Indian attention, and a team of experts from IAF went to Moscow to explore the possibility of using these engines for the HF-24 Mk.11 air-frame, and their manufacture in India under licence. But these engines could not be used in the Indian air frame ; if Indians were to use them, either the engines or the airframe were to be modified. Indians were unwilling to change the airframe, as it had become a matter of prestige for them ; moreover, it would take some time to give effect to the changes. The Soviet Union ultimately agreed to modify the engine to suit Indian needs ; and an agreement was reached in July 1962 for the manufacture of these engines in India.

When the negotiations for these engines were proceeding, the Russians seem to have raised the question of their latest MIG-21 as a substitute for the RD 9 engines, as it would take some time to redesign and modify these engines.[33] Indian experts were favourably impressed with the aircraft, and also gathered that the Russians might be willing to help India in manufacturing these planes under licence. No formal offer to sell these planes was, however, made.

The Indian air Force, anxious to match Pakistan's superiority in the air, suggested to the Government the purchase of two squadrons of Russian MIG-21 or French Mirage-111 fighters. As this would involve an expenditure of over £30m in foreign exchange, the Defence Ministry did not show much interest in these proposals at the initial stages. But the possibility of manufacturing MIGs in India seemed to be attractive, as this would reduce the dependence on foreign powers for aircraft. While the suggestion was being considered in secret, the news leaked out.

When reports of Indian interest in MIGs first came out in the newrpapers, it evoked a great deal of criticism in US at a time when the Congress was debating the foreign aid bill. The British were also anxious ; for, if the reported deal materialised, it would mean the loss of a valuable market, as India was one of the best customers of British aircraft. Moreover, there was some apprehension in Britain that if the Russian technicians were allowed to come to India with MIGs, British military secrets might be known to them as India was in possession of many classified equipment of British origin. In effect, this would mean the virtual end of "a clear understanding" between Lord Mountbatten and Nehru that the Indian Government would consult the British Government before any decision was taken about purchase or manufacture of aircraft for the Indian Air Force.[34] Nehru's undertaking was, no doubt, a delicate personal matter, and could not, therefore, be used by the British Government to prevent India from buying aircraft from any source of her choice. President Kennedy and Prime Minister Macmillan entered into urgent consultations to make an attractive counter offer to the Government of India, which would thwart the MIG deal.[35] The British Commonwealth Seeretary, Mr Duncan Sandys who was to visit India and Pakistan to explain his Government's position regarding the Common Market, would also discuss with Nehru the MIG issue. It is important to note that at this stage the Soviet Union did not make any formal offer to sell MIGs to India, nor did the latter make any proposal regarding their purchase.

Public opinion within the country now began to crystalise on the question, and because of the interference by the British and American governments, a seemingly non-political issue acquired political significance. Mr H.V. Kamath, a Member of the Lok Sabha, voiced the feeling of the House when he expressed his resentment against interference by outside Powers in what was considered to be a matter for India alone.[36] An Indian weekly wrote editorially on 2 June, 1962, under the title 'Freedom to Purchase Arms' that the past practice in the matter of arms purchase had given rise to a widely-held belief "among those who should know better that India followed a convention of buying arms from no other source than Britain and France". Arms requirements should be tailored to the needs of changing circumstances, and, therefore, commented the paper, India should assert "her right of choosing her sources of supply to suit her requirements and convenience."[37] The MIG deal, which should have been based on purely technical and commercial considerations, now became a matter of prestige for the nation—a fact which left little room for the Government to manoeuvre.

On June 15, Mr Duncan Sandys arrived in New Delhi for consultations with Nehru. He brought with him some compromise proposals and suggested that India should buy supersonic fighters from UK, US, and the Soviet Union, and test them under varying conditions for one year before finally deciding which planes should be manufactured in India.[38] Nehru was reported to be willing to consider the suggestion, and 'diplomatic sources' revealed that he had assured the visiting British

Minister that India would consult the British government before taking any final decision on the MIGs.[39] Some political commentators in India interpreted it as a sort of quid pro quo arrangement in return for an assurance by both Britain and the United States that India would be spared embarrassment over the Kashmir problem, which was then being discussed in the Security Council. When Mr Duncan Sandys returned to London, a section of the press reported that Britain had offered to sell BAC Lightinings to India and to help her in manufacturing them under licence.[40]

But the Prime Minister's hopes of UK-US behaviour in the United Nations were soon belied when the representatives of both the countries voted in favour of a resolution[41] in the Security Council that brought up once more question of plebiscite to decide the future of Kashmir. Nehru told the Parliament in no uncertain terms that both the British and American governments had deliberately misrepresented Indian views on many important issues.

He then declared that although India depended on aid for the successful implementation of the Five Year Plans, the Government of India would not ask for aid if it meant giving up the country's independence, in any respect.[42]

In July three senior officers of the Indian Air Force led by Air Vice-Marshal Harjinder Singh left for Britain to evaluate the performance of the BAC Lightning. The team had been advised to convince the British that India was more interested in manufacturing fighter aircraft under licence, though some purchase would be made as a stop-gap measure. But the IAF team reported that the BAC Lightning was no match for MIG. The Indian Government also reportedly sounded the US State Department for the possible purchase of Mcdonnel F-1015 and the French Dassault Co. for the purchase of the Mirage-111 fighters ; but no satisfactory reply came from these sources.[43] By the end of July the Government had decided in principle to buy Soviet MIGs ; and an Indian team left for Moscow on 31 July to discuss with the Russian authorities the question of the production of these planes in India and the following month the Soviet Union reached an agreement with India to sell 12

MIG-21 fighters, and to provide assistance for the production of planes of this model in India. The terms of the deal were also favourable as payment was to be made in rupees—an offer which could not be matched by any of the manufacturers in the West.

Some doubts were raised about the availability of MIGs after the Sino-Indian conflict of 1962, but these were finally dispelled with the arrival of four planes in Bombay in the February of the following year. By the middle of April 1963, the Government had chosen the sites for the manufacture of the plane at Nasik (for airframes) and at Koraput in Orissa (for the engines); in October of the same year discussions were going ahead for setting up a factory for the manufacture of guided missiles.

The analysis of events leading to the Indo-Soviet MIG deal, and their impact on India's relations with UK (and US) suggests some important conclusions. The Government of India had, no doubt, the right to make military purchases where it liked; but Britain's anxieties were also understandable. The British government could not view with equanimity the possibility of losing the Indian market to the Soviet Union. Moreover, as a result of the longcooperation between the British and Indian air forces, the latter came to acquire some classified information. There was some apprehension in London that if the proposed Indo-Soviet MIG deal went through, such information might be leaked to the Soviet Union. However, it appeared to many political observers that the attitude of the Western powers, especially of the United States, was formed by certain illusions and prejudices against Krishna Menon, the then Defence Minister of India.[44] In USA emotions ran so high that President Kennedy found it necessary, more than once, to pacify the critics of the Government of India by asserting that India was certainly within her rights to buy planes from any country of her choice.

In UK, the belief—created by reports in a section of the press—that India had turned to the Soviet Union with ulterior political designs was based on two assumptions: (1) that Britain had comparable aircraft to spare, and (2) that she was willing to sell them to India, and to help her in manufacturing these. Both these assumptions proved to be incorrect. When Mr Duncan Sandys came to India, the Government had not yet decided on the purchase of MIGs. He requested the Indian Government to evaluate the performance of the BAC Lightnings before taking any final decision on the purchase of supersonic fighters. A section of the British press circulated the news that Mr Sandys had offered Lightnings to India at, 'reduced' price ; but this was not true. In fact, the Indian team which had gone to London found that neither the English Electric Company (the manufacturers of Lightning) nor the British Government had anything concrete to offer. Therefore, the position was that, wrote the London correspondent of an Indian daily, India did not turn down anything, because "there was, quite simply, nothing to accept or reject."[45]

The final decision to purchase MIGs had been taken after a number of considerations. These were not only cheaper than any other Western aircraft, of comparable merit, but also more suited to India's needs.[46] The Lightnings could not reach the Mach 2 speed which was necessary if India was to meet Pakistan's superiority in the air. Moreover, the Soviet Union agreed to help India in manufacturing these planes—a primary reason for turning to MIGs. Above all, payments were to be made in rupees.

The MIG deal had some important consequences for the future of Indian defence. It meant, in the first place, a significant breakthrough in the Indian arms market by the Soviet Union—a market for which she had been trying for a long time. At the same time it signalled the end of an era of complete dependence on the West, especially on Britain, for the purchase of arms and equipment, and for their production within the country under licence.

III

The Sino-Indian Conflict And After : Politics Of Military Aid

The Sino-Indian war in October-November 1962, and the events following, underlined the changes in New Delhi's attitude towards Britain as the supplier of arms. A shift of emphasis from London to Washington, and finally to Moscow, was clearly discernible. So far as India's relations with the West were concerned, this was a period of missed opportunities. When the hostilities between India and China broke out, Britain was one of the first countries to give unqualified support to India's stand on the border conflict ; and later on, in response to an Indian request for arms, UK joined US and other friendly countries for an emergency airlift of arms to India.[47] But most of the emergency arms-aid during the period came from US supply depots in West Germany.

Within a week of the unilateral declaration of cease-fire by the Chinese on 22 November, a high-level Anglo-American mission arrived in New Delhi led by Mr Duncan Sandys and Mr Averell Harriman respectively, to study India's long-term need for arms. On 27 November, Mr Sandys and the then Indian Defence Minister Mr Y.B. Chavan, signed an agreement governing the use of the arms supplied to India by Britain. The agreement stipulated that these arms could be used only to defend India against China and that facilities would be given to British representatives "to observe and review" the purpose for which they were being used. The arms and equipment supplied under this agreement would be free of payment within certain financial limits.[48] On 22 December, President Kennedy and Prime Minister Macmillan announced in a joint communique, after their meeting at Nassau, an emergency arms aid of £45m. to India, to be shared equally by the United States, and the United Kingdom and the Commonwealth.[49]

The British and American gestures were highly appreciated in India, and relations with the West had never been better in recent years. But differences soon began to appear between India and her Western friends over a number of issues. During the Sandys-Harriman mission in November 1962, it was made known to the Indian government that the British and the American governments could not commit themselves to any long-term programme of arms aid to India without a satisfactory solution of the Kashmir dispute.[50] Pressure was brought to bear on India to reopen negotiations with Pakistan for a settlement of the intractable Kashmir problem.[51]

As suppliers of arms, UK and US were obviously justified in expecting that Pakistan and India, instead of deploying their armies against each other, should compose their differences and combine their strength against China. A solution of the Kashmir dispute would have paved the way for such cooperation. But any satisfactory settlement of the long-standing dispute would require considerable concession by both sides. Anglo-American pressure on India to agree to negotiations with Pakistan at a time when Indians were still smarting under the shadow of a military defeat, appeared to be sheer diplomatic arm-twisting even to most moderate Indians and gave rise to a wide-spread feeling of anger and resentment.

As the threat from China receded, other causes of disagreement between the British and the Indian governments appeared. Indians thought that China would renew hostilities on a bigger scale within eighteen months ; but such a possibility was discounted by the British as well as by the Americans. Differences also arose in their assessment of the nature and quantity of weapons required by India to meet the threat posed by China. The Anglo-American emergency arms aid consisted mainly of infantry weapons to re-equip India's existing armed forces. The US Government also sent some C-130 transport planes to India, on temporary loan, to facilitate the movement of weapons and stores to the forward areas in the Himalayas. Any long-term programme of rearmament would, however, call for a close study of India's needs. On 30 January, 1963, a joint US-Commonwealth air mission arrived in New Delhi to study the long-term needs for India's air defence. While the reeommendations of the mission were not disclosed, it soon became apparent that Indians were disappointed. High on the list of India's requirements was the provision for the purchase of at least two squadrons of supersonic fighters. The Anglo-American assessment was different ; they did not think it necessary for India to have supersonic aircraft to fight China, and they were unwilling to supply such aircraft to India as these would offend Pakistan and raise a storm of protest from Rawalpindi.[82]

India's grand design to rearm and expand the defence forces —with a larger role for the air force and the navy—seemed to be out of step with the trend of thought in London and Washington. The defence-planners in India conceived of the possibility of a joint attack from Pakistan and China in view of the growing collusion between the two states, whreas US and UK were concerned with the threat from China. A round of discussions held in New Delhi in April 1963 between the Indian leaders, and Messrs Dean Rusk, Duncan Sandys aud Lord Mountbatten, the then Chief of the Defence forces in Britain, revealed these differences. The correspondent of *The Times* wrote from New Delhi about the disappointment in Indian official circles with both Britain and the United States [53] It was the attitude of Britain which was resented more, and there was a suspicion that she was not only restricting her own assistance to India but also persuading the United States to do likewise. The Indian Minister for Economic and Defence Coordination, Mr T.T. Krishnamachari, visited Ottawa, Washington and London during the summer of 1963 to discuss with the respective governments the plan for India's defence, and to persuade the United States to supply supersonic planes to India. The original Indian request for military aid totalling £ 536m., spread over a period of three years, was believed to be too high both in London and Washington. But the figure was considerably reduced after detailed dissussions in U.S.. India nevertheless expected a contribution of £ 120m. from Britain over the next three years.[54] But Mr Krishnamachari failed to receive any such commitment from London. However, a few days later, a joint communique was issued from London after talks between President Kennedy and Prime Minister Macmillan at Birch-grove, pledging long-term military assistance to India.[55] The timing of the communique was important, as it came just after the announcement of the Government of India's decision to accept the Soviet Union's invitation for talks on the supply of military equipment to India. The American Government had already taken the decision to continue to supply arms to India and the decision was communicated to the Government of India through diplomatic channels. What was particularly significant about the Birch-grove declaration was that the U.S. President also secured the British Government's commitment, although the bulk of the assistance was to come from America.[56] By August 1963 it became clear that so far as the U.S.-Commonwealth aid was concerned, the United States was prepared to shoulder three-quarters of it.[57] While India welcomed the joint Anglo American declaration for long-term assistance, she was obviously disappointed with their refusal to supply supersonic planes for the Indian Air Force.

During the border conflict with China the weaknesses of India's air defence system became particularly exposed inasmuch as almost all the populous cities in eastern and northern India were vulnerable to aerial attack by the Chinese. Towards the end of the conflict, Nehru had appealed to President Kennedy for help to protect the Indian cities from Chinese air attack.[58] When the war was over, top priority was, therefore, accorded to the strengthening of India's air-defence, and Indian officials were still thinking in terms of a tacit air-defence agreement with U.S.[59] When the U.S.-Commonwealth air defence team came to New Delhi in January 1963, vague reports of a western "air umbrella" were circulated in the press. What transpired between the Government of India and the air defence mission was not clear ; probably Nehru wanted a joint declaration by the Western powers that if China attacked India, they would be prepared to give India military support. Such a declaration, he thought, would act as a deterrent to the Chinese. But the very vagueness of the terms "air umbrella" and "air shield" gave rise to all kinds of speculation about the implications of any scheme in which India would be roped in an alliance with the West, especially with U.S.. Criticisms against the scheme were voiced by different sections of political opinion in India, particularly by the Communists and the left-wing of the Congress, leading to considerable soft-pedalling of the issue by the Indian Government. On 1 February Nehru told a group of M.P.s that the newspaper reports on the 'air umbrella' for India to be provided by Britain, the United States and the Commonwealth air forces were not correct.[60] However, the criticisms voiced aginst the so-called "air umbrella" scheme, and the government's inept handling of the issue created misgivings in Washington and brought a sharp rejoinder from the then U.S. Ambassador, Professor Galbraith, who said in a press conference in New Delhi that United States was not offering the Indian Government anything they did not ask for.[61] The matter was temporarily settled by Nehru's intervention in the Parliament. On 23 February he stated in the Lok Sabha that speculations in the press about the establishment of foreign bases in India and plans for an 'air umbrella' were incorrect and greatly exaggerated.[62]

After Mr Krishnamachari's visit to London and Washington in the summer of 1963, the decision to hold periodic joint air-exercises between Indian, American and British-Commonwealth Air forces was reported in the press.[63] However useful it might have been for India from the military point of view, politically it was an embarrassing decision for the Government. For, at home it revived the Communist criticism of an 'imperialist conspiracy', and even a pro-West paper like the *Times of India* was critical of it. But the Government of India was also apprehensive of the fact that excessive publicity to it might damage New Delhi's relations with Moscow. The Government's policy was, therefore, to play down the whole thing, and to emphasise that the air exercises were being held to train the Indian Air Force personnel in the use of radar and other communications equipment.[64] The Western view, however, was that the joint exercise would be held to prepare the British and American squadrons to come to India's help in case of an emergency.[65] These differences did not contribute to the improvement in India's relations with Britain and the United States. Joint air exercises were held between I.A.F. and the British and American air forces in November 1963. Indians took the opportunity to substantiate their claim that the Indian Air Force needed supersonic aircraft, as the Himalayas acted as a barrier to the radar screen. But India failed to acquire supersonic interceptors from US.

The first phase of the programme of expansion and rearmament of the defence forces in India ended with a round of visits to the Soviet Union by an Indian military mission. The team, led by a senior official of the Government of India, S. Bhoothalingam, left for Moscow on 16 July, and returned to New

Delhi a month later, on 15 August, 1963. The Indian team concluded an agreement with the Russian authorities for the supply of certain weapons and equipment to India. In his statement to the Lok Sabha a few days later in September, 1963, the Defence Minister, Y.B. Chavan, without disclosing the details of the agreement, described it as satisfactory.[66]

The decline of Britain's importance to India as the supplier of arms

That Britain was no longer the principal supplier of arms to India was quite evident from the annual *Report* for 1963-64, published by the Ministry of Defence.[67] Britain's contribution to India's new defence build-up was only marginal. During 1963-64, the transport fleet of IAF had been substantially increased by the purchase of a number of An-12 heavy transport planes from the Soviet Union, and 16 Caribou medium transport planes from Canada, for which the Canadian Government had provided the credit, in addition to the gift of 8 Dakota aircraft. The United States supplied 24 Packet aircraft under the military assistance programme : and HAL was to manufacture 29 Avro-748 aircraft at Kanpur, under licence from a British firm. A number of helicopters had also been acquired. The Soviet Union had agreed to supply MI-4 helicopters under deferred payment agreement ; and some Aloutte helicopters were to be purchased from France. The Indian Air Force would also indigenously produce these for meeting future needs. The US Government had agreed to provide sets of powerful static radar installations and related communications equipment ; and had given, as a temporary measure, some mobile radar installations, to provide limited air coverage, and for training the IAF personnel.

The British Government's contributions related mainly to electronic and communications equipment.[68]

The second phase of India's rearmament programme was devoted to long-term planning. Mr Chavan told the Lok Sabha on 23 March 1964 that the Government was working on a Five-Year Defence programme.[69] On an invitation from the US Government the Defence Minister visited Washington in

May 1964 for talks on India's Five-Year Defence Plan; and New Delhi had high hopes about the outcome of this visit. He was also to have visited UK at the end of his American tour, but had to hurry back to New Delhi due to the sudden death of Nehru. Later on, towards the end of August, he visited Moscow.

In his statement to the Parliament on 21 September 1964, the Defence Minister outlined India's Five-Year Defence Plan, and the foreign military assistance which she was likely to receive for the implementation of the Plan.[70] This clearly showed that India no longer looked to UK as the main supplier of arms and equipment for the defence forces.

The US Government had agreed to supply:

(I) An immediate credit of $ 10m for the purchase of defence articles and services.

(II) A military grant assistance of $ 50m for the US fiscal year 1965 (July 1964-June 1965). This would include continued support for India's mountain divisions, six defence communications equipment, transport aircraft support and road-building equipment for the Border Road Organisation.

(III) A further credit of $ 50m to be available during the fiscal year 1965. An artillery plant, to be set up at Ambajhari, would be financed with this.

The statement continued that successful implementation of the defence plan would require continued assistance from US "at the current levels in respect of both grant assistance and credit assistance", which meant that India expected to receive $ 110m annually by way of grants and aid from US. The US authorities also agreed to hold periodical talks between the two governments to determine further US assistance in relation to India's defence effort.

As for the Soviet Union, agreements had been concluded with the Russian government for the extension of the agreement reached in 1962 for the production of MIG-21 planes in India. The Soviet Union now agreed to provide plants, and machinery, jigs and tools for the early establishment of MIG factories in India. The Soviet Union also agreed to supply a certain number of MIG-21 aircraft to enable the Indian Air

Force to reequip three of its fighter squadrons, and to supply a certain number of light tanks. While the financial value of Soviet aid was not revealed, the Western sources put it around $ 130m.[71]

As for British aid,[72] Mr Chavan said that the British government had agreed to give a loan to enable construction of frigates in India. The UK government had also agreed to provide facilities for placing an order for a modern submarine for the Indian Navy.

It was quite apparent from Mr Chavan's statement to the Parliament that it was only for the reorganisation and expansion of the navy that India looked to Britain for assistance, primarily because almost all the vessels of the Indian navy were of British origin. But even in this sphere, British response was halting.

The need for submarines for the Indian Navy had long been felt, and the matter acquired some urgency after the Himalayan conflict of 1962. By April, 1963, the Government had accepted in principle the need for submarines for the Navy, and asked the Naval Headquarters to submit proposals. Earlier in the year press reports suggested that the Government was interested in the purchase of submarines, and that order might be placed abroad. Though Britain would be an obvious choice, in view of the close association between the navies of the two countries, other markets, especially the Swedish and the American, were also being explored. Foreign exchange difficulties prevented the possibility of purchasing from Sweden. Washington had also been approached ; when Chavan visited US in May 1964, the matter came up for discussion with the authorities. But the US Government expressed inability to supply submarines to India principally because this would offend Pakistan .

The British government's initial reaction to the Indian request was cautious. Apparently the British government's view was that the Indian Navy would have only a limited role in India's defence, and that the submarine was not necessary for defence against China.[73] However, during Chavan's visit to London in November, 1964, Britain offered to sell one submarine of the Second World War origin, as this was the only one which could be made immediately available to India. But the offer was rejected. Another British offer for the construction of an 'Oberon' class submarine was under the consideration of the Government of India, but ultimately this was also rejected as the costs were too high.[74] An alternative arrangment was, however, agreed whereby the Royal Navy would provide training facilities for the training of Indians in modern submarine, for two to three months a year. But this did not end India's quest for submarines for the navy, and in the autumn of the following year an agreement was reached with the Russian government for the purchase of submarines for the Indian Navy. Mr Chavan had also discussed the possibility of purchasing from Britain three destroyers for the Indian Navy to replace some of the obsolete ones ; but failed to get them. The visit ended with the signing of an agreement for a £ 4.7 m British loan for the construction of three Leander class frigates in Mazagaon dockyards at Bombay.[75] Though the Joint Communique issued at the end of the talks said that the British Government had assured Mr Chavan of their desire to cooperate with the Indian authorities in solving problems relating to defence supplies,[76] Mr Chavan failed to secure all that he wanted. This was partly due to the fact that his visit came at a time when the British Government was engaged in an urgent review of their own defence policy.

Because of the failure of the British government to supply submarines to India, the latter turned to the Soviet Union for the same. The supply of Soviet submarines to the Indian Navy filled a very important gap in India's naval build-up.

During the Indo-Pakistan war of 1965, both the UK and the US governments suspended their military assistance programmes. Supplies to Pakistan were also stopped by both. The purpose was to prevent the escalation of the conflict by putting an end to the supply of arms to the combatants. But the British embargo hit India hard, as this in effect "stopped not only the supplies of arms and equipment to India under aid but even purchases from Government stocks. Commercial purchases, though not embargoed, were in effect suspended."[77] This was achieved by postponing the issue of export licences. This created, in the language of an official publication, "a strong reaction in India reflected by all shades of opinion, and caused considerable strain on Indo-British relations."[78] The Defence Minister told foreign correspondents at a news conference in New Delhi, on 28 September 1965, that the Indian government strongly protested to London for interference with the supply of defence articles that had already been paid for.[79] Other countries such as France did not stop such supply even during the fighting,[80] and it was being suggested in New Delhi that India should learn her lessons and try to reduce overwhelming dependence on Britain for the supply of defence materials. However in March, 1966, the British government decided to revoke the restrictions on the supply of military hardware to India, and the U.S. government also decided to resume the supply of non-lethal weapons to India on a selective basis.

IV

Defence Of India And The Declining Importance Of Britain

In the preceding pages we have seen how India's dependence on Britain in respect of the supply of arms and equipment gradually declined. A number of factors account for this. In the first place, with the development of the industrial base, most of the conventional arms and equipment for the army can now be produced within the country. India has almost been compelled to resort to autarchic practices in defence production for economic, political and strategic reasons. The 1965 war with Pakistan revealed the dangers of excessive reliance on foreign powers for the supply of spare parts and components of arms, at the hour of need. India is now producing almost all her infantry requirements, and all these weapons are of the post-1960 model and currently being used in other developed countries.[81] Indians are also developing their own mountain guns, and producing L-70 anti-aircraft guns under Licence. Indian defence industries can meet substantial portion of the needs of the air force, and to some extent, even the needs of the navy. But in respect of sophisticated weapons, India still has to rely on foreign Powers. The Government's policy in this matter has been to cast the net as wide as possible in order to get the best available terms, and also to reduce dependence on any one power, or group of powers. But whether they have succeeded in achieving this goal is a different matter. The real position seems to be that reliance on UK has been replaced by reliance on the Soviet Union. This is a situation for which the Western countries are partly to be blamed. Since 1962, no major weapons-system (like tanks, frigates, submarines or aircraft) has been purchased from UK. Most of them had to be purchased from the Soviet Union, or are being built in India under licence from various countries. With the gradual phasing out of British weapons from active service, most of which were purchased during the mid-fifties, dependence on Britain for arms is likely to decline further.

By the end of the 1960s Britain lost her position as the principal supplier of arms to the three wings of the defence forces.[82] At the same time, reliance on the Soviet Union increased. Besides supplying light tanks, supersonic aircraft, and submarines, the Soviet Union has made a valuable contribution to India's armoury by supplying some Guideline SA missiles to the Indian Air Force. During the 1960s India had very few guided missiles in active service ; but she will have to concentrate on missiles technology in the years ahead, as guided missiles are becoming an essential weapon of modern warfare. Already, by the middle of the sixties, India was producing some guided missiles.[83] However, the defence forces needed more sophisticated weapons—more sophisticated than the ones India could produce.[84]

It is not only in the matter of supply of arms that Britain's influence in India declined, her capability to defend India in case of a major war declined too, especially since the late 1960s. During the 1950s Britain's military presence in South and South East Asia was an important force for the maintenance of stability in the region. Specially important was the presence of the Royal Navy in the Indian Ocean region. Weak as it was in the past, the Indian Navy is not sufficiently strong even today to defend India's vital interests as a maritime power. It was developed to guard India's long coast lines. While it was sufficiently strong to deal with India's principal adversary in the region, Pakistan (which was demonstrated during the Indo-Pakistan war of 1971), in the event of a prolonged conflict with a major power like China, the Indian Navy would not be able to protect the vital sea-lanes, and may have to depend on friendly foreign powers. But the credibility of the Royal Navy to act as a deterrent began to decline with the liquidation of the bases in the Indian Ocean, and most of all, with the announcement of a policy of military disengagement from the east of Suez.

The underlying assumption for British defence policy, till the middle of the sixties, was that UK had a special responsibility for the defence of the Indian Ocean region. The assumption was a legacy from the days of the empire when UK had vital strategic and commercial interests east of Suez, maintenance of which called for British military presence in the area. In fact, the preponderance of the Royal Navy in the seas, combined with the strength of the British Indian Army in the Indian sub-continent, had turned the Indian Ocean into a British lake. But after the liquidation of the empire in the east Britain had neither the capacity nor the need to act as the policeman in the Indian Ocean region. Nevertheless, successive governments in London accepted this role for Britain, largely because their conception of Britain's status as a world power was influenced by the nostalgic ideas of the days of the empire.[85] Usually criticisms against this policy were voiced by the party in opposition. The Labour party had for long been an advocate of a policy of reduction of British forces east of Suez, in order to strengthen the British Army on the Rhine. But when the Labour party came to power in 1964, it refused to surrender the global defence ambition of the previous Governments. As late as March 1965, Mr Denis Healey, the then British Defence Secretary claimed that Britain's military presence east of Suez was necessary not for "building of a wall against communism...nor (for) the protection of selfish British interests ; but in order to contribute to the maintenance of peace..."[86] In June 1965, Mr Harold Wilson declared, while opening the Nehru Memorial Exhibition, that Britain's frontier extended to the Himalayas and that she should use all necessary means to maintain India's political independence and territorial integrity.[87] A year later, on 15 June 1966, he told the Parliamentary Labour party that Britain's military presence east of Suez was important for countries like India. If Britain withdrew from South and South East Asia, India would have to depend either on one of the super powers, or she would go nuclear herself. In essence, both the Prime Minister and his Defence Secretary were advocating a policy under which Britain would retain her world role in a military sense.

But the British government had to change this policy and accept a role for Britain more in accord with her resources and capabilities. The most important cause accounting for this change was Britain's chronic balance of payments problem during the latter half of the 1960s. It was soon realised that Britain had not the means to maintain the posture of a world power.[88] In his Supplementary Statement on Defence presented to the Parliament in July 1967, Mr Healey said that the British government had decided to reduce the forces deployed in Singapore and Malaysia by half, during 1970-71, and to withdraw the forces altogether during the mid-80s.[89] It is significant to note that this decision of the British government was welcomed in New Delhi. Though Whitehall's decision gave rise to anxieties in some quarters regarding the maintenance of peace and stability in the Indian Ocean region, the Government of India's view was that the British withdrawal would not create any more power-vacuum in the area than the liquidation of the Empire had created.[90] This was as much a reflection of the diminishing importance attached to Britain in India's defence perspective, as of the desire to see the Indian Ocean region being a nuclear free zone, free of military bases and big-power tensions. The Conservative party which came to power after the general election in June 1970, was committed to a policy of participation in a five-power defence arrangement in South East Asia. But the process of withdrawal has gone too far and there is no realistic possibility of the revival of a strong British military presence in the Indian Ocean region.[90a]

With the considerable reduction of Britain's military strength east of Suez, her capability to help India in an emergency also declined. During the late 1960s, India's defence-planners reckoned with two types of threat to the country's security : (1) the possibility of a conventional war either with Pakistan, or with China, or with both at the same time, and (2) subversive guerilla war in the discontented pockets in the north-east frontier, with or without active aid and encouragement from Pakistan, or China or both. The possibility of an immediate nuclear attack by China was not seriously considered, and it was implicitly assumed that in any such eventuality either or both of the super powers would come to India's help.[91]

In none of these two kinds of threats to India's territorial security mentioned above, Britain's role could be anything more than marginal from the military point of view. She could render little help to India, if the latter was to fight another round of protracted hit-and-run battle with the Nagas or with any other hostile minority group in the inhospitable terrains of the vulnerable north-eastern sector of India's border. The solution in this case would be partly political and economic; and insofar as military measures were necessary, these would have to be in the nature of an anti-guerilla campaign on the classic Malayan technique.[92]

It is therefore, only in the case of a conventional war with an external enemy that India may be required to stretch her arms for help from friendly foreign powers. In any future Indo-Pak war of the type fought in 1965, or the one in 1971, Britain cannot be expected to extend military help to either of the combatants ; all she can do is to exert diplomatic or political pressure on both sides through UN, or in concert with the super powers, to bring an end to the hostilities.

Even in the event of a war with China, it is doubtful whether UK can be expected to come to India's help in the way it did in 1962. Moreover, Britain's conventional forces are so limited in manpower and equipment that after meeting her NATO commitments she does not have the military capability to make any substantial and effective contribution to India's defence efforts, in the case of a brush-fire war with China. During the Sino-Indian border war of 1962, Britain and the United States offered military assistance to India. In any future conflict with China, India will have to rely more on her own ; if she is to ask for external assistance, it will probably come from the Soviet Union. With the modernisation of her equipment and the strengthening of the forces along the Sino-Indian border, what remains a cause of concern to India's military planners is China's air power. China no longer enjoys the qualitative superiority over India's air force, as was the situation in 1962. But she has definite strategic advantages in that almost the whole of northern India's population centres and industrial complexes are within easy striking ranges from Tibet. The coverage provided by the US-built early-warning system, and by the installation of surface-to-air missiles bought from the Soviet Union may give some protection, but may not stand against heavy-density strikes. If India is compelled to ask for air cover, Britain does not have the capability to provide it.

Thus in the sphere of India's defence, Britain's influence has perceptibly declined over the last few years. The assumptions on which the concept of Indo-British co-operation for the defence of the Indian Ocean region were based, are no longer valid today. *Britannia* no longer rules the waves ; nor has Britain the imperial possessions in the East which necessitated British military presence in the area.

Britain is no longer the principal supplier of arms and weapons-system to India's defence forces, though many arms and equipment of British origin are still being used in India and will continue to be used in the near future. In the matter of training officers, India no longer depends on U.K. as most of the officers are trained within the country. For the training of officers in the use of specialised equipment, selected men are sent to various countries ; between 1962 and 1965, Indian officers were sent for training not only to UK, but also to the United States, the Soviet Union, Australia, Canada, and to a few other friendly countries. With the decline in the number of officers having their training in the British military institutions, the links at the higher echelons of the armed forces in the two countries have also declined. With the disengagement of substantial British military forces from South and South-East Asia, Britain's capability to give operational support to India's forces, in the event of an emergency, has also declined. The continuation of co-operation in the matter of training officers, exchange of information regarding scientific and technical developments, and holding of joint air and naval exercises from time to time —however limited their values may be—can maintain the diminishing link.

NOTES AND REFERENCES

1. K.M. Panikkar ; *Problems of Indian Defence* (Asia Publishing House, Bombay, 1960), p. 23.

2. See, for example, K.M. Panikkar ; *The Basis of an Indo-British Treaty*, p. 1.

3. See, K.M. Panikkar ; "The Defence of India and Indo-British Obligations" in *International Affairs*, January 1946, p 85.

4. K.M. Panikkar ; *Basis of an Indo-British Treaty*, p. 4.

5. Sir Syed Ahmed, a member of the Viceroy's Executive Council, also advocated Indo-British cooperation in the field of defence. See Syed S. Ahmed ; *A Treaty Between India and the United Kingdom* (ICWA, New Delhi, 1945).

6. See C.B. Birdwood ; *A Continent Experiments* (Skeffington & Son Ltd., London, 1946), Ch. VIII.

7. See A. Strachey ; 'Some Aspects of the Future Defence of New India' in *Asiatic Review* (April, 1947). Also G. Schuster and G. Wint : *India and Democracy*, pp. 322-37.

8. See, L.J. Kavic ; *India's Quest for Security : Defence Policies 1947-65.* (University of California Press, Berkeley and Los Angeles, 1967), pp. 22-28,

9. Cited in N.V. Rajkumar (ed.) ; *The Background of India's Foreign Policy* (All India Congress Committee, New Delhi, 1952), p. 90.

10. J. Nehru ; *Independence and After* (Publications Division, Ministry of Information and Broadcasting, Government of India, Delhi, 1949), p. 340.

11. *ibid.*, p. 277.

12. As Prime Minister Attlee told the House of Commous, on 25 February 1947 : "If India decides to leave the Commonwealth, the continued security of India will, of course, be a matter of great interest to the British Commonwealth. His Majesty's Government will naturally be very willing to enter into discussions with India as to mutual assistance in matter of external defence subject, of course, to the obligation of both parties under the United Nations Charter. See *Hansard*, (Commons), 5 Series, Vol. 433, col. 1879.

13. In 1954-55, the Indian Navy sent 108 persons to UK for training ; in 1959-60 the number dropped to 42. But the link has been maintained.

Some twenty officers, from all services go to UK each year to attend specialised courses, and some British officers also attend Staff Colleges in India. It is now recognised that Indians have become experts in high altitude warfare.

14. Central Office of Information ; *Cooperation and Consultation within the Commonwealth* (H.M.S.O., London, 1963).

15. In 1965, for instance, there were 14 service officers attached to the Indian High Commission in London, all of the rank of Adviser or Deputy Adviser ; in 1966, the number was 13. See, C.R.O. ; List 1965, pp. 54-55, and C.R.O. ; *Year Book of the Commonwealth 1966*, p. 217. Britain also maintained a large military mission in India.

16. See H.M. Patel ; *The Defence of India* (R.R. Kale Memorial Lecture, Gokhale Institute of Politics and Economics, Poona 1963), p. 15. Mr Patel was formerly the Secretary to the Ministry of Defence, Government of India.

17. L.J. Kavic ; *op.cit.*, p. 90.

18. *ibid.*

19. *Asian Review*, January 1956, p. 42 (Speech before a joint meeting of the East India Association and the Overseas League). Mr Gundevia was at that time the Indian deputy High Commissioner in London.

20. The names of Admiral Parry and Admiral Pizey are especially important in this connection.

21. L.J. Kavic, *op.cit.*, p. 117.

22. For details, see Raymond V.B. Blackman (ed.) ; *Jane's Fighting Ships 1969-70*, (London), pp. 143-50.

23. Illyushin-28s were offered at £60,000 apiece ; after strenuous Western lobbying it was decided to buy British Canberras at £250,000 each. See, M. Kidron ; *Foreign Investments in India.* (O.U.P., London, 1965) p. 118.

24. See, J.L. Sutton and G. Kemp ; *Arms to Developing Countries* 1945-65, (Institute for Strategic Studies, London, Adelphi Paper No. 28, October 1966) p. 36. This number, however, does not tally with that calculated by Kavic. For details, L.J. Kavic, *op.cit.* pp. 102-103.

25. See page 244.

26. *The Times*, 3 April, 1956. Also, the *Asian Recorder*, March 31-April 6, 1956, p. 759. Six years later on 23 June, 1962, Nehru made a statement to the Rajya Sabha which was slightly different in nature. While replying to a foreign affairs debate Nehru referred to the events of 1956. He said that India was considering the proposal for the purchase of Illyushin-28s from the Soviet Union, only because Britain had refused to sell the type of aircraft desired by India. But then the British Government intervened and pleaded with the Government of India not to buy Russian aircraft. A counter-offer was made to New Delhi, and ultimately the Government of India decided to buy British. See, *Parliamentary Debates*, (Rajya Sabha), Vol. XXXIX, No. 9, Cols. 1772-73.

27. *The Times*, 4 February, 1957.

28. L.J. Kavic, *op cit.*, p. 104.

29. *The Times*, 4 February, 1957.

30. *The Times*, 2 September, 1957.

31. See the Appendix, III, Table 1.

32. See report by K. Rangaswami in *The Hindu*, 9 May 1962. For the background to the Indo-Soviet MIG deal and the reaction of the British and American Governments to the proposed deal, also see, J. Nehru's speech in the Rajya Sabha on 23 June, 1962. *Parliamentary Debates* (Rajya Sabha), Vol. XXXIX, No. 9 Cols. 1769-1776.

33. K. Rangaswami ; 'The Truth about the MIG deal' in *The Hindu*, 19 June, 1962.

34. See Paul Gore-Booth ; *With Great Truth and Respect*, p. 290.

35. As reported by A.M. Rosenthal in the *New York Times* of 13 June, 1962. Also see, John K. Galbraith ; *Ambassador's Journal : A Personal Account of the Kennedy Years* (Hamish Hamilton, London, 1969), pp. 384-86.

36. *The Hindu*, 31 May, 1962.

37. *The Economic Weekly* (Bombay), 2 June, 1962.

38. Report by Romesh Thapar in *The Economic Weekly*, 23 June, 1962.

39. *New York Times*, 16 June, 1962.

40. See the *Sunday Telegraph*, 24 June, 1962.

41. S/5134.

42. See Nehru's speech in the Rajya Sabha on 23 June, 1962. *Parliamentary Debates* (Rajya Sabha). Vol. XXIX, No. 9, Col. 1775.

43. L.J. Kavic, *op.cit.*, p. 108.

44. See, for example, *The Observer*, (London), 17 June, 1962.

45. K. Shelvankar in *The Hindu*, 4 August, 1962.

46. Lt. Genl. B.M. Kaul, the then Chief of the General Staff of the Indian Army, had reservations about this. In a book published after his inglorious retirement from the army he wrote, about the MIG deal, that there was a general feeling in the Indian Air Force that the MIG aircraft was being thrust upon them by the Indian Government against their better judgment. He thought that the decision to purchase MIGs and to produce them in India was a deliberate policy decision of the Indian government to associate the Soviet Union in an important defence project at a time when tensions in Sino-Indian relations were increasing. See B.M. Kaul ; *The Untold Story* (Allied Publishers, Bombay, 1967) pp. 34-44.

47. The first shipment of British arms, mainly infantry weapons, reached India on 9 October, 1962.

48. For the text of the letter exchanged between Mr Chavan and Mr Sandys, see the C.R.O. release as published in *The Times*, 28 November, 1962.

49. *The Sunday Times*, 23 December, 1962.

50. See Mr Duncan Sandy's statement in the House of Commons on

3 December 1962 : *Hansard* (Commons) fifth series, vol. 668, Cols. 933-936. The relevant portion of the statement has been quoted in Ch. 3, supra. Also see, *Foreign Assistance Act of 1963*. Hearings before the Committee on Foreign Affairs, House of Representatives, 88th Congress, 1st session, Statement by J. Grant on 30 April, 1963. pp. 416-17.

51. For a discussion on the differences between Mr Duncan Sandys and the then American Ambassador to India, Prof. J.K. Galbraith, see Ch. 3, supra.

52. For Pakistan's objections to western arms aid to India see Mr Bhutto's speeches to the Pakistan National Assembly on 26 November, 1962, 4 December, 1962 and 17 July, 1962, later published in a single volume : Z.A. Bhutto ; *Foreign Policy of Pakistan : A Compendium of Speeches made in the National Assembly* 1962-64. (Pakistan Institute of International Affairs, Karachi, 1964).

53. *The Times*, 1 May, 1963. See also the editorial in *The Hindu*, 4 June, 1963.

54. *The Times*, 30 May, 1963.

55. *The Hindu*, 1 July, 1963.

56. *The Hindu*, 2 July, 1963.

57. See the report by the military correspondent of the *Daily Telegraph*, 4 August, 1963.

58. J.K. Galbraith, *op. cit.*, p. 456.

59. *ibid.*, p. 504.

60. *The Hindu*, 2 February, 1963.

61. J.K. Galbraith, *op.cit.*, p. 549.

62. *Lok Sabha Debates*, Fourth Sessions, 3rd Series, Vol. XIII, Col. 545.

63. *The Times*, 11 July, 1963.

64. See Nehru's statement in the Lok Sabha on 19 August 1963 : *Lok Sabha Debates*, 5th Session, 3rd Series, Vol. X1X, Cols. 1213-18.

65. See Report by Thomas Brady in the *New York Times*, 2 Sept. 1963.

66. *The Hindu*, 17 September, 1963.

67. See *Report, 1963-64* (annual) Ministry of Defence, Government of India, New Delhi, 1964, pp. 54-55.

68. *ibid.*, p. 49.

69. *Lok Sabha Debate*, 3rd series, 7th session, Vol. XXVIII, Cols. 544-46.

70. For details, see *The Hindu*, 22 September, 1964. Also *Report* 1964-65, p. 2.

71. *New York Times*, 13 May, 1964.

72. The financial value of British military assistance to India between 1962-63 and 1968-69 was £24.7m. See, Appdx. III. The total value of British military aid to India between 1950 and March 1965, according to the then Secretary for Commonwealth Relations, Mr Arthur Bottomley, was £ 16.63 m. For Mr Bottomley's reply, see *Hansard* (Commons), 5 series, vol. 710, 1964-65 session, Col. 249, Answers.

73. *The Hindu*, 13 July, 1964.

74. *The Hindu*, 21 November ; also *The Financial Times*, 21 November, 1964.

75. For details, see "Exchange of Letters between the Government of the United Kingdom and the Government of India...for assistance towards the Mazagaon Dock and Leander frigate Project." *Cmnd.* 2549.

76. For the text of the Communique, see *The Hindu*, 21 November, 1964.

77. See, *Report, 65-66*, (Ministry of External Affairs, Government of India, New Delhi, p. 57.)

78. *ibid.*, pp. 57-58.

79. *The Times*, 29 September, 1965.

80. *ibid.*

81. See K. Subrahmanyam ; 'Planning and Defence' in Paul Streeten and Michael Lipton (eds.) ; '*The Crisis of Indian Planning*'. Mr Subrahmanyam was formerly a senior official in the Ministry of Defence, and later the Director of the Institute for Defence Studies and Analyses, New Delhi (1968-75).

82. See Appendix III.

83. See, the statement by S. Bhagavantam, the then Scientific Adviser to the Ministry of Defence, in *The Hindu*, 28 March, 1966.

84. J.L. Sutton and G. Kemp ; *op. cit.* p. 18.

85. Walter Goldstein ; *The Dilemmas of British Defence* (Ohio State University Press, April, 1966).

86. Quoted by *The Economist*, 25 June. 1966.

87. *The Guardian*, 11 June, 1965. On 4 February 1965, in reply to a question by Mr E. Griffiths, Prime Minister Mr Wilson said that though India had not asked for any specific commitment from Britain as an insurance against aggression, if she "were to be the object of such aggression, we would, of course, immediately wish to consult her about means of assistance." See *Hansard* (Commons), 5 Series, vol. 705, 1964-65 session, col. *331*, (written answer).

88. See, Patrick Gordon Walker ; *The Cabinet*, pp. 123-29.

89. *Cmnd.* 3357.

90. See, *Report 1969-70*, (Ministry of External Affairs, Government of India, New Delhi), pp. 5-6.

90a. In 1971 the British Government proposed to set up a Commonwealth Study Group to examine the problem of defence of the Indian Ocean region. India accepted the proposal but later on withdrew from the Study Group in protest againt British sale of arms to South Africa.

91. For a different view on this point, see Lt. Genl. P.S. Gyani ; 'India's Military Strategy' in *India Quarterly* January-March 1967, p. 26.

92. See Dilip Mukherjee; 'India's Defence Perspectives' in *International Affairs*, October, 1968.

CHAPTER VII

CONCLUSIONS

RELATIONS BETWEEN states vary over a wide spectrum from the extreme of total enmity leading to war, to the other extreme of stable friendliness. If we try to trace the reciprocal relations among nations along some scale of diplomatic 'amity-enmity',[1] Indo-British relations since 1947 would most of the time be nearer the end of 'amity', though there were some fluctuations towards the other pole. Seen from New Delhi, one of the persistent causes of discord between Britain and India was the attitude of successive British governments towards the Indo-Pakistani conflict over Kashmir. Colonial and racial issues have also contributed to tensions between the two states. In spite of these differences, diplomatic relations between Britain and India have generally been friendly—rather dull and flat, compared for example to India's relations with the United States—with relatively few major fluctuations. An analysis of Indo-British relations in the years 1947-68 therefore consists, as we have seen, of accounting for the gradual decline in the intensity of their relationships. However, although the process of decline has characterised Indo-British relations as a whole, it is important to note that the rate of decline has not always been parallel in the three principal spheres of their inter-action—political, economic and military.

The evolution of Indo-British relations between 1947-68 went through a series of distinct though overlapping phases which bring out the nature of the changes in their relationships. For the first few years after independence (1947-50), the policy of the Government of India was to develop and maintain close links with Britain. This basic premise of Indian policy very largely explains the decision to continue membership of the Commonwealth. It was not a decision taken merely out of sentimental considerations for the past association between Britain and India. Indeed, if anything, the memories of this association created—in India—an ambivalent attitude towards the United Kingdom. The Government of India's decision was influenced ultimately, by considerations of mutual benefits that, it was believed, would follow from membership of the Commonwealth. Because of the close economic, political and military links between the two states (which it would have been difficult, if not impossible, to dismantle overnight) and also because of India's relative lack of experience in international diplomacy, good relations with Britain were one of the assets and aims of Indian foreign policy during the years 1947-50. There were some disappointments, notably because of the lack of British support in her quarrels with Pakistan, and in her disputes with South Africa. But disappointments and differences over these issues did not prevent general Indo-British consultation and cordiality in international affairs. During this period India's relations with the United States were cool but diplomatically correct, and relationship with the Soviet Union had not yet fully developed, primarily because of Soviet Russia's suspicions about Nehru's policy. Britain remained by far the most important external influence on the new Indian Government. But the flow of influence was not all in one direction.

In 1950 India exercised great influence on British foreign policy, especially on British policy in Asia, through her membership of the Commonwealth.[2] The British Government's decision to grant recognition to the Communist Government in China in 1950 was influenced by Indian views. Both the governments were in favour of China's entry to U.N. There was also substantial agreement between them at the initial stages of the Korean War.

However, it was with the deepening of the 'Cold War' that differences between the two governments began to appear as Indian policy shifted from a pro-West bias to an independent neutralist posture. In October 1950, the Government of India strongly advised against the crossing of the 38th parallel by the U.N. forces in Korea ; the U.S. ignored the warning, and when American forces crossed the 38th parallel, Britain supported the move. India was against the recognition of the Bao-Dai government in Vietnam, but Britain along with the United

States, Australia and New Zealand granted recognition. The Government of India were critical of the Western alliances which would, in their view, further increase tensions in an already ideologically divided world, and would retard the progress of decolonisation in Asia. Though ideologically opposed to the system of military alliances, India's criticism of NATO was initially mild. In June 1952, at the NATO Council meeting in Lisbon, Portugal tried to enlist the support of her alliance partners to the Portuguese claim of sovereignty over Goa. Nehru reacted sharply to this move, and thereafter Indian criticism of military alliances became more vocal and consistent. Indo-British relations suffered accordingly as, for example, in 1954 when the British Foreign Office adopted a partisan attitude in the Indo-Portuguese dispute over Goa. Progressively differences between alignment and non-alignment emerged as a major source of tension in Anglo-Indian relations during the mid-fifties. This was the period when Nehru was preoccupied with the idea of a resurgent Asianism, free from the domination of the West, and free from the blast of the cold war. Certain policies of the Western Powers seemed to frustrate these aims, and for this India blamed the United States as well as Britain. The extension of the Western system of alliances to South East Asia and the Middle East through SEATO and the Baghdad Pact—with Pakistan and Britain as members of both—was particularly disturbing to India and was seen in New Delhi as a threat to India's territorial security. Above all, they revived the memories of colonial domination of Asia by Europe, and were regarded in India as attempts to resuscitate the old system in a new disguise. At the Bandung Conference (1955) Nehru reaffirmed India's policy of non-alignment and warned that every step that reduced the 'unaligned' area was a dangerous step leading to war. India's worst fears about military alliances seemed to be confirmed in 1956 when Pakistan successfully raised the Kashmir issue at the SEATO Council meeting in Karachi and a few months later, at the Baghdad Pact Council meeting in Teheran.

An important aspect of this second phase (1951-56) of Indo-British relations was that in spite of their differences, the two governments continued to maintain a policy of close cosultation and even a 'working co-operation'[3] with each other in international affairs. Such co-operation and consultation served the interests of both. India was a newly independent state, important in her own right. She was also the acknowledged spokesman, if not the leader, of Asian- African states on such issues as colonialism and racialism. Because of her policy of non-involvement in the Cold War, and also because of her friendly relations with China, and with the Soviet Union after the death of Stalin, India was in a unique position to act as a channel of communication—through her membership of the Commonwealth—between the two sides in the Cold War. The British Government, therefore, realised that the success of British policy in Asia would be facilitated if they could secure the acquiescence, if not the support, of the Government of India. Co-operation with India strengthened Britain's views in Washington, particularly in matters relating to Asia, where there were differences between the policies of the British and the American governments. India also derived advantages from such co-operation as access to the British government in London enabled her views to reach a wider audience in the west. Indo-British compromise procedures were particularly effective during the negotiations leading to the cease-fire in Korea in 1953 and again, during the Geneva Conference on Indo-China in 1954. Though India was not a member of the conference, Krishna Menon, Nehru's Ambassador-at-large, played a very important role in it success. Consultations between the two Governments continued even on issues where their views were not similar.

The first major deviation from the principle of prior consultation with the Commonwealth came with the Anglo-French invasion of Suez in October 1956. In fact, one of the causes for Indian resentment against Britain's action, as voiced by the Opposition spokesman in the Indian Parliament, was this failure on the part of the British government to consult the largest member of the Commonwealth.

Suez was an aberration in Britain's post-war policy. The response of the British government to the Middle East crisis of 1956, arising out of Egypt's nationalisation of the Suez Canal

Company, was determined, to a large extent, by the personal biases and resentments of the British Prime Minister against Nasser, a conclusion which becomes evident from the study of his own memoirs.[4] Nevertheless, once the British Government had resorted to gun-boat diplomacy, the Indian reaction was predictable. The Anglo-French invasion of Suez was viewed in India as an attempt by the two imperialist powers to re-establish their influence in the Middle East through the use of force. The result of the Anglo-French move was disastrous ; it united the Arabs, divided the British, divided the Commonwealth, alienated one of Britain's closest allies, and outraged public opinion against Britain. It imposed severe strains on Anglo-Indian relations. The Government of India's ambivalent attitude to the Soviet Union's military intervention in Hungary in the same year led to further deterioration in their relations. But, above all, it was the Suez crisis which marked the turning point in India's relations with Britain. For the first time since India's independence the value of the special relationship with Britain through membership of the Commonwealth was called into question.

1956-57 were particularly bad years for Indo-British relations. Before the rumpus over the Suez crisis had died down, Indian resentments against Britain rose high because of the British Government's unfriendly attitude during the Security Council debates on Kashmir in early 1957. Nevertheless, the breach was never complete. There were a number of factors—India's economic difficulties and the consequent need for foreign assistance, and the British government's willingness and, indeed, need to repair the damage to Indo-British relations as to its diplomatic posture generally, as a result of the Suez crisis—which called for the continuation of close cooperation between Britain and India. There was a rare felicity of communication between the leaders of the two states which made reconciliation easier. As a gesture of reconciliation the British Prime Minister, Mr Harold Macmillan, visited India in January 1958. This, no doubt, helped to dispel much of the misunderstanding in the relations between the two states. But the Indo-British initiatives in international affairs as seen during the

Korean war and the Geneva conference on Indo-China (1954) could not be resumed. In that sense the special relationship that had developed between Britain and India, enabling them to coordinate their policies in a number of international crises during 1951-56, was at an end.

A number of developments account for this change. The Suez adventure had damaged Britain's international prestige and subsequently she lost much of her previous manoeuverability in international affairs. After 1957 there was also a decline in India's mediatory role, primarily because of her preoccupation with domestic economic problems, but also because of certain changes in the international environment—the beginning of a Russo-American detente, the emergence of militant anti-colonialism in the new states of Africa, and finally, especially after 1959, the deterioration in India's relations with China.

With the shift in emphasis in India's foreign policy—from the active mediatory role in international affairs in the early years to the quieter role in the post-Suez years,—the emphasis in Indo-British relations shifted to cooperation in economic and defence matters. During the second half of the 1950s India's economic plans ran into some difficulties which were dramatically presented to the world by the severe foreign exchange crisis of 1957. In September of that year the then Indian Finance Minister Mr T.T. Krishnamachari visited the United States, Canada, West Germany and Britain to secure economic support for the Plan. From London he returned almost empty-handed. He was disappointed with the British Government; nevertheless, in the following year the British government played an important role in establishing an international consortium of donor countries (the Aid India Consortium) to cordinate the aid given to India. Bilateral trade between the two states increased during the late fifties. British exports to India increased steadily between 1958-59 and 1960-61 partly because of the flow of aid which started in 1958; imports from India also showed improvements during the same period. Because of the 'swing-right' in India's domestic economic policy, exports of British capital to India increased considerably during the post-Suez years, particularly between 1959-60. Between 1959-61, India purchased large quantities of arms and equipment from Britain, as the three wings of India's defence forces were undergoing a programme of expansion and development during these years.

By 1960 there were few major issues in Indo-British relations, with the exception of the continuing differences over Kashmir. Even on the Kashmir issue the differences between the two governments were narrowed, as the emphasis of British policy shifted from insistence on plebiscite to direct negotiations between India and Pakistan. India also welcomed the change in British attitude towards the racialist regime in South Africa, and the latter's departure from the Commonwealth (1961) reaffirmed India's faith in the multi-racial character of that association. The enthusiastic welcome extended to the Queen and the Duke of Edinburgh during their official visit to India in 1961 served to illustrate the depth of friendly feelings in India towards Britain.

Thus a fortunate conjunction of Anglo-Indian interests helped to repair, if not undo, the damage caused to their relationships by the Suez affair. However it is possible to note a new phase in their relations beginning in 1961, the onset of which was marked by a period of strain. A number of roughly coincidental events during the latter part of the year contributed to tensions in their relations. Some were the result of a reassessment by Britain of her own needs and priorities ; but they were interpreted differently in India, as they affected Indian interests. In the summer of 1961 the British Government announced the decision to apply for membership of the European Economic Community which provoked much adverse criticism in India and other Asian Commonwealth member-states. Shortly after this the British Government introduced legislation in the Parliament to control immigration from the new Commonwealth. But to most Indians (as well as to many Britons) this came as a shock, as a blow to their concept of the Commonwealth as an association based on the free movement of people, and, racial non-discrimination.

At much the same time as these developments came the Indian annexation of Goa, in December 1961. The Government of India's action in Goa was a deviation from the earlier pledges for the settlement of the dispute through peaceful means. Though it was largely acclaimed in Africa and Asia, as well as by the states in the Communist bloc, it tarnished India's image in the West. The spate of criticism in Britain created anger, dismay and resentment in India.

The diplomatic row over the Indo-Soviet MIG deal (1962) further aggravated the tensions. Yet once again, by the turn of events, conflict and amity were kept in the balance. Anti-British feelings receded in the wake of the military conflict with China in October-November 1962. Britain's diplomatic support to India, and the offer of military aid created a surge of pro-British feelings. On this occasion, however, the euphoria was short-lived. Goodwill for Britain soon turned into resentment as the British Government tried to put pressure on India for a satisfactory solution of the Kashmir dispute with Pakistan. Differences also emerged between the Indian and British Governments regarding the assessment of the threat posed by China, and the types of weapons needed to meet the threat. The years 1963-64 were the years of lost opportunities for the improvement of Indo-British relations. When the Labour Party won the elections in 1964, many Indians thought it would be easier to deal with a sympathetic Labour Government in London. The appointment of John Freeman, former editor of the *New Statesman*, as the High Commissioner to New Delhi in 1965 was probably a gesture to improve relations with India, and may be compared to the appointment of Professor John Kenneth Galbraith, one of the late President Kennedy's New Frotiersmen, as the US Ambassador to India in 1961. In the summer of 1965, the then British Prime Minister Mr (now Sir) Harold Wilson successfully mediated in the Indo-Pakistani dispute over the Rann of Kutch. But British diplomacy reached the nadir of its influence in India in September 1965 as a result of Mr Wilson's ill-advised statement during the war criticising India. India's reaction to the statement was strong and enduring.

During the 1960s there were also other causes of disagreement between the two Governments ; their attitudes to many issues of international politics were different—the nuclear non-proliferation treaty, the Sino-Indian conflict, Soviet domination of Eastern Europe, US intervention in Vietnam, the White minority regimes in South Africa and Rhodesia, to a name a few. This was not unnatural, given the differences between the two states in their geographical setting, historical experience, economic development and concepts of interests. By contrast, it is important to note that between 1947-68, there were few bilateral issues which created any major rift in Indo-British relations. The differences between the two states were often accentuated by old attitudes—the inability of the Indians to shake off some of their inhibitions inherited from the days of the Raj ; and the tendency of the British to behave in a way as if they were still the rulers.

The overall decline of British influence in India, particularly during the latter half of 1960s was parallelled, and may partly be explained by the diminishing importance of Britain in two vital sectors of Indian foreign policy—economics and defence. Anti-British feelings in India after the Indo-Pakistani war of 1965 probably accentuated the process. Between 1961-66 there was considerable decline in Indo-British trade, with imports from Britain declining at a faster rate than exports to Britain. Though UK remained India's most important trading partner during the period under review, Indo-British trade as a percentage of total trade declined beacause of a number of reasons : import-substitution by India, the influence of tied aid in changing the suppliers' share of imports, the deliberate policy of diversification of India's foreign trade and the redirection of Britain's foreign trade towards the high income countries of Europe and North America. When one considers the total involvement of foreign capital in India's economic development (in the form of foreign aid and investment), the United States' contribution far exceeded that of Britain. Since the mid-50's, moreover, the Soviet Union also became a supplier of capital to India's public sector ; Indo-Soviet trade increased too during the 1960s. India's economic dependence on Britain was thus progressively declining.

Britain's declining importance to India was also evident in the sphere of defence and security. Though Britain had never been formally committed to India's defence since 1947, there were some close links between the two states even in military matters. The organisation and training of the armed forces in India had close similarity with the systems prevailing in Britain. Till the Sino-Indian armed clash of 1962 Britain was India's principal source of arms, although the Government of India purchased the arms on commerical basis. With the conclusion of the Indo-Soviet agreement in 1962 for the manufacture of MIG fighter planes in India, the Soviet Union made a vital breakthrough in the Indian arms market. Since the Soviet Russia's involvement in India's defenee build-up has increased, while dependence on Britain as the supplier of arms and equipment declined almost dramatically after the Sino-Indian armed conflict of 1962. Britain's ability to help India in an emergency (like the one in 1962) declined too because of the considerable run-down of British forces east of Suez.

Two points, however, should be noted. First, during the 1950s and early 1960s, because of India's excessive dependence on Britain (in the spheres of economics and defence), the British government tried to put pressure on the Government of India on many sensitive issues at various times, either through the United Nations, or directly through normal diplomatic channels. The British government's action during the Security Council debates on Kashmir in 1957, the Anglo-American diplomatic pressure on India just before the Indian occupation of Goa in 1961, their attempts to block the Indo-Soviet MIG deal in 1962, and during the latter part of the same year their attempts to put pressure on India by linking up military aid with a satisfactory settlement of the Kashmir dispute, are some of the examples. Whether such efforts succeeded in achieving the desired aim is a matter of opinion ; but they served to embitter India's relations with Britain. With the loss of Britain's dominant position in India's defence and economic sectors she has lost much of this leverage, particularly after the Indo-Pakistani war of 1965.

The loss of Britain's position as the principal supplier of arms to India or as the predominant trading partner cannot be explained only or even primarily by reference to the political differences between the two governments. In 1957, after the traumatic experience of the Suez war, and during a period of tension in Indo-British relations (as a result of the latter's role during the Security Council debates on Kashmir), India finalised the decision to purchase Canberra bombers from Britain despite a Russian offer to supply Illyushin bombers at half the price. This was followed by the order for a large number of Hawker Hunter jets from Britain in the autumn of 1957, and Sea Hawk fighter planes for the Indian Navy in 1958. Perhaps one should not make much of this single incident. A number of reasons might have influenced the decision of the Indian government : India's dependence on Britain for other weapons and equipment, familiarity of the Indian Air Force with British aircraft and the pro-British inclination of many senior officials in the Services and in the Ministry of Defence, and finally, the reluctance of the Indian government to get too closely associated with the Soviet Union at a time when India needed financial aid from the West.

There is also evidence to suggest that political differences between the two governments did not necessarily lead to an adverse effect on their economic relationship, at least in the short run. Britain's involvement in India's economic development (by way of trade, aid and investment) increased steadily between 1957-58 and 1961 ; the decline which set in thereafter was the result, primarily, of the underlying changes in the economic sectors in both the states.

The shift in India's policy away from Britain started in the aftermath of the Sino-Indian conflict (1962), and the process was accelerated after the Indo-Pakistani war (1965). It was as much the result of disillusionment with British policy, as of a deliberate reordering of foreign policy priorities by India. The low-profile foreign policy of the post-Nehru era was different from the high-sounding moralistic posture of Nehru's foreign policy. The Government of India realised that India is primarily an Asian power and, therefore, in future India should be more interested in the developments in her neighbouring states in south and south east Asia. The Indian Prime Minister's visit to Nepal and Ceylon in 1966 and 1967, to Australia, New

Zealand, Singapore and Malayasia in 1968, and to Japan and Indonesia in 1969 were symbolic and underlined the importance attached by India to the states of this region. India emphasised the need for broad-based cooperation encompassing the whole area—as opposed to military pacts—as a means of ensuring the stability of this region. In 1968, she played an important role in establishing the Asian Council of Ministers under ECAFE.

With the virtual liquidation of the empire, and with the chronic balance of payments problem leading to the devaluation of the Pound-Sterling in 1967, a similar reassessment of foreign policy alternatives was also made in Britain. The implications of Britain's non-imperial role had for long been obscured by a number of factors—the existence of the Commonwealth which was taken as a substitute for a lost empire, the maintenance of military presence East of Suez, and the role of the sterling as an international currency. The purpose of the Duncan Report[5], despite all the criticisms voiced against it, was to draw attention to the realities of Britain's new non-imperial role as a middle-ranking European power. Britain's shrinking role in the world, the declining defence commitments overseas, the diminishing trade with the Commonwealth partners, and her accession to the treaty of Rome—all these showed that in the seventies she would be more concerned with matters nearer home, in Europe, than with those in distant India.

The British public at large showed very little interest in Indian affairs even during the heyday of the empire ; but the number of Britons who were interested in India declined, particularly during the 1960s. Because of Africa's sudden emergence in the international scene, events in Africa attracted more attention than those in India. Scant press coverage and occasional (tendentious) television reporting on India did not help to improve India's image. To the ordinary man in Britain India still remained the land of poverty, snake charmers, yogis and of Mahatma Gandhi.

There had also been a perceptible decline in academic interest on India, during the 1960s. In the field of economics and conventional history (down to 1900) the contribution made by the British scholars was still significant ; but in contemporary

Indian history and politics they had been overtaken by the Americans. There are South Asia Study Centres in the Universities of London, Cambridge and Sussex and a Study Groups in India still meets regularly at the Royal Institute of International Affairs, Chatham House, London. Nevertheless, as the older generation of British scholars (mostly 'old India hands') became less active, the study of Indian affairs in Britain had been seriously eroded during the 1960s, and the future seemed to many to be bleak.[6]

With the rise of a new social and political elites in India British influence is also on the wane. In the past, especially in the pre-independence days, the Anglicised intelligentsia constituted the dominant social elites ; having part of one's education in Britain was itself an advantage for a promising career in the civil service or in the professions. This continued for a few years even after independence. A large number of Indians still go abroad for higher studies and training ; but many of them now attend non-British universities. The Western-educated elite in India do no longer form a cohesive group, not even in New Delhi ; and do not carry with them ideas and practices particularly British.

Indo-British relations : Are they mature ?

The concept of maturity as applied to Indo-British relations is relatively new, and was fostered by the British Labour Government during 1964-70. During his visit to India the then British Foreign Secretary Mr Michael Stewart repeatedly spoke of the need for a 'maturer relationship' between Britain and India. But the meaning of the term 'mature' in the context of inter-State relations is still not very clear. Does it mean that the peculiarly involved and complex relationship which had grown up between Britain and India during the years since India's independence was immature ?

If the concept of 'maturity' meant relegating to history the era of love-hate relationship between Britain and India, if it meant that in future their relationship should be based on an objective assessment of each other's problems and difficulties, this should certainly be welcome. As the composition of the ruling elites in the two states changes, this may facilitate the development of such a relationship. The new generation of leaders who came to power in India in the post-Nehru era did not have the peculiarly ambivalent and sentimental attitudes towards Britain which Nehru and the men of his generation. had. In Britain, also, the new generation of political leaders —those who came to political prominence in the post-imperial years—are free from the nostalgic attitude of their predecessors, a nostalgia born out of a sense of regret for a departed imperial glory ; and, therefore, should be in a better position to deal with India on a footing of equality.

Consequent upon the loosening of links between the two states, occasions for conflict between them will also be less in future. Colonial issues were an important cause of friction in Indo-British relations during 1950s ; with the virtual death of classical European colonialism overseas, colonial issues will no longer be a significant cause of tension in Indo-British relations. The British government's attitude to the racialist regime in South Africa was another recurrent cause of disagreement in Indo-British relations, especially during the 1950s. With the crystallisation of opinion in the world against racial discrimination, policy towards South Africa no longer remains a major cause of conflict in Indo-British relations. Nevertheless, there is a possibility that in furture questions of race and colour may become a cause of tension in Britain's relations with the Afro-Asian states. Much will, however, depend on Britain's treatment of her own racial minorities. The Commonwealth Immigrants Act, 1968, gave rise to serious misgivings in India, and revived old feelings of racial discrimination by the British. The Government of India's cautious reaction to it, (and to the subsequent measures taken by the British Government to reduce the flow of coloured immigrants to Britain to almost a trickle) surely shows signs of realism.[7]

The most important prevailing source of tensions in Anglo-Indian relations towards the close of the period under review was the British government's attitude to the Indo-Pakistani dispute over Kashmir. But after the Indo-Pakistani war of 1965, there was a distinct change in British government's policy.

During his visit to India in 1968 Mr Stewart said that Britain's future policy in Kashmir dispute would be one of non-interference, unless both the parties requested the British government to intervene. This stance of the British government was quite consistent with the policy of withdrawal from the 'residual' responsibilities of the past.

Does it mean that in future Indo-British relations will be mature in the sense of being based on a non-emotive realisitic appraisal of their mutual interests ? For the future, it seems, Mr Stewart hinted at a relationship between Britain and India that would be friendly but inconsequential. Perhaps the main purpose of Mr Stewart's visit to India was not to strengthen Indo-British links, but to explain to India Britain's new non-imperial role.

By the end of the 1960s, relations with Britain no longer formed the principal concern of Indian foreign policy ; nor did India feature prominently in Britain's foreign policy. Each country's conception of its main national interests had undergone changes. For India the major threat to security was believed to be China, while the British thought that the main threat to world peace was the Soviet Union—at least this was the impression left by Mr Stewart. On the eve of India's independence, in 1946, K.M. Panikkar wrote eloquently on the need and necessity for an Indo-British treaty ; a quarter of a century later, in 1971, India concluded a 'Treaty of Friendship' not with Britain, but with the Soviet Union, and the British Parliament voted overwhelmingly in favour of joining the European Economic Community. Nothing illustrates better the changes in the international outlook of Britain and India.

For a few years after the Indo-Pakistani war of 1965, it seemed that Indians had virtually written Britain off. Partly, it was a reaction to the British government's policy during the war ; but it also reflected the declining importance of Britain to India. During the latter half of the 1960s India's foreign policy gradually moved from a position of equidistance from the two super powers to a position of equal proximity towards them. But with the beginning of a thaw in Sino-US relations, and with India's increasing dependence on the Soviet Union, maintenance of amicable relations with Britain, now a member of EEC, will be beneficial for India. Indeed the need for this was clearly demonstrated during the Indo-Pakistani war of 1971. However, in the late 1960s, the talk of maturity in Indo-British relations seemed to be an euphemism for the loss of ardour and of emotional ambivalence, for disenchantment and quiet disillusion, for reappraisal of each other's needs and priorities with mutually lowered expectations.

NOTES AND REFERENCES

1. See, K.E. Boulding ; 'National Images and International Systems' in James N, Rosenau (ed.) ; *International Politics and Foreign Policy* (Free Press of Glencoe, 1961). Also see, Arnold Wolfers ; 'Amity and Enmity among Nations' in A. Wolfers ; *Discord and Collaboration,* (John Hopkins Press, Baltimore, 1962).
2. See Patrik Gordon Walker ; *The Commonwealth* (Mercury Books, London, 1965), p. 315.
3. Peter Lyon ; *Neutralism* (Leicester University Press, 1963, p. 125).
4. Anthony Eden ; *The Full Circle : Memoirs of Sir Anthony Eden,* (Cassell, London, 1960).
5. Cmnd. 4107.
6. See, Hugh Tinker ; 'The Rediscovery of India', review article in *International Affairs*, Jan. 1969. Also see, D.A. Low ; "South Asian Studies: Finding the Next Generation" in *South Asian Review,* January, 1969. Lipton and Firn, however, are not so pessimistic. They point out that there has been a revival of interest in India in the 1970s, particularly among the younger generation of scholars, working in specialised centres, who are less emotionally involved than the old India hands. See, M. Lipton & J. Firn ; op cit, p. 153.
7. If the Government of India's cautions reaction to the Commonwealth Immigrants Act (1968) showed signs of 'maturity', the over-reaction to the Louis Malle affair (1970) did not.

APPENDIX I

Chronology of Important events affecting Indo-British Relations (1947-65)

	1	2	3	4
Year	Political	Economic and Technological	Adminis-trative	Military
1947	U.K. : Parliament passes the Indian Independence Act (July 1947) The British Government transfers power to the Indian Government. (15 August, 1947) India : accepts Kashmir's accession. (27 October, 1947.) India : refers the Kashmir dispute to U.N. (31 December, 1947)	U.K. and India : Financial Agreement regarding sterling balances. (14 August 1947)		Infiltrators from the Pakistani territory enter Kashmir (24 October, 1947) India : Sends troops to Kashmir. (27 October, 1947) India : sends troops to Junagadh.
1948	U.K. (and U.S.) : propose arbitration on Kashmir. U.K. : passes the Nationality Bill.	India : Industrial Policy Resolution. U.K. and India : Financial Agreement.	India : the IAS and the IPS created as successors to the two all India services created by the Raj—the Indian Civil Service and the Indian Police.	India : sends troops to Hyderabad. (13 September 1948)

1		2	3	4
Year	Political	Economic and Technological	Adminis-trative	Military
1949	India : decides to continue membership of the Commonwealth even after the adoption of a republican constitution. India : recognises the Government of the Peoples' Republic of China.	U.K. and India : both devalue their currencies		India : accepts cease-fire in Kashmir. (1 January, 1949) U.K. : NATO
1950	U.K. : recognises the Government of the Peoples' Republic of China. India : adopts a republican constitution. U.K. : grants recognition to the Bao Dai Government in Vietnam.	U.K. and India : Participate in the Colombo Conference (January)		U.K. and India support U.N. police action against North Korea (June). India : opposes the crossing of the 38th parallel by the U.N. forces in Korea. (October)
1951	U.K. : re-affirms in the Security Council that the ultimate disposition of the Kashmir state would be made through the holding of plebiscite, suggests arbitration on points of disagreement between India and Pakistan.	India : launches the First Five Year Plan. India and U.K. : agreement on preferences		

	1	2	3	4
Year	Political	Economic and Technological	Administrative	Military
1952	India : protests against Portugal's efforts to raise the Goa issue at the NATO Council Meeting in Lisbon.	The Commonwealth Economic Conference in London (27 Nov. —11 Dec.) rejects restrictionist trade policies.		
1953	India : mediatory role in the POW negotiations at the end of the Korean War.	U.K. and India : Financial Agreement.		
1954	India : signs agreement with China on Tibet. (April, 1954) U.K. : sends note to India advising against the use of force in Goa.			U.K. : Joins SEATO. U.K. & India : cooperation for bringing to an end the French Colonial war in Indo-China. (Geneva Conference) India : Military purchases from Britain.
1955	India : criticises the western powers at the Bandung Conference. The British Foreign Secretary visits India.	U.K. and India : Agreement for the peaceful uses of atomic energy.		U.K. : joins the Baghdad Pact.

	1	2	3	4
Year	Political	Economic and Technological	Administrative	Military
1956	India : protests against the SEATO Council's discussion of the Kashmir issue.	India : Industrial Policy Resolution. India : enters into an agreement with a British Consortium for the Durgapur Steel Project.		India : purchases Centurion tanks from Britain. India : sharply reacts to the Anglo-French attack on Egypt ; mild criticism of Soviet military intervention in Hungary.
1957	U.K. : re-affirms the need for plebiscite in Kashmir ; suggests the introduction of U.N. troops in Kashmir for the purpose of demilitarisation.	India : faced with a severe foreign exchange crisis ; liberalises the terms of foreign investment.		India : decides to buy Canberras for IAF, and acquires INS-Vikrant for the Indian Navy.
1958	Prime Minister Macmillan visits India	The Aid-India consortium set up. U.K. and India : The Commonwealth Trade and Economic Conference in Montreal.		India : Criticises the landing of British troops in Jordan. India: purchases anti-submarine frigates from Britain.
1959		Agreement between India and U.K. for 'voluntary' limitation on the export of Indian textiles to Britain.		India : enters into an agreement with the Hawker-Siddeley for the construction of AVRO-748 planes in India.

	1	2	3	4
Year	Political	Economic and Technological	Administrative	Military
1960	U.K. : Prime Minister Macmillan delivers his 'wind of change' speech in South Africa.			
1961	Britain : role in the Congo crisis and India. South Africa leaves the Commonwealth	India : launches the 3rd 5-year Plan.		India : concludes an agreement with the Vickers Armstrong for the manufacture of Chieftain tanks in India. India : sends troops to Goa.
1962	U.K. : The Commonwealth Immigrants' Act (1962). India and U.K. : guarantee the independence and neutrality of Laos. (July, 1962). U.K. : Initiates bi-lateral talks between India and Pakistan on Kashmir (Sandys-Harriman Mission)	U.K. : applies for entry to E.E.C		India : concludes an agreement with the Soviet Union for the manufacture of MIG-21 planes. U.K. : emergency supply of arms to India (Nassau Declaration, December).
1963	U.K. and U.S. : declare that long-term arms aid to India is not related to the settlement of the Kashmir dispute.			Joint air exercises in India between Indian and U.S.-Commonwealth air forces. India and U.K. : both sign the nuclear Test-ban Treaty. U.K. (and U.S.) : pledge long-term military assistance to India.

	1	2	3	4
Year	Political	Economic and Technological	Adminis-trative	Military
1964	U.K. : supports the proposal for India-Pakistan negotiation on Kashmir. Commonwealth Prime Minister's Conference in London decides to set up a Commonwealth Secretariat.	U.K. : new fiscal measures affect the flow of investment to India.		India and U.K. : agreement for a loan for the construction of Leander class frigates in India.
1965	U.K. : mediates in the Rann of Kutch conflict between India and Pakistan. India : resents the British Prime Minister's statement during the Indo-Pak War. (Sept. 1965) Rhodesia declares UDI (November 1965). U.K. : moves the U.N. for economic sanction against Rhodesia. U.K. : New restrictions on Immigration from the Commonwealth Countries.	India : accedes to the Commonwealth sugar Agreement.	U.K. : The Foreign & Commonwealth Services are merged in the Diplomatic Service.	U.K. : suspends the supply of arms to India (September, 1965)

APPENDIX II

TABLE I

Direction of India's Trade with UK.

19-	Imports (Merchandise) (In Rs. Lakhs.)			Exports (Merchandise) (In Rs. Lakhs)**		
	1 Total	2 from UK	3 (2) as a % of (1)	4 Total	5 to UK	6 (5) as a % of (4)
48-49	542,92	152,36	28.6	423,31	98,28	23.2
51-52	863,48	158,13	18.3	715,69	189,66	26.5
52-53	670,07	140,99	21.4	578,07	123.29	21.3
53-54	572,06	144,98	25.3	530,66	151,33	28.5
54-55	656,44	153,36	23.3	593,98	189,41	31.9
55-56	678,99	172,69	25.2	597,43	166,15	27.8
58-59	856,17	158.63	18.5	568,97	164,23	28.8
59-60	960,77	194,30	20.2	639,55	178,85	27.8
60-61	1121,62	217,15	19.3	642,32	172,48	26.8
61-62	1090,06	200,15	18.3	660,34	160,94	24.3
62-63	1131,48	185,56	16.4	685,48	163,22	23.8
63-64	1222,85	171,46	14.0	793,24	163.67	20.6
64-65	1349,03	163,65	12.1	816,30	167,30	20.4
69-70	1582,10	102.59	6.4	1413,27	165,07	11.7

* Figures for the year 1957 were given on the calendar year basis, and as such have not been included here.

Source :		
For years 1948-49 & 1951-52	*Reserve Bank of India Bulletin*,	Oct. 1953
,, ,, 1952-53 to 1954-55	,, ,, ,, ,, ,,	,, 1956
,, 1955-56	,, ,, ,, ,, ,,	,, 1957
,, ,, 1958-59 to 1962-63	,, ,, ,, ,, ,,	Nov. 1964
,, ,, 1963-64 to 1964-65	,, ,, ,, ,, ,,	,, 1966
,, 1969-70	,, ,, ,, ,, ,,	June. 1975

** 1 Lakh equals one hundred thousand.

TABLE IA

India's Principal Trading Partners (Outside the Communist Bloc) April 1968-March 1969

(Rs. million)

Export (f.o.b.)			Imports (c.i.f.)	
Value	% of total	Total	Value	% of Total
13,600.2		of which	18,616.2	
2,015.1	14.8	Britain	12,78.7	6.9
2,342.7	17.2	U.S.A.	5,750.6	30.9
1,114.8	8.2	E.E.C.	2,336.5	12.6
1,583.3	11.6	Japan	1,153.0	6.2

Source: Foreign and Commonwealth Office; *A Year Book of the Commonwealth 1971* (H.M.S.O., London, 1971.) p. 725.

TABLE II

Direction of Britain's Trade with India (in £m).

	Imports (merchandise)			Exports (merchandise)		
Year	1	2	3	4	5	6
19-	Total	from India	(2) as a % of (1)	Total	to India	(5) as a % of (4)
'48	2078.04	96.35	4.6	1581.80	96.12	6.0
'49	2274.70	98.96	4.3	1786.40	117.13	6.5
'54	3373.93	148.38	4.4	2674.24	114.81	4.3
'55	3880.90	158.96	4.0	2905.42	130.16	4.4
'57	4070.81	157.48	3.8	3324.41	176.41	5.2
'59	3983.38	142.64	3.5	3330.13	171.39	5.1
'60	4540.66	148.46	3.2	3554.80	150.48	4.5
'61	4395.14	144.93	3.2	3681.50	151.81	4.0
'62	4487.22	135.94	3,2	3791.07	116.50	3.7
'63	4812.74	140.74	2.9	4081.04	136.64	3.3
'64	5696.08	141.34	2.4	4411.64	128.87	2.9
'65	5751.09	128.34	2.2	4727.97	114.08	2.4
'66	5946.79	119.10	2.0	5046.95	95.41	1.8

Source: The Trade figures have been taken from the various volumes of the *UN Year Book of International Trade Statistics.* For 1948 and 1949 *Year Book* 1951 (p. 255), for the years 1954 and 1955, *Year Book* 1956 (p. 596), for the years 1959 and 1960 *Year Book* 1961 (p. 671), for the years 1961-1964 *Year-Book* 1965 (p. 813) and for the years 1965 and 1966, *Year Book*, 1966 (p. 852).

TABLE III

Outstanding Foreign Business Investment in India from mid-1948 to end 1962

(In Rs. Crores)

Country	Mid-48	end-53	end-55	end-57	end-59	end-6o	end-61	end-62
Canada	—	—	—	—	—	—	6.5	7.3
W. Germany	0.1	0.1	2.4	3.1	5.0	6.4	10.7	12.0
UK	206.0	326.4	365.9	390.6	389.6	432.3	446.2	482.8
USA	11.2	30.0	39.6	57.2	67.7	73.0	95.9	108.9
Switzerland	5.3	6.0	5.7	5.8	6.6	7.9	9.3	10.8
Japan	—	—	—	—	—	—	3.2	3.3
Sweden	—	—	—	—	—	—	4.4	7.4
All Countries	255.8	392.0	442.4	532.0	582.8	634.7	679.8	735.5

Sources : *Reserve Bank of India Bulletin*, April 1966, Statement 111, pp. 374-376.

TABLE IIIA

Gross and Net Inflow of Foreign Investments in India

Rs. Crores.

	1961		1962		1963-64		1964-65		Outstanding investments
	Gross	Net	Gross	Net	Gross	Net	Gross	Net	end-March
UK	18.9	13.8	26.3	20.9	27.6	13.7	33.9	25.7	529.3.
USA	24.2	22.9	14.8	10.1	43.0	41.4	45.4	39.3	193,2
Others (inc. internation-al insts.)	17.6	8.2	17.9	7.1	30.9	12.8	37.0	12.7	213.3
Total	60.7	44.9	59.1	38.2	101.5	67.9	116.3	77.7	935.8

Sources : *Reserve Bank of India Bulletin, January*, 1967, p. 42, Table 6.

TABLE IV

Foreign Paid-up Capital in Manufacturing (Subsidiaries)—Countrywise Percentage Shares

COUNTRY	1960-61	1961-62	as at the end of 1962-63	1963-64 (Percentages)
UK	75.8	73.2	68.2	68.6
USA	8.5	9.8	10.5	10.1
Switzerland	3.5	4.7	5.2	4.8
Canada	3.8	3.4	2.9	4.1
France	—	—	2.8	2.8
Sweden	2.8	2.5	4.7	4.2
Others	5.6	6.4	5.7	5.4

Source : R.B.I. ; *Foreign Collaboration in Indian Industry—Survey Report* (Bombay 1968), Statement 1, p. 114.

TABLE V

Foreign Paid-up Capital in Manufacturing (Minority Capital Participation firms)—Countrywise percentage shares

Country	1960-61	1961-62	as at the end of 1962-63	1963-64 (percentages)
UK	57.2	50.0	45.1	44.5
USA	16.4	18.2	22.0	22.6
W. Germany	15.9	15.3	14.3	13.4
Switzerland	1.1	2.7	3.6	4.2
Others	9.4	13.8	15.0	15.3

Sources : R.B.I. ; *Foreign Collaboration in Indian Industry—Survey Report* (Bombay, 1968), Statement X, p. 121.

TABLE VI

Distribution of UK Private Investment in India by Industry Group (Rs. million)

Year	Plantation	Mining	Petroleum	Manufacturing	Services	Total
End-						
1953	703	80	606	970	905	3264
1955	862	90	791	990	925	3659
1960	981	125	1020	1266	931	4323
March-						
1963	1043	69	1231	1680	909	4932
1965	1137	71	1215	2009	958	5390
1967	1098	69	1029	2501	1173	5870

Figures exclude valuation changes arising from the devaluation of the rupee in June 1966.

Source : 'Indo-British Economic Relations' in *Newsletter*, 15 October, 1967 (Indian Investment Centre, New Delhi, p. 3.)

TABLE VII

British aid to India (Rs. millon).

Up to the end of	Loan authorised	Loan utilised	Grant authorised	Grant utilised
1st 5-year plan	—	—	5.2	0.4
During 2nd 5-year plan	1656.0	1644.9	5.7	5.8
During 3rd 5-year plan	3267.0	2300.7	13.4	10.8
During 1966-7	684.9	776.6	0.8	0.9
During 1967-8	558 0	736.3	0.8	5.4
	6165.9	5459.5	25.9	23.3

Source : *External Assistance*, 1967-68 (Ministry of Finance, Department of Economic Affairs, Government of India, New Delhi, 1969), p. 17.

TABLE VIII

British Aid to India

Percentage of UK's non-project aid to its total aid:

2nd Five-Year Plan	77 per cent
3rd Five-Year Plan	54 per cent
1966-67	100 per cent
1967-68	100 per cent

TABLE VIIIA

The non-project aid given consisted of the following : (Rs. million)

1. Balance of Payments Assistance	2970
2. Debt Relief Assistance	360
3. Kipping Loans	378.0
4. Food Relief Assistance	135.0
5. Others	198.0
	4041.0

Source : For Tables VIII and VIIIA *External Assistance 1967-68*, p. 12.

Note : For Tables VII and VIIIA Rupee equivalents are at the rate of £1/=Rs. 18.

TABLE IX

India's Regional Balance Of Payments on Current Account

Transfer Payments (Sterling Area) Rs. Crores

	1962-63	63-64	64-65	65-66	66-67*	69-70**
I. Official						
Dr.	—	—	0.3	0.3	0.5	0.8
Cr.	0.2	0.4	1.4	0.7	—	3.1
Net	+0.2	+0.4	+1.1	+0.4	—0.5	+2.3
II. Private						
Dr.	10.6	9.5	10.6	10.5	13.4	8.6
Cr.	24.5	29.8	25.5	50.5	37.9	40.8
Net	+13.9	+20.3	+14.9	+40.0	+24.5	+32.2

*Revised **Preliminary

Source : For the years 1962-63 to 1966-67, *Reserve Bank of India Bulletin*, March, 1970, Table 49, p. 526. For 1969-70, *ibid.* April, 1971, Table 44, p. 660.

APPENDIX III

TABLE Ia

Military jet aircraft delivered to India by different countries (1945-65). Figures include jet fighters, jet trainers, and jet bombers acquired by purchase, grant or licensed production.

Total aircraft acquired				Breakdown by countries of origin											
45-55	55-56	Total on hand, '65		45-55				55-65				on hand, '65			
1	2	3	4	1	2	3	4	1	2	3	4	1	2	3	4
120	558	678	500	SU	GB	US	FR.	SU	GB	US	FR.	SU	GB	US	FR
				—	50	—	70	12	387	—	159	12	387	—	110

Note.: SU stands for the Soviet Union, GB for Great Britain, US for the United States, and Fr. for France.

Source: J.L. Sutton and G. Kemp: *Arms to Developing Countries (1945-65)* (Adelphi Paper, No. 28, Institute for Strategic Studies, London, 1966) p. 36.

TABLE-Ib

Aircraft belonging to the Indian Air Force (IAF) at the end of the Five Year Defence Plan in 1969-70.

Total strength of IAF (personnel): 57,000

Total number of combat aircraft: 625, divided into 45 squadrons.

Type of aircraft:	*Origin*:
50 Canberra B91 light bombers	British (purchased in 1957)
8 Canberra PR-57 reconnisance aircraft	British (purchased in 1957)
120 MIG-21 Interceptors	Russian (some purchased between 1962-65, but mostly produced in India under licence.)
150 Gant Mk.1. Interceptors	British (produced in India)
150 Hunter F-56 fighter/ground attack aircraft	British (purchased during 1956-57)
60 Mystere IV fighter/fighter-Bomber	French (purchased in the mid-'50s)

25	HF-24 Marut IA fighter/ ground attack aircraft	Indian (produced in India with Bristol Orpheus engines).
8	Lockhead L-1049 Super Constellation maritime reconnisance aircraft	American

Agreement for 140 SU-7b ground-support aircraft was signed with the Soviet Union in January 1968.

The Indian Air Force also acquired some Guideline-2 SA missiles from the Soviet Union.

The Transport and Communications squadrons of IAF were also of mixed origin, which can be seen from the following table.

Table Ic

The Transport Squadrons of IAF :

80	C-47	aircraft of US origin
72	C-119	aircraft of US origin
24	Ill-14	aircraft of Russian origin
32	An-12	aircraft of Russian origin
30	Otter	aircraft of French origin
20	HS-748	aircraft of British origin, and
18	Caribou	medium transport aircraft of Canadian origin.

The Helicopter Squadrons of IAF :

109 MI-4 helicopters of Russian origin

100* Alouette helicopters of French origin, and

12 Bell-47 helicopters of US origin.

There were also about 35 Auster and 60 Krishak light observation aircraft.

* approximately.

Source : *The Military Balance* 1969-70 (Institute for Strategic Studies, London, 1969). pp. 43-44.

Note : These figures show the emergence of the Soviet Union as the major supplier for IAF. Most of the British planes were purchased in the mid-fiifties.

Table II

The Indian Army as at the end of the Five-Year Defence Plan :

Total Strength : 848000*.

Fighting Units : 1 armoured division, 2 independent armoured brigades, 13 infantry divisions, 10 mountain divisions, 6 independent infantry brigades, and 2 parachute brigades.

The armoured division consisted of :

Weapons :	*country of origin*
222 Centurion Tanks	Britain
250 M4A3 Sherman Tanks	US
50 Vijayanta medium Tanks	Built in India under licence from a British firm.
140 AMX light Tanks	France
150 PT-76	USSR
50 M3 Al Stuart light Tanks	US
450 T-54 and T-55 Tanks	USSR and East European countries

About 30000 artillery pieces, mostly British 25 pounders, but including some 300 100mm and 140 130mm guns supplied by USSR.

Between 12 and 25 anti-aircraft artillery units.

* According to the Defence Minister's statement in the Lok Sabha on 21 Sept. 1964, the strength of the Indian Army is fixed at 825,000. See. *Report 1964-65*, (Ministry of Defence, Government of India, New Delhi. 1965). p. 1.

Source : *The Military Balance 1969-70*, p. 43.

Table III

The Indian Navy as at the end of the Five-Year Defence Plan :

Total strength (men in uniform) : 20,000.

Number and type of vessels :

1	16000-ton aircraft carrier	(ex-H.M.S. *Hercules*)
2	Submarines *	(ex-Soviet F Class)
2	Cruisers	of British origin.
7	Destroyers/Destroyer Escorts	(one ex-Soviet Petya class, and rest of British origin).

3 anti-aircraft frigates of British origin
5 Anti -submarine frigates of British origin
2 other escort vessels
4 Coastal minesweepers, 4 Survey ships, and 16 other kinds of vessels, mostly of British origin, including some minor vessels built in India.

* According to *Jane's Fighting Ships 1969-70*, the Indian Navy had acquired 4 Russian Submarines.

Source : *The Military Balance 1969-70* p. 43, and Raymond, V.B. Blackman (ed) ; *Jane's Fighting Ships 1969-70*, (London), 1969.

Note : At the end of the 5-yr. Defence Plan the Navy was still dependent on UK for the vessels and their spare parts. However, the supply of submarines by the Soviet Union filled an important gap in the naval build up.

TABLE IV

Indian Army (British Officers)

		Year	
Category of officer	1 Jan. 1947	1 April, 1947*	1 Jan. 1948*
Regular British Officers Of the Indian Army	2583	2200	1100
Regular British Service Officers attached to the Indian Army	751	500	350
British Emergency Commissioned Officers of the Indian Army	6348	3700	2200
British Service E.C.O's attached to the Indian Army	7689	5000	350

*Estimated

Source : *Hansard* (Commons) Vol. 433, 1946-47 Session, *Col.* 130 ; written answer by the Under Secretary Of State for India, on 17th February, 1947.

Sandhurst-Commissioned Officers in the Indian Army

In 1959-60, of the 16 senior officers in the Indian Army, 13 were commissioned from Sandhurst, two had their education at the Royal Military Academy at Woolwich. Only one non-combatant officer (Director-General of the Armed Forces Medical Services) joined the Army after finishing his studies in India. But later he studied at the Royal Army Medical College at Milbank.

In 1968, of the six senior officers mentioned in the *Armed Forces Year Book*, only one graduated from Woolwich ; the rest were commissioned into the Army from the Indian Military Academy at Dehradun.

Source : J. Singh (ed.) ; *Indian Armed Forces Year Book 1959-60* (Bombay, 1960) pp. 865-77, and, S.P. Baranwal ; *Armed Forces Year Book 1968* (Guide Publications, New Delhi, 1968).

British military aid to India

(£000)

Year	1960-61 to 1965-66	1966-67 to 1970-71	1960-61 to 1970-71	value of loan outstanding (at 31.3. 1971)
Value	20,321.9	9483.9	29,805.8	4352.6
of which grants	20,144.5	4961.8	25,106.3	—

Source : M. Lipton & John Firn ; *Erosion Of a Relationship : India and Britain Since 1960* (O.U.P. for R.I.I.A, London. 1975.) Statistical Appdx. Table 11.7.

APPENDIX IV

TABLE Ia

Historical List Of Indian High Commissioners in London

(1) Mr V.K. Krishna Menon (August 1947—June 1952)
(2) Mr B.G. Kher (June 1952—December 1952)
(3) Mrs V.L. Pandit (December 1952—August 1961)

(4) Mr M.C. Chagla (May 1962—October 1963)
(5) Dr J. Mehta (December 1963—December 1966)
(6) Mr S.S. Dhawan (January 1968—September 1969)
(7) Mr A.B. Pant (September 1969—1972)

Source : Information supplied by the India House Library, Indian High Commission, London.

Table Ib

The size of the Indian Diplomatic Mission in Britain

Year	No. of personnel (Total)	of whom India-based	London-based
1962	1044	219	825
1965	935	205	730
1968	600	151	449

Source : Personal correspondence with the Indian High Commission, London.

Table IIa

Historical List of British High Commissioners in India

	Name	date of joining
(1)	Sir Terence Shone	November, 1946
(2)	Lt. Genl. Sir Archibald Nye	October, 1948
(3)	Sir Alexander Clutterbuck	October, 1952
(4)	Mr Malcolm Macdonald	September, 1955
(5)	Sir Paul Gore-Booth	November, 1960
(6)	Rt. Hon. John Freeman	April, 1965
(7)	Rt. Hon. Sir Morrice James	October, 1968

Source : Foreign and Commonwealth Office : *A Year Book of the Commonwealth* (H.M.S.O., London 1970). p. 27.

Table IIb

Number of staff employed in British Diplomatic Missions in India

Year	Total
1949-50	821
1956-57	661
1957-58	625
1958-59	634
1962-63	743
1965-66	889
1967-68	765

Source : For the years 1949-59, *Third Report From the Select Committee On Estimates*, Session 1958-59. See, Minutes of Evidence submitted by CRO to the Sub-Committee 'E' of the Select Committee on Estimates on 29 January, 1959, pp. 6-7. For year 1962-63, *Civil Estimates 1963-64* (H.M.S.O., London, 1964) p. 11-37 Appdx. Table-1. For 1965-66, *Civil Estimates 1966-67* p. 11-13, Appdx. Table IV. For 1967-68, *Civil Estimates 1968-69*, p. 11-13. Appdx. Table-IV. Of the total staff employed in India, only a small portion was UK-based. For example, in 1958-59, the number of UK-based staff was 89, it rose to 145 in 1966-67, before falling to just over 100 in 1970-71 (out of a total of 680). See, *Third Report*, p. 65, and M. Lipton & John Firn ; *op. cit.*, p. 172.

APPENDIX V

Indian Immigrants

TABLE 1

Indian Immigrants in Britain

Estimates Of Indian Immigrants in England and Wales :

Year	1951	1961	1966
Number	30,000	81,400	163,300

Source : E.J.B. Rose et. al. ; *Colour and Citizenship* (O.U.P. for the Institute of Race Relations, London, 1969) p. 97, Table 10.1

TABLE II

Net arrival of Indian Immigrants between 1955-68 :

Year	Number
1955-60	33,070
1961-30 June, 1962	42,000
1 July 1962-1967	95,850
1 Jan. 1968—31 Dec. 1968	23,147

Note : The sharp increase in the number of immigrants between 1961-30 June 1962 was due to the rush to beat the barrier sought to be erected by the Commonwealth Immigrants Act, 1962.

Source : For the period 1955-67, E.J.B Rose et. al ; *op. cit*, p. 83, Table 8.1. For the 1968 figures, Home Office ; *Commonwealth Immigrants Act 1962 & 1968* (H.M.S.O., London, 1969) p. 6, Table 3.

TABLE III

Breakdown of Indian Immigrant Population into Voucher-holders & dependents :

Year	Voucher-holders	dependents	Persons coming to settle not included in (1) or (2)	Total
	(1)	(2)	(3)	(4)
1 Jan. 1965—31 Dec. '65	3,794	12,794	539	17,131
1 Jan. 1966—31 Dec. '66	2,433	13,357	918	16,708
1 Jan. 1967—31 Dec. '67	2,175	15,822	1070	19,067
1 Jan. 1968—31 Dec. '68	1,864	13,718	2,565	23,147
1 Jan. 1969—31 Dec. '69	1,382	8,286	12,290	10,958

Source : For 1965, Home Office ; *Commonwealth Immigrants Act., 1962 : Statistics 1965* (H.M.S.O., London, 1956), p. 6, Table 3.

For 1966 & 1967, *Statistics 1966* (1967), p. 6, Table, 3, and *Statistics 1967* (London, 1968), p. 6, Table 3.

For 1968, Home Office ; *Commonwealth Immigrants Act 1962 and 1968, Statistics 1968*, (London, 1969), p. 6, Table 3.

For 1969, *Statistics 1969*, p. 6, Table 3.

TABLE IV

Age Structure of Indian Immigrants in Britain according to the 1966 Sample Census :

Age group	Male%	Fenmale%
0-4 years	1.5	1.8
5-9 Years	3.5	4.1
10-14 „	5.8	5.7
15-19 „	7.4	6.4
20-24 „	10.4	10.9
25-44 „	47.6	37.5
45-59 „	16.4	18.9
60-64 „	3.0	4.4
65 and over	4.4	10.3
	100.0	100.0
Total in Number :	(134,200)	(106, 390)

Source : *Report of the Race Relations Board for 1969-70* (H,M.S.O., London,) H.C. 309, pp. 60-61.

TABLE—V

Economic Activity of Commonwealth Immigrants according to the 1966 Sample Census :

Born in	Percentage economically active	
	Males	Females
India	88.9	38.4
Pakistan	94.4	26.0
British Carribean	94.0	65.6
Cyprus	89.7	46.0
All new Commonwealth countries	84.0	42.2

Source : *ibid*, p. 68.

TABLE—VI

Indian Students in Britain

Year	Total*	Full-time of whom	Post-Graduate	Under-Graduate
	1	2	3	4
1960-61	n.a.*	1513	776	737
1963-64	4129	1543	935	608
1968-69	3373	1153	846	307

This number includes full-time students in the universities as well as students in Technical Colleges, Inns of Court, Teacher Training Colleges and students taking professional training.

** n.a. = not available.

Source : For 1960-61, Duncan Row ; *Commonwealth Education : Britain's Contribution* (Central Office of Information, London,) p. 60. For 1963-64, *The Commonwealth Relations Office List 1965* (London 1965) p. 501. For 1968-69, *Foreign and Commonwealth Office : A Year Book of the Commonwealth*, 1970 (London, 1970) pp. 743-77.

The British in India

British Citizens in India

Year	Number	
March 1947	100,000	(British subjects of European origin)
December 1971	12,000	

Source : For the year 1947, *Hansard*, (Commons), 5 series, vol. 434, col. 931. Statement by the Under Secretary of State for Commonwealth Relations, on 10 March, 1947.

For the year 1971 : Estimates by the Foreign & Commonwealth Relations Office, as reported in *The Times*, 7 Dec. 1971. Between 2000-2500 British nationals resided in Pakistan, in 1971.

British Students in India

A few British students study in Indian Universities every year, but they constitute an insignificant proportion of the total number of overseas students studying in India. For example, in 1963-64, 4667 overseas students were studying in India, of whom only 15 were British. Of these 15, 6 were under-graduate students and 3 were post-graduate students in the Arts faculties of different universities. Five were studying for professional degrees—four in Medicine and one in Engineering. The subject of study of was not specified.

Source : *Education in Universities in India : A Statistical Survey* (Ministry of Education, GOI, New Delhi, 1969) pp. 107-08.

British Officers in India

In 1947, after the transfer of power, 121 British officers continued to serve under the Government of India. Of them 54 were formerly in the Indian Civil Service, 64 in the Indian Police and 3 in the Indian Political Service. Source: *Hansard* (Commons) 5 series, vol. 445, 1947-48 session, col. 1179, 11 Dec. 1947. Reply by Mr P. Noel-Baker, the Secretary of State for Commonwealth Relations.

Number of ICS Officers serving in India

Year	Number
1947	451
1968 (1 Jan)	117 (Total authorised cadre strength of the Indian Administrative Service as on 1 Jan. was 2459)

Source : For the year 1947, R. Braibanti ; "Elite Cadres in

the Bureaucracies of India, Pakistan, Ceylon and Malaya" in W.B. Hamilton et. al. (ed) ; *A Decade of the Commonwealth 1955-64* (Duke University Press, Durham, N.C. 1966) p. 277.

For 1968, *Civil List of the Indian Administrative Service as on* 1 January, *1968* (Ministry of Home Affairs, GOI, N. Delhi) 1968, p. 287.

APPENDIX VI

Organisations and Societies in Britain concerned with various aspects of Indo-British Relations :

Associations with economic interest in India :

1. India Pakistan and Burma Association (established in 1924 as the India-Burma Association). Aims : To protect and to promote the rights and interests of British associations and individuals engaged in industrial, trading or commercial enterprises in India, Pakistan and Burma or in trade between Britain and these states.

2. Joint Committee on India : The Committee was formed in 1945 to represent British trading interests in India and Burma. Pakistan was included in 1947. The Committee is composed of representatives of the British Insurance Association, Chamber of Shipping of UK, Federation of British Industries, London Chamber of Commerce.

3. The Confederation of British Industries.

Associations mainly interested in history, sociology, culture and traditions of the states in South-east Asia ;

1. Royal India, Pakistan and Ceylon Society : It was founded in 1910 by a small body of men, British and Indian, with a view to promoting a better understanding and appreciation of the history and culture of the states in South Asia. Originally known as the India Society, it was expanded in 1950 to include Ceylon. Its quarterly journal, *South Asian Review*, publishes articles on contemporary social and political developments in South Asian states.

2. Royal Asiatic Society : Mainly interested in the study of

history, sociology, institutions, customs, art, language and literature of the Asian states. Publishes a quarterly *Journal*.

3. Royal Central Asian Society : Founded in 1901, it seeks to maintain in UK a centre for the collection and diffusion of information about the social, cultural and political developments of the states in Asia. Publishes a quartely *Journal*.

4. The Royal Overseas League : Founded in 1910 it seeks to promote friendship and understanding among the people of the Commonwealth.

Formerly known as the Royal Empire Society, it is the oldest of the voluntary associations in Britain concerned with commonwealth affairs. Its object is to promote knowledge and understanding among the people of the commonwealth. It publishes a bi-monthly, *Commonwealth Journal*.

6. The British Council : Founded in 1934, it works for the promotion of wider knowledge about Britain and its people, and for the promotion of closer cultural links between Britain and other countries.

Academic Institutions and Intellectual Discussion Groups with Interest in Indian Affairs.

1. Institute of Commonwealth Studies (University of London)
2. Institute of Commonwealth Studies (University of Oxford)
3. India Study Group of the Royal Institute of International Affairs, Chatham House, London.
4. Institute of Development of Studies (University of Sussex)
5. The Round Table
6. The Royal United Services Institution, London.
7. The Institute for Strategic Studies (London).

Other Associations interested in the promotion of better understanding between Britain and India

1. India League : Founded in 1930, it included among its members both Britons and Indians. During the 1930s and 1940s, it campaigned for Indian independence. Since indepen-

dence, its activities have been directed towards the promotion of Indo-British amity.

2. Britain-India Forum : It exists to promote knowledge about India in Britain, and to this end organises seminars, and discussions on current affairs.

The list is by no means exhaustive. By virtue of her membership of the Commonwealth, India is a member of various other organisations and associations such as The Commonwealth Parliamentary Association, Commonwealth Agricultural Bureau, Commonwealth Advisory Aeronautical Research Council, Air Transport Council etc. Reference to such associations has deliberately been omitted as membership of these organisations is not open to a private individual. These are semi-official bodies, compssed of delegates appointed by the Commonwealth Governments.

For a list of such associations, see, Foreign & Commonwealth Office ; *A Year Book of the Commonwealth 1970* (London, 1970) pt. VIII.

SELECT BIBLIOGRAPHY

PRIMARY SOURCES :

Official Publications

Government of India :

Ministry of Defence ; *Brief Statement of the Activities of the Defence during 1956-57* (New Delhi).

„ *Brief Statement......During 1957-58* (New Delhi).

„ *Report* (annual) 1962-63 to 1968-69 (New Delhi).

Minstry of External Affairs ; *Report* (formerly *Annual Report*), 1962-63 to 1968-69, (New Delhi).

„ *Jammu and Kashmir White Paper* (N. Delhi, 1948).

„ *Kashmir Papers* (New Delhi, n. d.).

„ *Kashmir and the United Nations* (New Delhi, 1962.)

Aggression In Kashmir (N. Delhi, 1963.)

Ministry of Information & Broadcasting (Publications Div.) ; *Pakistan's Aggression in Kutch* (N. Delhi, 1965).

„ *When Freedom Is Menaced* (Speeches of Lal Bahadur Shastri, N. Delhi, 1965).

„ *Pakistan's New Attempt to Grab Kashmir* (N. Delhi, 1965).

„ *Let Pakistan Speak For Herself* (N. Delhi, 1965).

„ *Independence and After* (Speeches of J. Nehru 1946-49, New Delhi, 1949).

Ministry of Information & Broadcasting (Publications Div.) ; *Jawaharlal Nehru's Speeches 1949-53* (N. Delhi, 1954)

" *Speeches 1953-57* (N. Delhi, 1958), and *Speeches 1957-63* (N. Delhi, 1964).

" *India's Foreign Policy* (Selected Speeches of J.Nehru Sept. 1946-April 1961, N.Delhi, 1961)

Ministry of Finance ; *External Assistance* (annual), 1962-63 to 1968-69 (N. Delhi).

Ministry of Commerce ; *Foreign Trade of India* (monthly).

Planning Commission ; *Fourth Five-Year Plan—A Draft Outline* (N. Delhi, 1966)

Reserve Bank of India ; *Reserve Bank of India Bulletin* (monthly, Bombay).

" *Report on Currency and Finance* (annual), (Bombay).

" *Survey of India's Foreign Liabilities & Assets* (Bombay, 1953).

" *Survey of India's Foreign Liabilities & Assets* (1955)

" *India's Foreign Liabilities & Assets—a Survey Report* (1964)

" *Foreign Collaboration in Indian Industry—a Survey Report.* (Bombay, 1968)

Parliamentary Publications :

Lok Sabha Secretariat ; *Lok Sabha Debates* (N. Delhi).

Rajya Sabha Secretariat ; *Rajya Sabha Debates* (N. Delhi)

Pakistan :

Pakistan, Government of ; *The Story of Kashmir* (Karachi, 1951)

" *Reports on Kashmir by United Nations Representatives* (Karachi, 1962)

" *Kashmir : Speech Delivered to the Security Council on 11 May, 1964, by*

Pakistan, Government of ; *Mr. Zulfikar Ali Bhutto* (Karachi, 1964)

" *President Ayub on the Crisis over Kashmir* (Karachi, 1965)

" *Indian Aggression in the Rann of Kutch* (Karachi, 1965)

" *India Sets the Sub-Continent Ablaze* (Karachi, 1966)

U.K. :

Command Papers :

Cmd. 6350. *Lord Privy Seal's Mission.* (London, 1942)

Cmd. 6829. *Cabinet Mission* (London),1946

Cmd. 7047. *Indian Policy Statement of 20 February 1947* (London, 1947).

Cmd. 7195. *Financial Agreement Between the Government of the United Kingdom and the Government of India on 14 August 1947* (London, 1947)

Cmd. 7342 *Exchange of Letters...extending the Financial Agreement of 14 August, 1947* (London, Feb. 1948)

Cmd. 7472. *Exchange of Letters...extending the Financial Agreement of 14 August, 1947* (London, July, 1948)

Cmd. 8080. *Colombo Plan* (London 1950).

Cmd. 8953. *India : Financial Agreement* (London, 1953)

Cmd. 2276. *Report of the Committee on the Representational Services Overseas* (London, 1964)

Cmd. 2549. *Exchange of Letters...for assistance towards the Mazagaon Dock and the Leander Frigate Project* (London, 1964)

Cmd. 2901. *Statement on the Defence Estimates, 1966. Part. 1. The Defence Review* (London, 1966).

Cmd. 3357. *Supplementary Statement of Defence Policy 1967* (London, 1967.)

Cmd. 2979. *Commonwealth Immigrants Act 1962 : Control of Immigration Statistics 1965* (London, 1966)

Cmd. 3258. *Immigration Statistics 1966* (London, 1967).

Cmd. 3594. *Immigration Statistics 1967* (London, 1968)

Cmd. 4027. *Commonwealth Immigrants Act 1962 & 1968 : Control of Immigration Statistics 1969* (London, 1970)

Cmd. 4107. *Report of the Review Committee on Overseas Representation* (London, 1969).

Cmd. 2739. *Immigration From the Commonwealth* (London, 1965)

Cmd. 4715. *The United Kingdom and the European Communities* (London, 1971).

Parliamentary dsbates, accounts and papers :

Civil Estimates (annual) 1962-63 to 1968-69.

House Of Commons Debates : Official Reports

House Of Lords Debates : Official Reports

Estimates Committee : *Third Report From the Select Committee On Estimates : 1958-59 Parliamentary Session : The Commonwealth Relations Office* (H.C. 252, London, 1959.)

" *Seventh Report From the Select Committee On Estimates : 1967-68 Session : Overseas Aid.* (London, 1968)

" *Select Committee On Race Relations and Immigration, Session 1969-70 : Control Of Immigration.* Minutes of

Estimates Committee : Evidence by FCO and the Home Office on 17 May, 1970 (H.C. 17-XXVI, London, 1970) ; and Minutes of Evidence by the Home Secretary (H.C.-17 XXVI, H.M.S.O., London, 1970)

Publications by Govt. Depts. and Ministers :

Central Office of Information ; *Cooperation and Consultation in the Commonwealth* (London, 1963)

,, *Britain and the Process of Decolonisation* (London, 1970)

Commonwealth Relations Office ; *Commonwealth Relations Office List* (annual) 1950-65, (London), and *Commonwealth Relations Office Year Book 1966* (London)

Foreign & Commonwealth Office ; *A Year Book of the Commonwealth* 1968, 1969, 1970 & 71. (London)

United Nations Publications :

General Assembly Official Records : Verbatim Report 1946-65. (New York)

Security Council Official Records : Verbatim Report 1948-65 (New York)

Security Council Official Records : Resolutions & Decisions 1948-65. (New York)

Year Book Of International Trade Statistics (annual), 1950-66 (New York)

Collection Of Documents & Surveys :

Eayrs, J. (ed.) ; *The Commonwealth & Suez : A Documentary Survey* (O.U.P. London,1964)

Gwyer, M. & Appadorai, A. (eds) ; *Speeches and Documents on the Indian Constitution 1921-47*, Vol. II, (O.U.P., London, 1957)

Kumar, Girja, and Arora, V.K. (eds) ; *Documents on Indian Affairs* (1960, Asia Publishing House, London, 1965)

Lakhanpal, P.L. (ed.) ; *Essential Documents and Notes On Kashmir Dispute* (International Books, Delhi, 2nd edn., 1965)

Lok Sabha Secretariat ; *Foreign Policy of India : Texts of Documents 1947-64* (N. Delhi, 1964).

Mansergh, N. (ed.) ; *The Transfer of Power 1942-47*, vol. 1. *Cripps Mission* (H.M.S.O., London, 1970). Vol. II *Quit India* (London 1971), Vol. III. *Reassertion of Authority* (1971).

" *Documents and Speeches on British Commonwealth Affairs 1931-52*, Vols. I&II, (O.U.P., London, 1953)

Documents & Speeches on Commonwealth Affairs 1952-62 (O.U.P., London, 1963)

" *Survey of British Commonwealth Affairs : Problems of Wartime Cooperation and post-War Change*, Vol. II, (O.U.P., London, 1958)

Poplai, S.L. (ed) ; *Select Documents on Asian Affairs : India* Vols. I & II (O.U.P., Bombay, 1959)

Rajkumar, N.V. (ed.) ; *The Background of India's Foreign Policy* (All India Congress Committee, New Delhi, 1952).

R,I.I.A. *Survey of International Affairs* (various volumes), (O.U.P., London)

" *Documents on International Affairs* (various volumes, O.U.P. London).

Biographies, auto-biographies and accounts by participant observers :

Attlee, C.R. ; *As it Happened* (Heinemann, London, 1954)

Azad, A.K. ; *India Wins Freedom* (Orient Longman, Calcutta, 1959).

Brecher, M. ; *Nehru : A Political Biography* (Abridged edn. O.U.P., London, 1961).

" *India And World Politics : Krishna Menon's View of the World* (O.U.P., London, 1968) especially, pt.1.

Brittain, Vera ; *Envoy Extraordinary* (Allen & Unwin, London, 1965).

Bonarjee N.B. ; *Under Two Masters* (O.U.P., Calcutta 1970).

Campbell-Johnson, Alan ; *Mission With Mountbatten* (Hale, London, 1951).

Connel, John (pseud) ; *Auchinleck : A Biography of Field Marshal Sir Claude Auchinleck* (Cassell, London, 1959)

Eden, Anthony ; *Full Circle : Memoirs of Sir Anthony Eden* (Cassell, London, 1960)

Gadgil, N.V. ; *Government From Inside* (Meenakshi, Meerut, 1968)

Galbraith, J.K. ; *Ambassador's journal : A Personal Account of the Kennedy Years* (Hamish Hamilton, London, 1969)

George, T.J.S. ; *Krishna Menon : A Biography* (Cape, London, 1964).

Ghosh, Sudhir ; *Gandhi's Emissary* (Cresset Press, London, 1969.)

Hancock, K.W. ; *Smuts : The Fields of Force* (Cambridge University Press, 1968)

Hilsman, R, ; *To Move a Nation* (Doubleday, New York, 1967)

Kaul, B.M. ; *The Untold Story* (Allied, Bombay, 1967)

Khan, Mohammad Ayub ; *Friends Not Masters : A Political Autobiography* (O.U.P., London, 1967)

Lyttleton, Oliver ; *Memoirs of Lord Chandos* (Bodley Head, London, 1961)

Menon, K.P.S. ; *The Lamp And the Lampstand* (O.U.P. London, 1967)

Menon, V.P. ; *The Story of the Integration of the Indian States* (Longmans, London, 1956)

Macmillan, H. ; *Riding the Storm 1956-59* (Macmillan, London, 1971)

Moon, Penderel (ed) ; *Wavell : The Viceroy's Journal* (O.U.P., London, 1973)

Moraes, Frank ; *Jawaharlal Nehru : A Biography* (Macmillan, New York, 1956)

Nehru, J. ; *An Autobiography* (Bodley Head, London, 1942)

" *The Discovery of India* (Meridian Books, London, 1945)

Prasad, R. ; *India Divided* (Hind Kitabs, Bombay, 1947)

Pyarelal ; *Mahatma Gandhi : The Last Phase* (Navajivan Publishing, Ahmedabad, 1958)

Tuker, F. ; *While Memory Serves* (Cassell, London, 1950)

Tyson, G. ; *Nehru : The Years of Power* (Pall Mall, London, 1966)

Williams, F. ; *A Prime Minister Remembers : War and Post-War Memoirs Of the Rt. Hon. Earl Attlee* (Heinemann, London, 1961)

Wilson, H. ; *The Labour Government 1964-70 : A Personal Record* (Weidenfeld & Nicolson, & M. Joseph, London, 1971)

Private Papers :

Private Papers Of the Rt. Hon. Earl Attlee (University College Library, Oxford.)

SECONDARY SOURCES

Books & Pamphlets :

Ahmed, S : *A Treaty Between India and the United Kingdom* (New Delhi, 1945)

Anstey, V. ; *The Economic Development Of India* (Longmans, 4th edn. London, 1952)

Arnold, H.J.P. ; *Aid For Development* (Bodley Head, London, 1964)

Appadorai, A. (ed) ; *India : Studies in Social and Political Development* (Asia Publishing, London, 1968)

Attlee, C.R. ; *Empire Into Cammonwealth* (O.U.P., London, 1961)

Austin, D. ; *Britain and South Africa* (O.U.P., London, 1966)

Aziz, K.K. : *The Making Of Pakistan* (Chatto & Windus, London, 1967)

Barooah, D.P.* ; Indo-British Relations, 1959-60 (Stering, New Delhi 1977)

Bazaz, P.N. ; *Kashmir in Crucible* (Pamposh Publications, New Delhi, 1967)

Bamzai, P.N.K ; *Kashmir and Power Politics* (Metropolitan, Delhi, 1966)

Berkes, R.N. & Bedi, M.S. ; *The Diplomacy of India : Indian Foreign Policy in the United Nations* (Stanford University Press, California, 1958)

Bandyopadhyay, J. ; *The Making Of India's Foreign Policy* (Allied, Bombay/Calcutta/Madras / New Delhi, 1970)

Bhatkal, R. (ed.) ; *Political Alternatives in India* (Popular Prakasan, Bombay, 1967)

* This book came out too late to be consulted.

Bhutto. Z.A. ; *The Myth of Independence* (O.U.P., London, 1969)

Birdwood, C.B ; *A Continent Experiments* (Skeffington, London, 1946)

„ *Two Nations & Kashmir* (Hale, London, 1956).

Brailsford, H.N. ; *Subject India* (Gollancz, London, 1943)

Brecher, M. ; *The Struggle For Kashmir* (Ryerson Press, Toronto, 1953)

„ *New States Of Asia : A Political Analysis* (O.U.P. London, 1963)

„ *India's Foreign Policy : An Interpretation* (Institute For Pacific Relations, New York, 1957)

Brines, R. ; *The Indo-Pakistani Conflict* (Pall Mall, London, 1968)

Brown, M.B. ; *After Imperialism* (Heinemann, London, 1963)

Brown, N. ; *Arms Without Empire* (Penguin, Harmondsworth, 1967)

Buchanan, D.H. ; *The Development Of Capitalistic Enterprise in India* (Cass, London, 1966)

Burns, Alan ; *In Defence of Colonies* (Allen & Unwin, London, 1957)

Callard, Keith ; *Pakistan : A Political Study* (Allen & Unwin, London, 1957)

Caroe, Olaf ; *Wells Of Power* (Macmillan, London, 1951)

Chandrasekhar, S ; *American Aid and India's Economic Development* (Praeger, N. York, and Pall Mall, London, 1965)

Choudhury, G.W. ; *Pakistan's Relations With India* (Pall Mall, London, 1968)

Conan, A.R. ; *The Sterling Area* (Macmillan, London, 1952)

Conservative Overseas Bureau ; *Conservatives and the Colonies* (Conservative Political Centre, London. 1952)

Cross, James ; *Whitehall and the Commonwealth* (Routledge & Kegan Paul, London, 1967)

Das, Durga ; *India : From Curzon to Nehru and After* (Collins, London, 1969).

Das Gupta, J.B. ; *Indo-Pakistan Relations* (Djambatan, Amsterdam, 1958).

Dutt, R.P. ; *India Today* (Gollancz, London, 1946) ; *The Crisis Of Britain and the*
,, *British Empire* (Lawrence & Winshart, London, 1953)

Douglas-Home, A. ; *Great Britain's Foreign Policy* (Conservative Political Centre, London, 1961)

Edwardes, M. ; *The Last Years Of British India* (Cassell, London, 1963) ;

,, *Raj : The Story Of British India* (Pan Books, London, 1967)

Eldridge, P.J. ; *The Politics Of Foreign Aid in India* (Weidenfeld & Nicolson, London, 1969)

Finer, S.E. et. al ; *Back-Bench Opinion in the House Of Commons 1955-59* (Pergamon Press, London, 1961)

Foot, Paul ; *Immigration and Race in British Politics* (Penguin, Harmondsworth, 1966)

Goldstein, W, ; *The Dilemmas of British Defence* (Ohio State University Press, 1966).

Goldsworthy, D. ; *Colonial Issues in British Politics 1945-61* (Clarendon Press, Oxford, 1971)

Goodwin, G.L. ; *Britain and the U.N.* (Manhattan Publishing Co., New York, 1957)

Gopal, Ram ; *British Rule in India : An Assessment* (Asia Publishing, N. York, 1963)

Gopal, S. ; *Modern India* (Historical Association, London, 1967)

Griffiths, P. ; *The British Impact on India* (Macdonald, London, 1952)

Gupta, J.N.et. al. ; *Directory of Foreign Collaboration in India* (de Indiana Overseas Publications, New Delhi, 1968).

Gupta, S. ; *Kashmir : A Study in India-Pakistan Relations* (Asia, Bombay, 1966).

Hamilton, W.B. et. al (eds) ; *A Decade of the Commonwealth 1955-64* (Duke University Press, Durham, N.C. 1966)

Harrison, S.S. ; *India : The Most Dangerous Decade* (Princeton University Press, Princeton, 1960)

Hinden, Rita (ed) ; *Fabian Colonial Essays* (Allen & Unwin, London, 1945)

Hodson, H.V. ; *The Great Divide : Britain-India-Pakistan* (Hutchinson, London 1969)

Hussain, A. ; *Pakistan : Its Ideology and Foreign Policy* (Cass, London, 1966)

Indian Institute Of Foreign Trade ; *Foreign Trade Of India : Country Profiles* (New Delhi, 1968)

Institute for Strategic Studies ; *Military Balance* (annual), London, especially, 1965-66 to 1968-69 volumes

Institute for Defence Studies & Analyses ; *India in World Strategic Environment: Annual Review* (New Delhi, 1970)

Karunakaran, K.P. ; *India in World Affairs : August 1947-January 1950* (O.U.P,, Calcutta, 1952)

Kavic, L.J. ; *India's Quest For Security* (California University Press, Berkeley & Los Angeles, 1967)

Kipping, Norman & Donelan, M. ; *India : 1963* (Federation of British Industries, London, 1963)

Kidron, M. ; *Foreign Investments in India* (O.U.P., London, 1965)

Kirkman, W.P. ; *Unscrambling an Empire* (Chatto & Windus, London, 1966)

Kennedy, D. ; *The Security of Southern Asia* (Chatto & Windus, London, 1965)

Khera, S.S. ; *India's Defence Problems* (Orient Longman, New Delhi, 1968)

Kondapi, C ; *Indians Overseas* (O.U.P., 1951)

Korbel, J. ; *Danger in Kashmir* (rev. edn. Princeton University Press, Princeton, 1966)

Kundra, J.C. ; *India's Foreign Policy 1947-54 : A Study of Relations with the Western Bloc* (Groningen, Walters, 1955)

Lamb, A. ; *Crisis in Kashmir 1947-66* (Routledge & Kegan Paul, London, 1966)

Lee, J.M. ; *Colonial Development and Good Government : A Study of the Ideas Expressed by the British Official Class in Planning Decolonisation* (Clarendon Press, Oxford, 1967)

Legum, Colin & Marget ; *Crisis in Africa* (Pall Mall, London, 1964)

Lyon, P.H. ; *Neutralism* (Leicester University Press, Leicester, 1963)

Mankekar, D. ; *Twenty Two Fateful Days* (Manaktalas, Bombay, 1966)

Mende, T. ; *Conversations with Nehru* (Secker & Warburg, London, 1956)

Mansergh, N. ; *Commonwealth Experience* (Weidenfeld & Nicolson, 1969)

Martin, L.W. (ed) ; *Neutralism and Non-alignment* (Praeger, N. York, 1962)

Masani, R.P. ; *Britain in India : An Account of British Rule in the Indian Subcontinent* (O.U.P., Bombay, 1960)

Menon, V.P. ; *The Transfer of Power in India* (Princeton University Press, Princeton, 1957)

Menon, V.P.; *An Outline of Indian Constitutional History* (Bharatiya Vidya Bhavan, Bombay, 1965)

Millar, T.B. ; *The Commonwealth and the United Nations* (Sydney University Press, Sydney, 1967)

Miller, J.D.B. ; *The Commonwealth in the World* (G. Duckworth, London, 3rd edn., 1965).

Morris-Jones, W.H. ; *The Government and Politics of India* (Hutchinson, London, 1967)

Mosley, L. ; *The Last Days of the British Raj* (Weidenfeld & Nicolson, London, 1961)

Naoroji, D. ; *Poverty and Un-British Rule in India* (London, 1901)

Northedge, F.S. ; *British Foreign Policy : The Process of Readjustment 1945-61* (Allen & Unwin, London, 1962)

O'Malley, L.S.S. ; *Modern India and the West* (O.U.P., London, 1941)

Palmer, N.D. ; *The United States and South Asia* (Houghton, Mifflin, Boston, 1966)

Panikkar, K.M. ; *The Future of South East Asia* (Allen & Unwin, London, 1945)

" *India and the Indian Ocean* (Allen & Unwin, London, 1945)

" *Asia and Western Dominance* (Allen & Unwin, London, 1953)

" *The Basis of an Indo-British Treaty* (O.U.P., Bombay 1946)

" *Problems of Indian Defence* (Asia Publishing, N. York. 1960)

" *Foundations of New India* (Allen & Unwin, London, 1963)

Patel, H.M.; *The Defence of India* (R.R. Kale Memorial Lecture, Asia Publishing, Bombay, 1963)

Perham, M. ; *The Colonial Reckoning* (Collins, London, 1961)

Philips, C.H.
& Wainwright, M.D. (eds) ; *The Partition of India : Policies and Perspectives 1935-47* (Allen & Unwin, London, 1970)

Pillai, K.R. ; *India's Foreign Policy* ; *Basic Issues and Political Attitudes* (Meenakshi, Meerut, 1969)

Prasad, B ; *Defence of India* : *Policy and Plans* (Orient Longman, 1963)

Rajan, M.S. ; *India In World Affairs 1954-56* (Asia Publishing, London, 1964)

" *Post-War Transformation of the Commonwealth : Reflections on the Asian-African Contribution* (Asia Publishing, London, 1963)

Rao, V.K.R.V.
& Narain, D. ; *Foreign Aid and India's Economic Development* (Asia Publishing, London 1963)

Rangnekar, D.K. ; *India, Britain and the European Common Market* (R & K Publishing, New Delhi, 1963)

Reddaway, W.B. et. al. ; *Effects of Direct UK Investment Overseas* : *An Interim Report* (Cambridge University Press, 1967)

Reddy, T.R. ; *India's Policy in the United Nations* (Fairleigh Dickinson University Press, Rutherford, 1968)

Rose, S. (ed). ; *Politics in Southern Asia* (Chatto & Windus, London, 1963)

Rose, E.J.B. et. al. ; *Colour & Citizenship* (O.U.P., London, 1970)

Russett, B.M. ; *Community and Contention* : *Britain and America in the Twentieth Century* (M.I.T. Press, Cambridge, Mass. 1967)

Schuster, G. and
Wint, G. ; *India and Democracy* (Macmillan, London, 1941)

Segal, R.S. (ed.) ; *Sanctions against South Africa* (Penguin, Harmondsworth, 1964)

Shah, A.B. (ed.) ; *India's Defence and Foreign Policies* (Manaktalas, Bombay, 1966)

Sharma, B. L. ; *The Kashmir Story* (Asia Publishing, London, 1967)

Sharma, S.R. ; *India's Foreign Palicy : The British Interpretation* (Gyan Mandir, Gwalior 1961)

Shenoy, B.R. ; *Indian Planning and Economic Development* (Asia Publishing, London, 1963)

Shonfield, A. ; *British Economic Policy Since the War* (Penguin, Harmondsworth, 1957)

Spear, P. ; *India, Pakistan and the West* (O.U.P., 4th edn., 1967)

Steel, D. ; *No Entry* (Hurst, London, 1969)

Strausz-Hupe, R. & Hazard, H.W. (ed.) ; *The Idea of Colonialism* (Stevens, London, 1958)

Streeten, Paul, & Lipton, Michael (eds) ; *Crisis of Indian Planning* (O.U.P.. London, 1968)

Stephens, Ian ; *Pakistan* (Benn, London, 1963)

Sutton, G.L. & Kemp, G. ; *Arms to Developing Countries 1945-65* (Adelphi Paper No. 28, Institute For Strategic Studies, London. 1966)

Talbot, P. & Poplai, S.L. ; *India and America : A Study of their Relations* (Harper, N. York, 1955)

Symonds, R. ; *The Making of Pakistan* (Faber, London)

Tinker, H. ; *Experiment with Freedom : India and Pakistan 1947* (O.U.P., London, 1967

" *India and Pakistan* (2nd rev. edn. Pall Mall, London, 1967)

Venkatasubbiah, H. ; *Indian Economy Since Independence*

Venkatasubbiah, H. ; (Asia Publishing, London, 2nd rev. edn. 1961)

Venkateswaran, A.L. ; *Defence Organisation in India* (Publications Division, GOI, N. Delhi, 1967)

Vital, D. ; *The Making Of British Foreign Policy* (Allen & Unwin, London, 1969)

Walker, Gordon, Patrick ; *The Commonwealth* (Mercury Books, London, 1965)

,, *The Cabinet* (Cape, London, 1970)

Ward, B. ; *India and the West* (Norton, N, York, 1964)

Watt. D.C. ; *Personalities & Policies : Studies in British Foreign Policy in the Twentieth Century* (Longmans Green, London, 1965)

Wilcox, W. ; *India, Pakistan and the Rise Of China* (Walker, N. York, 1962)

Wint, G. ; *The British In Asia* (Faber, London, 1947)

Wint, G. (ed.) ; *Asia : A Handbook* (Penguin, Harmondsworth, 1969)

Wint, G. and Calvocoressi, P. ; *The Middle East Crisis* (Penguin, Harmondsworth, 1958)

White, John ; *Pledged to Development : A Study of International Consortia and the Strategy Of Aid* (Overseas Devleopment Institute, London, 1967)

Wolfers, A. ; *Discord and Collaboration* (Johns Hopkins, Baltimore, 1962)

Woodruff, P. (pseud) ; *The Men Who Ruled India*, Vol. 1. *The Founders* and Vol. 11 *The Guardians* (Cape, London, 1953 & 1954)

Woodhouse, C.M. ; *Post-War Britain* (Bodley Head, London, 1966)

Younger, K. ; *Changing Perspectives in British Foreign Policy* (O.U.P. London, 1964)

Zinkin, Maurice & Taya ; *Britain and India : Requiem for Empire* (Chatto & Windus, London, 1964)

Zinkin, Taya ; *India Changes* (Chatto and Windus, London, 1958)

„ *Letters from India* (Conservative Political Centre, London, 1958)

Articles :

Abdullah, Sheikh ; "Kashmir, India and Pakistan", *Foreign Affairs*, April, 1965

Alport, C.J.M. ; "Indian Policy and the Colonies", *New Commonwealth*, 12 October, 1953

Appadorai, A ; "The Foreign Policy Of India" in Black, E. and Thompson, K.W. (Eds); *Foreign Policies in a World of Change* (Harper, N. York. 1963)

Anand. R.P. ; "The Kutch Award", *India Quarterly*, July-September, 1968

Bajpai, G.S. ; "India and the Balance of Power", *Indian Book Of World Affairs* (Madras, 1952)

Banerji, A.K. ; "Unburdening an Imperial Legacy : Colour, Citizenship and British Immigration Policy" ; *India Quarterly*, October-December, 1976

„ "The Great Divide and the British Raj", the *Socialist Perspective* Vol. 1, No. 1.

„ "The Quest for a New Order in Indo-British Relations", *India Quarterly* July-Sep. 1977.

Barton, W. ; "Great Betrayal", *National Review*. Vol. 129, 1947

„ "Pakistan's Claim to Kashmir", *Foreign Affairs*, January, 1950

Bauer, P.T. ; "The Economics of Resentment : Colonialism and Under-Development", *Journal Of Contemporary History*, Vol. 4, No. 1., January 1969

Beaton, L ; "Anglo-Indian Relations : Are They Immature ?", *The Times*, 19 December, 1968

Birdwood, C.B. ; "The External Interests of India and Pakistan", *Asian Review*, April 1954

" "Kashmir", *International Affairs*, July, 1952

" "Kashmir Revisited" *Asian Review*, October, 1955

" "The Defence of South East Asia", *International Affairs*, January, 1953

Bhanukoti, V. ; "India's Trade With the East European Countries", *Foreign Trade Of India*, Vol. 14, June, 1965

Brailsford, H.N. ; "India's Two Nations", *New Statesman and Nation*, 10 May, 1947

Boulding, K.E. ; "National Images and International Systems" in Rosenau, J.N. (ed.) ; *International Politics and Foreign Policy* (Fress Press Of Glencoe, 1961)

Brecher, M. ; "Towards the Close of the Nehru Era", *International Journal*, Summer, 1963

" "India's Decision to remain in the Commonwealth", *Journal of Commonwealth and Comparative Politics*, vol. XII, Nos. I & II.

Buchan, A. ; "An Asian Balance of Power", *Australian Journal of Politics and History*, Vol. XLL, 1966

" "The Balance of Power in Asia After Vietnam", *Journal Of Royal Central Asian Society*, Vol. LVI, pt. 11, June, 1969

Campbell-Johnson, Alan ; "Reflections on the Transfer of Power", *Asiatic Review*, July, 1952

Caroe, Olaf ; "The Persian Gulf : A Romance", *The Round Table*, March, 1949

Caroe, Olaf ; "Problems of Power Confrontation in Inner Asia", *Journal of Royal Central Asian Society,* Vol LVI, Pt. III, October, 1969

" "The End Of British Rule : Storms Which Still Blow" in *The Round Table*, January, 1970

Charlton, E. ; "Some Sort of Relationship", *Asian Review*, Vol. 1., No. 1., November, 1967

Cohen, J.B. ; "India's Foreign Economic Policies", *World Politics*, July, 1955

Deakin, N, ; "The Politics of the Commonwealth Immigrants Bill", *Political Quarterly*, January-March, 1968

Desai, A.V. ; "India's Growing Military Problems : Reaching out to the Soviet Union", *The Round Table*, October, 1967

Donelan, M. ; "The Trade Of Diplomacy", *International Affairs*, October, 1969

Douglas-Home, C. ; "Military Power Consolidated", *The Times*, Supplement on India, 13 October, 1969

Dutt, Som ; "Security and Defence of South and South East Asia", *India Quarterly*, January-March, 1969

Emerson, Rupert ; "Colonialism", *Journal Of Contemporary History*, Vol. IV. No. 1., January, 1969

Fisher, M. ; "Goa In Wider Perspective", *Asian Survey*, April, 1963

Fontera, R.M. ; "Anti-Colonialism as a Basic Indian Foreign Policy", *Western Political Quarterly*, Vol. 13, June, 1960

Gangal, S.C. ; "The Commonwealth and Indo-Pakistan Relations", *International Studies*, July-October, 1966

Goodwin, G.L. ; "The Commonwealth and the United

Goodwin, G.L. ; Nations", *International Organisation*, Summer, 1965

Goodwin, G.L. "The Political Role Of the U.N. : Some British Views", *International Organisation*, Autumn 1961

Gopal. S. ; "The Commonwealth : An Indian View", *The Round Table*, Diamond Jubilee Number, November, 1970

Graham, Ian, C.C. ; "The Indo-Soviet M.I.G. Deal and its International Repercussions", *Asian Survey*, Vol. IV. No. 5, May, 1964

Gupta, S. ; "Indo-Pakistan Relations", *International Studies*, October, 1963

" "The Kashmir Question, 1947-60 : A Survey Of Source Material", *International Studies*, October, 1961

" "Our Foreign Policy : The Problem", *Seminar*, March, 1961

" "India's Policy towards Pakistan", *International Studies*, July-October, 1966

Gyani, P.S. ; "India's Military Strategy", *India Quarterly*, January-March, 1967

Harrison, J.B. ; "South Asian Studies : the Weak Link at the Schools", *Asian Review*, Vol. 2, No. 2, January, 1966

Harrison, S.S. ; "India, Pakistan and the U.S.", *The New Republic*, 10 August, 24 August, and 7 September, 1959

Hatch, John ; "The Opposition's Part in Colonial Policy" *The Listener*, 25 April, 1963

Hugh-Jones, Stephen ; "India's New Military Strength", *The New Republic*, 19 December, 1964

" "British Attitude to the Indo-Pakistani War" *Economic Weekly*, 16 October, 1965

Illchman, W. ; "Political Development and Foreign

Illchman, W.; Policy : The Case Of India", *The Journal Of Commonwealth Studies*, Vol. IV, No. 3, November 1966

Ingram, D.; "Commonwealth Communications—The Press" (mimeo.) (Institute of Commonwealth Studies, London, 1967)

Ispahani, M.A.H.; "The Ire Of Pakistan", *Asian Review*, Vol. 1., No. 1., Nov. 1969

Jackson, Colin; "Time to Remember India", *Venture*, October, 1956, Vol. 8, No. 5

Kapur, H.; "The Soviet Union and Indo-Pakistan Relations", *International Studies*, July-October, 1966

Kaul, Ravi; "The Indian Armed Forces in the 1970s", the R*oyal United Services Institution Journal*, March, 1971

Khan, Ayub; "The Pakistan-American Alliance: Stresses and Strains", *Foreign Affairs*, January 1964

Kidron, M.; "From High Indignation to Indifference : Asian Commonwealth attitudes to Britain's Entry", Rounds 1 and 2 in P. Uri (ed.) *From Commonwealth to Common Market* (Penguin, Harmondsworth, 1968)

Kondapi, C.; "India and the United Nations", *International Organisation*, Nov. 1951

Kumar, D.; "The New Community and the Developing Commonwealth", *The Round Table*, October, 1971

Lall, Arthur; "Change and Continuity In India's Foreign Policy", *Orbis*, Vol. x., No. 1, Spring, 1966

Lee, Jennie; "Socialists Can be Proud of India" in E. Thomas (ed.); *Tribune 21*, (Macgibbon & Kee, London, 1958)

Levi. W.; "The Evolution Of India's Foreign

Levi. W. ; Policy", *The Year Book of World Affairs* (Stevens, London, 1958)

" "Kashmir and India's Foreign Policy", *Current History*, June, 1958

Lewis, W.A. ; "The Colonies and the Sterling", *The Financial Times*, 16 January, 1952

Lipton, M. and Bell, C. ; "The Fall in Commonwealth Trade", *The Round Table,* January, 1970

Lipton, M. and Firn J. ; "Drawbacks in Withdrawal", *The Times*, Supplemement on India, 13 October, 1969

Limaye, M. ; "National Apathy", *Seminar*, July, 1962

Low, D.A. ; "South Asian Studies : Finding the Next Generation", *Asian Review*, Vol. 2, No. 2., January, 1969

Lyon, P. ; "Foreign Policy Of India" in F.S. Northedge (ed.) ; *Foreign Policies Of Powers* (Faber, London, 1969)

" "Kashmir", *International Relations*, Vol. III. No. 2, October 1966

Mansergh, P.N.S. : "Commonwealth and the Future", *International Studies*, July 1969

Millar, T.B. ; "Kashmir, The Commonwealth and the United Nations", *Australian Outlook*, Vol. 17, No. 1., April, 1963

Miller, J.D.B. ; "The C.R.O. and Commonwealth Relations", *International Studies* Vol. II, No. 1., July, 1966

Molesworth, G.N. ; "Some Problems of Future Security in the Indian Ocean Area", *Asiatic Review*, January, 1946

Mukerjee, D. ; "India's Defence Perspectives", *International Affairs*, October, 1968

" "The Search for a Realistic Indo-British Relationship" in *The Statesman*, (Calcutta), 6 December, 1968

Naik, J.P. ; "Soviet Policy On Kashmir", *India Quarterly*, January-March 1968

Nehru, J. ; "Changing India", *Foreign Affairs*, April, 1963

Northedge, F.S. ; "British Foreign Policy" in Northedge, F.S. (ed); *Foreign Policies Of Powers.*

Pandit, V.L. ; "India's Foreign Policy", *Foreign Affairs*, April, 1956

Panikkar, K.M. ; "The Defence of India and Indo-British Obligations", *International Affairs*, January, 1946

Patel, H.M. ; "Realities of the Situation", *Seminar*, July, 1962

Pizey, M. ; "The Indian Navy Today", *Asian Review*, January, 1956

Prentice, R. ; "Aid : The Elusive 1 Per Cent", *New Statesman*, 17 October, 1969

,, "Aid : What Went Wrong", *New Statesman,* 13 August, 1971

Ray, J.K. ; "India and Pakistan as Factors in Each Other's Foreign Policies". *International Studies*, July-October, 1966

Rose, Saul ; "The Foreign Policy of Britain" in Black, E. & Thompson, K.W. (eds) ; *Foreign Policies in a World Of Change.*

Salazar, O. ; "Goa and the Indian Union : The Portuguese View", *Foreign Affairs*, April, 1956

Sandys, D. ; "The Modern Commonwealth" in *C.R.O. List*, 1963. (H.M.S.O., London.)

Sharma, K.K. ; "Anti-British Pick in Cotton", *Financial Times*, 9 July, 1971

Shonfield, A ; "The Duncan Report and its Critics", *International Affairs*, April, 1970

Siddiqui, A. ; "Pakistan's External Environment",

Siddiqui, A. ; *Asian Review*, Vol. 2. No. 2, July 1969

Strachey, A. ; "Some Aspects of the Future Defence of New India" in *Asiatic Review*, April, 1947

Stewart, M. ; "Indo-British Relations" in *Foreign Affairs Reports*, Vol. XVII, No. 12, December, 1968

Strange, Susan ; "The Commonwealth and the Sterling Area", *The Year Book of World Affairs*, 1959. (Stevens, London, 1959)

" "Suez and After", *The Year Book Of World Affairs 1957*

Thinker, H. ; "Colour and Colonization", *The Round Table*, Diamand Jubilee No., November, 1970

" "Rediscovery of India" review article in *International Affairs*, January, 1969

Tyson, G. ; "Foreign Investments in India", *International Affairs*, April, 1955

Walker, Gordon, Patrick ; "The Commonwealth Secretary", the *Journal of Commonwealth Political Studies*, Vol. 3, No. 1., November, 1961

White, John ; "Private Investors Confident", *The Times*, East of Suez Supplement, 7 January, 1969

Yarwood, A. T. ; "The Overseas Indians : A Problem in Indian and Imperial Politics at the End of World War One", *Australian Journal of Politics and History*, Vol. XIV, No. 2, August, 1968

Younger, K. ; "The Colonial Issues in World Politics" in A. Creech-Jones (ed.) ; *New Fabian Colonial Essays* (Hogarth Press, London, 1959)

" "Britain's Point of No Return", *The Year Book of World Affairs 1968*

Zinkin, M. ; "Britain as World Power ?" *The Listener*, 26 November, 1964

Zinkin, Taya ; "Indian Foreign Policy : Interpretation of Attitudes" *World Politics* January, 1955

" "Are the British Racists ?", *Economic Weekly*, 20 November, 1965

Unpublished Dissertations :

Sharma, V.B.L. ; *Strategic Aspects of India's Foreign Policy*, London University Ph.D. thesis, 1958

Wagenberg, R.H. ; *Commonwealth Reactions to South Africa's Racial Policy* (1948-61), London University Ph.D. thesis, 1966

List of Persons Interviewed :

Mr E. Charlton
Rt. Hon. John Freeman
Lord Gore-Booth
Mr S. S. Khera
Mr R. A. Longmire
Mr Victor Martin
Mr W. H. Morgan
Mr A. W. Redpath
Mr Apa B. Pant
Mr Maurice Zinkin

INDEX

M.

N.

O.

P.

Q.

R.

S.

T.

U.

W.